D0569826

All Over the Map

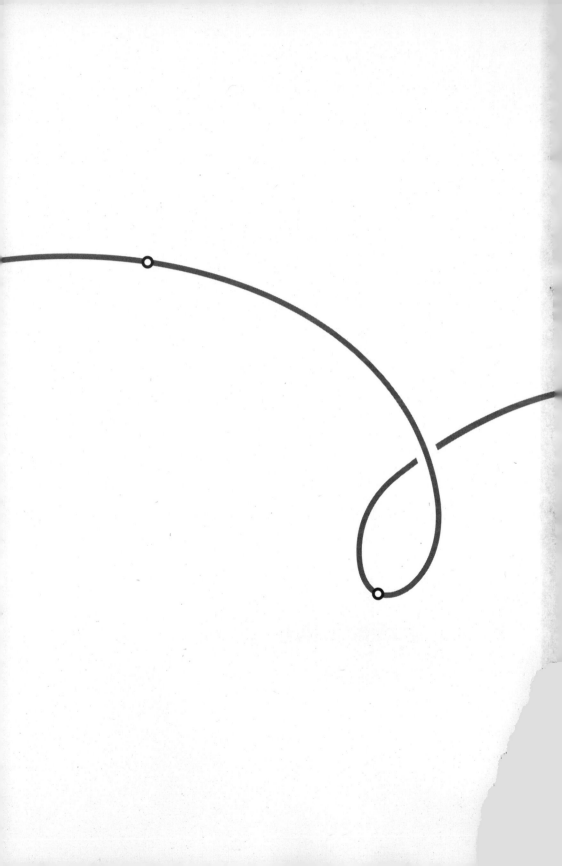

RON JAMES

ALL OVER THE MAP

Rambles and Ruminations from the Canadian Road

DOUBLEDAY CANADA

Doubleday Canada and colophon are registered trademarks of Penguin Random House Canada Limited

Excerpt on p.vii from "The Country of the Young" by Al Purdy, *Beyond Remembering: The Collected Poems of Al Purdy*, edited by Sam Solecki, 2000, Harbour Publishing, www.harbourpublishing.com

LIBRARY AND ARCHIVES CANADA CATALOGUING IN PUBLICATION

Title: All over the map : rambles and ruminations from the Canadian road /
    Ron James.
Names: James, Ron, 1958- author.
Identifiers: Canadiana (print) 20200212028 | Canadiana (ebook) 20200212044 |
    ISBN 9780385671132 (hardcover) | ISBN 9780385671149 (EPUB)
Subjects: LCSH: James, Ron, 1958- | LCSH: Comedians—Canada—Biography. |
    LCGFT: Autobiographies.
Classification: LCC PN2308.J35 A3 2021 | DDC 792.702/8092—dc23

Cover design: Andrew Roberts
Cover photo: Ed Kowal

Printed in Canada

Published in Canada by Doubleday Canada,
a division of Penguin Random House Canada Limited

www.penguinrandomhouse.ca

10 9 8 7 6 5 4 3 2 1

 Penguin
Random House
DOUBLEDAY CANADA

To June, Cayley and Gracie,
who were always there
when I went elsewhere.

Go ahead, chase fame. See what that does to your soul.

—Billy Connolly

Follow your bliss.

—Joseph Campbell

Look here
You've never seen this country
it's not the way you thought it was
Look again

—Al Purdy

CONTENTS

FOREWORD

All Over the Map is a travelogue through time; a road trip between one comedian's ears, taking pit stops in the past and present, that embraces the mysteries of people and place.

That comedian is me, by the way, and I wouldn't be writing the book were I not one—I'd be busy in the lab with other nuclear physicists, playing with boron.

That's a lie. You need good marks in math to be a nuclear physicist, and I repeatedly flunked that subject in school, because I'd rather talk than think. I'd also rather hit the road, looking for laughs, than deal with a nuclear meltdown in a cooling tower any day . . . so there's that, too.

By the way, when I write "mysteries of people and place," I don't mean the run-of-the-mill mysteries, like "Are sasquatches real, and if so, why does the only existing film footage of them look like a neighbour running through a backyard in a hair suit they sewed in their man cave?" Or "Was the last recorded sighting of the serpent

Ogopogo—which legend says swims in British Columbia's Lake Okanagan—authentic, or the result of the claimant enjoying a magic mushroom–induced afternoon? (Perfectly plausible. I certainly saw my fair share of giant lizards after scarfing a mittful of shrooms at a folk festival or two back in the day. Believe me, a trio of seven-foot salamanders singing backup for Valdy in 1978 was a vision a twenty-year-old kid could have done without.)

Perhaps the most enduring of Canadian mysteries is: "How many mosquitoes, over what period of time, does it take to drain you dry of blood while you're attempting to fill your bucket with the blueberries you're picking north of Temiskaming? (Actually, it's 729,623, in under five minutes. How about that? Maybe I *am* good at math.)

At the risk of pushing the envelope into hypothetical realms of the fantastical, the mystery I'm referring to is the tactile connection of spirit to place. It's the soul note that connects you to the authentic. I heard it ringing Sunday-morning clear when touring cities, towns and whistle stops along 7,821 kilometres of our nation's connective tissue: the Trans-Canada Highway. The hidden boons accrued in a call to adventure answered, occurred when I crossed paths with fellow pilgrims who, unprompted, shared their stories that in the telling, delivered a currency far greater than a payday's treasure.

Whether in coffee shops, hotels, planes, street corners, food courts or bars, when these strangers started talking, I'd just listen. When they were done and disappeared to where they'd come from, I wrote it all down so I wouldn't forget. I'm glad I did, because those conversations took place well before we were forced to close off the real world we actually walked through in exchange for the digital one we don't. They happened before everything changed. They happened before a worldwide pandemic shifted our psychic paradigm, dramatically altering daily life, crippling economies, gutting government infrastructure and, at this writing, leaving 3.6 million global casualties in its wake.

The performing arts suffered a particularly devastating blow. Throughout the global village, those places where practitioners of the myriad disciplines that comprise the profession once plied our trades—theatres, stadiums, bars, clubs, concert halls—were shuttered to protect audiences and performers alike from an invisible enemy ten times more contagious than the common flu. This killing of *authentic* social contact made social media's *inauthentic* contact a mandatory lifeline. What for me had once been a live audience seated in theatres, suddenly became an *unseen* audience, seated somewhere in cyberspace. With everyone housebound, Zoom became cyberworld's ubiquitous delivery system. Where I'd once stood onstage hearing laughter, I now stood in my living room . . . hearing, well . . . nothing at all! (Given the contemptibly quiet crowds I'd weathered in my first few years in stand-up, the irony wasn't lost on me. You gotta love it when life comes full circle, eh?)

Streaming gigs live from my living room certainly kept my mojo workin' and threw a few bucks in my kitty, yet every performance felt as if I was delivering my set to fellow earthlings from a space capsule orbiting the Nebulon galaxy. Authentic connection is not the medium's strong suit.

My Covid-enforced dependence on technology can't be entirely blamed on the virus, though. I'd already become prisoner to the dopamine release that a smart phone's "ping" delivers to the neocortex. With each one, the brain's receptors experience such an orgasmic hit of adrenalin it's a wonder there's not a discharge of fluids! The thing about receiving a dose of dopamine, though, is that in less than an hour, you'll be wanting another one. Its buzz is fleeting. Ephemeral. Empty calories. A soul note, on the other hand, is not just a passing sensation, but one of permanence. It echoes through time, by setting its anchor way down deep to where spirit abides. It's what those fellow pilgrims I chatted with felt compelled to share and I felt privileged to hear. That makes this their book as much as it does mine.

I started writing *All Over the Map* three years ago in my Old Town Toronto condo, never imagining that I'd be writing the second draft during an Atlantic Bubble–mandated quarantine—cocooned in a sanctuary by the sea that made my Nova Scotia province of origin the safest place *in . . . the . . . world* during the summer of 2020—to ride out the plague. During the fourteen days indoors, neighbours and friends brought me food or reached out via text, asking what was needed. Their kindness personified the unifying phrase: "We're all in this together."

This wasn't unique to the East Coast, either. Despite all the mixed messages the public received from authorities as to how to beat the virus—and the virulent idiocy of the anti-maskers with their conspiratorial belief that COVID-19 was a Bilderberg/New World Order/ illuminati star chamber–orchestrated *plan*-demic supported by evil Big Pharma, George Soros, Beijing billionaires, Russian oligarchs, Bill Gates and his Silicon Valley minions busy planting microchips in our bloodstream for mind control shenanigans, a couple of Masons named Bill and Reg playing shuffleboard at the Okotoks Legion and that pair of giant lizards beneath the White House living on a diet of Republican babies snatched by Hillary Clinton riding a broomstick— Canadians for the most part prioritized the common good. We wore masks, washed our hands and kept our social distance as we fought to "flatten the curve" of globalism's first plague, the impact of which will be felt for generations. Provided, of course, the Martians don't invade first. Which, given the consistently bizarre geopolitical plot twists in our planet's daily narrative, would not surprise me in the least. By the time the paperback edition of this book hits the stands, the entire planet could be under alien bondage with me doing hard labour in the zinc mines of Thompson, Manitoba guarded by Martians with ray guns. (I'm sorry. Do outer space invaders even use ray guns? They probably just stare at your forehead until it explodes, right? Okay. I stand corrected. So, no ray guns. Apologies for the 1930s Buck Rogers–level of reference for Martian weaponry, but the only science fiction I read is an occasional op-ed in the *National Post* by Conrad Black, and that's just for the sesquipedalian rush of it all. By the way, I bet Conrad Black *is* a Martian.)

Even with the majority of Canadians following protocols at the start of the pandemic, the ineptitude of Canada's political class was staggering when it came to managing it. Our national travesty saw 81 percent of deaths from COVID occur in elder care homes. The populist dominions of Doug Ford's Ontario and François Legault's Quebec led the nation in geriatric deaths. Privately run elder care facilities were the most notorious offenders. Owned by stone-cold corporate profiteers, these warehouses to the hereafter hired devalued workers to care for devalued lives who were as disposable as the diaper they were wearing that hadn't been changed in a week. Perhaps when these heartless totems of capitalist greed meet their Maker, their reward will be that crowded corner in a very special place in hell.

"Move over, Bernie Madoff—Mike Harris and Chartwell's board of governors just arrived!"

By the pandemic's second wave, the frustratingly slow procurement of vaccines by Canada may have showcased our prime minister's skills at reading a teleprompter, but when inoculation rates put our G20 nation thirty-third in the world, I bet there were plenty days Trudeau had wished he'd stayed a snowboarder in Whistler. At one point we were behind Slovenia! In layman's terms, that meant Melania Trump's third-cousin Igor got the jab before our essential workers!

But when the third wave arrived, carrying a host of lethal variants, it hit with a tsunami's impact. Canada's most populous province, Ontario, suffered a near collapse of its public health care system and a mind-boggling projected loss of 15,000 lives a day, all thanks to the science-defying arrogance of Premier Doug "Big Daddy" Ford and his cabal of Conservative henchmen, whose mismanagement of everything from vaccine roll-out to paid sick leave was nothing short of criminal. I swear the man had a better grasp of supply and demand when he was a community college drop-out selling hash from the trunk of his father's Cadillac!

Yet during COVID's initial assault, the communal response of Canadians stood in stark contrast to that colossus to our south. The next-door neighbour we once knew and admired slipped its moorings, drifting into far more dangerous waters of the Rubicon we were all crossing over. That will happen when you choose to follow the petulant diatribes of an intellectually compromised paranoid POTUS, whose pathological narcissism, moronic dictates and unmitigated cruelties were enabled by a cabal of lickspittle sycophants, fawning toadies, billionaire kleptocrats and delusional legions of evangelical Christians whose blind obedience to that American id run amok made a mockery of everything the Saviour stood for. Whatever happened to love thy neighbour as thyself? Someone should have told them when "me" trumps "we" everyone loses. When the richest, most technologically advanced nation on Earth couldn't even put personal protective equipment into the hands of front-line workers when it had once succeeded in putting a man on the moon, I figured the *least* they could have done was try to put their president up there!

Thankfully, the oozing cyst on America's body politic was removed by Joseph R. Biden. Yet two weeks before the new president's inauguration, the poison festering in the bowels of a Republican Party evacuated its rancid effluvia into the streets of Washington, metamorphosing into a flesh-and-blood mob of mouth-breathing batshit-crazy conspiracy-addled zealots in MAGA hats hell bent on death and destruction in their Capitol building and looking to put the coup in koo-koo.

And that was only 3,000 of the 74 *million* Americans who still believe the election was stolen. Good ol' Uncle Joe may personify the "better angels of man's higher nature" but besides wrestling a pandemic to the mat, making America *sane* again will be the toughest task.

I mention all this because I couldn't discuss a life spent as a foot soldier in the trenches of Canadian show business without a nod to the allure of America's. The war wounds incurred pursuing an acting career in the attrition-littered arena of Los Angeles another lifetime ago taught me a fundamental lesson: the individual is responsible for his or her own happiness. Unfortunately, that clarion call to self-empowerment courtesy of the Enlightenment, has, over the past forty years, fallen hostage to neoliberalism's feverish pursuit of mammon, where the road to "happiness" has been hijacked by a Gordon Gekko level of greed whose hunger for acquisition could never be satiated. Once "more is never enough" became the mantra America chanted, even getting by in the Land of Plenty was seen as losing . . . and I was barely doing that in the early '90s.

Ironically, not grabbing the grail I'd sought in that Los Angeles of long ago proved instrumental in siring a radical shift in my perspective. After three years, I realized the creatively fulfilling life I wanted would not be hand-delivered by someone else but had to be sought for and fought for by me. Once I returned to Canada, I decided to put that epiphany into action. If something came of it, bonus! If not, given the debt I'd incurred chasing Hollywood's golden goose, I'd better start turning a buck soon or else I'd have to sell a kidney.

Hitting the road in search of employment is nothing new for those of us born to the Maritimes. "Going where the work is" has been as integral to that region's identity as staying put. We're tartan nomads, driven beyond the familiar for a better run at a new day.

Even though I've called Toronto home for more than forty years, learned my stock in trade and raised a family here, that other somewhere I'm from is encoded in my DNA. Because no matter how far we roam, Maritimers never really leave "back home." Our need to return every summer is not dissimilar to that of the wily Pacific salmon—stay with me—which, after a lifetime spent swimming strange waters, suddenly finds its internal compass at the mercy of Earth's magnetic pull, bearing it back to its river of birth.

Perhaps our annual return is an attempt to reclaim something that's been lost. To reconnect with the place where, once upon a time, you genuinely *belonged*. To feel a continuity of spirit with those now gone, whose presence once coloured the tapestry of your life. The ability to channel the timeless feels all the more possible in landscapes of the familiar.

Just a heads up . . . the content of this book does on occasion bounce around a bit, as you've no doubt already noticed. Think of your reading experience as playing a pinball game with a man suffering attention deficit hyperactivity disorder (ADHD) in charge of the flippers. It's the way my mind works. A diagnosis a couple of years ago gave a name to what I'd experienced for a while: serotonin and norepinephrine do a daily tap dance on the floor of my frontal lobes, making my ability to concentrate on one subject at a time somewhat of a challenge. Multi-tasking is another man's forte. On the other hand, standing onstage in front of a thousand people, my synapses cutting and pasting two hours of content at the speed of thought from a combination of memory and spontaneously created material, is not an issue. Apparently, that ability is an attribute of the ADHD-afflicted.

It's a peculiar superpower though. Sometimes I wish I had the talent to hold my breath underwater for ten minutes instead, so I could be a Polynesian pearl diver. How cool would that be?! I would never have been forced to battle blizzards a yeti wouldn't wander as I drove through Rocky Mountain passes to a gig. Instead, I'd be running a pearl-diving business from a beachside shack in Bora Bora. Mind you, *were* I a pearl diver, I would have to contend with tiger sharks, one of the more notorious man-eaters of the South Pacific. They regularly grow to thirteen feet in length, sporting a head full of sharp-as-obsidian serrated teeth, as they prowl Oceania's shallow warm waters and bays, looking to satiate the bottomless appetite of the apex predators that they are. (See what I mean?)

On the following pages, you'll also find reflections on nature's fury and the humbling wonders I've been privy to while chasing a living crisscrossing the vast expanse of the Big Wide Open. There are opinions about the industry I'm in and some recounting of experiences I've had in some television shows that I've done.

The nano-second pace of change during these years of the plague may mean some of the observations about current events have an even shorter shelf life than is usual for topical content. So here's hoping they aren't too irrelevant by the time the book reaches your hands. (Then again, if the Martians have invaded in the meantime, my concern is a moot point anyway, so there's that.)

Memories of failure, fear, loss, change, redemption and challenge are here too, with occasional pit stops taken to times long gone when life was spent amongst those I'm from in a world that was, whose heartline hum I feel beating still.

Chapter One
CROSSING THE THRESHOLD

I was behind the wheel of my '99 Toyota 4Runner, overlooking Lake Superior, that vast inland sea the Ojibwa call Gitchi-Gami, when a logging truck came barrelling full tilt round a hairpin turn with all the malevolence of a bad dream. We were suddenly jousting for dominance on an empty stretch of the Trans-Canada Highway, running through the heart of the Canadian Shield scoured granite-hard by retreating glaciers you'd swear had just left yesterday. I'm willing to wager that Joseph Campbell wasn't driving this ribbon of widow-making asphalt when the wizened sage coined his galvanizing phrase: "Follow your bliss."

Nevertheless, I was doing exactly that: a stand-up comedian bound for eight one-night stands, playing towns strung sentinel lonesome round the frozen lip of Lake Superior. Surrounded on all sides by jaw-dropping, iconic geography that would have given the Group of Seven a collective woody, I was doing my best to dodge a cannonading steel leviathan threatening to bounce me off its Peterbilt logo into the afterlife, where my dubious end would be marked by one of those ubiquitous white crosses coyotes happily hop the highway to piss on. I was so far out on the edge of forever that if our world ended tomorrow, it wouldn't register up there until a week later!

Moose rule that country, and they have developed a taste for highway road salt with all the feverish addiction a junkie has for Afghani smack. At any moment, I expected to collide with six hundred kilos of stunned ungulate, standing clueless in the middle of the highway . . . licking it. The impact would have most certainly sent that swamp donkey caterwauling arse-over-antlers through the windshield, rendering me comatose in a blur of fur, blood and bone.

As my now-gone father used to warn, "It's not the moose landing on your lap that'll kill you, Ronnie. It's their flailing hooves beating your face to a pulp once they're *in* the car does that!" I was in no rush to test Dad's claim, having once seen a substantial hoofprint on the forehead of his third cousin once removed.

Speaking of moose, after my show in Atikokan, Ontario, an audience member handed me a seven-and-a-half-pound sirloin tip moose roast. I remember thinking that America may have a multi-million-dollar Hollywood star system, where talent can ride a comet-worthy career trajectory from obscurity to forty-foot-tall neon billboards advertising your latest film in every corner of the known world, but you know you're on the right showbiz road in Canada when locals in towns beyond the pale are paying you in butchered game. You just don't get post-show perks like that when you're playing Vegas. When someone hands you a brown paper bag dripping with blood in *that* town, it's probably got the head of a Teamster in it!

Atikokan, the canoeing capital of Canada, is an iron-hard outpost of 1,500 souls, perched on the edge of boreal forest, home to a labyrinth of waterways that bandy-legged voyageurs once paddled to reach the heart of a wild continent back in a fur-trading day when beaver was king.

What kid who canoed at summer camp didn't fantasize about being a voyageur? Living a life paddling the wilderness in a birchbark canoe full of your crusty habitant pals, all of you smelling ripe as an old diaper, with nary a care in the world. In actuality, it was a will-killing, ball-busting gig. When you weren't running Class V rapids capable of pulverizing your vertebrae to the consistency of tapioca pudding, you were portaging seventy-five pounds of pemmican through mosquito-infested *terra incognita*, shackled to servitude by corporate overlords in Montreal, all for a feudal wage. (Though they were still paid better than most Canadian comedians are for a gala set at Just for Laughs today!)

Outside Atikokan, I bunked at the only nice hotel on the tour, the White Otter Inn, sitting beside the Voyageur Route of the Trans-Canada Highway. An elderly bartender there told me that as a kid growing up in town, he'd seen Dan Blocker—the guy who played Hoss on the long-running 1960s television series *Bonanza*—stocking up on supplies for summertime fishing trips he was taking in-country. Other showbiz notables of the day would drop in from time to time too, he said, should they happen to be gigging a short plane flight away in Michigan. He swore the likes of Dean Martin, Jerry Lewis and other Rat Pack pals were seen stepping from a plane loaded down with hooch and hookers, headed for a luxurious fishing camp that catered to Las Vegas royalty. Now *there's* a vision of the Canadian wilds we never saw on *Hinterland Who's Who* when we were growing up: a taciturn, monosyllabic Ojibwa fishing guide, watching the Nutty Professor cast for muskie from the boat with a Vegas showgirl on his lap while yelling, "Nice lady!" and scaring the fish.

Rivers were Canada's roads once, snaking through a forest primeval, carrying commerce to wild dominions eons before RE/MAX was a cottage country catchphrase. I was following lines on maps born as corridors in some Clovis-point dreamtime, when First Peoples stumbled windward, bent and bowed, in search of meadows green with game. Next came explorers, trappers and settlers, escaping the rat-choked, scab-picking, syphilitic alleyways of the Old World for the pine-scented, fresh-air freedoms of the New. Mind you, after one winter of tooth-spitting, gum-bleeding eighteenth-century Montreal scurvy, you'd be damn near whimsical for a case of Parisian clap!

If life is all about the journey and not the destination, that seminal winter tour was my first step across the threshold into a wider world of wonders that, twenty-five years later, I'm still giving thanks for.

Before I made the move to Los Angeles in 1990, my approach to career had been the usual co-dependent actor/agent relationship, where you *hope* they will score you an audition so you can *hopefully* score whatever role they sent you out for. That approach exhausted itself during the relentless pursuit of too-few-and-far-between paydays; a gruelling run compounded by Biblical calamities of riots, floods, fires and earthquakes. Nothing alters perspective quite like a 6.7 seismic how-do-you-do that gets you and your loved ones huddling beneath the kitchen table as the ground below your shaking townhouse turns to Jell-O.

Lesson learned: there is a price to pay for Paradise.

After three years of chasing a moving target, I was done down there. I was done with agents. I was done waiting for a break. I was done being broke. (Well, not quite.) I was done waiting for my life to start. And I was most certainly done waiting for someone else to start it for me. It was time to set a new compass bearing.

Upon my return to Canada, I shifted the paradigm. Instead of being an actor who depended on others to feed me and mine, I became a comedian who fed them himself. Picking the best eight minutes worth of "bits" from a one-man show I'd written about my three years in Los Angeles, called *Up and Down in Shaky Town: One Man's Journey Through the Californian Dream*, at thirty-eight I started over and stepped onstage at a comedy club called the Laugh Resort, for that ego-crushing crucible called "amateur night."

To this day, the memory spooks. Those eight minutes scare you spitless *and* buck naked shitless as the glaring solo spot threatens to burn a hole straight to your soul with a merciless determination befitting the judgmental eye of God. That's why those of us who answered the call do it . . . because we *have* to.

Five years were spent honing my act, playing Canada's laughably lean club circuit for a paltry wage, until mouths to feed and a mortgage to pay bade me move beyond the parochial limitations of the Big Smoke and blaze a trail playing small-town theatres in lands beyond the pale. Granted, the theatres I played weren't exactly Carnegie Hall. In fact, they weren't even theatres! They were smoke-choked Legions, community centres, church basements and school gymnasiums, all housing a quality of acoustics only a mime could love. Still, there was an authenticity to it all. It was tactile. It had a real you could feel.

Back then, many comedians and their agents were prone to the prejudice that trying to break into "soft-seat" theatres in Canada wasn't worth the effort. Where's the career trajectory in playing a high-school auditorium on a Friday night in Dryden, Ontario? (Well, none actually . . . but the gig paid three times more for one show than the Toronto clubs did for five, so there's that.) "Why bother with Canada?" went the mantra, when the incantatory juju of that American woman's siren song said a life flush with riches beyond the realm of reason was but a hop across the US border and a green card away.

Everyone believed that when it came to stand-up comedy, validation in the Land of Liberty was the only option worth pursuing. I begged to differ—naively perhaps, but if people in a host of other professions never had to leave to actualize their livelihoods, why should a comedian? Most importantly, that inaugural tour ignited my faith that a worthy stand-up career could be built in Canada. So, I stayed here stringing my trap line from Corner Brook to Courtenay-Comox, and over several years as the gigs increased and crowds grew, I came to realize that hearing one thousand people laughing in a country I call home sounds *exactly* the same as hearing one thousand people laughing in a country I don't.

Working homegrown stages didn't depend on the pursuit of a predominant myth every Canadian comic once embraced: that a killer set at Montreal's internationally renowned Just for Laughs festival would lead to a career in the States. That once the appointed and anointed saw you catch lightning in a bottle at the world's biggest comedy festival, you'd be plucked from obscurity and suddenly find yourself surrounded by a team of perpetually tanned Los Angeles handlers and managers so secure in their assessment of what's funny, they never laughed. As if by teleportation, you'd awaken to a eucalyptus-scented breeze on a sunny southern California morning, signed to a lucrative network development deal where you'd live under glorified house arrest in a charming bungalow on the Warner Bros. lot, dreaming up television shows while you kicked a bag of money around the floor. In actuality, the odds of that happening were so infinitesimal, you'd have had better luck finding Oak Island gold.

It's easy to understand why we believed this was possible. Comedic status in Canada has always been measured by whether or not you're successful elsewhere. Ask any of us who have seen that look of pity cross a certain kind of Canadian's face when they ask whether we perform in the States and we answer no. Their reaction says, "Well, I *guess* you're doing okay, despite that big hairy ear growing out of your forehead."

Yet, even after a very rewarding seven-year run across Canada, with three specials to my name and more in the works, the thought of taking another run at America still percolated. But I finally committed to keeping my feet firmly planted in Canada thanks to an encounter with my comedy hero at a Just for Laughs post-show party in 2007. It was none other than that Glaswegian wizard . . . Mr. Billy Connolly.

If a person can have a religious experience laughing themselves into a state of grace, then watching this man's first HBO special in 1991, during a soul-sucking year-long run of unemployment in Los Angeles, was most definitely mine. This uncensored force of nature threw himself from one end of the stage to the next, delivering a rollicking, profane and fearless ninety-minute set as he extolled the virtues of his fractured tribe. Billy's performance elevated me to that alternate state of awareness I imagine alien abductees must walk forever, after they've been beamed back to the cornfield they'd been snatched from. (It's always a cornfield.) Nothing is ever the same again. I remember thinking, *That's my tribal song, too!* And I felt I'd be sinning against my purpose in life if I didn't try to sing along. Simply put, it was a calling.

Standing tall above the schmoozing Montreal crowd, filled with comedians, hangers-on, managers and agents, Billy—with his shoulder-length white locks, General Custer–like goatee and a cigar pinched between his teeth—looked every inch the hermitic sage wandering pilgrims would seek for words of wisdom. I was hoping his insight might help me step beyond what I had been told countless times: that my Canadian content severely limited my chances of achieving a *real* career.

Despite Billy's affable nature, I was hesitant to approach, aware of the boundaries famous people prefer you'd respect when you see them in public. Fans can be intrusive. Forceful. Unpredictable. I presume that's why film festivals erect red ropes at their star-studded premieres. Should the likes of Brad Pitt or Scarlett Johansson, say, ever decide to step *beyond* the boundary and mingle with the crowd, the pack's euphoria could easily shift into a feeding frenzy worthy of *The Walking Dead* and before you know it, there's blood on the ground and an actor's lost a finger.

I stood before Billy on the receiving end of a piercing stare that said he did not suffer fools. I spoke.

"The only reason I'm here," I said, "is because fifteen years ago, I saw your HBO special when I was church-mouse poor and out of work in LA. It was my Saint-Paul-on-the-road-to-Damascus comedic epiphany."

He laughed and said, "I hope you don't open with that!"

I mustered my courage and, with all earnestness, asked, "How did a working-class welder from the Glasgow docks become an internationally renowned comedian?"

He plucked the cigar he had pinched between his teeth and, with a fiery-eyed defiance, barked, "That's a question about fame! To hell with fame! Just do what you do and sing your song!"

Lesson learned: sages confirm what pilgrims already knew in the first place.

This alchemist of the calling whom I watched, mesmerized, as he spun gold from straw during a blistering two-and-a-half-hour set at Hamilton Place later that same year, knew that to pursue fame was to court the Promethean fire. What mattered to him was the pure joy of performance. You could see it in every concert of his. This tartan shaman tapped into the life force! Every performer worth their salt is tuned to that frequency, but success breeds fame and fame fuels the engine of celebrity—and no one does celebrity quite like America. It's why our national media feeds on theirs, because the phrase "Canadian celebrity" is a glaring oxymoron. You don't get a street named after you in Scarborough for starring in three seasons of *The Littlest Hobo*.

Because Canada has no star system, we have also mostly dodged Scientology's pernicious ruse of using Hollywood celebrities to recruit future disciples. It's one thing to hear a pitch from that über movie star "gone clear," Dianetics deity Tom Cruise, on how a cruel interplanetary warlord named Xenu dropped billions of his people into an active volcano from DC-8s 75 million years ago, but I'll bet the house not many of my countrymen in search of a messiah are going to join a cult because buddy from *Murdoch Mysteries* told them to.

I'd met celebrities at Toronto's iconic Old Firehall during my days as a rookie actor on the Second City mainstage, when the cast of *SCTV* would hire me on occasion. That group of comedic illuminati were dedicated, consummate actors/writers already at the top of their game in 1983. Although they were certainly accommodating and profession-ally welcoming, to say I was intimidated in their company is a glaring understatement. Chatting up Eugene Levy while he's fine-tuning an impression of a drunken Henry Kissinger for a Joe Flaherty–hosted *Maudlin o' the Night* sketch, as Andrea Martin threads the needle on an Edith Prickley bit, while Marty Short runs up and down the halls channelling an uncannily obnoxious and accurate Howie Mandel impression—for eight hours *prior* to shooting—was not encouraged. Know your boundaries, kid. You learned your lines, hit your mark, hopefully didn't suck, cashed the cheque and paid the rent. I realize now, I was witness to a remarkably talented cast whose groundbreaking series had miraculously harnessed the zeitgeist, creating a standard of comedy that still stands the test of time forty years later.

In 2017, I was asked to perform a ten-minute audience warm-up set for the shooting of *SCTV*'s Netflix special, directed by Martin Scorsese and moderated by Jimmy Kimmel, at Toronto's historic 2,500-seat Elgin Theatre. That stage, along with its sister theatre the Winter Garden, once welcomed luminaries of the vaudeville circuit like Buster Keaton, as well as far lesser-known acts such as . . . "Wanda! The Seal with a Human Brain!"

You read that correctly. I tried to imagine the owner travelling the dirt roads of that gruelling North American vaudeville circuit of 1910 with a seal as a sidekick. Did it ride beside him on the bus with the other acts as they watched him throw a glass of salt water in the seal's face every half hour? Seals have to be wet or they die, don't they? Where do you find seal food in the Midwest? As far as I know, there's not a lot of herring to be found in Toledo, Ohio. I'm sure a seal wouldn't settle for a grilled cheese if the diner was out of squid. Tell me that wouldn't make a great film? If Clint Eastwood could make two movies with an orangutan in a truck, then surely a barking seal on a bus could fly. No? Let the idea germinate for a bit, and I'm sure you'll see its potential.

I'd last performed at the Elgin in 2003, when Conan O'Brien came to town for three sold-out shows after America's fear of SARS had ravaged Toronto's film and tourism industries. It's not an exaggeration to say the city lost its collective mind. Nothing gets Torontonians damp in the pants faster than American recognition. I was getting messaged from people I hadn't heard from in thirty years, asking me for a ticket.

"I could get you a kidney quicker!" I barked.

The night of the *SCTV* taping, the Elgin was humming with the electric anticipation of a jam-packed audience come to honour their homegrown Emmy Award–winning comedy heroes. Meanwhile backstage, the real showbiz machine was in gear . . . Hollywood was here! The *SCTV* cast were gracious and warm, all exuding a generosity of spirit devoid of the standoffish attitude one might associate with their status. I'd logged more than a few kilometres looking for laughs since they'd hired a kid for half a dozen sketches in the early 1980s, and for once, I believed the invitation had been honestly warranted.

Jimmy Kimmel entered, surrounded by a coterie of carcinogenically tanned LA handlers, all wearing dismissive, nonplussed looks unique to the perpetually unimpressed. I'd bet good money they wouldn't raise so much as an eyebrow of expression even in the presence of a talking, card trick–performing cat riding a unicycle. In a roped-off area stood the most influential and revered director of our age, Martin Scorsese himself. This diminutive presence of such peaceful disposition stood in direct juxtaposition to his cinematic pedigree, whose palette of lyrically orchestrated violence made it hard to imagine him giving directions to Robert De Niro and Joe Pesci in that infamous *Goodfellas* scene, where they put the serious boots to the head of Billy Batts in their bar. There was a side of me that wanted to slip into the De Niro impression I'd honed over the past thirty years and yell, "Marty!! When do I get my close-up?!" But, having been schooled in a respect for boundaries, I thought otherwise. (Besides, there was also a chance Scorsese's personal security detail—who, my imagination assumed, were blending in as that couple of thick-necked IATSE union dudes in the corner—were also very handy with their boots.)

You have to understand, it's not every day a working Canadian comic is involved in an event like this. I love the road and every town or city played, but my touring world is so far removed from the rarefied air of high-stakes showbiz, I might as well be a medieval juggler working market day during the annual shaving of the simpletons. (I'm not sure they actually had those days, so apologies to whatever simpleton was simple enough to buy this book and is now simply offended.) Prior to getting the invite from *SCTV*, I was actually feeling fortunate for having just sold out two shows in Sarnia . . . on weeknights!

If readers will indulge me a tangent . . . for those living east or west of Ontario, Sarnia is known as Chemical Valley, thanks to the sixty or more chemical plants, fertilizer facilities and oil refineries whose industries daily dump a devil's brew of carcinogens into the air and water. Locals seem to take it in stride, though. Granted, the bartender at a certain watering hole may be sporting a mysterious seven-pound cauliflower growth on his chin . . . that changes colour with the seasons . . . but that's a small price to pay for a truck in the driveway and a job at Dow Chemical. Besides, there's really no need to worry: union health benefits would cover the removal of any facial tumours incurred as a result of slopping up an industrial-sized spill of ethylbenzene that's already melted some poor bastard's feet off clear to the shins.

My Elgin set went exceptionally well. The laughs roared up from the seats with the fury of rogue waves. It felt redemptive, especially since I'd been fired from the Second City mainstage thirty-five years prior. The invite came from the man who did it, impresario Andrew Alexander. To be asked to deliver a set before this august body of talent hit the stage was testimony to his faith in my abilities. Even though he'd been the one to hand me my pink slip, he knew the improviser I tried to be in 1983 wasn't the stand-up I'd become.

Second City was the best place for any eager young actor to learn the craft of character-driven ensemble comedy, where scene structure and spontaneity worked in tandem to create, as high priestess of the form, Viola Spolin, put it, "something wonderful right away."

Yet, despite Second City's indisputable opportunities for creative growth, a sword of Damocles hung over the place, where whispered names of the unceremoniously fired stood as portents of how quickly you could be "disappeared." Oblivious to the fate about to befall them, one minute, an actor was in the cast, and the next, their backstage dressing room booth was occupied by a hungry wannabe who'd been watching the show every night from their perch at the back of the theatre in vulture's corner, when they weren't at home sticking pins in a voodoo doll that resembled the actor who just got the boot.

After five years and three shows with the organization, the sword fell on me. Given how light I'd become in the nightly improv sets, (from whose scenes we built each new show), it came as no surprise. Feeling that I wasn't pulling my weight, a gnawing insecurity took hold, fuelling an anxiety that stifled an innate comedic intuition that, up to this point, had served me well my entire life.

Suffice it to say, every time I opened my mouth I felt I should shut it, and every time I shut it, I felt I should speak up. To quote my father, "Jesus Murphy, Ronnie! A man wouldn't know whether to shit or go blind!"

Among those of us who started together in the Touring Company, pressure to succeed in the major leagues of Toronto's mainstage compromised what had once been a have-your-back brothers-in-arms camaraderie, earned in the fight for laughs surviving tough gigs in ugly rooms and long drives on winter roads in a crowded van, where we vacillated between being a mirthful gang of ribald young satirists and a seething crew of battle-crusted veterans expressing contempt for whatever idiosyncrasies might manifest themselves in the close quarters of a vehicle gone ripe with a winter's worth of stale marijuana smoke, Big Macs, and a vegan member's sneaky flatulence. (The only difference between that van and the submariners of *Das Boot* is that we weren't speaking German.)

As eager disciples of the form, we had progressed from beginner to advanced in Second City's improv classes. If you passed their twice-yearly auditions, you won entrance to the Touring Company where this aforementioned van sat parked outside the front doors of Toronto's historic Old Firehall Theatre at 110 Lombard Street. Once aboard and on the road, you were now a card-carrying member of a club that was the first step to youthful ambition realized. Unless of course, after two weeks, two months or too long for your own good, you still stunk up a scene, had no comedic timing, couldn't improvise to save your life, were way too weird even for a comedy troupe, missed your onstage cues or got on everyone's nerves in the van by telling boring stories that lacked punchlines. In that case, during one interminable drive back to Toronto through another February midnight after suffering another hellish gig spent moiling for comedy gold north of "Why Were We Ever Booked in This Hillbilly Holler in the First Place?", you'd be thrown from the moving vehicle and left to suffer the vicissitudes of a cruel season, when, come spring, what was left of your bones would be ground to potash by enterprising farm-hands and sold to the nurseries that dot the fertile soil of the Holland Marsh. Or worse . . . just ignored.

The bonus of suffering Ontario's winter roads was a summertime residence at Deerhurst Resort, in the heart of Muskoka cottage country. In 1981, Deerhurst was hardly the sprawling corporate retreat it would later become, but getting paid to hone your funny in what was really the Canadian Catskills before audiences of vacationing Torontonians was as good as it gets.

Our cast rented a defunct turn-of-the-century hotel called Portage Station that in its late-nineteenth-century salad days of parasols, top hats and Victorian manners, catered to affluent passengers arriving on the Muskoka steamship lines. By the time of our tenure, it had sat empty since its short-lived role as a liquor licensed summertime party palace, which in its late twentieth-century incarnation catered to the caramel tanned Topsider wearing aryan eyed sons and daughters of Muskoka blue bloods, who when they weren't fraternizing with the locals they'd forget about in September, were incurring DUIs for rolling Daddy's beamer in the ditch on the dirt road drive home. The place came complete with an institutional-sized kitchen and a dance floor with a working disco ball that we'd turn on and laugh at in praise of our bizarre good fortune. Our stately white elephant sat on a hill with a commanding view of a lake surrounded by forest, where young lovers could steal away to hidden glades in those elfin woodlands and shag with the zeal of docile house cats recently gone feral. Life was good.

We performed at Deerhurst Resort twice a week all year long for whatever corporate group was on retreat (and once for a lone pair of newlyweds who, we assumed, couldn't afford a trip to Vegas), diligently making the Wednesday and Saturday drive for our 8 p.m. show, regardless of what hellacious weather nature was throwing our way. In that neolithic age of travel, the only place to grab a meal on Highway 11 during our 11 p.m. drive back to Toronto was a forlorn service station and adjoining small diner run by a grumpy man and his sad wife. When the seven of us entered, jabbering non-stop, sporting our ravenous post-show "food faces", the couple eyed us much in the way one would if surprised by euphoric outpatients who had suddenly shown up in your kitchen right before bedtime, talking loudly, touching stuff, and eating your Frosted Flakes.

I'm back at the Elgin now. (Stay with me.) I remember making a point of keeping my set "universal," so it could be understood by any Americans in attendance unacquainted with our nation's regional idiosyncrasies, such as the size of the potholes on the streets of Inuvik in spring, or the impact of a chinook's dropping barometric pressure on manic-depressives in Lethbridge. Actually, my keeping it universal was for the benefit of Torontonians, too. When you consider your city to be the centre of the universe, knowing the price of a dozen eggs in Pangnirtung is not a priority.

(Truth be told, I'm so Canadian, most *Canadians* don't know what the hell I'm talking about!)

After my Elgin set I was standing in the wings watching the show when the head of Netflix, Ted Sarandos, came up to me and said, "That was a great set." I thanked him and said, "You've certainly seen a lot of comedy."

"Yes, I have," he replied, looking down at me from his six-foot, seven-inch height with a paternal smile unique to those with a net worth of six *billion* dollars. "And that was a great set," he said again.

As a minion scurried him away, while throwing a surly, proprietary stink eye back at me, I figured that at sixty years of age, I'd finally gotten my big break. It would only be a matter of time before Netflix rolled out the welcome mat.

Lesson learned: age might only be a number, but in television, if that number's over fifty, it's a number that carries COVID.

Judging a Canadian performer's worth against American standards is unfair, but perfectly understandable, especially when 80 percent of our population lives so close to the border, we're practically looking up Lady Liberty's skirt! The incantatory spell of her siren song has for generations heralded the promise of dreams made manifest. At least in my business. After all, America invented television. They knew, and still *do* know, entertainment. They set the standard. Granted, Canadian television might be light years from where it was in the 1970s but still, back then *The Beachcombers* coming on CBC on Sunday night just meant *The Wonderful World of Disney* was over!

It was the same for our leaders as well. During America's golden era of postwar prosperity in the early 1960s, when President Kennedy and Jacqueline Bouvier Kennedy were the shining, sexy young couple of Camelot, just next door in dour Canada, jowly John "The Farmers' Friend" Diefenbaker and his main squeeze, Olive, were stepping over cow pies at a tractor pull in Girvin. Sure, eight years later a cape-and-fedora-sporting Pierre Trudeau dating Jill St. John may have bought us some cred with the paparazzi, but the die had been cast.

We grew up watching American comedians whose subversive voices inspired an entire generation of stand-ups. No way could the likes of Richard Pryor, George Carlin or even the Smothers Brothers have developed in our "peaceable kingdom." Nor could the man I'd talked to at JFL, Billy Connolly. No Canadian television network would have given that comedic force of nature a ninety-minute special, out of which he spends twenty minutes imitating farting sled dogs. (I love how he doubles down on the bit, too—pushing it farther and farther and revelling in the unapologetic, unbridled puerile joy of it all, while trumpeting an operatic impression of Arctic canines passing their raw, seal-meat-supper-powered ass gas into the wind. Google the clip. In fact, watch *any* clip of Billy Connolly. If you don't think he's funny, throw this book away right now!)

These socially disruptive voices simply could not have developed here, because the cultural illuminati and network gatekeepers during the era that made them could be prudes when it came to comedy. And not just in television, either. Even live acts suffered at the hands of puritanical censorship. It's why the trail-blazing, uncompromisingly profane and hilarious comedy team of brothers MacLean and MacLean had to fight a charge of immoral content all the way to the Supreme Court of Canada in 1977, all because they dropped a fusillade of f-bombs in their act, which an adult audience had paid *expecting* to hear! It's not like Mr. Dressup pulled a drunken Finnegan out of the Tickle Trunk and the first thing the puppet did was take a whiz onstage. (I know puppets don't pee; I'm just making a metaphoric allusion to describe how surprised an audience would be had they paid to see these totems of innocence fully expecting innocuous repartee between the duo—lauding access to colouring books and crayons on a rainy day as a soothing cure for the mumps for instance—but instead, were subjected to an inebriated Finnegan defiantly taking the act in a surprising new direction.) Even though adults had made an adult decision to hear the brothers MacLean, a Sault Ste. Marie prosecutor with political ambitions and a sense of propriety far more conservative than the comedy duo's fans thought their act would do irreparable harm to the moral fibre of society, perhaps even incite a level of anarchy resulting in everything from a rise in teenage pregnancies to a drop in softwood prices. So, he pressed charges. But the brothers won. Twice.

Angry iconoclasts are distrusted in a country whose motto is "Peace, order and good government." That call to arms says, "Be nice, follow the rules and keep the noise down." On the other hand, America's motto—"Life, liberty and the pursuit of happiness"— amounts to "This way for hookers and blow, bro!" That's why so many Canadian-born comedians headed for the States. Not for hookers and blow, I mean, but to rock the apple cart in a country with 365 million people. Not thirty-seven million. You can have half the population of America hating your act and the other half loving it . . . which is still roughly *five times* the population of Canada. That's some decent wiggle room.

So, before you think I've sold my allegiance to America, I haven't. I was merely giving context to why Canadian comedians head south. (I know, it's a stretch.)

There's another reason these comedy legends could never have built their acts here. It's because the origins of our two nations were diametrically opposite. Canada wasn't sired by the smoke and fire of revolution, while America was. When her Thirteen Colonies gave England the boot in 1776 by raising an army of fighting farmers who beat the Yorkshire pudding out of a professional British one, she canonized a distrust of authority stoked by stirring catchphrases from their deified Founding Fathers such as "Give me liberty or give me death" . . . a sentiment actualized during COVID by the many who refused to wear a mask.

Canada's founding fathers, on the other hand—if you can give such immortal status to a gang of mutton-chopped lawyers harbouring such deference for the monarchy that they'd have bronzed one of Queen Victoria's turds to use as a paperweight—took a far more measured approach when they *legislated* our country into being. Where Canada was a benign delivery from the womb of Mother Britain, America's was a crack baby breech birth that chewed off its own umbilical cord.

To the untrained eye, it would appear Canada is clinically short on rebels, when in reality, that role has been played by Indigenous leaders who have fought settler privilege and the colonial mandate of expansion since before Confederation. During the nineteenth century, leaders such as Chief Poundmaker and Chief Crowfoot of the prairie Assiniboine and Sioux, to the fearless Mohawk of the Oka standoff, the Heltsiuk of Bella Bella who saved the Great Bear Rainforest from Enbridge pipelines, and the Wet'suwet'en of British Columbia, who refused company bulldozers entry to their lands, thus galvanizing a nationwide Indigenous blockade of railway lines, were bona fide Canadian rebels standing in defiant opposition to the status quo. Honouring the treaties and Supreme Court decisions signed in good faith by the Crown would be a step in the right direction, but when influence-peddling corporate interests in collusion with government proxy hold all the aces in the deck, it's no wonder solutions seem impossible. I don't get it. Oil and mining companies can pollute the country with impunity and it's business as usual. When I was a homeowner and dared to burn a few fall leaves in my backyard, the SWAT team showed up!

Perhaps the most famous of these land defenders is Manitoba iconoclast Louis Riel, who fought the right fight for his Métis people in the North-West Rebellion of 1885. His reward was to be hanged by John A. Macdonald's Conservatives. One hundred and forty years later, and well into the twenty-first century, successive governments—Conservative *and* Liberal—have refused to pardon the man. You know you must have been doing something right when Ottawa hates your guts that long! Louis disrupted the white Anglo-Saxon status quo, and nothing pisses off old white dudes more than telling them they can't have it their way—which is what rebels do.

Of course, Riel didn't have to get laughs while he did it, though maybe his men laughed behind his back when he started talking to angels in the clouds and had the bright idea of moving the Vatican to Batoche, Saskatchewan. (Then again, anyone who has spent time in a Roman Catholic seminary as Louis did, shouldn't be surprised if they come out of the experience susceptible to hallucinations.)

But I'm getting ahead of myself.

In 1997, I'd heard of an event called Contact, a marketplace where performers of all stripes could set up a booth, advertise their act and do fifteen minutes of it for an auditorium full of people who had the authority to book you in their theatres and the clout to write a cheque. After my set, a dozen of them did just that—which was unusual, because theatres wanted nothing to do with comedians in those days. We were anathema to their more refined tastes.

The only experience Canadians had of seeing homegrown stand-up comedians on television in the mid-'90s was CBC's *Comics!* This series brought the art form into the nation's living rooms for the first time ever. *Comics!* was filmed in front of a live studio audience, and every comedian got a thirty-minute set that acted as a calling card for club owners and bookers, who could see an actual audience validate a comedian's performance with their laughter and applause. When few homegrown comedians were scoring a coveted eight-minute televised gala set at Just for Laughs, *Comics!* was giving us the incredible luxury of half an hour of national airtime.

Lorne Elliott's radio show *Madly Off in All Directions* did much the same, providing comedians with what Steve Patterson and CBC's *The Debaters* offer many today: national exposure and a payday.

The Comedy Network, with its promotional tag of "Time Well Wasted," had yet to be born, but when it was, parent company CTV handed rare ninety-minute specials to Ottawa-born bulletproof act, Jeremy Hotz, Brampton's own Russell Peters and myself. I shot my one-man show *Up and Down in Shaky Town*, and damned if CTV didn't play it every New Year's Day for seven years in a row! Nary a penny came my way in residuals, though, because in Canada, we're bought out for 100 percent of our fee, which means a show can be played in perpetuity—until Joggins, Nova Scotia, is once again attached to the Horn of Africa. But at least I could take vicarious pleasure in knowing I was helping some hurting buckos sweat their way through a hangover while they watched me do the "Liquor Barn" dance.

Truth is that more often than not, the moving target I never hit a lifetime ago in LA was far from the studios of Hollywood legend. My worlds were the vast casting houses I shared with dozens of other struggling members of the Screen Actors Guild, all of us desperate to land the bread and butter of the performing proletariat: television commercials. Everyone hoped to score a coveted and lucrative national campaign that would keep the bills from prowling round their mail slot like wolves over a litter of blind piglets in the snow. The first commercial I got down there saved us a winter of purgatorial gloom.

Do you remember those years when you were so broke, you had to scour the house for suitable Christmas gifts? I remember phoning my mother and asking, "So, you liked the pot holders, then, Mom? Yes, that's the way they make them in California . . . covered in crusty food with burn marks on them."

I'd moved down to do a television series created by a couple of talented Toronto Second City actresses, Deborah McGrath and Linda Kash. They'd sold it to Ron Howard's company, Imagine Entertainment, and it was syndicated nightly to independent channels across America. *My Talk Show* was a quirky, original concept set in a suburban home in the fictional town of Derby, Wisconsin, where a woman and her neighbours (including me) chatted up celebrity guests on a living room couch. At first, the guests were bona fide celebrities of the day, such as William Shatner, Martin Mull and Jim Belushi. But as the ratings took a nosedive, the show's booker—rebuffed, I assume, by agents who'd sooner see their A-list clients cutting a ribbon at the opening of an abattoir than chatting with us—began scouring showbiz purgatory for anyone who once had a modicum of television notoriety. Someone opened the gates at the "Where Are They Now?" compound, and every network personality from yesteryear who was still capable of functioning in public unescorted by orderlies got a day pass.

Werner Klemperer, who played Colonel Klink on *Hogan's Heroes* in the '60s, showed up, as did a Romanian plate spinner who'd gained fame on *The Ed Sullivan Show* and was still going to lunch on that appearance—thirty years later! They tried to get Bob Denver of *Gilligan's Island* fame, but were told, "There's not a chance. Besides, he's a very difficult guest."

No kidding he's "difficult"! Who wouldn't be the exact opposite in real life of that happy-go-lucky, sailor-hat-wearing, goofy man-child he played on a television show decades ago—a guy whose persona was forever fused in public memory thanks to endless reruns that never paid him a penny in residuals? That's not a career; that's a curse!

Chubby Checker also visited the set and lip-synched to "The Twist." That's right, *lip-synched*. In the hallway after shooting was done for the day, the man whose song had started a worldwide dance craze in 1960 after he sang it on Dick Clark's *American Bandstand* told me he used to work at a chicken-cutting plant. (Not the subject I'd open a conversation with, but to each his own.) He was an uncomfortably close talker too, whose pleading eyes, moist either with melancholy or medication, made me wish I wasn't an actor with his back to the wall offering no avenue of escape but a simple Sardinian shepherd leading his flock to pasture nurturing no dream of Hollywood glory.

I will bet good money that shamanic novitiates, well into the throes of an ayahuasca-induced hallucinogenic-shape-shifting vision quest, could never reach the level of surreality I did while listening with rapt attention to Chubby Checker's dissertation on his stolen American Dream.

"I noticed with all the choppin' of chickens we were doin'," said Chubby, "that we were throwin' away perfectly good chicken parts."

(I had a good idea that the parts he was referring to wouldn't even make the cut on the menu at Fat Jerry's House of Organ Meats.)

"After I got my big break, I left the plant, but the idea of doing something with all that wasted chicken stayed with me. One day I told my manager the idea. He said, 'You are crazy, man! That's why they throw it *away*! Ain't nobody gonna want to eat a bowl of chicken dicks!'

"Well," Chubby continued, "soon as my song was no longer number one, what did that no-good scoundrel do? But steal my idea and invent . . . mock chicken! That's right! *Mock chicken* is my idea! Chicken made with other parts of the chicken is . . . ?"

"Mock chicken," I answered.

He poked me in the chest. "You got it! Sonofabitch manager *stole* my idea! He got the credit for inventing mock chicken, became a billionaire, and Chubby," he lamented, arms outstretched at the injustice of it all, "he's still singing the 'Twist'!"

If that's not pathos, good reader, I'm Burton Cummings.

Vince Edwards, the actor who played neurosurgeon Dr. Ben Casey from 1961 to 1966 on ABC, also joined us, as if released from the kind of coma his television character was always pulling patients out of. I don't remember much about him, other than that his girl-friend was from New Brunswick, and when he found out I was born in the province next door, he made me say hello to her on the phone. We talked about the Magnetic Hill, McCain shoestring french fries, K.C. Irving's billions—and how the Bay of Fundy's infamous tidal *bore* is the most aptly named geographic phenomena in the world. (Look, it might be a big money maker for Moncton where tourists stand and wait for this expectant wall of water to come racing up an estuary that heralds the rise of the world's highest tides but sweet Jesus, people, I've made bigger waves in the tub after eating a break-fast burrito!)

Mostly, though, I remember the servile and sallow-faced execu-tives from Imagine Entertainment who roamed the hallways before every show, poring over the previous night's Nielsen ratings sheet. Once the numbers began their fiery nosedive to oblivion, they stood in the shadows, wearing faces wracked with feigned concern, all the while wringing their manicured hands like Pontius Pilate looking for someone to crucify. Our bane was a particularly unctuous and insipid courtier, still sporting a disco dance-floor perm twenty years after its best-before date who wore a sweater wrapped round his neck like some dime-store Gatsby and called everybody "family." Right. So did Charles Manson.

On Tuesday, our cast photo was in *Newsweek*, accompanying a piece that lauded us as this year's "cult show to watch." On Thursday, we were cancelled. And on Monday, I was chest-deep in a hole on the actor Robert Urich's front lawn with a local pal's father's landscaping company, tugging at the roots of a rotted bush. The man who played Jake Spoon on the riveting mini-series *Lonesome Dove* walked out the front door dressed in knee-high leather riding boots with a polo helmet tucked under one arm while nonchalantly swinging a mallet made for the sport with the other. The dude looked every inch the baronial master of his San Fernando Valley domain ready for an afternoon engaged in the sport of kings. My pal greeted him with "Hi, Bob!" and pointing down to me said, "This is my friend Ron. He's an actor, too." "Really?" he responded with all the feigned interest a Hollywood star could muster while staring at a mud-smeared troll-in-a-hole. I would have happily taken a break from my digging to discuss the merits of the Stanislavski method and its impact on contemporary American cinema, but oddly enough, Jake Spoon didn't seem psyched for a chin wag. Go figure?

Suffice it to say that when the dust finally cleared, I found I hadn't made the kind of money you'd associate with American TV. In fact, I hadn't made the kind of money you'd associate with a manager of a mini-putt course. I was supposed to make three grand a week with sixty-five shows guaranteed, but after a palace coup at Imagine resulted in a new head of development replacing the *old* head of development who supported the show, a bloody gutting of our original group was under way, and out of an eight-person writing and acting team, three were left standing. What had been three thousand dollars a week at sixty-five shows guaranteed in 1990, became fifteen shows guaranteed at four hundred and fifteen bucks an episode. You read that right. Four *hundred* and fifteen. Taxes took 30 percent of that, and I *still* got audited by the IRS for the thirty-seven thousand dollars I made that year—correct again, *thirty-seven*—because the H&R Block accountant at the mall I had paid to do my taxes (who also played an accountant once in an episode of *Mannix*) put a decimal point in the wrong place. I know. Seems unfair.

The same year that the California aerospace industry bottomed out, taking sixty thousand jobs with it and throwing an entire state into recession, the IRS figured an actor from Canada who netted three hundred and fifty dollars a show after taxes on a now-cancelled series, whose family car was a second-hand '79 Dodge Colt that left an oil slick so thick on the floor of the garage that every time he pulled out of the driveway, there was a dying sea bird flopping in it, was the cause of the collapse.

Because of the plodding nature of bureaucracy, the IRS never notified me of my arrears until I was safely back in Canada. What had started out as two thousand dollars owing had now, thanks to interest, doubled to four.

The IRS agent and I spoke half a dozen times on the phone, and each time we did when I'd confidently inform him that, "You have no jurisdiction over me here," I swore I heard the ventricles in that bureaucrat's ice-cold heart crystallizing on the other end of the phone.

"We have ways of making life very difficult should you ever cross the border again," he warned.

The IRS has an elephant's memory and a fearsome reputation for pursuing their quarry with a Nazi hunter's zeal. Simon Wiesenthal with a team of Mossad agents and a list of of residents with German last names at an old folks' home in a hidden corner of Paraguay couldn't hold a candle to the dedicated hitmen of Washington's tax department when they were hell-bent on retribution. Not going to lie, a little shiver still goes up my spine every time I hand my passport to an American customs agent. I'm worried my long-gone tax infraction will show up on their computer screen and I'll be whisked into a soundproof room on the wrong side of Toronto's Pearson Airport, for a pistol-whipping courtesy of Homeland Security.

Every Canadian who chases Hollywood's grail has an experience uniquely their own. That just happened to be mine. Hats off to the perseverance of my fellow countrymen who also went south and managed to scratch out a career in a nation that knows no middle ground. In America, you're either winning or you're not. Victory is the only option. Anything less, and you've lost. So, after three years of trying to make something happen there, I returned to Canada and made something happen here.

But I didn't do it alone. Once upon a time I had a wife who really had my back. She said, "When we move home to Toronto, you can't do the same thing you've always done. You can't just wait for your agent to phone with an audition and hope you get it. You've got to approach your career differently." So, I did. Unfortunately, becoming a comedian wasn't what she'd anticipated, which is why I live alone now.

That's a shorter way of saying: The road became my priority and I returned from my tours an exhausted, emotionally depleted, cranky bastard who used up all his funny for paying audiences, so that once he crossed the threshold of his own home, he transformed into a moody, distant cur tucked into a corner reading another tome on the Battle of Stalingrad. Suffice it to say, a mechanic's car isn't always clean, and a comedian's home isn't always funny.

After a few years of booking rooms on my own, good fortune saw me fall into partnership with an exemplary producer of unimpeachable honesty, business acumen and integrity: Terry McRae of Shantero Productions. The Contact event got me booked for a night at the Academy Theatre in Lindsay, Ontario, a show that was supposed to be attended by townsfolk, as well as one hundred and fifty members of the Cadillac Club. I guess owning a Cadillac isn't enough; you also have to spend weekends and holidays amongst your Cadillac kin, all wearing jackets sporting Cadillac logos, with whom you'll share esoteric information on everything from finding spark plugs for your '61 El Dorado to how owning such a vehicle makes you so much better than the proles who can only afford a Dodge Neon.

This tribal allegiance is not terribly dissimilar from that of Civil War re-enactors. (It's very dissimilar, actually, and I'll admit the analogy's a stretch, but bear with me . . . *again*.) Like Cadillac Club people, Civil War re-enactors lead lives of normalcy during the week, but come Saturday, they'll be amongst their own, running through a field, clutching a period-piece rifle in 102-degree heat, dressed from tip to tail in mid-nineteenth-century regimental uniforms made of wool, so they can pretend they've caught a bullet in the breast at the Second Battle of Bull Run. Get this, though: once you're "shot," you've got to stay where you've fallen, under the blistering sun . . . *for the rest of the day*. Oh, what fun! If that's what it takes to feel a sense of belonging, I'd sooner live alone in a cave, subsisting on rainwater and toe jam.

In the re-enactor world, authenticity is everything. Meticulous attention to detail is paramount, from the make of their uniform buttons to using toothbrushes made of horsehair. I guess they draw the line at dysentery. (Wimps.) If getting as close as possible to authentically experiencing the horror of battle without time-travelling to 1863 is their real modus operandi, then I have a suggestion: shoot yourself in the foot, let gangrene set in and have a drunken buddy dressed as a battlefield surgeon saw it off in a cornfield under the hot sun, while you bite down on a piece of wood and pass out. There you go: time-travelling problem solved.

I just realized that anyone reading this book who belongs to a Cadillac Club has probably just drifted it across the room in a pique of anger. My sincere apologies. Dying of a fake suppurating chest wound is far more unusual a hobby than talking engine size with a Cadillac owner in a mall parking lot in Lindsay, Ontario—which, I guess, is where most of the Cadillac Club was the night I was performing, because only two of the clowns showed up. Counting the townsfolk who *did* come, that made forty-one. The theatre held six hundred. My take for the night was supposed to be eight hundred dollars, but with the loss the theatre took at the door, we agreed on four hundred.

A month later, Terry McRae and his son dropped in looking to see if the artistic director who ran the theatre had ever booked comedians. The artistic director held up my photo and said, "This guy is pretty good." Lesson learned: it's not always about the money.

I learned the hard way about the importance of a great producer after leaving Terry's company for bigger Toronto agencies . . .

twice, thinking they'd take me to "the next level"—whatever that was supposed to be. The decision was spawned by an ego-driven belief that where you're *at* isn't as good as where you *should be*. But, in fact, where I *was* was exactly where I have always wanted to be . . . just working!

Shantero and I started our first tour in April 1999 with half a dozen theatres along Ontario's Highway 401. We sold out the 1,000-seat Centrepointe Theatre in Nepean and added an encore date, too. I couldn't believe my good fortune! Terry did what no other promoter in Canada had the guts to do for a relatively unknown comic looking to play theatres: he put his own dollar on the line, took the risk, rented the theatres, landed local radio stations as sponsors and advertised aggressively on that medium and in print, never seeing a penny of federal largesse or corporate funding to fuel our engine. A work ethic worthy of biblical Job did that, and with forty years spent running acts this wide country over, that taciturn Scotsman, despite COVID's impact on live touring, is still in business.

When I first hit the road, the tech revolution was in its infancy, and it took me a while to get on board. (After all, I'm from a day where a hashtag was something you got from doing hash *knives*.) Not to disparage social media entirely, because I enjoy sharing photos on Instagram of meals I've made, rivers I've run, hikes I've taken and tomatoes I've grown . . . but I still don't know *why*. I don't know why it matters that someone in Salmon Arm, British Columbia, "likes" the garden I planted on the deck of my Toronto condo, but the dopamine it releases in the brain's pleasure centre does a great job of making me believe it *should*. ("Pleasure centre." Sounds like a sex club in Berlin where you'd catch chlamydia, COVID-19, Zika virus,

SARS, Ebola and a bad case of Bactrian camel ass rash just by ringing the doorbell. Out of curiosity, of course.)

The nanosecond pace of technological change made the sale of my specials on DVD obsolete overnight. From 2007 until 2013, I'd stay for an hour in the lobby after every show, autographing copies for patrons who'd purchased them. By 2015, this bit of extra income had suffered the dodo's fate. There are now a dozen boxes of my final four specials, shot between 2013 and 2017, holding up a wall in a Toronto storage space. Now I know how buddy felt who invested a family fortune in buggy whips, five years after Henry Ford flooded the market with Model Ts.

Here we are at the end of the chapter, and you're no doubt wondering, "Whatever happened to that logging truck?" (I didn't forget.) Well, with half the boreal forest's worth of logs strapped to its carriage and its ass end swaying into my lane, I cut hard for the shoulder.

As it blew past at an unholy clip, barely a sliver of Eucharist away from introducing me to dead relations, I let loose with:

"Slow down, ya bastard! You're carrying wood. It will keep!"

Chapter Two
TWO DAYS IN SASKATCHEWAN

A cold and sepulchral ice fog smothers the coulees of the Qu'Appelle Valley while the vacant eye of a reluctant sun makes a feeble attempt at breaking through the grey mantle of sky. If the ceiling were any lower, it would be in my lap. Squinting through the car's windshield, I swear I see antlered silhouettes of mule deer moving wraithlike in the distance. Hitting one would most certainly turn this ergonomic nightmare of tin and plastic I've rented from Avis into a piece of abstract art.

The Yellowhead Highway is streaked with bloodstains where many of the ungulates have met their Maker, leaving nothing but a smear of deer between the double lines and a pair of spindly legs poking up at unnatural angles from a mound of pink meat and fur on the soft shoulder.

I'm always travelling this corner of the country when winter has the land in a hammerlock and the sweetgrass smells of a prairie summer seem as far away as Chief Poundmaker's childhood. Every Canadian comic hits the road when it's under frigid siege, and people are looking for a night of laughs to take the edge off the long haul towards spring. They know from experience that there's an undeniable visceral charge you get from watching stand-up performed live, cocooned with others in a packed theatre, as opposed to watching it on TV, alone at home in your pajamas. (That observation can't help but feel bittersweet as I write these words in April 2021. With live performance forced into the realm of cyberspace, we've become acutely aware how important a *shared* experience really is.) For a few hours, stand-up puts strangers seated shoulder to shoulder all on the same page channelling the same life force. Laughter releases a cascade of endorphins through their collective nervous systems, lightening the load of the daily struggle. Or, as a cab driver in Sault Ste. Marie once said to me, "It's a vacation for the soul, Ronnie."

Stand-up creates an umbilical relationship between audience and comedian. It is symbiotic, proving that laughter is an affirmation of what it means to be human. After all, we're the only species in the animal kingdom that *can* laugh! (As much as I love meerkats, you never see them getting together as a group beneath the monkey tree to watch one of their own imitate the time he saw a hyena get gored in the arse by a warthog.)

As mentioned, I'm fortunate enough to have a competent producer in my corner, one with an impeccable pedigree and unimpeachable reputation. Unlike other producers who are content to book a tour, take their commission and then subcontract its execution to others, the indomitable Terry McRae (now joined by sons Patrick and Robin) not only books his theatres with a deposit a year in advance, garners sponsors and drives publicity with his one-stop shop, he also commits to driving every kilometre his acts do.

Thankfully, the man had the presence of mind to keep a map on his desk when he booked a tour. When I foolishly left his family's boutique operation for other outfits with star-studded rosters, their assurances that they would take me to "the next level," whatever *that* is in Canada, proved shamelessly long on promises and laughably short on substance. Upon signing with them, I entered a world of such cartographic ignorance, my tour must have been booked by a room full of drunken interns in blindfolds, seated at a table cluttered with empty shot glasses opposite a map of Canada on a wall riddled with darts they had thrown in imitation of a frat house drinking game. One February tour I took a pass on, designed with no regard for my personal safety, would have had me criss-crossing the Rocky Mountains through avalanche country for back-to-back gigs 640 kilometres apart along the killer Coquihalla Highway, a road that was surely designed by an optically compromised engineer who bought his degree at a Honduran flea market.

This is the sort of touring hell you suffer when you're an eager rookie in the Yuk Yuk's comedy mines, where the vast majority of Canadian comedians have honed their chops. They learn to weather brutal driving conditions, drunken patrons and paltry paydays, yet persevere, because stand-up is what they've been called to do. You've got to tip your hat to four comics in a no-name beater living on fast food and faith, bound for a one-nighter at a biker bar somewhere north of nowhere whose owner knows where the bodies are buried. They'll be bunking at a funky, down-at-the-heels motel whose cigarette butt–burned carpets reek from decades of sloppy sex, cheap whisky and the Pine-Sol the maids used in a futile attempt to scrub the stink of hopelessness away.

My early dues-paying years on the road had nothing on that level of suffering. For one thing, I travelled in a van with a cast of actors—because, well, I wanted to be one. What I didn't know then was that the basic job requirement for most actors is the ability to survive *not* being employed as one.

After graduating university, I landed a gig in a Wolfville, Nova Scotia–based puppet company. You read that right: puppets. Over the years, this well-run and very professional company has gone on to win many awards and global acclaim. But back then, we weren't flying to Beijing and Krakow, as they eventually would, for international puppet festivals where marionettes are revered and puppeteers drink for free in the company of municipal officials and art councils run by disillusioned communists. No, we were driving to elementary schools around Nova Scotia, performing in that equity-wage rite of passage known as "children's theatre."

The morning it all went horribly south, we were encircled by preschoolers in a very small, smothering-hot gymnasium after a night spent eating pickled eggs and drinking skunky draft in a New Glasgow Legion.

This particular production never involved puppets, which were reserved for older children who could survive the sight of an actor wearing a frightening face mask, standing seven feet tall in boots with wooden blocks on them, dressed as Gitchi Manitou of Mi'kmaq myth. (White people expropriating the cosmology of an Indigenous people never played on that company's conscience forty-two years ago. It was a much different day. However, had we played any First Nations reserves, I'm sure the locals living there would have enlightened us—and justifiably so—as to why we shouldn't.)

What we were performing that morning was a counting game for four- to six-year-olds. I played a character called Baby One, who ambled round the floor on knee pads, holding a rattle. I was twenty-two years old, with a bachelor's degree in history. "Pride goeth before a fall," they say. I clearly had none, so I was safe. I'm not sure if Laurence Olivier kicked his career into gear doing children's theatre, but in the days of early hunger hoping for a foothold in a precarious industry, I felt I had hit the jackpot.

My pal was playing . . . the Chicken. He never wore a full chicken suit, as our prop budget was limited. After all, we were supported by government grants in what was then called a "have-not" province. (I'm told that Canada's greatest Shakespearean actor, Colm Feore, had the full and pristine chicken suit during *his* years in children's theatre, but that's Ontario affluence for you.) The Chicken wore a mask fashioned from scuba headgear that had a red rubber glove glued to the top. Inside the fingers of the glove were cigar tubes, so that they would stand up straight like a rooster's comb, even though my pal was not a rooster, but the Chicken. (Given our demographic, costume gender accuracy was a moot point.)

The Chicken's face was entirely visible, and the pores on his forehead were leaking the swill we'd been quaffing the night before. The droplets were beading into a dank, cold sweat, as the nauseating reek of pickled eggs that had been quietly fermenting in our colons overnight began to silently sneak from their recesses and permeate every corner of that very small, equatorially stifling-hot gymnasium. The children seemed oblivious to the deadly attack of chlorine-level ass gas that, without a shadow of a doubt, would have buckled every troop to their knees in the trenches of Passchendaele. But not here. They were transfixed . . . on a chicken and a baby.

Everyone gets punchy after a long theatrical run, no matter what the play. I'm not saying a counting game for preschoolers can hold a candle to *Come from Away*, but I *am* willing to wager that even those incredibly talented actors, performing in the most heart-warming musical since the von Trapp family ran from Nazis in *The Sound of Music*, will, as we did, slowly start to lose their minds. More than likely, they'll stay the course, because they're all talented professionals of the highest order. I, on the other hand forty-two years ago, was not.

Children seated three rows deep on the floor surrounded us in a semicircle. One of the other actors had some scene-chewing monologue about the number three, and he'd just left the stage with a confident strut, exuding a self-serving satisfaction worthy of a young Peter O'Toole after delivering a show-stopping soliloquy in the West End. It's pretty hard to justify that level of ego when your entire audience has entered the gymnasium attached to each other's mittens.

Maybe that's why my pal started clucking louder than usual. Maybe it had dawned on him sometime the night before, when we were drunk in a Legion—*again*—that whatever plans he had of escaping this internment to become the next Robert Duvall were as gossamer-thin in delivering on that dream, as a desert mirage would be to a lost and dehydrated Englishman hallucinating a naked duchess with a tray of tea and crumpets.

The Chicken had hit what journalist Malcolm Gladwell would later describe as the "tipping point." It's the moment where the gloves come off, where what had once mattered no longer does. Another idea popularized by Malcolm is that one must dedicate a minimum of ten thousand hours to achieve proficiency at one's chosen craft. This morning would witness no such perseverance from the Chicken—nor his sidekick. Other puppeteers may assail the heights of the profession and become the willing muse of every marionette maker in Leipzig, but for us, that dream was dead.

What, at the start of our tour, had been a gentle, happy-go-lucky *cluck-cluck-cluck* any barnyard chicken would make while scratching in the dirt, on this notorious morning became a painful howl: *booo-deck! booo-deck!* It was nothing short of a *cri de coeur*, delivered with all the gusto a journeyman actor, still drunk at 9 a.m. and dressed as poultry, could muster. The young man had been cold-cocked by the realization that his hope of stardom had dematerialized before his eyes with all the indifference of a ghost at dawn. So, why fight it? With a dangerously flushed pallor and spit arcing in great sprays of gesticulation, the Chicken's wilful display of anarchy bade the Baby step "off book."(*Off book* is a theatrical term that means, you are no longer in need of the script because you've memorized all the lines for whatever role you're playing, which in my case was no lines at all.)

As the Chicken moved towards me with a louder and far more aggressive *booo-deck*, I upped my tormentor's ante. Licking the suction cup on the bottom of my rattle, I stuck it to my forehead, crossed my eyes for maximum effect and launched into a nonsensical garble of baby speak. Great paroxysms shook the Chicken's squatting body as he fought boldly to stay in character, but that battle proved futile. He was choking instead . . . but in a good way—the way you choke on your own spit when you're laughing your hole off!

I waddled round the gymnasium on padded knees, shaking the rattle that was stuck to my head, as cherubic faces of wide-eyed children exploded in fits of laughter, accompanied by the applause of their appreciative teachers. Don't tell *me* I can't play a room!

Not everyone was laughing, though. From behind the curtain, I saw the steely-eyed stare of the company's senior member. Beside him was the actor who'd just delivered the galvanizing monologue on the number three—who, in his bloated moment of messianic bliss, believed he'd soon be the recipient of the David O. Selznick Lifetime Achievement Award from the Academy of Motion Picture Arts and Sciences. Soon as I got backstage (I mean, behind the black curtain suspended on poles beside the bathroom), the company's senior member hissed at me:

"I have never seen such unprofessionalism in my life!"

"Unprofessional? Give me a break," I replied, with the rattle still stuck to my forehead. "How can playing to a room full of preschoolers be considered remotely professional, when most of the audience still goes to the bathroom in their pants?" Which, forty-two years later, is exactly the standard I shoot for in my shows today!

Lesson learned: if the ushers aren't wiping the seats down after a show, I haven't done my job.

On the Trans-Canada Highway between Regina and Saskatoon, an iron effigy of the animal that once darkened the plains in a moving blanket of meat on the hoof sits beside an erratic dropped as a glacial afterthought when sheets of ice once receded to oblivion. Called a "buffalo stone," it commemorates an animal that once numbered eighty million strong and moved mighty as Jehovah from the treeline to Texas with nary a mini mall to block its passage. On their way to calving grounds in eons gone, they'd stop at boulders such as this to scratch their hairy rumps free of winter fur. (Because it's hard, I guess, to scratch your bum when you've got a hoof not a hand. Chalk another one up for man.)

I'm bound for a gig in Prince Albert, a town with little over thirty-five thousand people and the sweet, six-hundred-seat EA Rawlinson Centre. It's the last substantially populated community before rolling hills of aspen give way to northern boreal forest, peat bogs and moose pasture. Besides being home to three prisons, Prince Albert is also where jowly ol' John Diefenbaker, Canada's thirteenth prime minister, was raised. The legacy of this Conservative is a tarnished one, thanks to his decision in 1959 to cancel Canada's state-of-the-art supersonic fighter jet, the Avro Arrow. That decision resulted in the loss of fifteen thousand jobs and more or less scuttled our fledgling (but innovative) aerospace industry.

In fairness to the man who spent the latter years of his political life ostracized from power, mumbling to himself behind stone pillars in the Parliament Buildings, he did appoint the first woman to cabinet, and he passed Canada's Bill of Rights—whose scope and legal force were increased a decade later by Pierre Trudeau's Charter of Rights and Freedoms. Diefenbaker also "allowed" Indigenous people to vote . . . finally.

(By the way—Quebec didn't give Indigenous people the right to vote until 1969. That's right: two years *after* Expo 67. And to think it's francophone culture that plays the victim card.)

On occasion, I've been the recipient of condescending judgment from snotty urban cognoscenti as to why I'd perform way up in Prince Albert. Well, for one thing, it's a great theatre; for another, performers are essentially hunter-gatherers. We may not follow the buffalo for sustenance, but the metaphor is an apt one. Follow the herds / follow the gigs. Kill a buffalo / "kill" an audience. Get food / get paid. Eat buffalo meat on the prairie / eat rubbery chicken wings in a roadhouse bar post-show. Sleep, wake up in the morning and keep moving / sleep, wake up in the morning and keep moving . . . but forget a raincoat, sweater or scarf in the hotel room.

Compared to the almost twenty years I spent chasing a buck as an actor in Toronto and LA, waiting for the phone to ring with news of an audition for roles in an occasional film, commercial, or guest spot on some long-forgotten television show, a comedian's road allows for a connection with an audience that can't be manufactured, rigged or jigged. Great lighting and editing can't help when you're walking the high wire, pinned to a solo spot. Every comedian standing alone onstage, with nothing but a microphone and memory, channeling the energy of a packed, expectant house, experiences a fundamentally satisfying reward in knowing that whatever quotidian demands bedevil their audience's daily march through life's bright fury are for ninety minutes, to quote my 89-year-old Cape Breton-born mother, given "a kick in the arse with a frozen boot straight out the friggin' door."

Ticket sales are down in Prince Albert compared to my visit two years ago, when I did two sold-out shows. Maybe seeing my noggin on television once a week in the series has something to do with it? Maybe the numbers are dropping because there's more to keep people at home, rather than leave the house to brave a wind chill just to see a show? Maybe it's because the marketplace is glutted with acts like never before? There is certainly no doubt that, since the collapse of the American economy in 2008, every comedian's manager down there with a GPS has happened to discover a country north of them, that up until now, they never knew existed. Seems everyone but Peaches and Herb was touring an act that year.

Pulling my suitcase into the lobby of a Ramada Inn, I'm greeted warmly by the receptionist, Jocelyn, an elegant woman in her late forties whose co-worker is a younger woman with a five-year-old daughter she's raising herself. The woman has a tattoo on her arm to commemorate the death of a friend, and she tells me of time spent as a volunteer, chatting through plexiglass with lifers in the penal system. She is their only contact with the outside world, except for the hour a day they get for exercise in "the yard." After a day spent dodging mule deer, it feels good to share a communion of spirit, connecting to something deeper than the sole purpose of my visit.

Jocelyn tells me she's a single mom who raised three boys herself in a "tough town with plenty of crime."

"There's lots of drugs, murder and domestic violence. We're the last stop before the North, and you know the North—it's a wide-open halfway house with no curfew," she says, rolling her eyes. There are legions of criminals wandering our North, and despite the haunting beauty of its primal landscape and the hamlets and towns strung along the treeline, the region also attracts an odious detritus from "down South," come to prey on the despair born from isolation and unemployment, in a place where winter hangs around for seven months of the year.

"We don't need F-18s in the North," Jocelyn tells me. "We need social programs, with cops on the ground, nurses, schools and teachers. We need infrastructure." She says the crime in Prince Albert is getting out of hand, but when I tell her we raised our two daughters in Toronto, she says, "I'd hate to raise my children there! It's too big and dangerous!" Poor Toronto. It will never win in the eyes of the rest of the country.

There's a spine of resilience I admire in her straightforward, no-nonsense way of speaking. She is direct, forthright and refreshingly matter-of-fact. I'm still smarting from my recent separation and its emotional toll when she asks me how my wife deals with the long stretches I'm away from home. I tell her she doesn't anymore, because we're not together.

"When I was getting standing ovations, she was getting another load of laundry," I confess. "It's a creatively fulfilling life for me; for her, not so much."

She nods knowingly with a nuanced sigh unique to those who have weathered the emotional fray of love lost, whose scar tissue might sit tough around their heart, but not tough enough to harden it.

"A month after my divorce, my parents were killed in a car accident. I had three small boys to raise myself, with no family to rely on. I did it. Don't know how, but I did. They're all teenagers now. I have a cabin in Weyakwin. It's good for my soul to go there. In fact, it's not too far from where Johnny Cash, June Carter and John Jr. used to come to fish. Lots of locals in La Ronge still remember him. He was just real people."

I wonder if the Man in Black had a wandering eye for a lithe summertime-tanned Jocelyn walking past his table at a La Ronge diner. Trying hard not to stare, but losing the battle, I bet Johnny couldn't help but stop in mid-sentence to do just that, when he'd receive a sharp boot to the shins beneath the table and a reprimand from June saying:

"Eyes forward! You are *not* on the road now, Johnny!"

Jocelyn has bought her youngest something from Avon. I didn't know Avon still existed. (Avon Soap-on-a-Rope was a standard Christmas gift in the 1970s. I hadn't had that in my shower since "everybody was kung-fu fighting!") Her son's Christmas gift is a toaster emblazoned with a Montreal Canadiens logo, but when the toast pops up, burned into the bread is . . . a Toronto Maple Leafs logo. Maybe the coolest little gift ever! We share a good laugh. You don't get a moment like that at the front desk of a high-end Hilton in Vegas.

Nor do you get comped the King Henry Suite in a Ramada Inn that caters to travellers in a four-prison town. My themed suite had a plush indoor/outdoor royal blue carpet decorated with gold crowns, where in the middle sat a matching contoured blue velvet lounging couch. I assumed that was there in case enthusiastic occupants couldn't make it all the way to the four-poster king-sized bed, covered in a canopy rimmed with ornate gold-braided tassels. I guess nothing makes a former inmate forget ten years of incarceration faster than having a shag in a setting fit for a jester.

Most hotels on tour are airless, generic franchises lacking any attribute you could call remotely unique. However, there was once a hotel in Belleville, Ontario, that's long since burned down, whose rooms were named after the Fathers of Confederation—and the Sir George-Étienne Cartier room had a stripper's pole in it. It did! A stripper's pole! I'm willing to wager there was more bacteria on that adult novelty item than on a toilet seat in a shantytown rub 'n' tug! I know the French love their peelers, so given that Cartier hailed from Quebec, I assumed the pole was in keeping with the province's cultural appetite for lunchtime lap dances. I'm not sure if Cartier enjoyed the occasional lap dance, but there was no stripper's pole in the D'Arcy McGee suite. Just sayin'.

My show only brings in four hundred or so patrons. Small turnout, given the long drive, and I bemoan the turn of events, worried that the market has changed for good—as it probably has. All the same, you do your show, and on this night at the Rawlinson Centre, I deliver a tight two-hour performance without breaking a sweat and have an excellent time. Still, there's the worry that the money made wasn't worth the kilometres driven. It's something that's still gnawing at me the next day, when I head into the Safeway supermarket for a Starbucks.

While I'm putting cream in my coffee, a young Indigenous man extends his hand for a shake and speaks to me.

"Hey, Ron James. My family and I saw you a couple of days ago in Regina." Like most in Saskatchewan, his face is open and friendly, exuding the unpretentious affability unique to flatlanders. Sure, people might stumble with an Orwellian lethargy through winter's gloom on the downtown streets of Regina, but it being the seat of provincial government, I chalk that mood up to a life spent moiling in the bowels of bureaucracy, praying they'll not lose their marbles before their civil servant's pension provides clemency. That's when flatlanders make a beeline for a British Columbia retirement community where relentless winter doesn't break them so hard, they're found in May curled in a fetal position behind the couch, and wearing nothing but a Roughriders toque.

I once pulled in for breakfast at a roadside diner outside Lloydminster where half a dozen farmers were enjoying their morning coffee. They called me over to tell a joke, and although the last thing a comedian wants to hear is a joke, this one wasn't bad. "You can tell this one onstage in Regina: Why can't a government employee look out the window in the morning? 'Cause they'd have nothing to do in the afternoon." The table roared in agreement. I noted they were all farmers having coffee on a working day but decided not to share my observation.

I remember seeing the Indigenous kid and his family during a noisy breakfast at Regina's Delta Hotel, in a pictureless room with a brutal buffet. He was surrounded by a pair of brilliant red-haired older sisters, their husbands and little ones, a white-haired matriarch and her husband. Their dairy-fresh faces stood in contrast to the high cheek-bones and brown complexion of his heritage. It was Saskatchewan Roughrider game day, and the place was filled with fans bedecked in the colours of a team that personifies their prairie heart. During Roughrider game day at that hotel several years earlier, I bumped into a family stepping off the elevator. From the youngest child of ten to the parents themselves, all were wearing hollowed-out watermelons on their heads. Naturally, I asked why they were all wearing melons on their melons, and they stared quizzically as if there was something wrong with *me*.

We sit in the Safeway, enjoying our coffee. Initially, we talk of the game and Saskatchewan's collapse in the fourth quarter. Then the kid opens a door to his life and the universe drops another ruby in my lap.

"I love Don Burnstick, the Native comedian. He got me through an awful lot of pain. How to not let what others say define me but let *me* define me."

The kid tells me he has lived with racism every day of his life. "Up in Birch River, my dad ran a buffalo ranch. Twenty-five hundred head. Some of those bulls were three hands high. Heads like trucks. We steered clear of them during the rut and calving season. It's great meat! Just great. Always cook it on low heat, or else it will be too tough," he advises. "Mom used to comb the buffalo fur off their heads and put it in our boots. Some warm! Trust me, when it's minus-45, you want some buffalo fur in your boots. Ironic, eh? A Native kid working on a white man's buffalo farm!" He laughs, then just as quickly lapses into pensive reflection.

"I had to learn to stand tall. I had to make those kids at school not make me believe who they said I was. They used to call me 'chink,' because I look Asian. 'Hey chink. Chink!' they'd yell. I developed a temper. It was boiling in me. So, in grade seven, I started taking karate outside town, but only after three guys in my class pinned me against the fence after school. One of them, the ringleader, was a big, stupid hillbilly. His buddies had shovels. They held my arms, and he punched me hard in the stomach. I went down, and they kicked me. I started taking karate after that. I'm a second-degree black belt now. About six months after they beat me, I got him alone." He smiles with a satisfaction born from righteous retribution. "The dumb hillbilly.

"'Who's the brave one now without his pals? Let's go. One on one.'

"I could tell he was scared. He took a swing. I stepped back and planted a punch in his throat. He started to cry.

"'You want some more?' I asked him.

"The big baby reported me to the principal's office. The principal and the vice-principal wanted to expel me. I said, 'You try that, and I'll have the television cameras and newspapers here tomorrow. The mission statement of this school says, "Every child should feel safe." I don't.' They backed off."

"Did the kids back off, too?" I asked.

"No. My buddy and I were walking down the hill after school one afternoon. I see a bunch of kids at the bottom with bats and hockey sticks. I turned to him and said, 'This doesn't look too good. Have you got my back?'

"'Thur,' he says . . . 'cause he had a lisp. I say, 'Thur? This is no time to be calling me "thur."'

"See? Don Burnstick makes everything funny.

"When I walked toward those kids, I turned around and he was gone. So, I ran that gauntlet of bullies myself. Thanks to them, I only have 20 percent vision in my right eye. It's why I couldn't join the army. I wanted to help people. I wanted to make a difference somewhere. So, instead, I'm making it here."

He looked at me with a conviction that belied his nineteen years and pointing his finger emphatically on the table declared: "Hey. I'm not an Indian. I'm a Native! The only way a person effects change in this world is by changing themselves first. I want to empower young Native kids. Tell them there's another way. They need to believe it's possible to be better than some people say you can be. Stephen Harper was wrong when he said the residential school is an ugly chapter in our history that is finally closed. No way! It's a generational disease! And it's my generation that will make a difference. Not the government, but us!"

He drained his coffee.

"Everybody should do what they can to make it better, right?"

With a nod of his head, the kid turns on his heel disappearing into a world he's dedicated to making a difference in.

Chapter Three

ADIDAS MEXICANA

Last time I saw my namesake before his stroke, I was seated at the kitchen table in that old house of his with no foundation. It sat at a precarious tilt, sinking into its lot on Steeles Hill, overlooking the once-booming coal town of Glace Bay, Cape Breton. Another stand-up tour of Atlantic Canada had brought me full circle to my birthplace for a gig at the Savoy Theatre, where, in a world when black-and-white television with one channel to watch was the only option, raucous gangs of children dropped twenty-five cents every Saturday afternoon to sit, mesmerized, watching matinees in garish Panavision.

The day after my show, I dropped by to see Uncle Ronald. Other than his niece, who kept house and cooked for him, the seventy-eight-year-old man lived alone. I sat with my back to a well-worn La-Z-Boy on the opposite side of the room where an almost-blind mutt called Mork lay sleeping.

"Don't sit dere, b'y, in case a'nudder rat comes up tru' da' floorboards.

I'll need a clear shot," he warned, patting the barrel of a pellet gun that rested beside his chair.

My cousin Diane reprimanded him.

"Ranal'! Ronnie might want you to say hello first. Jesus, eh? No friggin' manners," she said, looking at me and laughing, her red cheeks flush with life as she flipped the haddock in the frying pan. If they start handing out Orders of Canada for unsung saints who fly below the red-carpet radar, my cousin deserves one. She was the only one in the family who could spar with him. Her voice had the mischievous, rollicking cadence of an accent heard on the other side of the Canso Causeway, that harkened me back to a grandmother's kitchen where cousins smeared butter on gingerbread cookies as aunts chattered sparrow-fast over steaming-hot cups of King Cole Tea cut with canned Carnation milk. My gentle grandmother's Broughton-born sapphire eyes twinkled with goodness from a rocking chair, where she sang ancient songs in Gaelic to grandchildren whose faces have long since turned to age, their parents either gone or going.

"Ranal'! Ronnie doesn't want to hear about you shooting the rat. He's eating," my cousin declared.

Uncle wasted no time clarifying.

"Ronnie knows I knows he's here. He's right in front of me. But if I have to start shooting again, all's I'm sayin' is, he fuckin' well better duck!"

It's not every day you get a good rat story anymore, vermin having been eradicated from pretty well every kitchen I've had the pleasure to visit. But apparently, in Uncle's home, rats still crawled up on occasion from their cozy warren beneath the floorboards for a gander.

My cousin put plates of haddock with boiled carrots, potatoes and canned peas before us. Between forkfuls that Uncle kept lodged somewhere between his palate and esophagus (as was his wont when talking and eating at the same time), he told me about his duel with that rat. Did I mention he embraced profanity with the zeal a penitent would holy scripture?

"I heard Mork whinin', eh? I says, 'What's da matter, buddy?' And then I sees the little prick on the arm of the chair. A filthy fuckin' no-good goddamn-rat! Hissin' at me, too. Hissin'! In me own house! I says to Diane, 'Get me my pellet gun. I'se de last one he'll ever hiss at!'"

As she ladled more peas onto his heaping plate of food, my cousin interjected.

"I didn't know what he was gonna do with the pellet gun," she said, looking at me in disbelief. "He can barely hold a cup o' coffee without spilling half of it for shaking!"

Uncle held his hands out in front of me, oblivious to how badly they shook.

"Steady as a surgeon's, b'y."

He went back to the rat story.

"So's I cocked me pellet gun seven times. Raised da t'ing. Aimed. Squeezed da trigger . . . and, with a finger pointed between my eyes, said . . . 'Right dere!' I nailed it. And ho-leeee fuck! Out she squirted, b'y! Blood. Nutting but blood! Spraying like a Jesus garden hose. It was like da . . . da . . . da . . ."—searching for the right word, he exclaims—"da *CIS* show on TV."

Diane corrected him.

"*CSI*, Ranal'. *CSI*." She looked at me, laughing.

"Whatever it's called. Da t'ing staggers and falls off de arm of de chair to da floor. I puts two more pellets in da belly of the little fat bastard but . . . he's not dead yet!"

Uncle had his dinner stuffed in one cheek, and as he became more animated, bits of haddock and peas were falling out of his mouth.

"Den', holy ol' Jesus, doesn't he run into my bedroom and crawl up on da bedpost . . . sits right on top of 'er and starts hissing again . . . wit' da blood spraying everywhere." Much like his dinner was doing to me. I felt wet food hit my face.

"Then that rat—you'se got to give him points for being tough—didn't he rise up to his full rat height on that bedpost, like he was claiming it for his own? I says, 'That's the last time you'll raise your little rat arms at me, you son of a whore,' and *pow! pow! pow!* I puts t'ree more pellets into da little prick and he dropped. Dead."

He finally swallowed his food, and pointing at my face with his fork, said:

"You got peas stuck to your cheek, b'y."

Three years later, another tour brought me across the Causeway, but there'd be no visit to Steeles Hill. The stroke had hit fast one winter afternoon, ending his life in his own house and beginning what would be the last four years of it, at Cabot Lodge in Sydney. The home was a well-run, antiseptic and brightly lit gateway to the hereafter.

He lay prostrate on the bed, drilling me from the pillow with those defiant eyes of steel blue.

"How are you doing today, Uncle?" I said. He didn't answer, but his eyes did. Gauging. Judging. Evaluating.

"Holy fuck, b'y! Are you'se ever bole-legged!"

I roared laughing. He was his cantankerous self again, and a far cry from those first few days after his stroke, when he slipped in and out of consciousness in the hospital room.

"Good to see you, too! It's nice to know the stroke didn't kill your sarcasm."

"I wasn't being sarcastic. I was being honest. You're some bole-legged."

My Uncle Ronald. In an age where being politically correct, or even polite, is an expected social norm, he had clearly never received the memo. He never knew how *not* to say what was on his mind. There was no filter—ever. He was who he was, and you got what you got. In a world of posturing and pretense, his disposition was to tell it as he saw it, which made his moments of warmth all the more authentic.

Uncle was the only boy in a family of five sisters. They all lived in a simple house my grandfather built by himself with money made working in "the pit." The pit was a euphemism for the coal mine, which one relative once told me "was prison with wages." It's difficult to fathom the fortitude that made such a race of men who toiled, as the song says, "where the rain never falls, nor sun never shines." Crews piled into a metal cage that travelled gut-liftingly fast down a shaft drilled into the black belly of Earth, finally stopping a mile below the ocean floor. For eight to ten hours—day or night shift—miners pounded away under Dickensian conditions against a wall of coal with pick and shovel, in a rat-infested, dangerous, dark, claustrophobic world, for a feudal wage. I'm ready for a couple of cold beer after being onstage for two hours . . . and all I do is talk!

I swore the smell of that workingman's fuel was hanging in the air the day I visited Uncle. It was evocative of the steady employment the industrial heartland of Atlantic Canada could once lay claim to, back when coal was king and, as my eighty-nine-year-old mother recalls, "A person couldn't fit a dime between the shoulders on miners' payday for the size of the crowds shopping Saturday mornings on Commercial Street. No, they couldn't. Sure, you could try, but you couldn't. Mind you, I wouldn't want to try and fit a dime between a coal miner's shoulders. He'd puck your face off!"

Fifteen kilometres up the road at the Sydney steel plant, the best girders used to rebuild postwar Europe were made, and every smelter our wide country over used Cape Breton coal to fire the furnaces of their "satanic mills." I guess in a less environmentally enlightened day, one man's hell was another man's heaven, especially when there are mouths to feed. Take that, William Blake.

"He never really started drinking hard until he joined the army," they all said. Most letters home, from wherever Uncle was stationed, spoke of peeling potatoes on KP. Once he was discharged, he never held a job very long. Grade eight education doesn't bring you much at the best of times, but you could still land something steady back then if you wanted to.

When I was little, I never knew him not to be prisoner to the bottle—and not just pleasantly toasted, but hopelessly hammered, staggering three sheets to the wind up a quiet daytime street. Everyone worried. Phones rang between the sisters, wondering where he was or what he was getting up to.

"Is he driving again? He'll kill himself, if not somebody else first."

We sat watching TV in Uncle's room when a lost-looking man in a baseball cap stood staring vacantly through his open door. Looking at the man, then back to me, Uncle said:

"That's the son of a whore who stole my slippers."

"Does he have Alzheimer's?" I asked.

"I don't know, but he fuckin' well will if I gets a hold of him."

You gotta love that level of belly fire, especially in someone who's bedridden.

At this point, he'd been dry for forty-three years, with AA's *Big Book* beside his bed, which he read with diligence every morning. When I was little, he disappeared into the Big Smoke. Another Maritime refugee "gone down the road" looking for a better one, but finding a dead end instead. If full-blown alcoholism is the major leagues, then the fist-fighting coal town road of the early 1950s was the farm team. By the time you won your Stanley Cup in booze, you'd certainly earned it.

Perhaps a Christmas card would arrive for one of the sisters during his lost years. Or a cheque requested for a "bus back home" that was always cashed, but the ticket never bought. Still, despite all those haunted nights spent shivering in lonesome alleyways or flea-ravaged flophouses, he survived to wrestle his addiction to the mat. Once he did, his kindness knew no bounds and gift-giving came easily. Whether rent and groceries for a sister and her kids, Christmas and birthday gifts for a small army of nephews and nieces, or, in later years, a car to a grandnephew and graduation gifts for all of us. That was Uncle.

I remember that summer day he materialized as if from the ether in front of our house in Halifax. I remember it mostly because I was wearing a brand-spanking-new pair of Adidas Mexicanas I'd bought with my own money. When you're a shamelessly short twelve-year-old red-headed kid with a size four foot that only fits a two-stripe, bush-league, Canadian-made North Star but not the unattainable Adidas everyone in the hallowed ranks of the chosen was wearing, and you suddenly find yourself springing down the street sporting a brand new pair you bought yourself with hard-won lucre made delivering the Halifax *Mail-Star*, it was as good as life could ever get. No longer would you feel a kinship with the barefoot Amish farm boy taking his prize pig to market.

I saw a Casino taxi pull up in front of our house. That never happened. Nobody took cabs in the daytime, least of all to our place. A man slid from the back seat, double-fisting two-quart bottles in wrinkled paper bags, and staggered up the driveway, disappearing into the backyard.

This would be the "visit" that would see him institutionalized in the Dartmouth asylum, where he'd begin his long journey back to the light. That imposing brick matron sat (and still does) on a big green lawn on the opposite side of the harbour from Halifax. "Going across the bridge" was the local euphemism for being institutionalized. It's the way we talked back then, because no one knew or understood what it was like to be broken. No one cared to know what it was like not to be singing the song the rest of us knew all the words to.

We'd pick him up on Sundays for supper at the outpatient door. Wraith-white he stood, looking strangely incongruous in the morning sun, like some gothic apparition who'd forgotten to flee for the shadows at daybreak. He'd squeeze into the back seat of Dad's Plymouth between my younger sister and me, all pale and shaky, his hair matted, staring straight ahead.

"It's like deer were sleeping in it," I said to my sister later. She was a wide-eyed six-year-old who, although four years younger than me, was far more sensible . . . and still is.

"What do you mean?"

"Well, you know when deer sleep in a field of tall grass, and how in the morning, it's all matted down?"

"Kinda."

"Well, Uncle's hair is like that. Only with deer, you don't see white scalp and dandruff."

"If it snows, you do." (See what I mean?)

Mom always cried when Uncle appeared. He was her baby brother, and she saw his face forever pressed against the kitchen window in their childhood gone. He was all wide-eyed and sad, watching her and other neighbourhood kids play outside on a summer's day, but he was forbidden to join them because the house was quarantined for scarlet fever, and he had it.

Uncle hated for his food to touch. Carrots couldn't touch peas, nor peas potatoes, and he'd have to separate them on the plate. Well, when you're only a week into a thirty-day detox program, a steady hand is not one of your strong suits. His attempt to preserve a standard that anchored him to a world he was trying hard to return to was an effort worthy of Sisyphus. He'd ever-so-carefully raise his knife and fork from the table setting, the utensils threatening to slip from his fingers for the shaking. Then he'd lower that fork and knife to the plate, where the sound of them rattling on the porcelain was worthy of a Buddy Rich drum solo. Accompanied by our mother's gentle sobbing from the end of the table, he'd persevere, oblivious to the rest of us. Dad kept his head buried in his food, glancing up occasionally from the plate. My sister and I stared, marvelling at Uncle's defiant persistence in bringing those peas to his mouth. Despite their propensity to adhere to his fork with the consistency of mercury, he somehow managed to manipulate one lone survivor to his mouth. Once there, his cracked, chapped lips would wrap around that lone pea, to be savoured with the reverence a confessor would the Eucharist.

Our father made valiant attempts at small talk.

"So, plans for the week?"

"No." A rim shot rattled the plate as the knife pushed peas to the fork.

"Watching the Expos?"

"Yep." He raised the fork. All the peas would fall . . . except one. He'd get a bead on it. His eyes focused and his lips pursed with concentration. Then down went Sisyphus to the plate again, and another hard slog up his hill.

As mentioned, when I saw Uncle step from the cab, I was wearing a brand-new pair of rare and covetable Adidas Mexicanas. They had three shiny black stripes running down a body of burnt yellow-coloured suede. Put simply, they shouted, "Cool!" Today, you can buy any kind of running shoe in any size, anywhere, at any time. Not so in 1970. To see a pair—in size four, at that—sitting bright as a new dream in the front window of Phinney's Sporting Goods on Barrington Street was nothing short of miraculous. I imagined myself ripping up the track in the Olympics, where I'd stand on the podium, giving the Black Panther salute, even though I was a four-foot-ten, freckle-faced white kid who ran like the "bole-legged" man Uncle would one day in a far-off future bluntly declare I was. Never again would I wear the embarrassing two-stripe Canadian-made North Stars, whose paper-thin soles evaporated before the summer did.

(Phinney's, by the way, was a sporting goods store that also sold grand pianos. It wasn't uncommon to see one kid trying out new goalie pads while another tried out a Steinway. How's that for eclectic? "Will it be a Victoriaville hockey stick for the lad, ma'am, or the sheet music for Tchaikovsky's *1812 Overture* in E-flat major?")

The Adidas in Phinney's window were clearly an aberration. They must have been custom-made for a fleet-footed, diminutive Cuban sprinter whose daily steroid injections had caused a sudden growth spurt. I assumed he'd defected during a stopover in Gander, Newfoundland, while on his way to the Eastern Bloc for a Warsaw Pact track and field meet. Upon arriving in Halifax, he probably pawned the Adidas, box and all, at Phinney's, picking up a few extra bucks to start his new life. (How he got to Halifax from Gander remains a mystery I've yet to invent.)

I followed Uncle into the backyard, where he sat in a lawn chair, taking a long pull from one of the bottles.

"Hi, Uncle. How ya doin'?"

All bleary-eyed, wrung-out and wasted, he looked and said, "I hope you don't turn out like me, just 'cause you got my name b'y."

The thought struck me as absurd at the time, though now I wonder if I hadn't flirted with a drinking problem myself, having spent most weekends after the age of sixteen making a valiant effort to get there. The quest every Friday or Saturday night was to get someone to go into the Nova Scotia Liquor Commission for you. One pal could go all Lon Chaney Jr. on a whim and grow a full beard overnight. He'd stop shaving Wednesday, and by Friday evening, his look was so full-on Wolf Man, the only thing that could stop him from sauntering out of the "Commission" with a few pints of vodka was a silver bullet. The vodka would be poured into a skunky hockey water bottle and mixed with orange Tang, to be guzzled in the Camp Hill graveyard on bone-cold winter nights before high school dances. Sporting a bad case of "Tang lips," you stepped through the gymnasium doors with a courage primed by Smirnoff that propelled you into dance moves worthy of *Soul Train*—until the whirlies hit during a waltz to "Colour My World."

After a kid from a school in Dartmouth passed out drunk in the snow and almost froze to death, we started trying to get into taverns underage, and the seedier the waterfront watering hole, the better. One crusty refuge was home to Maltese stevedores and gangrenous whores who reeled round the floor in a liquor-pig ballet while sucking back skunky draft from rotgut kegs whose pipes hadn't been cleaned since Sir Charles Tupper caught his first case of Cumberland County clap. A two-ton Stygian vixen we called Enormous Doris sat beside the door to the men's room, furtively eyeing her prey. A young man was wise to give this nightmare a wide berth, for if one of her meaty tentacles should reach out and snatch you, up that skirt you'd go, never to be seen again! Having to use the toilet in that tavern, as opposed to just the urinal, tested the limits of courage. The seats danced with microbial spores carried from diseased ports of call from forgotten corners of the seven seas. They had not seen so much as a thimble's worth of disinfectant since the 1919 Spanish flu came through and killed the janitor.

There were no picture IDs then, and whether or not you were carded depended on the judgment of whoever was working the front door. This place had an ex-welterweight for a doorman called Winky McLeod, whose claim to fame was having fought a thirteen-round donnybrook against a ranked Russian middleweight during his days in the navy.

Winky was an imposing presence who sported a crewcut and a weathered face covered by half a dozen razor nicks. When you have to go out in public with more than five pieces of Kleenex stuck to your shaving cuts, I figure it's time to change the blade. The years he'd spent in the ring after that fight had left his noodle pummelled into such a state of punch-drunk grace, it was not uncommon to see

Winky swinging at shadows of former opponents while on duty, instead of watching for underage patrons.

You could always get into the Pirate's Quarters when Winky was bouncing, provided you walked in on his "bad side." That was the side where his eye, well, "winked" non-stop. The lid was covered in such lumpy folds of scar tissue, the doctor who stitched him up must have been convicted of crimes against humanity at Nuremberg.

But on that summer's day of then, with a *Mail-Star* bag slung over my shoulder, pockets heavy with quarters and springing down the street sporting brand new too-cool-for-school running shoes, Uncle's worry that I'd "turn out like him, just because I had his name," warranted only one response.

"There's no way that will happen, Uncle. Look what I'm wearing: a brand-new pair of Adidas Mexicanas I bought with my paper route money!"

I don't know how long or arduous Uncle's climb to sobriety was, but the man got there, finding hope, support and, most importantly, salvation in church basement meetings surrounded by an AA tribe of seekers all like him, just looking to find their road home.

Twelve years after I bought those Adidas, I also found myself in Toronto, only I was chasing an acting career and bartending at an Italian restaurant to pay the rent. The other bartender was also called Ron, and he was my senior by about, oh, five hundred and twenty-seven years. He was Nosferatu in a bartender's bowtie, with unsettlingly luminous raptor-length fingernails, and to this day, I swear the ectomorphic apparition cast no shadow. The owner of the restaurant carried herself with the haughty air of the Cosa Nostra doyenne she was. I recognized her husband from a documentary of the time about the mafia in Canada. He and three Tony Soprano prototypes always had lunch at the back of the restaurant. Their laughter was more a gurgle than a guffaw, and I imagined they were sharing stories of the body they had just dumped in Hamilton Harbour. Angelina called me "Stupid," because I had the same name as the other bartender and because I only knew three beers: Keith's, Oland's and Moosehead—none of which were available in Ontario. I really missed back home.

One quiet afternoon when I was wiping the counter for the umpteenth time, daydreaming about being cast opposite Al Pacino in Coppola's next cinematic masterpiece—even though the only thing I'd landed in a year's worth of auditioning was as a background extra in a CBC series lost to time—a customer walked in and introduced himself. A man in his late forties, his voice had that familiar accent—not as thick as if he still lived on the other side of the Causeway, but nonetheless, there it was.

"I'm your Uncle Ron's pal Danny, from Glace Bay, but I live in Mississauga now," he said. "We grew up together. He told me to give you this." He handed me an envelope with ten $20 bills inside and a note that said:

"Don't spend this on sneakers.
Uncle"

Chapter Four

THE LAND OF OPPORTUNITY

I owe Alberta a debt of gratitude, as do many Atlantic Canadians who once reaped big boons in the Land of Opportunity.

The Canadian West was sold that way from the very start. In the late nineteenth century, colourful posters of waving golden wheat under sunny prairie skies recruited the downtrodden, disenfranchised and oppressed from European backwaters, promising 160 acres of free land to those willing to take the bait. What those 160 acres turned out to be was gristle-hard prairie in a land so mean, it could eat you. I guess the government lied. Really? There's a first.

The immigrants' first homes were huts built of sod. You heard me—sod. *There's* a cozy crib for a first winter in the New World: a house built of dirt. Today, there's not enough profanity in the English language to get me through an afternoon trying to install a ceiling fan. But living in a house of sod? Life must have really sucked in the Old Country if that was considered winning the lottery!

They came all the same—legions of nineteenth-century serfs, driven by the hope of a fresh start in a country where you could be all that you wanted and not who you were. From Ukraine, Iceland, Moravia, Poland and Russia they came, leaving behind oppressive feudal backwaters where bad guys with big moustaches kicked you comatose just for looking happy. Hopping rusty steamships for a sea-sick ten-week bounce across the stormy Atlantic, they stepped ashore at Pier 21 in Halifax to be deloused by dockside authorities and stared at by local herring chokers selling skunky Ten Penny, then took a week-long train trip to the parcel of paradise that awaited them in the West.

And if you lasted in your new world of opportunity, the reward was to drive your body hard from dawn until dusk with no vacation ever, until you dropped dead in the field while pushing a plow at the ripe old age of fifty-seven. I'd like to see our self-help yoga-junkie generation suffer that torment.

The dream was the same for those of us born to lobster blood. When the oil boom hit, Alberta's clarion call to riches rang loud and clear, and the pilgrimage to the Promised Land was on. The East hadn't seen such an exodus of that magnitude since Charlton Heston parted the Red Sea! The only thing missing was a biblical soundtrack accompanied by images of fast-moving Israelites and slow-moving Egyptians.

From Gambo to Saint-Louis-du-Ha! Ha! and all points in between, the learned and the lost fixed their eyes to the horizon and made a beeline for where tomorrow was shining bright as a new dream. Some never made it as far as Alberta, though. I heard tell of one guy driving west who stopped for a leak on the road in Saskatchewan and just disappeared. He was last seen wandering the wheat, chasing a thought.

It was a time of plenty, with plenty of money to be made. Down payments on a home in the foothills, complete with a two-car garage, shortly followed by a new truck and Harley to fill it. Millionaires were everywhere, and the manifesto preached from the boardrooms to the bedrooms said it was absolutely possible for you to become one, too. Thanks to the gooey black gold called bitumen that drove a turbocharged economic engine, Calgary shirked its dusty moniker of Cowtown, as skyscrapers rose overnight in testimony to its good fortune. Fort McMurray tripled its population in two years.

Fort Mac was the tough Athabaskan country Peter Pond travelled in 1795 with his Chipewyan guides, paddling their way upriver to a fur-bearing El Dorado that was now the gateway to a different one: the oil patch. Pond was, as his biographer Barry Gough writes in *The Elusive Mr. Pond*, "a hard man in a hard trade." Well, as much as things change, they stay the same.

Fort Mac was the kind of industry town where someone with a high school diploma could pull down 350 grand a year, working 24/7/365 for Syncrude, driving a truck the size of a duchy while sharing a two-bedroom apartment with six pals, all living on Kraft Dinner, canned wieners and crystal meth. Fort Mac, in its Wild West heyday, made an episode of *Deadwood* look like Sunday supper at the Waltons'.

One particular evening, I was headed to an infamous local pub called the Oil Can for a bite to eat. In the parking lot, draft-goggle patrons spilled from cabs into the street at the pub's front door, which opened to billows of second-hand smoke so Turkish-whorehouse thick, a person could lose three years off their life before they finished their first beer.

It made no nevermind, because the place was packed to the rafters with the singing, dancing, drinking proletariat, all doing their best to blunt the reality of doing hard time in this frozen outpost of the boreal forest.

Out the door tumbled a gang of rig workers on a two-week furlough. The leader of the posse was a ferociously tattooed, steroid-stoked, muscular bull of a man whose eyes bulged red from sockets shadowed by a proscenium brow on a shaved and leonine-sized skull. He looked closer to something King Minos might have kept in a cave on Crete than a human being. His entourage hopped and purred around him, punching the night air with fisted cigarettes and grunting laughter. I'm willing to wager that when rampaging Visigoths took their first dump in a fountain during the sacking of Rome, they looked like these guys.

The leader of this testosterone-fuelled freak show barked, "Let's hire a fuckin' cab and go to New York fuckin' City!"

This got the posse howling support, when suddenly from the bar doors burst half a dozen bleached blond sirens wearing dangerous-looking stilettoes and micro-miniskirts, their arms wrapped tightly round their vulnerable breasts in a futile attempt to protect them from the hyperborean level of cold. One of them downed the last of her fluorescent shooter and threw the glass into the street. Curses flew. People laughed. Another planted a big red kiss on the top of the leader's shaved head.

"We're going to New York fuckin' City!"

The leader spread a line of cocaine on his thumb, and a woman with chapped nostrils snorted it up. Others stood in line, waiting their turn, when someone said, "Watch out for the cops," and someone else said, "Fuck the cops!" Then, one of the women yelled, "I did!" The leader doubled over with laughter. The others were overcome with knee-slapping guffaws.

It was minus-30 (at least), and everyone was in T-shirts. Suddenly, like a flock of birds that for no apparent reason will suddenly veer from what seemed their intended course, the posse headed back inside. One of the women wondered aloud as she ran to catch up: "We're still going to New York City, right . . . right?"

I woke in my hotel room the following morning to an overwhelming smell of diesel fumes. Looking out the window, I saw an army of Dodge "Ram Tough" trucks idling in the parking lot—with nary a driver nor passenger in them. (It put me in mind of a short story Stephen King might write, where all the vehicles in a Maine coastal town inexplicably get possessed and kill their owners by swallowing them between the seat cushions, trash Main Street, then drive hell-bent into the sunset for a night of biblical reckoning.)

Whatever hole in the ozone was being punched open by the trucks' billowing exhaust was of little concern to the owners. When you're pulling down some serious scratch in "the patch," it's safe to assume one's personal impact on global warming does not weigh heavily on one's conscience. I felt the righteous anger of environmental concern rise in my chest and thought, "Hey, that's not right. I'm going to march right downstairs and tell them to turn those engines off"! But the feeling went away two seconds later when I realize they'd probably leave their carbon footprint on my face.

When oil was selling at $142 a barrel in 2006, every time a car blew up in Baghdad, two new trucks appeared in every Albertan's driveway! Everybody was making money.

Once, when playing the city of Kelowna, I met a retired couple from Cape Breton who were riding their bikes along the boardwalk. They owned the very first Subway franchise in Fort Mac.

"There were lineups round the block, Ronnie!" the man said. We worked fourteen-hour days, seven days a week, for fifteen years. The town is filled with good people. It gets a bad rap, but it gave us everything." He pointed to a beautiful condominium overlooking Lake Okanagan. "That's ours," he said proudly. "Not bad for a guy with only grade eleven who made sandwiches for a living, eh?"

If you came with a willingness to work, the West gave back what you put into it.

That roaring Alberta economy built me a house in Toronto. We ran a tour every two years from 2004 until 2018. During the winter of 2006, we had non-stop encore dates across Alberta that kept us on the road from November to March, filling theatres from one end of the province to the next. We'd start our tour in Lethbridge, at the 475-seat Yates, head up to a sweet 700-seater in Medicine Hat, then over to the Memorial in Red Deer, where one year we sold out that 680-seat room just shy of half a dozen times. Add the 1,700-seat Jack Singer in Calgary, the state-of-the-art 2,000-seat Winspear in Edmonton, a 600-seater in Grande Prairie and several sold-out shows at Fort Mac's Keyano College, and we were living large. For once, I felt creatively *and* monetarily fulfilled.

Those of us who ply our trade in the feast-or-famine fields of the self-employed know a run like that is rare as a Stanley Cup parade on Bay Street. After all those years of beating the bushes for a gig worth celebrating, it had finally come to fruition. They were very good years . . . and they're over.

Dependence on the fossil fuel nipple made diversification a dirty word in Alberta, and the thought of saving money for a rainy day anathema to the ethos of the Promised Land. Suggesting a sales tax was sedition. Only a pessimist would think those days would ever end . . . but they did.

Time moves on, and industry, just like people, has to move with it. Marching backwards to the wrong side of history never got a person anywhere. The undeniable facts surrounding climate change altered the equation forever. Let the science deniers and conspiracy-addled true believers buy the first round at their next Sons of Odin run fundraiser. The earth is teetering on the precipice of climatic catastrophe. The polar ice caps are melting. A nuclear-level conflagration of forest fires annually rages across Australia and Western North America. Sea levels are rising at an astronomical rate. Biodiversity is imperiled and mass extinction of species a pending reality. I'm not willing to wait for the planet to rise another two degrees before we take our foot off the gas of runaway consumption. Jason Kenney and his United Conservative Party can victimize themselves into a self-delusional state of frenzy while they scapegoat the rest of us for their failure to adapt to changing reality, but I'll side with science, thank you . . . and that's coming from a guy who flunked the subject in high school!

"It's you!"

Her voice bounces across the restaurant of Calgary's Delta Hotel with that unmistakable, rollicking Celtic lilt of the Cape Breton highlands. I'm staring at a face, all rosy-cheeked and smiley-eyed, warm with welcome. I don't know this waitress who's greeted me, but I know where she's from. It's the unpretentious, informal greeting of a "Caper"—my mother's people, the other half of me.

"Didn't know you were in town. Some shows coming up?"

"Yes," I say, but I know her query is just an opening to start talking. They *all* talk. And can they talk! At eighty-nine and still going strong, my mother can do two hours without breaking a sweat talking about the colour beige!

"What part of Cape Breton are you from?" I ask.

"Inverness," she says. "I'm Lena McIntyre from Inverness."

Inverness sits on the western side of the Cabot Trail. Winters are long and mean and summers are short and stunning. A one-time working-class town of coal miners and fishermen who laboured either under or on the iron-hard Atlantic is now home to a world-class golf course and equally impressive hotel. (It can't be that good though, cause there's no royal theme room or suite with a stripper's pole. Just sayin' . . .)

My father knew Inverness in another day, when he and his union brothers at the Maritime Telegraph and Telephone Company bunked in boarding houses while installing dial tone systems for a people who had previously relied on party lines, back when the click of a neighbour's receiver guaranteed your business was now everyone else's.

I just sit there listening, as her life tumbles out. She says she's closer to seventy than sixty and has been out west since she read an article in *Maclean's* magazine back in 1976 about the "land of opportunity."

"I had to come west—and thank God it was here to come to," she says emphatically. "Because I had no choice. I was the oldest. Yes, I was, and left with all seven children to take care of after 'the accident.' There was nothing in Inverness for them to do back then. Nothing. No Girl Guides or Scouts, and with that many to feed, I couldn't afford hockey gear or skates. Nothing."

I put down my fork and decide it's best to let my eggs get cold this morning. I can have eggs anytime.

"Our parents were coming back from visiting my aunt and uncle on the other side of Kellys Mountain. That Sunday, the radio called for snow, and as the day wore on, it was coming down hard and getting worse. So Da decided to leave before dark, because he had to get back to Inverness for work at the pit in the morning. I was with them and remember heading to the door, about to put my coat on, but Ma stopped me. She had the oddest look on her face and said, 'No, you stay here, Lena. Two is enough from one family for Him to get tonight.'

"See, she knew. *She knew!* I'm still not sure why she got in that car, or even let Da pull it out of the driveway. Maybe she felt it was just their time. I don't know. I'll never know. Turns out they hit some hard driving not far from home, with the snow awful bad. That's when a truck came out of the blizzard on their side of the road. Da cut for the shoulder, lost control and hit the only tree standing in a farmer's field. Both were killed instantly. That's when my world changed. Changed forever, in fact. It was 1966. I had just turned seventeen. Was left with all the little ones to care for in that great, big house.

"You'd think the church would have helped more, what with all of us confirmed and never once missed Mass before the accident. Think again. The priest did the bare minimum. Bare minimum!" Her face gets fierce with determination now. "The Catholic church is great for making you afraid of hell and damnation, but hell will freeze good and solid if they'll ever see me put so much as a nickel in the collection plate again."

"It seems cruel for the church not to help you. I always thought small towns rallied round each other during times of tragedy," I say.

"Oh, don't get me wrong. Everyone did . . . at first. But after a while, people forget. They move on with their lives. Besides, they were scared around us, because we had ghosts."

Now, there's a word you don't hear every day over scrambled eggs and bacon at a Delta Hotel. I feel the goosebumps rise.

"Ghosts?"

"Yes," she says, so matter-of-factly that I'm the one who feels stupid for asking.

"It wasn't the ghosts of my parents, but ghosts that had always been on the property. I don't know who they were or why they were there, but two were nice, while one was mean. Mean as a March wind, it was! It would push you! Yes, it would! You'd be walking in the field and see these three balls of light coming at you, when suddenly, down you'd go with a shove."

Who was I to question her story's validity? Having heard of premonitions from my own people, I'd be the last one to doubt the woman. Dad said his Aunt Hilda, who lived next door to us in Halifax, had seen her husband, Albert, standing outside their house one afternoon. Nothing unusual about that, except he was across town in the veterans' wing of Camp Hill Hospital, dying of cancer—at the exact same time she saw him on the sidewalk, staring up at the house, dressed in his World War II navy blues.

I can still see that proud wraith, sitting on his porch while that rude disease chewed away at him. Wrapped in woollen blankets even during summer's hottest days, his racking cough could shiver me. Aunt Hilda was my grandmother's youngest sister, born at the turn of the century along Newfoundland's southwest coast, on Red Island. Once home to a thriving community and schooner fleet, whose people were indentured to St. John's cod merchants, it is now home to nothing but forgotten graveyards swallowed by the feral growth of forest.

Uncle Albert fought in the Battle of the Atlantic, as did all those Newfoundlanders from my father's side. Some were merchant marines, sailing on floating time bombs laden with petrol in convoys bound for Russia. Or they rode out gales through North Sea winters, protecting those very convoys in corvette navy ships, sometimes encased in so much ice, the extra weight threatened to sink them faster than the German U-boats hunting them. They were hard men of a harder world who carried the weight of the history they'd witnessed behind their eyes.

"Ronnie, my son," the crusty sea dog would bark, "go get me a pack of Zig-Zag tobacco at the store . . . and keep the change for yourself." Returning with the package, I'd sit and watch him gingerly sprinkle what was killing him into a rolling paper, which the nicotine-stained fingers of one hand would dexterously roll to tightly packed perfection.

Aunt Hilda told Dad that Uncle Albert was just standing on the sidewalk, looking up at the house. She opened the front door and called his name. He waved, turned and walked toward the corner, where McKay's Pharmacy used to be. By the time she made it out the door and down to the sidewalk, he had disappeared into the ether for ports unknown.

"His spirit had come to say goodbye," she told Dad, "because his body could not."

Maybe Dad knows where he went, because he's gone now, too. Born in 1932 on a pimple of Newfoundland granite called Vatcher's Island, to a Hobbesian world of toil, he'd tell how the old ones talked of premonitions. They put great stock in dreams, too. I think it's because they were tuned to life in a deeper key and not burdened by information overload. Their channels were cleaner.

"People stopped coming up to the house because it was the one with the ghosts. Like they were my fault!" Lena says. "I didn't know what they were doing there, either! So, I got on with the work of raising that family. I had two jobs, one sewing clothes and the other working at the IGA, while the two oldest boys got work on the boats or digging coal in the pit. Once they started getting big, they'd sit down at the table for dinner and shovel their food in, then be gone. I said, 'To hell with this.' That's when I got chopsticks.

"You bet I did! I gave them all chopsticks. Ever try to eat mashed potatoes and peas with chopsticks? That's how I got to know what went on in their day. They had to sit and answer my questions while they tried to eat dinner!" She roars with laughter, slaps me on the back and heads to another table.

Other diners come in. Lena seats them and returns. She's not done talking yet.

"I came here myself and got a job. It was a good job, doing secretarial work at an advertising agency. Flew those kids out, one or two at a time. Thirty years later, they've all done well, too. They're teachers, tradesmen, with a few up in the oil patch. Once they got out on their own, I went and married a fellow from California. Yes, I did. Real good-looking, too . . . like I was once," she says, winking while throwing an elbow into my arm.

"We lived in Santa Cruz. He wasn't a bad man, but he was all about image. His looks. He was a surfer. Loved nothing more than to be out on the water or looking at himself in the mirror. We had a son. He's a good kid who never seemed to click with his father, perhaps because he had too much of me in him—too much of the Caper. I'd take him back to Inverness for a few weeks during summer vacation. We stayed longer during the year his dad and I split up.

"One day, out of the blue—he's about seven years old, I guess—he says, 'I like it more here than California. Back there, people care about what's on the *outside*, but here, everyone cares what's on the *inside*. What you look like and what you've got, doesn't matter so much here.'"

It's not lost on me that this is the same place where the priest was stingy with kindness after her loss, and I say as much.

"That was more than forty-five years ago. Places change. People change. That's why I'm going back to the family home and we're opening up a B&B. Time to do something for me."

I remember the ghosts and ask if she's worried they might scare away clients.

"Jesus, no! A few ghosts in the house will be great for business! It's eating potatoes with chopsticks they'll have to worry about!"

She drives that elbow into my ribs again, roars laughing and heads for the other table.

They live close to the weather out west. To say it's not for the meek is an understatement.

Before my meniscus tore and the wonky knees of mid-life hobbled my daily run, I made for the streets in whatever city I found myself for my daily six kilometres. Calgary was easily one of the best cities in the country for that. No hills! Just the great, flat pathway beside the Bow River. During a morning jog, if you caught a strong tailwind along with your endorphin buzz, you could be in Regina by dinnertime.

I pushed my luck running one minus-40 morning when sweat froze my eyelids shut in ten minutes. The brutal temperature did nothing to impede the city's hard-core cyclists, though. From out of a frigid dawn they came, a mounted cavalry of commuters astride their mountain bikes, all pumping, snorting, grunting and wheezing their way to work, looking every inch a devilish horde from some

Nordic hell arriving for a day of reckoning, each bedecked in neon-coloured, down-filled Gore-Tex parkas, toques, big, floppy mitts and beards of crusted ice home to foot-long snot Popsicles they no doubt sucked for sustenance.

These hardy westerners cycling through a frigid morn would have given Shackleton's suffering crew a run for their money in perseverance.

When I had a rare day off on tour, I always made for nature to look for quiet corners of country where I could slow it all down. Although the jewel in the crown of our national park system is considered to be the mountain town of Banff, I was always taken with the raptor-rich skies and sweeping vistas of southern Alberta. Standing small on one of those sun-smiley meadowlark mornings, watching the wind rule the rolling plains beneath a big belly of blue, even the most rabid of atheists couldn't help being moved to start singing hymns forgotten. Appropriately so, for that corner of the West is home to many communities of Hutterites and Mennonites, whose agrarian simplicities can rock an urbanite's reality. I held a door for a family at a hardware store in Lethbridge, and seven daughters walked out wearing bonnets and calico dresses, looking every inch like extras from *Little House on the Prairie*. Father strode out next, in bib overalls and straw hat, wearing the beaming pride of procreation worthy of an Old Testament patriarch.

He was yelling at his sons across the parking lot: "Zebediah! Aaron! Malachi! Slow down and wait for Mother!"

And then came Mother. Poor woman was pushing a stroller with a toddler in it and another in tow, dragging her tired limbs with that shell-shocked stare of overworked moms everywhere who've spent the last fifteen years in the diaper-wet trenches of baby raising, thanks to a love of Jesus, her husband's seed and a womb fertile as the green valleys of Canaan.

You've got to admire a people with the discipline to shirk the trappings of contemporary society. Sure, the gene pool might be shallow and home dentistry standard practice, but you're never going to wait for Bell customer service to pick up while you grow a bubble on your brain. Plus, no matter what political party is running the country, it's always 1857 in the barn!

Whenever I was headed south for a show in Lethbridge, I always made it a point to visit the UNESCO World Heritage Site of Head-Smashed-In Buffalo Jump. Of all the stops I've made criss-crossing the West, these four thousand hectares rising above a rolling plain cut by the serpentine path of Oldman River haunts like no other.

From 5800 BP until AD 1850, Indigenous people used natural barriers of hills, coulees and depressions to drive bison towards a cliff, where the herd barrelled over the edge and dropped to the ground ten metres below. The spirit of place is a tangible presence here, and the Blackfoot people, whose reserve it abuts, are the guardians and docents in charge.

During one visit, a guide walked me along the path and told me the river's name in Blackfoot. He pointed out a mountain way down south, too, that was used for vision quests. When a weasel, entirely white save for a black strip across its upper lip, popped its head up from behind a boulder to stare at us, the guide told me it was my spirit animal.

I said, "I'd always thought my spirit animal would be a monarch of the forest, like a grizzly bear."

"Hey," he said, "beggars can't be choosers."

We had a good laugh. Indigenous people have a whole different rhythm to their funny. An economy of words. They cut to the truth quicker that way. Way back in 1986, I went whale-watching off Tofino on Vancouver Island. The tour was run by a local Nuu-chah-nulth man and his young son. I stepped aboard their boat wearing my new 35-millimetre Minolta camera. He took one look at me and said, "What are you taking pictures for? Can't remember?"

As the sun started to slip behind the horizon, the guide blessed the day in a tongue that had been around, as the title of that book says, "since the world began." It was a privilege.

I got to thinking about those settlers who were given 160 acres of free land to farm. It wasn't really free. It was the home of the Blackfoot, Cree, Piegan and Shoshone and every other people of the plains who'd been displaced by the building of our national railway. The guarantees of Treaty 7, signed in good faith with the Crown, were ignored and the territory confiscated by pork-barrelling corporate fat cats aligned with imperialist Ottawa politicians who were fuelled by the prevailing Victorian myth of Darwinian determinism and its doctrine of racial superiority, a pretext for dominion over brown, red and black peoples cloaked in the economic policies of late-nineteenth-century colonial paternalism. Of course, I'm paraphrasing.

In Lethbridge, I found a funky coffee shop whose walls were lined with paintings by local artists that was run by gregarious, moon-faced millennials making muffins and cappuccinos. With Joni Mitchell on the speakers singing, "I could drink a case of you and still be on my feet," the tiny place held a Canadian morning in its hand.

Outside, the southern Alberta sky was a cobalt blue. I was feeling content with the response I'd received to the five new pages of content I'd broken in the night before. Breaking in new material in the clubs ended ten years earlier, when I stopped playing them, so anything new had to go from the page to the stage. I like the anticipatory belly hum that comes before the curtain rises, as I wonder which of the thoughts I've scribbled on a legal pad that afternoon might hit the bull's eye tonight.

That's the luxury of doing a two-hour show. It allows you room to roam. In the early years, I got bent out of shape so easily before dropping in new content. No more. And I have the road to thank for that. "Stage time, stage time, stage time," as George Carlin said. It's what you need to learn your trade. After all, the first hammer a carpenter picks up, he doesn't build a mansion. Show business feeds on that Jiminy Cricket, "When you wish upon a star, your dreams come true" malarkey. Well, here's a wake-up call, kids: not if you suck, they won't! There are no shortcuts.

Lesson learned: anything worth doing well always takes time.

I made the unfair assumption the man entering the café was experiencing homelessness, as his clothes had the dusty look of someone who's spent time on the streets. Then I noticed a self-assurance in his stride typical of those who are comfortable moving through the world at their own pace. Although I'd travelled plenty throughout southern Alberta, I'd forgotten how many people live much closer to the land down here, which proved I'd been in Toronto too long. His corduroy jacket, with its wool sheepskin lining, was well broken in, and a Royal Tyrrell Museum patch was emblazoned on the shoulder. Seeing as he was well over sixty, I figured he'd outgrown the fascination with T. rex a while ago and probably just worked there.

He sat beside me at the window counter and started buttering the scone he'd ordered. "That's some title for your book," he said.

I was reading *Death of the Liberal Class*, in which Chris Hedges postulates that America's Democratic Party sold its soul to big business long ago, making room for the rise of a virulent strain of aggressive right-wing Republicanism. The party FDR had once guided with a steady hand through the Great Depression and the Second World War had divested itself of its traditional role as champion of the workingman when it failed to address the corporate plunder and abuse that was driving a third of the United States into neo-feudal penury. Given President Biden's $1.9 trillion stimulus package, the correction is underway.

The gentleman did not sit to the right or left politically. He was a thinker who told me he graduated from university in the early 1960s with a degree in geography and lived in a yurt.

"There's something different about living in a circular house," he said.

"And what's that?" I asked.

"Don't know," he answered. "Haven't figured that out yet."

He started to talk.

"Those guys who taught me in the early '60s, who'd fought in the war? They had convictions. They saw and did things over there, and it *tempered* them. When they got home, they wanted to live a life of value. The government knew it, too. They *encouraged* it. In America, they called it the GI Bill. The government helped you get started again. It was their way of thanking you for your contribution to the war effort. For turning away the tide of fascism. Today, soldiers come back from Afghanistan and our government provides them with nothing. Politicians are great for waving the flag, but they provide nothing for the returning troops but crappy housing and an opioid habit. Counselling for their mental health problems, if they're lucky.

I'm not sure what we're fighting for anymore in Afghanistan. Neither is the rest of the world. I can live in a changing Lethbridge, yet the ironies of a world in collision are all around me. Fundamentalist Hutterites and fundamentalist Muslims living side by side.

"The other day, I saw a woman in a hijab do a double-take when eight Hutterite women walked past her, dressed as if they were headed for an outing in the 1860s. Both were wearing the uniform of their tribe. According to enlightened standards, they're oppressed, but by their standards, they are happy in their roles.

"Lethbridge is changing. In the early 1980s, it was still a ranch town. Cowboys who hadn't seen but a horse's head and a gopher's ass for months would come here to drink and whore. It worked! I was ranch-raised. Roping. Riding. I grew up outdoors. My folks loved me, but life was hard. It was *real*, though. Look at that daycare centre across the street in that federal building." He threw his head towards a generic government box across the street, void of any personality or charm. Its austere architecture would be right at home in a forgotten corner of the Soviet bloc.

"The poor little kids are dropped off in the morning and spend all day *indoors*! May as well be in a padded cell. Never see so much as a grasshopper or ant, even! Never have a cranky tomcat scratch you. Never seeing or smelling the world around you.

"You know what Thomas Hobbes said?"

I shook my head.

"'The first virtue is courage.'"

He drank his coffee. "Some things don't make sense to me. How and why is it the Mounties can kill a poor drunken cowboy, or take Neil Stonechild for a midnight death march outside Saskatoon, taser a delusional Polish man to death in a Vancouver airport, or blow a kid's brains out in Smithers just for getting lippy, yet—*yet*—a cocaine kingpin in Calgary can walk free 24/7 and nobody 'accidentally' puts a bullet in his brain?" He rose to get his coffee replenished.

I was just another dude in the coffee shop, having his morning java before he sat down. Someone at the counter mentioned I was on TV, though, and I saw both of them look over. When he returned, his tone had changed. He was tentative. Less relaxed. It's weird, the effect television has. I wanted to say, "Relax, it's Canada. All fame means here is I might score a round or two for free north of the treeline."

"So, you're Ron James? How about that. You stay put, and the world comes to you." He took a sip of coffee. "You're not gonna put anything I said in your show, are you?"

"No," I said, but I was thinking, *If I ever write a book, I will.*

It was 8:30 a.m. and the sun was nothing more than a feeble rumour, poking meekly through spirals of smoke rising from stacks of industry. A raven on the roof outside my window stood with a frozen Timbit in its beak. Or maybe it was an eyeball he'd scavenged from the head of a dead drifter somewhere in the hinterland? The morning was draped in a curtain of purgatorial half-light.

As for me, I couldn't ask for more perfect weather. This was the kind of Stygian gloom that gets patrons packing theatres with hopes of laughing their worries away. Otherwise, they could snap one morning and run naked through traffic, singing a Carpenters song.

The Starbucks sat in a big-box park across the street, and although I could see the logo from the hotel parking lot, the intersection I needed to cross to get there was murderous. All I could hear was the cacophonous roar of sixteen-wheelers bound for the oil patch. I should've turned back and taken my rental car. But with all the driving and flying I'd been doing for days on end, my legs were in desperate need of a stretch. They felt cramped and swollen with arterial thrombosis, and I worried that if I didn't begin to move them soon, they'd become lifeless appendages of bone and tissue.

The notion of waiting out eight hours until showtime in a claustrophobic, bone-dry hotel room is daunting. A comedian killing a day in a hotel can feel closer to a gangster who has ratted out the Mob and is now in the witness protection program, waiting for his disguise to arrive so he can walk the streets in anonymity, safe in the assurance that no hit man sent to exact revenge would ever suspect "that rat bastard" is the guy in an orange fright wig and a polka-dot clown suit, hopping up and down by the flower shop. Which, by the way, I witnessed from my Holiday Inn hotel window *every time* I played Peterborough, Ontario. The person in the clown suit must have been on bennies, or an aerobics teacher, or paying off a Faustian bargain with the Devil himself to put that much energy into a workday, that involved bouncing up and down—*outside . . . in the wintertime*—in a clown suit. I always wondered why the owners of the flower shop who employed the clown wouldn't have rented one of those whacky thirty-foot blow-up stick people instead, that you see in the parking lots of used car dealerships, flailing their arms about like a drowning person.

I watched that Peterborough clown for two hours one February afternoon when it was minus-27, and never once did they falter. Arctic vortex be damned. Snow Goose parkas were pulled tight around the heads of passersby. Not the clown. The person in that polka-dot jumpsuit just kept on givin' 'er! Nary a move was mailed in. Nary a breath taken for rest. If audiences ever enjoyed my shows in Peterborough, they have the clown to thank. No way was I ever *not* going to give it my all, when on the frozen sidewalks but five blocks south of the theatre, a clown was dancing in the cold with the commitment of someone hoping to save their soul from the fires of eternal damnation.)

The Grande Prairie intersection was not what you'd call "pedestrian friendly." There were no sidewalks. With sixty billion dollars a year in profit being pulled from the oil patch, pedestrians were not a priority here. I wondered if anyone had ever crossed this road on foot and lived to tell the tale. The walk signal appeared as a contemptible flicker . . . a tantalizing tease as if to say, "Go ahead, Ron. Try it. Now! Run across the street! Go! Now! Run!"

"Oh . . . SMUCK!! Too late, bro. You're dead."

There were no sidewalks to walk to either, just a ten-foot bank of razor-sharp crystallized snow. Industry's infrastructure whistled past on flatbeds moving full tilt through rough country, spewing a toxic soup of diesel and smoke. I clearly needed that Starbucks. Even though the hotel coffee was complimentary, after one sip I remember thinking, *If this coffee's a compliment, my wake-up call must be a kick in the nuts!*

Speaking of coffee, when I hit the road twenty years ago, Tim Hortons had already established itself as an iconic Canadian brand. It has since fallen far on the consumer scale of favourites, no doubt because others like myself took a sip of their 7,123rd cup one morning and thought, "Wait a second. This tastes like shit!" There was a day, however, when Holy Communion couldn't hold a candle to the religious reverence our nation held for the chain. A Canadian's need for donuts and a morning kick-start of java produced a level of worship heretofore reserved only for the Saviour's suffering.

When the reverence was at its dizzying peak, to disparage the chain from the stage was to denigrate the essence of what it meant to be Canadian. You could feel the barometric pressure drop and the audience pull out faster than a teenage Lothario in the back seat of his father's '72 Chevy. "It's only coffee and donuts!" I would rail from the stage. "Canadian soldiers didn't brew it on Vimy Ridge after they took that hill from the Hun!" And I'd hear crickets. But woe betide the cocky elitist who deigned to pass judgment on what is still affectionately called Timmies.

But how does love of country become righteously equated with enjoying a maple-glazed cruller and a double-double? The chain had no historic significance we could hang a hat on to warrant its anointed status—unlike, say, pemmican, which you can't find anywhere unless you've got an in with a Cree trapper and his wife somewhere north of The Pas.

The light turned, the walk signal blinked, and with only the ferric taste of adrenalin as company, I bolted hard for the other side, praying I'd make it to safety before being nailed so hard by a truck that the raven from the rooftop would be treated to another eyeball. My knees hadn't entirely gone to hell yet from all the years of running, and although I could hear cartilage flopping in my meniscus as I ran, I made it safely across just as a large garbage truck blared its horn. As I turned to flip the driver the bird, he began to wave. A huge smile crossed his face. The passenger window rolled down, and he yelled, "I'm coming to the show tonight, you funny little bole-legged bastard!" I wondered if he knew my uncle.

In twenty years on the road, I'd seen Grande Prairie go from a high-plains town of forever prairie to a sprawling suburban landscape of shopping malls and highways. A guy I knew from Halifax was making his living as a school principal in a small town two hours west, and regardless of what fury nature was throwing down, he and his wife along with another couple never missed a show of mine. I appreciated that a great deal. It reconnected me to the place I'd left several lifetimes ago, where in high school days Roman Catholics from St. Pat's and Protestants from Queen Elizabeth duked it out after Saturday night dances, hacked each other on the hockey rink or bruised each other good during Wanderers Grounds football games. We were now just Maritime exiles enjoying post-show pints in the Promised Land a love of comedy had brought together.

Their neighbour told me her immigrant story. She arrived from Poland in a mink coat and high-heeled shoes in the cab of her uncle's pickup truck after flying from Gdansk to Edmonton via Frankfurt. Her uncle was a hog farmer, and when this woman from fashion-conscious Europe opened her eyes after sleeping away the four-hour drive from the airport, she found herself parked outside the farmers' Co-Op on a bone-cold, muddy Monday morning in November 1981 in a desolate Grande Prairie that, no doubt, felt less welcoming than Poland after the blitzkrieg. Her uncle and his wife thought she'd like a cup of coffee, and this was the only place you could get one for 250 kilometres.

"I walked into the place," she said, "and there were no women, just men wearing bib overalls and rubber boots covered in muck. I cried every day for a year." And yet, twenty-five years later, she was still there. That was the West for you.

Having finally scaled the snowbank and made it across the street alive, I was safely tucked into the corner of that Grande Prairie Starbucks with my Moleskine notebook and a cup of coffee, when this giant of a kid loped towards me, covering the floor from end to end in three long and determined strides.

The young man was in his late twenties, and he had a ruddy complexion and wide smile. Callused hands the size of small tennis racquets poked from a weather-worn Carhartt jacket indicating a life of outdoor labour, that guaranteed should an issue arise where a physical solution was needed once all diplomatic channels had been exhausted, you'd want those gorilla-sized mitts fighting on your side.

"You're that funny guy from TV, but I don't know your name."

It's Canada. They never know your name. Even though this conversation occurred twelve years ago, it happens all the time. I told him I was Peter Keleghan, and he didn't know who he was, either.

(That is how it always happened. People would see me seated by myself at a coffee shop in some corner of the country, and they'd just start talking. Connections of this sort happened to my mother a lot, too. She'd be riding the bus in Halifax when an unknown lady would sit down beside her, and twenty minutes later, she'd know all about the polyp they found on the ovary of a Pekingese dog owned by her second cousin's daughter, who ran away to Boston and married a jazz musician her family wants nothing to do with.)

When he wasn't working in Fort McMurray on a drilling crew, the kid told me, he lived outside Grande Prairie on his parents' six-hundred-acre farm. But today, he was making a rare visit to town.

"It's too noisy here," he said. "I like our ranch. It's so quiet. You come to town and everything's moving. No one is still."

I told him I live in Toronto.

"Toronto? I can't imagine why anyone would ever want to live in a place like that. But I guess you have to, being in show business and all, eh? I mean, if you want to work in the oil business, you have to be here."

"I might live in Toronto," I said, "but the country's my home. I've got the best of both worlds. I get to make a living seeing Canada from coast to coast, and by living in Toronto, I can walk to the Air Canada Centre when the Leafs are playing."

"But the Leafs suck," he said, laughing.

(This conversation *did* take place before Auston Matthews, Mitch Marner, John Tavares and the rest of those multimillionaire wunderkinds showed up in hopes of revitalizing a franchise synonymous with fifty-seven years of losing. If entering a rink before the game dressed to the nines in tailored suits, looking every inch a gaggle of pimps on a catwalk, guarantees a team the Stanley Cup, Toronto should be seeing a parade very soon.)

"That may be the case, but I 'bleed blue,'" I assured him. "I've been hoping for my Buds for fifty years. You have to keep the faith. I just want to see them win the Stanley Cup . . . in colour!"

He laughed and said he'd gone to Edmonton once to see the Oilers play.

"Never again!"

"The game couldn't have been that bad," I said.

"The game was great, but the city was *way* too noisy! There was nothing but horns and sirens and banging everywhere. It was non-stop noise. All we hear on the farm are the cattle and the wind. I love the sound of wind. It just rolls over the prairie. It's so simple, and it doesn't cost a penny. Everywhere you go costs money, but that doesn't. I don't like leaving but I have to. Why?"

And he answered his own question: "Because you gotta make money. Work on the drilling crew, though? It's very dangerous. No one pays attention to safety. You're supposed to, but it's ignored.

That's the last thing on the list when you're looking to get your day in. Safety's the last thing on anyone's mind."

That point was made very clear to me a few years later in Brandon, Manitoba. I was at the hotel bar for a pint, when a couple of seriously liquored compadres looked at me, all wobbly eyed, and shouted, "We're coming to your show tomorrow!"

I said, "It was tonight. You missed it."

The guy in the Harley shirt and biker beard looked at his buddy and said, "Shit. How'd we miss that?" His spooky-eyed and very intense wingman yelled, "'Cause we're too busy making money!" And he downed a couple of beers in a gulp. (I hadn't seen drinking prowess of that calibre since Latta emptied a forty of Donini in one Herculean guzzle, back in '76 at the infamous Acadia Wine Bee.)

Even though it was an hour shy of last call, they demanded I have a drink with them. I respectfully took a pass, letting them know I had to be up at 7 a.m. for my two-hour drive to the Winnipeg airport to catch a flight back home to Toronto.

The guy in the Harley shirt said, "Toronto sucks." (It's something you hear an awful lot west of Mississauga.)

The intense one bored a hole in my head with his stare and said, "Buddy! I'm gettin' up at 4 a.m.! Running a safety course for seventy guys in my work crew."

I thought, *What kind of safety course can a guy who is shitfaced at 12:30 a.m. possibly run a few hours from now?*

"What is it you do?" I inquired, hoping it didn't involve explosives.

And I kid you not good reader, this teetering and sloshed-to-the-eyeballs hombre declared—with pride, I might add—"I'm in charge of pipeline welders for Enbridge."

"Money breeds crime," the kid in Starbucks said. "We went up to Fort Mac with a six-man crew, and three of them got mugged buying their smokes!"

He told me this in the glory days of the boom, long before the big fire came and turned thirty years of dreams to ashes, coming perilously close to claiming the entire town. I remember how the nation rallied round to help, donating everything from airplane flights back to Atlantic Canada to clothes and food. A big bin sat for two weeks in a storefront on King Street East, right around the corner from my downtown Toronto condo. It gradually filled up with clothes until it was shipped out for the needy of Fort Mac. For a country with the second-greatest national land mass on Earth, it's surprising how small-town Canada feels when tragedy strikes. But in 2006, when Fort Mac was seeing record numbers of newcomers every day and real estate prices had skyrocketed into the realm of the absurd, the province and the oil companies were fighting over whose fiscal responsibility it was to fix the four-foot potholes on Main Street, and to put chalk in schools and bandages in hospitals. Highway 63 from Edmonton was a two-lane killer with a gruesome attrition rate that neither government nor the oil companies made a move to fix for years. During the height of the Iraq War, the highway to the Baghdad airport was safer to drive!

The kid excused himself, and I went back to my journal.

Moments later, I looked up, and he was standing over me, holding a ceramic Starbucks cup.

"Here you go: a gift from me to you. A cup goes around the world. Let people know that just because we drill for oil, doesn't make us bad people. We're all just trying to make a living in this hard world."

Chapter Five
THE CANADIAN WINTER

I like to think of myself as a winter person. I'm sure the polyglot Celtic gene pool I'm descended from has something to do with it. Our blood is far more suited to soup-and-sweater weather than sweating in the tropics, getting semi-comatose on a margarita drip. In actuality, my genetic disposition is far more conducive to staring at a winter campfire, getting semi-comatose on a rum toddy drip.

Short of channelling our inner *ursus* and slipping into a cave for a winter's worth of blissful torpor until the crocuses come again, the only option when it comes to dealing with winter is to survive it. After all, the Inuit managed to eke out an existence from a pitch-black, frozen world of ice, rock and lichen five thousand years before Netflix, when the only light for eight months was a thin strip of blood-red sky stretching across an infinite horizon. (I bet staring at *that* got old in a hurry.)

In his book *Arctic Dreams*, Barry Lopez tells us the Inuit had a word for the time of year when forever night dropped the weight of life on their shoulders: *pereloneq*, which no doubt can be loosely translated as "One more day spent sitting in this igloo under total darkness listening to old Uncle Tulimak fart, and I'm running buck naked on the tundra." Too bad they never had the option of bolting for Florida like we do.

The pilgrimage of snowbirds for sunny Florida is easily several generations old. I've been envious on occasion when I see Facebook posts from retired friends enjoying a lunch of mahi-mahi tacos on a lanai in their exclusive gated community, especially when I'm suffering through a third polar vortex two weeks into February. It sounds lovely, but spending your golden years amongst pistol-packing, mammon-loving, science-denying Republicans does not stoke my northern mojo. I'd cross the line of expected social decorum by saying the right thing to the wrong person at the first neighbourhood barbecue and be shunned faster than a shoplifting Mennonite. That is far too steep a price to pay for a tan in February.

Sure, studies may say a prolonged respite from winter's hard haul adds an extra ten years to your life, but the notion of spending those precious years growing melanoma blisters on my pale leprechaun skin while sporting Bermuda shorts hiked up to a droopy set of "man cans" is a nightmare on par with an emergency root canal performed with a pointy stick.

When it comes to the sun, let alone a killer tropical one, I'm already doomed! Clinical studies say five serious sunburns in childhood result in an 80 percent risk of getting skin cancer today. Then fit me for a wig and sign me up for a dozen bouts of chemotherapy now. *Five* sunburns? I've been covered in thermonuclear welts every summer since I was six!

That's why winter gets my vote. It's a season to be embraced, and many Canadians share my sentiments. Fingers turned black with frostbite after a gloveless day spent tobogganing on Mount Royal are standard badges of honour for those born in Montreal. I've seen entire families, *sans* hats or mitts, gleefully barrelling down that mountain face-first into the kind of wind chill that would have turned Frontenac back.

Those who like to ski live for winter. From Mont-Tremblant to Whistler, ski runs are ruled by fearless young snowboarders riding a piece of fibreglass at ninety-seven kilometres an hour down icy back bowls at an angle so sharp it would make Pythagoras puke!

Snowmobilers are rabid for the season as well. Soon as the first snowflake falls, they're pacing the living room floor with the enthusiasm of a Labrador retriever on the opening day of duck season.

Even ice fishing helps people get through the season. I'm not sure why it's called a sport, though. Sitting in a clapboard shack a Third World shepherd wouldn't shit in—that's heated to Amazonian jungle levels—while staring at six empty holes in the hope the perch will bite makes it seem a stretch to call it a sport. (Then again, professional darts matches are preferably played drunk, and that's called a sport, so they could have a point.)

It is said that smell is the most transformative of the five senses, and for the most part I agree, but with one exception: hearing your skates carve the ice of a frozen pond is a sound that sings a soul note in praise of the eternal. Simply put, it is transformative. Every time I do, I want to end the day in flannel pajamas, watching the Leafs play the Habs on a black and white TV while I eat a plate of home-made beans.

A couple of Januarys ago, while staying at my cottage in Nova Scotia, the mercury dropped to a perfect minus-20 for several windless nights in a row. Within three days, nature's magic had delivered such a bump-free, lump-free, frozen sheet of glass on the local pond, so smooth you'd swear it had been Zamboni-glazed to perfection by elves the night before. After breakfast, I hooked my Tacks over my hockey stick, stuck a puck in my pocket and headed down the road to commune with the timeless. I hit the ice with the confidence of that high school hockey god I never, *ever* was. House league pedigree be damned! I skated that day like I was born for the majors! Look at those Paul Coffey rinkwide strides! Had there been NHL scouts hiding in the cattails around the pond that day, I'd have most certainly had my call up to "the show."

All alone, and all day long, I pushed that circle of frozen rubber up and down the ice, oblivious to whatever woes bedevilled the world. With every stride I was fourteen years old again, playing shinny on frozen Chocolate Lake in the company of forever pals when those now gone were flesh and blood, moving immortal under a winter sun that cast our shadows long as life itself, back when all our gods were the same.

A lot of Canadian kids at one time or another have entertained the dream of making the NHL. Truth be told, I knew as early as peewee I would not be playing in the majors. It was after I got my first pair of skates. They were hand-me-downs from a cousin and came with buckles on them. *Buckles.* They looked as if some old fella had doctored up a pair of polio boots in his shed.

And my mother was selling me hard.

"Look at those skates your cousin gave you. They're practically brand new!" she exclaimed. "Those are really nice skates."

She saw the doubt behind my eyes—the abject refusal of an eleven-year-old son to buy her ludicrous spin.

"What? You don't like those skates? They're perfectly good skates. Yes. They. Are."

No, I thought, *they're a piece of shit*. I suppose the shaking of my head was as much a reaction to the clearly corrective footwear I was holding as to the audacity of her pitch.

She saw my head shake, and in turn, I caught her full fury as her voice began to rise in crescendo.

"You're lucky to even have skates! Your father never had skates when he was growing up in Newfoundland. Poor little fella, if he didn't wake up Christmas morning with a boner he never had a friggin' thing to play with!"

"I know, Ma. I know Dad had it tougher than me," I cried. "I know he moved from Newfoundland to Halifax when he was seven years old and had a paper route in the morning and one in the afternoon and even sold mackerel from a horse-drawn cart on Saturday mornings in the wintertime when he wanted to be playing shinny with his buddies on frozen Chocolate Lake, but he came home instead and gave the money to Nanny for rent, cause his dad was sick in bed with ALS and his older brothers were in the corvette navy, protecting convoys from the German U-boats prowling the North Atlantic. I know, I know . . . but there's fuckin' buckles on my skates! Leprechauns have buckles on their skates."

(Fifty years later, I can assure you I never had the guts to drop an f-bomb on Mom. I've added that for dramatic effect. Also, I am now very grateful I never had the Junior Tacks all the better players had. There's not a lot of laughs to be had, listening to somebody reminisce about how cool they once were.)

If you're wondering, I eventually did get what passed for a half-decent pair of hockey skates. Bauer Black Panthers. Strange that a style of skate would have been named after a black militant group who, besides distributing food to the poor of Oakland, California, also advocated armed overthrow of "the man." Purchased at Canadian Tire with money saved delivering newspapers, the thirty bucks I paid for them was literally a steal. *Someone* had conveniently changed the sticker price on the box. Life was simpler then.

When you're a kid, looking cool while playing sports was half the battle, especially if, like me, you weren't that good. Back in 1970, I tried to talk my father into buying me a Victoriaville hockey stick with a fibreglass blade that cost three dollars and twenty-one cents. This was beyond the realm of reason for a man whose toy at Christmas was, well . . . which explains his apoplectic reaction in Cleve's Sporting Goods. Although frightening at the time, I now understand it was perfectly reasonable for someone whose idea of a Saturday night treat in 1942 was splitting the head of a newly stewed rabbit with his brother Jack.

"Three dollars and twenty-one cents for a GD hockey stick? A hockey stick?! Lord Jesus, Ronnie! Bobby Hull doesn't have that slap-shot because he's got a fancy hockey stick. He's got that shot because he built his wrists up milking cows on the farm!"

"Then get me a cow, Dad," I said, "'cause I can't lift the friggin' puck!"

My protests were ignored, so I had to settle for the sixty-nine-cent Hespeler, the worst hockey stick on the market. I swear they were made of balsa wood. They were basically kindling with tape on them. After one shot, they shattered. The only thing they were good for was staking tomatoes in the garden come summer.

Not so today. Everything has got to be top of the line for kids playing the game, and half the time, it's their delusional parents setting that standard. Reality is so distorted for some hard-core hockey parents—the ones grooming their kids from birth to be the next Sidney Crosby. Soon as the umbilical cord is cut, the kids are practically thrown on a rink when they're still wet. Seal pups get less ice time! How about before you start mortgaging the house to keep little Bobby in gear, you do a reality check? He's eight! Let him be a kid first.

Of course, the vast majority play for the love of the game, and that's never more obvious than during hockey tournament weekends. Stay at any hotel when half a dozen teams have laid siege to it, and it becomes blatantly clear they're having a riot. Mongol hordes were easier on the furniture when they were sacking Constantinople! Back and forth from the games room to the pool; up and down the elevators barefoot, soaking wet and screaming; pillaging the candy, pop and ice machines all night long . . . and that's just the parents!

One afternoon I stepped into the hallway with my bags headed for my hotel room during a hockey tourney weekend and got corked in the cojones with a hard orange hockey ball shot by kids playing pickup hockey in the hallways—with their moms playing nets! That's the kind of quintessential Canadian tableau Krieghoff would have painted.

For a country known for saying "sorry" too much, we never apologize for loving this violent sport. A typical injury list during the playoffs reads like a casualty report from a Civil War hospital tent. But unlike wounded soldiers, they're expected to keep playing. It's why I have to laugh when professional baseball players are out for six weeks with a hangnail. When Sidney Crosby had his face reconstructed after getting hit by a seventy-five-mile-an-hour slapshot, he was back on the ice to win the Stanley Cup that same year.

I met an elderly gentleman over breakfast at the Delta Hotel in Saint John almost twenty-five years ago. People have always given me a window on their world. They wanted to let me know there were moments in their lives that mattered, and perhaps that in the sharing, the moments would live on longer than they. He was easily in his late seventies then, so I guess this story has. In a body bent over and hobbled by time, he had the gruff voice of those Canadian Legion lifers who are permanently seated by the shuffleboard table with a draft in hand. I'd not been on TV very much way back then, so when he addressed me by name, I was taken aback. Sometimes I thought these strangers were apparitions who materialized from the ether just long enough to share their stories. I never knew where they came from or where they were going. They just appeared, told their stories, and in the blink of an eye were gone.

"How are ya, Ronnie? I used to be six-foot-four. Not anymore. Time, Ronnie. Time. It's a son of a bitch!" the old man said. He continued . . .

"I used to play in the Wood Chopper's League back in '49 up by Lake Huron. It's the seventh game of the playoffs, and we're playing for the trophy. We're in the dressing room at the end of the second period, and the game's all tied up, 2–2. Our star centre was buckled over in tears. 'I can't go back out, Coach. I can't. It hurts too much.'

"Piles, Ronnie. He had a cluster of piles growing on the crack of his arse you'd swear were a cluster of grapes." And then, with a hand on my shoulder, he offered a conscientious courtesy: "I'm not bothering your breakfast, am I?"

"Of course not," I said, thinking, *It's not every day you get a great hockey story involving festering piles anymore.*

He grew taller in the telling as his posture straightened.

"Our team doctor learned his trade on the battlefields of World War II. He looked at Reggie, our centre, then back at us, and said, 'Pin his arms to the table, boys,' which we did . . . much like in the hazing, but I don't have time to get into that now. Then that doctor dropped Reggie's hockey pants and sliced those piles off with a straight razor! No freezing! He whipped a handful of ice and a bread poultice dipped in mercurochrome on the crack of his ass! Thirty minutes later, we were skating round the ice with that trophy."

"How did he do it?" I asked.

"Who?" he grunted.

"The guy with the piles," I said. "How did he get the winning goal?"

"Christ, Ronnie, *I* got the goal. Poor Reggie sat on the bench crying, and barely walked again." Then he roared a great, gravelly laugh, punched me in the arm with a bony fist and said, "Put that in a book someday."

So, I did.

Unless you live in the frigid West, the days of backyard rinks and frozen ponds are disappearing. No one can depend on a consistent run of cold weather anymore.

Lake Ontario acts as a bulwark to cold and snow in Toronto, so instead of an enjoyable white winter, the mild temperature drapes a funereal grey curtain over the city for weeks on end. That's when seasonal affective disorder kicks in. Lethargy rules. Moods darken. The weight is real. *Pereloneq!*

No amount of time spent on the elliptical, releasing endorphins at the gym, can chase the blues from your system. Your body is in dire need of a dose of vitamin D, well beyond the thousand milligrams you're getting from that bottle of Lakota every morning. You need to feel some *real* sun on your face, and the best place for that is far closer to the equator than Toronto, so to the tropics you go. (Of course, those lacking the necessary scratch for a Caribbean vacation can opt for a trip to the local tanning salon instead, where they'll receive a generous dose of ultraviolet light to chase the SAD from their system. Mind you, too-frequent visits could turn testicles to raisins or a uterus to dust, so it's your call.)

No matter how intense your love of the season, everyone hits a winter tipping point. Mine was at the tail end of a gruelling twenty-five-date tour of Ontario, on a blistering-cold March afternoon in Pembroke. As I pulled my suitcase from the 4Runner in a Best Western parking lot, I failed to realize I had not zipped it shut, and the entire contents spilled to the ground. While a profanity-laced diatribe danced from my cake hole, I watched the wind carry my clothes far across the parking lot in a dozen different directions. (You just know this kind of stuff doesn't happen to comedians playing Vegas.)

Just as I was about to go chasing my Stanfield's into the bush, a group of snowmobilers miraculously materialized from the forest adjacent to the hotel and began picking up, then returning, my clothes. I thanked these apostles of winter whose faces were covered in reflective visors and their bodies in thermal suits made for rocketing across snowy fields and through woodlands at eighty kilometres an hour . . . drunk. Feeling like a lost member from a party of polar explorers who'd been saved by the Inuit, I watched as my benefactors headed back to the forest from whence they'd come, leaving me with enough to survive the elements until I found sanctuary—or, in my case, the reception desk.

And that's when I decided to take my family to an all-inclusive resort on Mexico's Riviera Maya. We would join legions of pale, sleep-deprived Canadians at the airport at 3 a.m. for the 6 a.m.

flight, so psyched to be putting the snow and cold behind us, we'd have duct-taped ourselves to the wheel wells to escape.

We took a charter flight on Air Transat. I'll wager conditions were more humane on a POW troopship. At five-foot-three no one has ever accused me of being tall, but some legroom wouldn't have hurt. It's not like I was a seven-foot first-round draft pick for the Toronto Raptors, but Jesus H. Christ, a ventriloquist's suitcase would've had more room! Arterial thrombosis was swelling my joints and we hadn't even left the ground yet. A person needed to be a ninth-level yoga master just to get the cup to their lips for a sip of the brake fluid they were passing off as coffee.

The plane was packed with 498 punchy, sun-hungry travellers drawn from the vast and sprawling armies of the middle class, bound for the Yucatán sunbelt. Everyone still wore their pale winter skin, too, so after ten minutes in the tropics, those not smeared in 60-plus sunblock would very soon be starting to bubble.

On landing, we were processed by a listless, couldn't-give-a-shit-if-you-were-bringing-in-yellowcake-uranium Mexican customs official, then herded onto shuttle buses for the resort and driven for an hour past bone-crushing, corrugated-tin-hut, spooky-eyed poverty, where scrawny village dogs sporting pendulous nipples suckled their rabid broods beneath diseased palm trees. I got really indignant.

This is a crime, I thought. *We've got to help those people.*

Suddenly, our opulent hotel appeared through the jungle mists like some magical kingdom in the clouds, and the feeling went away.

"Well, those people are probably happy in their own way," I thought, as a hotel waiter put a Mai Tai in my hand.

The hotel's massive buffet had the kind of spread you'd see rolled out for a Third World dictator, while outside his stately palace, his people are eating old shoes and dog shit. The North American masses were wobbling up and down the aisle in all their gluttonous glory, heaping their plates with gravy-drenched meats and heart-seizing sweets, one cream puff away from having a five-alarm coronary in the surf.

You do get to engage with Americans on these trips, and it's always an eye-opener to meet some of the neighbours we share a continent with, whose government can spend sixty billion dollars a year on intelligence yet have half their country be comprised of the geographically clueless.

I overheard a conversation at the buffet table between a couple from Georgia and a woman from Saskatchewan. With her exceedingly polite Southern drawl, the Georgia peach inquired as to where the Canadian woman was from.

"Saskatoon, Saskatchewan," I heard her reply.

"Where did she say she was from, dear?" asked the husband.

"Damned if I know," was the reply. "She was speaking another language."

That's rich, because the entire week I had been listening to a cacophony of Appalachian accents the likes of which had not been heard since callbacks for *Hee Haw*'s road show.

Canada is not immune to garish patriotism. If you've ever believed there's no such thing as the "ugly Canadian," drop by Señor Frog's in Cancún during happy hour and the myth of our peaceable kingdom and her genteel citizens will be forever debunked. You'll see gangs of muscle-bound, party-hearty bros and their bleached-blond Gold's Gym sirens, all sporting NHL team's jerseys happily face-first in tequila Slurpies, singing Stompin' Tom's "The Hockey Song." And that's just the first night. By midweek, those cyborgs will be sitting in the shade at poolside, wrapped tip to tail in gauze, suffering such severe sunburn that as soon as they get home, they'll be losing half their asses to skin grafts.

Mexico spooks me. If you get murdered in Mexico, they will never find who did it. *Never*. Mexican cops are so hopeless, they couldn't catch a killer during a game of Clue! If you're murdered on the Riviera Maya, there are always two versions: the Mexican version and the truth. You can just imagine the conversation between you and the detective.

"It is clear the victim jumped from the balcony of his hotel room."

To which you would counter, "But he's been shot in the head."

Whereupon the detective, with a dismissive shrug would say, "Then he must have pulled the trigger on the way down."

Case closed.

The dogs are reading the vibe in Mexico, too. I have never seen a dog wag its tail there. Last time I was in Tulum, I was petting one for an hour at an outdoor café before I realized it was dead.

Returning home can be a different story. Here's a tip: remember your parking spot. Today, of course, we can use our phones to take photos of the spot. However, back in the Stone Age—say, ten years ago—a person had to write their parking spot down. Imagine! To forget was to flirt with death. I recall seeing a family, still sporting flip-flops, shorts and tank tops and carrying a Sherpa's weight in duty-free swag, wandering the parking lot at Toronto's Pearson Airport on a frigid February night, looking for their car because they'd forgotten their spot. I bet by the time they finally found it, half of them were suffering hypothermic shock. Mom probably showed up at work the next morning still sporting cornrows, a nice tan and both thumbs black with frostbite. Had she stayed home in Canada, a good pair of mitts would have prevented that.

Chapter Six

OUT WHERE MY MOJO LIVES

A stage with only a microphone is freedom made manifest. There you answer to no one but the audience, who provide a comedian with the luxury to line up the planets and make sense of the chaos we're all walking through—in the language of laughs. The audience is the great litmus test of what works and what doesn't—unlike network television, where gaggles of censorious lawyers skilled in arcane semantics vet your satire, and network apparatchiks who've drunk the corporate Kool Aid enact executive dictates. On the other hand, a non-televised run of live consecutive dates in packed theatres is not held hostage to institutionalized standards. On the road, the inmate runs their own asylum.

I once believed a television series was the grail at the end of the trail and the summit of creative achievement. Granted, playing to sold-out theatres on my own and shooting a well-received one-hour comedy special each year in a different Canadian city was a hell of a lot better than working for beer tickets before a room of sarcastic

Toronto comedy snobs at the Rivoli, but still, it wasn't enough. I had to land the coveted television series, but when that happened, I soon discovered that feeding a medium with an insatiable appetite for *content*, placed far greater demands on *creative* than the one-hour specials ever did.

For one thing, those first five one-hour television specials had a wealth of material whose laughs had been honed diamond-hard touring the regions I'd eventually feature. The bits with the strongest legs would act as adhesive to the overall narrative of the seventy-five-page script I'd write, memorize and shoot. It was a great system that had worked for seven years: hit the road, write new content—some thematic to the region I was touring and some not—keep what works, lose what doesn't, return to Toronto, lock myself away in my office come summer to bang it out on the computer, then shoot the special in the fall before a paying theatre audience, edit it down from the one hundred minutes we'd shot, to the forty-five it had to be and then deliver it to network.

Although I wrote the first five one-hour specials myself, the final four were co-written with the erudite Windsor, Ontario–born Paul Pogue, and the Winnipeg, Manitoba–raised scholar Scott Montgomery, whose collective comedic intelligence, soul and work ethic not only made me a better comedian but a more enlightened person as well. When I missed three weeks because of my father's passing in August 2017, a consummate stand-up and son of the Canadian Shield, Wawa-born Pete Zedlacher, stepped into the room to cover for me on that final special until my return. Executive producer Lynn Harvey brought a thirty-five-year television pedigree to the table and set an unimpeachable standard of production value from our very first collaboration. Everyone from lighting, set decoration, direction and editing was instrumental to the success of those specials as a New Year's Eve viewing tradition seen by millions of Canadians in our coveted 9 p.m. time slot—not just the guy with the microphone. Lesson learned: success is always a team effort.

Although the last place I ever wanted to find myself at fifty-two was fronting a TV series with sketches, *The Ron James Show*, which ran for five years, found me performing them before a live CBC studio audience who sometimes weren't very *alive* at all. Watching a neon applause sign light up in corners of the studio, as if it were tazering the comatose awake, was anathema to everything I believed. Still, you address the mandate of the ones cutting the cheque, put your shoulder to the mule and plow.

The writing room for the series was headed by multi-award winning Garry Campbell, who besides an affable and accommodating nature brought to the table thirty years' experience as a comedy writer in both Canada and LA. Along with me, Gary led a platoon of hard-working foot soldiers whose gregarious *esprit de corps* delivered twenty pages of original stand-up each week for thirteen weeks, as well as four new sketches and an animated cartoon that eventually had to be drawn, cast, voiced and edited. It was more than a blast working with the best sketch actors in Toronto (of whom 95 percent had earned their comedy chops in the Second City) but in order for the public to watch a show, a network had to promote it. Oh, well. Our series wasn't the first and certainly won't be the last to lose that battle. Looking back on several episodes in those earlier seasons and the time spent addressing an executive's vision besides searching for our own creative path, CBC's shunning could easily be construed as a blessing in disguise.

Why they never publicized the show after greenlighting it is a mystery on par with the riddle of the Sphinx. We were bounced around the dial and given seven different time slots for reasons known only to God and whatever inaccessible network mandarin at the top of the food chain was then calling the shots.

. Compare that to the warm welcome received at every theatre stretched across Canada (all of them, as I write, rendered hauntingly quiet by COVID-19's curse). Some are shiny new two-thousand-seaters like the brilliant Winspear in Edmonton; there's the thousand-seat Centrepointe in Nepean and the haunted eight-hundred-seat Grand in London. There's a sweet seven-hundred-seater in Belleville, called the Empire, whose renovation by local Royal LePage–owning guitar maestro Mark Rashotte eighteen years ago also had the tertiary impact of revitalizing the downtown core. Although we shot our *West Coast Wild* special at the impressive two-thousand-seat Royal in Victoria, British Columbia, we play the funky thousand-seat McPherson in Chinatown when on tour with Shantero whose audience always turns up with their laughing pants on, just as they do on the other side of the country, in the Confederation Centre in Charlottetown. There's a city that loves laughing! Only 150,000 in the entire province, yet they fill that theatre half a dozen times a year in support of stand-up comedy.

Several turn-of-the-century houses, like the Burton Cummings (formerly the Walker) in Winnipeg, the Capitol in Moncton or the Avon in Stratford, Ontario, carry the spirit of those who once toiled on an unforgiving vaudeville circuit, when luxury was a hotel room without bed bugs. (Apologies to those theatres not mentioned. My editors at Penguin Random House suggested listing them all would sound too "inside baseball" and I'd like to get another book out of them.)

By the time this book hits the stands, you will have seen me in the twenty-fifth anniversary of the Ha! Festival, shot in Halifax in

October 2020, when the largest city in the Atlantic Bubble was proudly COVID-free. So confident were the producers their zone was virus-free, audience members weren't required to wear masks and they were seated onstage at tables just an arm's length away from the performers. I didn't discover that until I stepped onstage. Not going to lie: it came as a shock. I remember thinking, *If there's a hidden carrier in the pack who suddenly starts sneezing, this room will be intubating in bulk!* I'd been assured all necessary precautions had been taken, and I had no reason to doubt them. Knowing the CBC's aversion to bad press, I doubted they'd relish being held responsible for pollinating a room full of people with the plague. It wouldn't have made for a great opening story on *The National*.

Besides, after the loss of more than a year's income, and worse, the ability to actualize my calling, once I heard the first laughs from that room, Ebola-carrying rats and flying Zika monkeys could not have moved me from the mike. This is what I'd so desperately been missing the past seven months: the sight and sounds of people sitting shoulder to shoulder, laughing together.

Though we only got the bare minimum of publicity to let viewers know when the television series was actually *on*, I did get invited to participate in CBC "Culture Days."

The mandate of Culture Days was to sell the CBC to the country and let the people know we were there for them, because I guess no one knew—or something. After serving time in a cold tent with an inadequate heater, meeting people on the lookout for something free to do on a rainy Tuesday afternoon in April, you attended a party where regional executives spent a great deal of time telling a room packed with other executives, headset-wearing publicity people, television actors, newscasters and radio personalities all drinking wine and snorting up a cracker-load of finger food, how great a job they were doing. When we were interviewed on camera, it was our job to sell the season's lineup to whatever members of the public were couch-surfing in the hinterlands and wishing they had HBO.

At one of these functions, I was seated beside an actor with a couple of movies under his belt in the States who was now starring in his own CBC television series. I tried to make small talk, which, given his obvious lack of interest, proved a challenge.

"Congratulations on the series," I said.

What a liar. I didn't watch it. Okay, I did catch it . . . *once*. A scene where a polar bear had wandered into a kitchen. It was the world's only trained polar bear, a species of *ursus* notoriously averse to taking orders, buckets of free seal meat or not. Wild animals change the dynamic of a set because, well, they're *wild*.

Indulge me a tangent here. Years ago, while living in LA, I shot a corporate training film (I know—here he goes again with more stories about the glamour of Hollywood) where we had chimpanzees on set. The use of chimpanzees is, thankfully, not permitted in the Canadian film industry, because our more enlightened nation knows that a chimp is but one chromosome away from being proficient at calculus. We were shooting in some nondescript warehouse in the San Fernando Valley, which, given the post-coital reek of our fetid dressing rooms, had clearly doubled quite recently as a pornographic film set. There was an odoriferous barnyard hum in the air and the floors hadn't been cleaned, to quote the homemade vernacular of my late father, "Since the Year of the White Mice." (When that infamous year actually occurred and the impact it had on civilization are unknown. But rest assured, good reader, scholarly discussions on par with Socratic debate occupied many hours—seated round canoe-trip campfires with pals during times gone, all pleasantly baked on Gaspereau homegrown—trying to figure that one out.)

Howie Mandel's OCD would have been off the charts had he been shining his black light into those crusty corners of our dressing rooms. But Howie would have never been shooting a corporate gig with a baby chimp in a diaper. Why? Well, because Howie had a legitimate career, that's why! And he had a career not only because of his stellar and unimpeachable gift for hosting game shows, talent contests and pulling a surgical glove over his head for his closer but because he had a great agent, and I did not. My agent was a cranky, barrel-bellied little dude called Ernie Dole, whose sad, bare office was a second-floor walk-up on Ventura Boulevard, squeezed between a karate studio and a beauty parlour. Anytime I dropped in for a meeting, I always heard kicks and grunts coming through the walls. I was never sure whether someone was getting their hair done or the shit kicked out of them. Or better yet, getting their hair done *while* getting the shit kicked out of them. (I bet people pay for that in Amsterdam.)

Ernie's dyed-blond perm was complemented by a volcanically red face, while his daily ensemble from tip to tail was always black pants, red shirt, red suit jacket and black tie to match his shiny, pointy, black, zippered dress boots. It wasn't hard to imagine him as a lesser satanic minion, running the Tilt-a-Whirl in a forgotten corner of hell's midway, which, given his office and the status of my acting career, he probably was.

Ernie's star clients were a couple of little people, Billy and Eric. They were actors, but primarily wrestlers; in the waning days of what went by the now politically incorrect moniker, "midget wrestling," where entertaining rednecks who hadn't received this memo still provided them plenty of work on the county fair circuit. Their current claim to fame, however, was having come off a good run as "special business extras" in the Val Kilmer movie *Willow*. (I know, I'm going back. By the way, special business extras are one step above background extras, meaning they get fed and you're not allowed to hit them.)

Billy and Eric carried themselves with a regal indifference to the rest of the world. They entered the room with a three-foot-seven swagger that said, "Get out of my way, or I'll flip you faster than a drugged calf at a dime-store rodeo." As a five-foot-four man who's been the recipient of more than his fair share of short jokes his entire life, I couldn't help but admire their defiant king-of-the-hill confidence. Oh well, at least I was working. Granted, it was with a chimpanzee, but that never hurt Ronald Reagan.

The animal wrangler had a doozy of a claw mark running from under his collar up to a horribly mauled eye socket. Apparently, a surly chimp in his menagerie had taken umbrage with its direction and made a point of protesting by using its six-inch fangs and gnarly jungle strength, which could snap the femur of a forest roaming dik-dik in half without blinking. Little-known fact: a simian's first line of attack is to—wait for it—chew your face off! That's right . . . *chew*! So next time you're thinking about picking up an orangutan for the family because everyone's tired of owning a cat who does nothing but eat, sleep, shit and sit at the window, licking itself comatose all day long, best to stock up on goalie masks first. Just saying.

So, to get back to where I started, a polar bear is a very difficult animal to train, as it's the only bear that will deliberately stalk and kill a human being. Therefore, taking down an extra who's standing beside the craft-services table, staring mindlessly at their own reflection in the whistling aluminum kettle, too self-absorbed by their daily fantasy of one day getting a speaking role to actually hear the bear coming, would be a breeze.

I watched the show for ten minutes, and when nothing happened other than actors screaming and running around in circles (much like they do at award shows), I changed the channel and found a nature show, where biologists happened to have drugged a female (non-thespian) polar bear for radio collaring.

By the way, I bet those scientists have some great blooper reels, like when the bear suddenly jolts awake because they never gave it enough dope, and even though it's sitting glassy-eyed and wobbly in its semi-comatose state as poor ol' Elvis on the toilet, it manages to muster enough energy to grab one of the eggheads by the leg. While he's screaming like a man being eaten alive (which he is), one of the other scientists acts quickly and shoots another loaded dart into the polar bear's ass. Thankfully, the bear is out cold before it can make a meal of his colleague's appendage, which is now being pulled, horribly mangled and bleeding, from the drooling jaws of Nanuk.

If I had been the scientist who was bitten, you can guarantee I'd be getting mileage out of *that* close call for, oh . . . the rest of my life! It would be the moment at one of those boring dinner parties you shouldn't have gone to in the first place, where you hit your tipping point discussing bourgeois inanities and accidentally spill the third Scotch you should never have poured in the first place. That's when "the attack" would be mentioned.

The other guests would cast knowing glances at each other with an eye-roll. Someone would excuse themselves and bolt for the loo.

A whispered "Oh please, not again" would be heard, but I wouldn't notice, because I'd be back on the sea ice of Lancaster Sound with my leg in the mouth of *Ursus maritimus*. In an instant, I'd roll my pant leg up and plop it on the dinner table. The other guests would squirm in their chairs, but I'd be too self-absorbed to notice as I regaled them with the damage left by the creature's seven-inch fangs, when my leg was pulled from its hungry jaws and the meat scraped clean to the tune of 357 stitches, whose hideous purple scar was now shining bright as the silverware no one was using anymore because I had wrecked dinner . . . *again*.

It would be the only topic of conversation on the way home in the car too.

"No one gives a shit that a bear had your leg in its mouth," she'd say. "No one! It's not like you were hunting it, wounded it and it back-tracked the sea ice to stalk you. The poor thing was drugged. It didn't even know it was your leg. The bear was so high, it could have been licking its own balls and wouldn't know it! You bring it up all the time—'Look where the polar bear almost chewed my leg off! Look!' Nobody cares! Why does everything always have to be about *you*?!"

And that's when I would mumble, "It couldn't lick its own balls. It was a feeee-male." Then I'd shut up and drift back to that day on the ice floes of Lancaster Sound when I'd never felt more alive.

Anyway, back to the original gist of the story.

"Thank you," the lead actor said, as sincerely as someone who fakes emotion for a living can. I could tell by his stone-cold stare that he was already bored shitless with me.

"You sure are getting lots of publicity. They are really behind your show," I said, hoping he'd say my show was great.

"Yes, they are treating us like gold. I couldn't ask for more."

I could ask for way *more,* I thought. Like a solid time-slot, for Christ's sake. Secretly, I was more jealous that buddy got to work with a man-eating polar bear. I worked with a baby chimp wearing a diaper. Comedians get different perks.

So, as I've done my entire life, I made a joke.

"Actually, CBC publicity is investing more time in our promotional campaign by organizing a Girl Guide cookie drive on our behalf, and we get to keep the money they make selling the chocolate ones."

Not a great joke, but a joke, nonetheless. It was delivered *as* a joke, with a cynical tone honed over forty years spent doing just that but it did not find purchase. It hit the brick wall behind his eyes and died instantly as he stared at me with the doleful expression of a child who's seen his first dandelion seeds fly to the wind.

"The Girl Guides are donating money earned selling cookies to your show? That's wonderful! Just wonderful!"

How do you respond to that? You don't. You shut up, because you know you've fallen into a valley of the comedically clueless.

Someone walked by our table and asked if I was doing another comedy special and I replied, "No. I have a series now" but they made a face like I was joking and kept going. With interest piqued, the star said he and his Hollywood pals wanted to start doing some stand-up. "You know," he said offhandedly with that carefree nonchalance of the uninitiated, "just working some stuff out at the clubs. Any suggestions?"

For a fleeting second, I thought about enlightening the actor, giving him exactly the "suggestions" he was looking for—insights that might help him in the new-found "hobby" that he and his posse of confident young LA actor bros would soon be dabbling in. After all, they were just looking to "work some stuff out." The inference was clear. It's always the same. A familiar, patronizing curiosity. Everyone thinks it's easy. They always do. After all, how hard can it be? You just walk onstage, stand in front of a microphone and start saying the same stuff that made your friends laugh. The only difference is, you're *onstage* . . . in front of an audience. But that *is* the difference! *The* difference, in fact. Stand-up is an exponential leap from real life to the high wire. It's why everyone *doesn't* do it. Stand-up comedy is the kind of job that 99 percent of the world would run from faster than the undead at daybreak.

Only those of us who have been bloodied in battle know. We remember all too well that baptism of fire called "amateur night." The step you took from behind the curtain to the stage might as well have been into the void of empty space, with you untethered from the mother ship. You have never, *ever* felt more alone. Your heart is trying to escape from your chest and bolt for home. Why did you ever come here?! Rivers of perspiration flood the palms of your hands as your mouth opens to speak. Your tongue conspires. It will not work. You have no spit. Your tongue is stuck to the roof of your mouth with the adherence of a tenacious mollusc to a government pier. *Open your mouth, open your mouth*, your brain says, knowing full well survival depends on it. It opens, but your mind goes blank. You can't remember your act! You had it memorized and everything! You see nothing but black beyond that terrible solo spot that's drilling a hole in your forehead while the coiled contempt of the audience for the comedian you have the audacity to believe you are expresses itself as a deafening silence. Your joke lands dead-sloth flat at your feet as your soul slides off the stage into the cigarette-butt-strewn street, while the quiet of the room screams, "*Get off!*"

Then, the next amateur night, bruised but not beaten, you try again—but they laugh this time. And that's enough to keep you coming back, until you have an act that's good enough to warrant a pauper's payday that will hopefully get you farther on up the road.

Instead, I told the movie star it's best to stick with what works. And I went to get some finger food.

Chapter Seven

PIT STOPS

On *The Ron James Show*, there was a regular two-minute travelogue called "Road Odes," where we tried to capture a quirky sense of the personalities of towns and cities across the country, much as my earlier specials did. It didn't work. CBC's *Still Standing* succeeds far better in this regard, where a comedian travels to rural corners of Canada, interviewing small-town locals in the first half of the show while gleaning material about their town for the stand-up comedy set he'll later perform for an appreciative audience in town.

Something happens when you're about to put non-professionals on camera. Soon as they hear the word *action*, things get weird. The gregarious old gentleman who, moments before had been full of charming anecdotes about the history of the town in which you're shooting, suddenly goes stone-cold quiet while others practically turn into the singing frog from the *Merrie Melodies* cartoons, but unlike that frog, they never shut up. When the crew and cameras were gone, I found people were far less intimidated. People felt safe to be themselves and some shared stories of substance that, from my experiences, I've come to believe are better served by the written word.

We were on a shoot in St. Andrews, New Brunswick for a couple of days when I took a walk around town. Sitting on a peninsula jutting into Passamaquoddy Bay, St. Andrews-by-the-Sea is one of those charming Maritime towns so close to America, you can practically reach out and grab a mittful off their money tree—which, by the looks of the stately nineteenth-century mansions round town, many wealthy families once did. Founded in 1783 by affluent United Empire Loyalists who were exiled after siding with Britain in the Revolutionary War, St. Andrew's well-preserved historic architecture is so evocative of another era, you can almost hear the ghosts of Irish cholera victims coughing up a lung in the local coffee shops.

Sitting on a hill, dominating the town, is the very majestic and supposedly haunted Algonquin Hotel. It's rumoured that after spending summer vacations here as a kid, Stephen King used this imposing old matron as his inspiration for the Overlook Hotel when he wrote *The Shining*. In its turn-of-the-century heyday, the hotel catered to filthy-rich industrialists like railroad magnate William Cornelius Van Horne, who summered in this playground of the privileged when he wasn't in the Rockies, barking demands at Chinese labourers forced to hang half-naked from a cliff face in straw baskets filled with dynamite. St. Andrews catered to the anointed of the Gilded Age, where wealthy white fat cats like Cornelius would take in the salt air, play croquet, eat lobsters, get drunk and wife-swap.

That's a lie. I think Cornelius was allergic to lobster.

A funky gallery sits at the end of the main drag, where genteel shops reeking of lavender potpourri and all selling the same thing are packed with swag-happy tourists looking for something more to bring home from their Bay of Fundy trip than the chunk of lobster meat stuck in their annoying molar's food trap, that nothing short of being shot in the mouth with a water cannon will remove.

The gallery is different than those craft shops. For one thing, it doesn't look like an anal-retentive Martha Stewart SWAT team had hit it overnight, surgically cramming placemats, scented candles, lighthouses and bottles of jam in every spare corner. This place is a riot of disorganization, bursting at the seams with authentic relics of Canadiana: exquisitely hand-carved wooden boats, Mi'kmaq-made snowshoes from the 1870s, walking sticks, wooden carvings of forest animals, and at every turn are paintings: kaleidoscopically coloured folk art canvases of owls, caribou, raven, deer, moose and bear, travelling the myth-rich dreamscape world of shape-shifters.

"Just putting these images on canvas is how I make sense of the world," the proprietor says. His name is Brian, and he's a David Crosby look-alike who's been running the gallery for ten years or more.

I tell him I feel the same way about stand-up. In a world that's increasingly fractured and polarized, getting a thousand people from different walks of life on the same page for two hours lets me know we're not so different from each other after all.

The place is authentic, and I say as much, adding, "What's here is exactly what *isn't* sitting in the stores on Main Street. That's the kind of stuff you'd give a grandmother."

"Much appreciated. I try to keep it real here," he says. "A world traveller came into my shop a few years back and asked what the hell is going on in the stores uptown. 'I want to buy something made in St. Andrews,' he said. 'I don't want to go home with a tiger lamp made in Indonesia!'"

Brian is clearly obsessed with bears, because their likenesses are everywhere in his shop. Carved Indigenous bear masks of West Coast origin, carved local figurines and unique fetishes from Bavaria. Those figurines are synonymous with German folklore, where a frequent running theme involves a bear dropping by a woodsman's humble abode in human disguise on a snowy night in search of shelter and a feed of strudel. If refused, he eats the woodsman, trashes the cabin then poops in the fireplace. (It's not my joke. German folklore is notoriously scatological.) "Bears won't suffer a lack of hospitality" is the moral there, I guess.

"Mom told me that as a little kid, I dreamt of bears all the time," he confesses, "and woke yelling about them. Thing is, since I started painting, I don't dream of them anymore. Bears were my messengers and they helped release my inner voice.

"The inner voice," he emphasizes, "is what it's all about. It's about trusting yourself. It doesn't come from your head, either, but your heart."

Strangely enough, I'd just finished listening to George Carlin's autobiography on CD, posthumously read by his brother. Carlin talked about finding his authentic voice, and how once he did, he stopped worrying what people thought about what he said, and he just said what he thought. He also stopped worrying about getting laughs, apparently, because when I saw him onstage in Vegas in front of 2,500 people six years before he died, he never got a single one during a ninety-minute set and never really cared to. Seriously, not one laugh. That takes guts. If I didn't hear belly laughs every thirty seconds from the audience, I'd commit hara-kiri as a closer.

"Dad was a peacekeeper who wore the blue helmet. Proudly, too. It's why I keep it on my desk. Good energy. Good karma." Although it seems incongruous among the other historic relics and paintings on display, its presence is soothing, reminding me of Canada's valued contribution to the world before America's imperial march to forever war after 9/11 altered the equation, and the preservation of peace took a back seat to the perpetuation of conflict.

He continued: "We were stationed in Lahr, Germany, not far from the Black Forest, and we'd vacation there. Every little inn has its own bear effigy at the front desk. The Germans revere bears."

Knowing full well I'm invoking Godwin's Law, which postulates that online conversations reach their nadir as soon as someone mentions Hitler, I go for it all the same.

"Too bad the Germans switched their reverence from bears to buddy with the odd little moustache back in the 1930s," I say. "It could have saved them and the rest of the planet a world of hurt."

"Funny you'd bring up Hitler," he says.

"If you knew me, not so much," I say, laughing. "My daughters used to rib me mercilessly about my choice in reading material. 'Hey Dad, we see you've bought a new book, and it's not about the Battle of Stalingrad. Is everything okay?'"

"Do you believe that energy travels in things?"

I guarantee you this is not a conversation being had in the craft stores up the road.

"I suppose . . ."

"There's a friend of mine in town who had a terrible year. Her husband passed away suddenly, and soon after that she got in a very bad car accident. Nothing was working out, so I told her to get rid of a painting she had. Her father had been at the Nuremberg Trials in 1946. I'm not sure what he did there, but he came back with one of Hitler's paintings. She kept it in a drawer. I saw it once, but I wouldn't touch the thing. It was of a factory: dark, mean, cold and depressing. What stayed with me were the belching smokestacks."

"It gave off a terrible vibe," says Brian. "Anyway, her daughter came home one day and mentioned I'd remarked about the painting. 'Mom. I think about that thing you've got in the drawer and how it should be sent away or destroyed.' So, that's what she did. She sent it off to the Canadian War Museum. As far as I know, it's buried in the vaults, where it belongs. Life has gotten better for her ever since."

Despite the claustrophobic heat of his small gallery, grape-sized goosebumps rise on my arms. Lesson learned: never buy any sketch at a lawn sale that might have been drawn by Hitler.

You have to feel bad for the Germans, though. Picking two world wars like that, and even though it's been seventy-five years since the end of the second one, and despite their enlightened environmental ways that set an example for the rest of the world, they still take serious flak for the egregious sins of their grandfathers. Maybe that's why they have an inordinate predisposition to saunter nude on every beach in the tropics? Not to stereotype an entire nation as unapologetic nudists, but you can always count on seeing more than a few on any tropical beach, splayed on the sand like drying codfish in the sun as if to declare, "We no longer have anything to hide!"

Some like the fog, too, and swear by its healing properties. In fact, there's a white elephant of an abandoned hotel on the Aspotogan Peninsula, along the South Shore of Nova Scotia, that was built specifically to attract those German tourists who believe in the benefits of walking naked in the fog. The place went bankrupt, though, because the fog was so thick, they couldn't find it. (By the way, while vacationing in Nova Scotia, if you should chance to see somebody walking naked toward you through the fog . . . don't say hello in German . . . run!)

We speak of bears again, and their haunting presence in the imagination of man. I tell of the first grizzly I saw walking a Yukon side road at dusk. Watching that monarch of the wild move with self-assurance into the enveloping night lent a predatory power to its measured stride that made me really glad I was in a truck.

I'd been up in Whitehorse for a couple of shows and got the invite from local businessman Craig Hougen to join him and a couple of pilot pals for a day of fishing in Dry Bay, Alaska. Two hours before dawn, we drove from Whitehorse headed for the small air strip in Kluane National Park, where we'd follow the Tatshenshini glacier down to the sea. Once in Alaska, I spent a day of uncontested bliss at the foot of the St. Elias Range, standing waist-deep in waders under a sky of cobalt blue pulling twenty-pound chinook from the Pacific Ocean on ten-pound test. It was the best day of fishing I'd ever had in my life. With the sun sinking behind us at the close of the day, our small plane taxied off a frugal strip of grass that laughably passed as a runway and lifted us above the alluvial plain of delta for the flight back to Kluane.

As we climbed the crest of a rolling green hill, my eye caught an object out the window. I remember thinking, *That's a weird place for somebody to sit and watch the sun go down.* It wasn't a somebody though, but a monstrous bear reclining comfortably on the hill with arms crossed—pardon me . . . *paws* crossed—looking every inch a man on the porch of his cottage.

"That sight never left me," I tell Brian. "The only thing missing was a pipe in its mouth and a cold brew in its paw. The bear just looked *so* human."

"That's because they practically *are*," says Brian. "The Natives knew it, too. In fact, the Tlingit tribe of the Yukon thought bears were *half* human. It's why they never ate them."

"I used to dream of bears all the time before I started stand-up," I tell him. "I'd be taking a walk in the forest along a gentle path, when this bear would suddenly show up, blocking my way. It chased me up a tree, but as I continued to climb, it climbed, too, pushing me ever farther out on the limb. Soon as I started stand-up, the dreams stopped."

"Because you found your inner voice," he says.

"But now I dream I'm standing naked onstage in front of an empty room, delivering lines that don't make sense into a microphone that doesn't work."

"You might want to ask a professional about that," he said. "I'm just a painter."

Leaving with paintings of an owl, a caribou and a carved reclining bear holding a metal bowl on its belly that may or may not have sat on the mantle at Berchtesgaden, I hope I'm carrying good karma into the world. I'm sure whoever bought the tiger lamp made in Indonesia at the Main Street store has never had that thought cross their mind.

Easily six-foot-four, almost toothless, with white sideburns, a goatee, an affable charm and an accent closer to Maine than the Maritimes, the man townsfolk called Ol' Ben was seventy-four years old then and a keeper of memories. Seated on a bench in front of the town hall, he beamed when I said hello, and it wasn't long before the sage started talking.

Pointing at a busy boardwalk, Ol' Ben says, "We'd play on that beach right there all day long when we was kids—dig periwinkles, clams and have a boil. Now all the kids are doing is gettin' in shit! Smoke in their mouth, pint in their pocket and a head full of wacky tabacky. We were too busy to get in trouble.

"During the war, the boats would come in. All those navy ships. One day, I must've been about eight years old, the corvette *St. Stephen* towed in a captured German U-boat! The captain gave my buddies and me a tour." He points, eyes shining. "Yis, sir. Right down the'ah where all dem to'rists is. Yis. I'll nevva forget it.

"People tells me my memory is good. I say I can't remembah what happened yistaday, but I sure can tell ya what this town was like sixty-five years ago!

"I used to work at the lobstah plant. All kinds of fish was in the hahba back then. Flounda. Halibut sometimes, too, would be there, and always lots of herring, but all the herring's gone now. Caught in weirs by all those monstah ships. Only mackerel come in now.

"I'll tell you a story, God's honest truth. Fellah used to sit ova' the'ah by the post office when two people from Nebraska showed up. Nevah seen the ocean befowa. Want to bring some home in a glass jar. Ol' Jim tells 'em, "Well, if you is, you best be only filling yo' jar halfway full o' water, 'cause when the tide rises, that water's gonna rise up and ovaflow de top of 'er!" And as true as I'm sittin' here, those people from Nebraska believed him!

"God knows how long that half-full jar with Bay of Fundy water sat on their kitchen shelf with them waiting for it to ovaflow. God knows."

If predictions are on target, our planet's turbocharged run to climatic oblivion will soon make a February morning in Canada humid as high noon in the Jurassic period. Therefore, it could be argued that winter no longer defines our national character as it once did. I beg to differ. Why? Because there's Winnipeg. Winter *owns* that city! This is the place where *thoughts* freeze. It's a teeth-splitting, will-killing cold that comes flying with a fury across the treeless flatlands, straight from the lair of a Norse demon there weren't enough virgins in the Viking village to satisfy. Winter is not just a noun in Winnipeg, it's a station of the Cross, where wind-worn survivors suffer the elements with a masochist's conviction.

And they built a city there! What were they thinking? Six immigrants bound for Calgary got off the train for a smoke, lost three fingers in five minutes to frostbite, and said, "If it's colder than this farther west, to hell with that. I'm staying!"

Then there was God's second curse: spring! What were the early settlers thinking when they set up shop smack dab in the middle of a Red River flood plain? If the river wasn't spilling biblical levels of water over its banks, its perfect breeding grounds were launching airborne armadas of blood-sucking mosquitoes who, to this *day*, hold 'Peggers hostage for weeks on end every single summer. And after finally getting warm, the locals start praying for the winter cold to come again and kill the bugs, before the malathion that the city sprays on the bugs kills *them*!

The popular vernacular used to describe the spraying is "fogging." Sounds less carcinogenic, I guess. In the Maritimes, "foggy" means you can't see the beach. In Winnipeg, it means "Keep the kids indoors!"

Some people don't mind the malathion, but the positive outlook of the 'Pegger I was talking to was very disconcerting.

"Sure, I may have lost all body hair and there's a tumour on my spleen the size of an eggplant," he seemed to brag, "but it's the first night I've been able to sit outside on the porch since May."

Then, more power to you, brother!

Winnipeg exists for those of us who never caught lightning in a bottle or won a prize in a Cracker Jack box. Winnipeg is the big-boned girl who was always the bridesmaid but never the bride.

Ultimately, Winnipeg is the same as most of us: forced to do the best you could, when you could, with what you were given. Forced to fix your eyes to the horizon, grit your teeth in the face of the gale, put one foot in front of the other and just . . . keep . . . going. Because when you're this far down the road, it takes more effort to look back than move forward. (Besides, the blizzard has probably covered your tracks and the wolves'll get you anyway!)

Don't be thinking you'll be getting home from Manitoba frostbite-free either, just because you dropped top dollar for that double-fleece-lined Patagonia ski toque. You'd best be sporting a lid peeled from the back of a fur-bearing creature of the boreal forest. Fur is what you want on your noggin there. Sure, that fox hat with the legs and tail still on it might get some radical anti-vivisectionist chucking a bucket of pig's blood in your face on the streets of Manhattan, but it will keep Jack Frost from wearing your ears as trophies in the 'Peg. (And you won't have a pair of weird-looking, mummified black prunes sticking out of your head as topics of conversation. Just sayin'.)

Life has always been hard there, let alone getting there. Canada never had legions of prairie schooners crossing the western frontier, because they couldn't get through the curtain of spruce forest round Lake Superior. In fact, way back in 1860, they tried to build a wagon road from Thunder Bay to Winnipeg, but only got forty kilometres built in eleven years. Anyone who has ever braved that section of the TCH knows they're still working on it!

In the days I played Rumor's Comedy Club, they'd put us up at the Fort Garry Hotel, just up the street from the Forks, a beautiful park of pathways where the historic Red and Assiniboine Rivers meet smack dab in the continent's middle. One typically bright and sunny prairie winter afternoon, with the temperature sitting at a cozy minus-a-million, I saw an old lady feeding the squirrels and asked, "Do you feed them every day, madam?" To which she replied, "No. Only when it's warm."

Besides Toronto's Laugh Resort, Rumor's at the time was the best-run independent comedy club in the country. In fact, it was the *only* other one. For years, the management had been notorious for favouring American comedians, but when most of them got famous and too expensive to book, the club started hiring us. A paid flight out, paid hotel room, cab to and from the club, and once you were there, all the free burgers, fries and chicken wings your arteries could handle. Life in the fast lane.

Winnipeg Comedy Festival founder Lara Rae regularly headlined the club, whose vision of thematically structured stand-up performances, first televised in 2002, has mushroomed into CBC's highest-rated comedy festival series. Another stalwart player in the Winnipeg comedy scene is Big Daddy Tazz (the Bi-Polar Buddha), whose annual gala benefit performance at the iconic Pantages Theatre and year-round, non-stop dedication to the cause has raised thousands of dollars for mental health. There's a generosity of spirit that permeates the comedy community in that town, where getting paid will always take a back seat to supporting those in need.

Unlike Toronto and Vancouver, whose attentions are forever focused southward when it comes to entertainment, the media in the 'Peg really support their own. The *Winnipeg Free Press* entertainment editor, Brad Oswald, has diligently covered club, theatre and festival appearances for the past twenty-five years, while Geoff Currier at CJOB, and broadcasters at other private stations and at local CBC radio, don't shy away from vigorous promotion, either. The welcome mat Winnipeg rolls out makes it a pit stop in a place that always lets you know you're wanted.

As I pulled my luggage through a three-foot snowdrift to get backstage in Cornwall, Ontario, my mind drifted back to Los Angeles and its world of endless summer another lifetime ago. We lived there in a townhouse community at 6146 Coral Pink Circle. *Coral Pink Circle.* Sounds like something you'd catch swimming in the shallow end of a public pool that hadn't been treated with chlorine. The community sat on a hillside that used to be an orange grove, but was no longer because developers tore it down to make room for people like us. When I found that out, the convenient environmentalist in me got all stirred up—"That's not right! We ought to do something about that!" But then we went shopping at Target, bought three T-shirts and a pair of pants for seven bucks, and the feeling went away.

In California, the consumer was king. I used to buy forty ounces of Captain Morgan dark rum for $9.95 at a place called the Liquor Barn. *The Liquor Barn.* A theme park to booze . . . and a temple of homage for any Maritimer.

"What're you doing today, Ron?"

"Nothing at all. Just perpetuating a regional stereotype and dancing on down to the Liquor Barn is all! 'Oh, the Liquor Barn. The Liquor Barn. We're all going to the Liquor, Liquor Barn!'"

There were deals to be had around every corner, and the intoxicating lure of the Golden State's bounty was never more apparent than when Maritimers came to visit. I lost my dad for days on end in the tool department at Sears. Every time he went to the mall, he brought home a new wrench.

"Have a gander at that, Ronnie b'y. Two feet of tungsten-steel, chrome-wrapped wrench. A buck ninety-five. Steel, b'y. *Steel!* You don't get that at Canadian Tire."

"No, Dad, you don't. But you *do* get fake money that's good for trips to the Third World."

(I gained first-hand knowledge of the versatility of the now-defunct Canadian Tire "money" when, during a 1974 high school trip to Spain, our group crossed the Straits of Gibraltar for a day trip to Morocco. At a leather store in the ancient casbah, where one-eyed Arabs stood looking medieval with falcons on their shoulders and street urchins tried to sell our teachers hash, several of us bought leather jackets with that "currency." I know . . . that's just wrong. Karma had the last laugh, though, because back in Spain, forty-eight hours later, those smooth leather jackets began to . . . grow hair. That's correct, hair. To this day, somewhere in my eighty-eight-year-old mother's basement, there's a plastic-wrapped, orange-coloured leather coat with a simian-like strip of fur running down its back. Apparently, the tanning process for soaking leather in North Africa involves camel urine, whose odoriferous properties love to secrete in the rain. I did mention I'm from Halifax. It can be very wet there, so wearing a semi-hairy leather jacket that smelled of camel whiz to a high school dance worked wonders in guaranteeing you'd be sitting out the last waltz.)

And even when you're doing what you love, what you know you were *born* to do, the road still gets old. A nomad's calling, this. Forever on the move. A life built one gig at a time. Nothing comes for free. The road takes no prisoners, and comedy doesn't suffer fools. When I was getting standing ovations, my wife was getting loads of laundry alone at home. Not a lot of laughs at her end. Plays and dance recitals missed. Birthday wishes sent long distance. Arguments left hanging when there were planes to catch. Not what she signed up for.

The road lingers long after you've pulled into your driveway, too. It takes a week to decompress. You're nocturnal. Fidgety. Still on your own time with your system still in perpetual motion, racing from gig to gig; still tuned to the driving pulse and pace of the tour. This is a perfect calling for those who can't sit still. (The fact I got this book finished is a miracle in itself!) Shows line up like dominoes, one after another. On the night of a performance, new bits written that day slide shotgun shell–smooth into the chamber and hit the mark. Laughs explode like clay pigeons picked out of the air. The adrenalin rush of it all . . . you can finally do something right! You've finally found something you don't suck at! Is it a blessing or a curse?

The time I went fishing after the Whitehorse gig was the first of several visits to that magical corner of Canada that has called me back half a dozen times since. People up there tell of the Yukon's supernatural pull. "If you come here once, you'll come here again."

A few winters back, I hung out for a couple days in a cabin at Tagish Lake. A woman who ran a store in town named Nancy Huston offered it to me. She'd seen the show the night before and it was her way of saying thanks. People are like that up there.

It had been unseasonably mild that January, but the day I went for a walk in the woods was after a flash freeze had hit and turned the slush to stone. Following wolf tracks in a light dusting of snow up a mountainside, communing with nothing but my breath and heart-beat, a few hours in, I noticed grizzly bear tracks—frozen now, but made in the slush but a day before. Perhaps it had felt a rumbling in its tummy and risen from winter slumber with the warmer weather in search of a snack? Omnivore or not, should we cross paths its Snickers bar most certainly would be me!

I turned on my heel and made a beeline for the road. Remembering I'd been forgetting to make noise so the animals will hear you—because if they don't, and you surprise the wrong ones, they *will* eat you—I broke into a song. A rousing rendition of "Battle Hymn of the Republic" at the top of my lungs, actually. (And because I'm Canadian, I knew all twenty-seven verses.) Racing to my car, out of breath and giddy with relief to be alive and not dragged semi-conscious and bleeding to a bruin's cave, I drove back to the cabin, slept, and woke ready for my drive to Whitehorse, where I'd catch my plane back home.

It was one of those winter mornings you only get in Canada's North. The constellation of Orion was sitting so clear on the horizon, his sword looked sharp enough to cut me. Outside the town of Carcross, I saw a lone figure standing beside the road with a thumb out . . . hitchhiking. It was 6:30 a.m. during a minus-35 Yukon dawn.

Soon as I passed, I stopped the car and thought, *If it's a serial killer, it's going to take them an hour and a half to get the butcher knife out from beneath the layers of Gore-Tex.* So, I backed up and opened the passenger-side door. A weathered face belonging to an elder Indigenous woman poked its way into my car. She pulled her hood back and smiled, saying, "Whoa. Good vibes in here, eh?"

She told me her name was Helen and she was on her way to Sunday church service at the Salvation Army in Whitehorse. I pulled away and we started talking.

"What are you doing way up here?" she asked.

"I was working in Whitehorse but had a few days off, so I hung out at a cabin in Tagish Lake and went hiking in the woods."

She sat straight up in her seat and looked at me in disbelief.

"By yourself?"

"Sure."

"Whoa," she warned. "God was watching out for you."

"Why?"

"The mild weather has the bears confused," she explained. "They're coming out of hibernation early and they're hungry. One of them is eating the dogs down by the lake and taking everything but the head."

Remembering the story from Tlingit folklore of a shape-shifting she-bear who kills and then eats her suitor, I found myself thinking, *I hope my passenger isn't one of those; otherwise, she's going to really trash this rental car.*

I said, "Oh, no worries. I was singing 'Battle Hymn of the Republic' really loud, and my voice is so out of tune, every wolf or bear within 120 kilometres would have had their paws over their ears."

Her hands went up in the air, and she howled with laughter.

"Oh, my goodness," she said, smiling. "You should be a comedian."

Chapter Eight

MAGNETIC NORTH

Watching the Yellowknife airport empty of passengers as we waited for the ride from our outfitter that never came, I found myself second-guessing the decision to take my fifteen-year-old daughter kayaking to the Northwest Territories. I remember thinking, *If this tour operator has forgotten to pick us up here in a truck, what's to stop him from forgetting to pick us up in a bush plane on the tundra when the trip is over?* Once the Chef Boyardee ravioli ran out, I'd be trying to feed us by recalling the rabbit-snaring skills my father saw as elemental to survival.

During his high-school days in the early 1950s, he'd snare them in the winter on the outskirts of Halifax, then sell them by the pair for a buck fifty to a barber in the city. Why a barber bought them I haven't a clue, but every time I heard that story I visualized a satisfied customer, sporting a new trim, sauntering out the door swinging a pair of dead rabbits by the feet.

"Jesus, that was big money back then, Ronnie!" he'd say. He went on to advise me, "If you know how to snare a rabbit, you'll never go hungry."

Thankfully, once I moved to Toronto in 1980, I got all the food I ever needed from the same place most people do: the grocery store. Besides, once I landed an agent in '82, expertise in rabbit snaring was not a necessity in my line of work. An actor would need skills appropriate for . . . well . . . *acting*, and since I came from a Second City background, where we learned to think on our feet, deliver a punchline and take direction, that skill set more often than not involved auditioning for television commercials. Booking one of those kept the bills at bay for at least awhile, because as everyone in the legions of the self-employed knows, just because the pot is laden with lard today, don't get too cocky, because you could be licking it tomorrow.

Still, work was work. Plus, it garnered peculiar stares of recognition from strangers trying to figure out where they knew you from, so you kind of *felt* like you were in show business. In truth, doing commercials put you one step away from being an organ grinder's monkey.

The audition process involved sitting in a casting room with a dozen other hungry actors, trying to pump life into thirty seconds' worth of inane script some coked-out copywriter from Ogilvy and Mather had written during a molar-grinding 3 a.m. pique of creative genius. When the casting agent called your name, you entered a bare room and stood thirty feet away from several uninterested-looking people seated at a long table covered in fruit plates, half-eaten croissants and Styrofoam coffee cups.

One was a producer from the production house charged with budgeting the commercial. Another was somebody behind a video camera hired to film you, so they could review the auditions afterwards. Another was the director. Also sitting amongst them was the person who had the final say, the client: a pinched and buttoned-down corporate suit, looking about as comfortable as a duck on skates. They were fawned over by a shamelessly sycophantic advertising executive, who hung on their every comment with the kind of desperate attention one would give an oncologist's biopsy report.

Every now and then, you'd get a director who empathized with the pressure an actor was under in trying to pump life into five lines about toothpaste at 9 a.m. while standing before a row of stone-cold expressions that said, "I'd rather be home, waxing my Mercedes."

Several commercial directors took a different tack. Matthew Vibert was one of them. He'd honed his chops as a first assistant director on the five-continent cinematic adventure *Quest for Fire*, as well as dozens of other feature films before he started directing commercials. It may seem insignificant to the uninitiated, but simply by getting up from his chair, crossing the floor, shaking your hand and discussing in non-condescending, professionally relatable terms what kind of performance the clients were looking for, the man instinctively equalized the status levels in the room. Making that extra effort—which many of his profession did not—let you know you mattered. By that one simple move, suddenly those strangers staring at you from behind the table weren't so intimidating anymore. It made a process that, for many just looking to make rent, was an exercise in desperation seem not so bad at all. Every actor in the waiting room afterwards said as much, too. Even if they knew they weren't going to book that ad in a million years, at least they left feeling less of a monkey than when they walked in.

Given that this was the audience an actor had to win over to land the "spot," it was all the more remarkable when you did. If it weren't for booking commercials when I was starting out, there's a good chance I would have been roaming Toronto's urban greenbelt, snaring rabbits for supper as Dad had suggested.

The owner of the eco-lodge that was a three-hour bush plane flight north of Yellowknife went by the name of Tundra Tom. That moniker should have been a dead giveaway that weird energy was afoot, but who was I to question a handle like that? His name had a reassuring alliterative ring that clearly validated him as a stalwart true son of the North. Tundra Tom. That's a cartoon I would have been glued to the tube watching in grade six! Each episode would find Tundra having daring adventures all over the North, accompanied by his trusty Inuit sidekick, Ulu (also deadly with one), who always showed up in the nick of time to save Tundra from certain death at the hands of Colombian drug cartel hit men. (Okay, the last part needs work. Perhaps a B story involving Wanda! The Seal with a Human Brain. No? Anyone?)

Websites were still in their infancy when I booked the trip, and Tundra Tom's was very impressive. Besides having endorsements from every major nature photographer in the business, there was a photo of Tundra himself. It showed a middle-aged man whose wide, welcoming smile and ruddy complexion exuded character carved by the elements, while atop his leonine skull sat a weathered and very well broken-in Tilley hat. The thing looked as if it had once passed through the digestive tract of a barren ground grizzly and then been chewed for sustenance by subterranean voles in nocturnal warrens all winter long. Casually leaning on the wing of a bush plane, Tundra Tom looked, if nothing else, authentic.

As for the term *eco-lodge*, I now realize the name had been used with a flippant disregard for accuracy. I'm not sure what standards an outfitter's lodge had to meet in order to warrant the label *eco*, but if it meant running a rudimentary rat nest of plastic pipes around the property from the lake for water, a scattering of empty oil drums and discarded plane parts, Quonset huts sinking sideways into the melting permafrost, a menu whose major food group was canned peas, and a staff of semi-feral wanderers Tundra Tom had found panhandling on the streets in Yellowknife dressed in shirts held together by safety pins that weren't already sticking out of their face, then I guess *eco-lodge* was spot on.

The most appealing aspect of Tundra Tom's website was this: the lodge sat on the migratory route of what was then the 325,000-strong Beverly caribou herd. And where there are caribou, there are wolves . . . and wolves are cool.

The symbiotic dance of survival between *Canis lupus* and its prey had held my imagination since Farley Mowat's classic *Never Cry Wolf* was required reading in public school. Farley was, and still is (for my money, at least) the author who, more than any other, sired my generation's imagination of Canada's North. When my tours took me to the storybook village of Port Hope, nestled along the Ganaraska River in southern Ontario, I would visit with him and his wife, Claire. Their cozy cottage was straight out of Hobbiton and filled with memorabilia from a life fully realized. I was thrilled when Farley—eighty-eight years of age at the time of my visit, with nothing but a frugal collection of wispy hair now left of his once trademark bushy beard—lived up to his reputation as that cantankerous raconteur of legend, and cracked a bottle of London Dock well before noon. I remember thinking, *Farley's what Yoda would be like if he enjoyed a drink of rum!*

After lunch with this bona fide veteran of the bloody Battle of Ortona and survivor of a character assassination at the hands of *Saturday Night* magazine in the 1980s, we stood in his living room, musing.

"Well, there it is," he said, nodding. "A lifetime." We were looking at a wall of shelves running from floor to ceiling, containing the forty-eight books he'd written, all with matching copies in what appeared to be every language except the dialect of the Kalahari Bushmen. Clearly, Farley's love of the North had resonated with readers the wide world over. That he never let the truth get in the way of a good story, as Farley was fond of saying, didn't seem to cripple his popularity.

We'd not be standing with our knapsacks in the Yellowknife airport, looking forlorn and stunned, had we taken an easier vacation and gone to say, Disneyland. When we lived in Los Angeles, the very child I was now taking kayaking happened to be addicted to the Disney Channel. Trust me, the living room can feel like a small world after all when that song plays constantly. It was her religion. I'd later joke that if you wanted your child to believe in Jesus, all you had to do was slap a set of mouse ears on the Saviour's head. Then I'd launch into the *Mickey Mouse Club* theme song, only with different lyrics:

"*Who's the Son of God who was born in Galilee?*
J-E-S U-S-C H-R-I-S-T.
Jesus Christ! Jesus Christ! He cured a leper rotting on the road!"

It's clear I don't share the reverence for the Disney fantasy that the truly devoted do—those who gain fulfilment watching their children's eyes sparkle with unmitigated joy as legions of minimum-wage employees perpetuate the myth of the "Happiest Place on Earth" by toiling in the trenches of Mousewitz eight hours a day, dressed as Donald, Mickey, Goofy, Minnie or Fuckface Magoo. (I stand corrected. There is no such character as Fuckface Magoo, although if there were, he'd be my favourite.)

Speaking of Disneyland, I was once seated in a Jasper, Alberta, café, killing a free day on tour listening to a local hiking guide tell bear stories. If you want wild, it's not Banff you go to, with its tour-bus traffic jams, kitty-corner Starbucks and strip of stores selling everything from skis to thirty-million-year-old fossilized crocodile coprolites (which I bought); it's the Rocky Mountain town of Jasper, a four-hour drive north from Edmonton.

The guide was telling me how he took a family of four from Anaheim, California, on a hike behind the impressive Jasper Park Lodge one beautiful spring morning in June. They were forty-five minutes into their stroll along a forest path that opened to a meadow where a herd of elk and their newborn calves were grazing, birds singing and bees buzzing. Disney animators could not have sketched a more bucolic tableau had they placed a knock-kneed Bambi in that meadow, chatting to Thumper himself.

Instead of a cartoon, though, these visitors who lived but a stone's throw from the Magic Kingdom got a far closer look at the natural world than they'd bargained for. As they continued quietly along the path that skirted the meadow, minding not to spook the herd, the parents remarked to their ten- and twelve-year-olds how this was the real thing and not some animatronic creation of Disney "Imagineers." In fact, some calves had just slipped fresh from their mammalian yolk sac to solid ground but minutes before, and, still funky with goo, had begun taking their first wobbly steps in the big wide world.

Unbeknownst to them and their mothers, not thirty yards away there stalked a primal reality hardwired to break the blissful reverie of this California family's idyllic morn.

When the natural balance is about to be radically altered, the birds always seem to sense it first, and on this particular morning everything with a beak ceased its happy chirping. A foreboding silence fell. Even the gentle breeze stilled. The elk raised their heads and with the fury of a runaway train there burst from the forest six hundred and fifty kilos in a blur of fur and fangs. In a nanosecond, a grizzly bear was in the middle of the scattering herd all running pell-mell for safety, save for a lone calf who'd been staring at butter-flies. With one calibrated swipe from the bear's paw, it was conveniently sliced in two. Struck dumb with fear, the family saw the grizzly bury its face in a pink stew of the still-wiggling ungulate and flagrantly embrace the circle of life. There's a scene that would require very different lyrics from Sir Elton's song.

"The parents wanted to sue me!" he said. "They held me responsible for their children being traumatized for life. Mom was crying, the children were crying and Dad wanted to punch me in the face. I told them, 'I don't control nature. I am not God. Blame God, not me!'"

He looked at me and said, "They lived next door to Disneyland. If *that's* not cause for trauma, I don't know what is."

Which is why, I suppose, we were visiting Yellowknife in August, about to experience ten days of mosquito-biting onslaught, paddling sub-arctic finger lakes and following wolf tracks atop sandy eskers way up north in the Land of the Little Sticks. Because you don't get *that* at Disneyland. You also don't get a narcoleptic, chain-smoking drunk as a tour operator, so it all balances out, I guess.

When a shuttle van pulled up from our hotel, discharging passengers for a later flight, we hopped in.

"What brings you to Yellowknife?" the driver asked.

"My dad and I are going kayaking for a week," my daughter piped up cheerfully, "with some dude called Tundra Tom."

At the mention of the man's name, the driver's eyes went saucer-wide with alarm as he looked at me in the rear-view mirror.

"Not *the* Tundra Tom," he said in a voice dripping in portent.

"You mean there's more than one?" I said half-jokingly, knowing full well that the man who had failed to arrive at the promised time was the same one whose name had made the blood drain from our driver's face.

"Good luck," he whispered, and gripping the steering wheel tightly, stared straight ahead, never mentioning the name again, as if doing so would curse those who heard it.

The gentleman at the hotel's reception desk was a dead ringer for Christopher Lee, who played Dracula with regal malevolence in those Hammer horror movies in the 1950s and '60s. Tall, gaunt, pale and imperious, sporting a set of incisors and cowl worthy of the Count himself, the only thing compromising the illusion was his Newfoundland accent. It's not every day you get to chat at a hotel's reception desk with a vampire who sounds as if he's from Fogo Island.

"You'se is in room seven-o-hate, m'son."

I swear that Newfoundlanders are the lost Tribe of Levi. Perpetual wanderers they are, driven by necessity to step beyond the economic limitations of home in search of a better run at a new day. The definitive accent is heard anywhere there's employment. Your plane could go down in the thickest jungles of the Congo, and dollars to donuts, within twenty-four hours, a Newfoundlander would be knocking on the broken window. You'd still be strapped in your seat, semi-conscious and bleeding while he'd let you know in an accent thick as a pot of fish 'n' brewis that "I was busy trapping monkeys for the Chinese circus, me son, when I seen de plane go down las' night. So, I machetes me way t'ru de jungle to see if der' was anybody from *'ome* on it."

It must be hard to leave a place so rich in personality, where the people stir the spirit as much as the land does. Where women punctuate the end of their sentences with "Yes, my love," "Yes, my little darlin'," "Yes, my honey . . ." A waitress told me that management asked them to stop talking like that to tourists because "The come-from-aways thought we was coming on to them and their wives was getting pissed off." This was the same waitress who, when I was wrestling with whether or not to have my second plate of cod tongues fried in pork scraps because I was worried about my high cholesterol, said, "That's no problem, my love. Have a'nudder glass of red wine and it'll balance 'er right out."

On another occasion, I stepped from my room in a Grand Falls hotel early one morning and said to housekeeping, "I'm heading out for a run and will be back in an hour. You can make up my room now if you'd like."

"No way! You just woke up. It's still right stinky in der'!"

St. John's is one of the the best cities in the country to work off a feed of fish and chips, and on one windy autumn day electric with character, I headed out for a stroll to Signal Hill, a national historic site where a noonday gun still barks religiously from that rocky promontory rising 167 metres out of the great big sea it commands a view of. Besides falling to England during the last battle of the Seven Years' War in 1763, it's also where Italian geek Guglielmo Marconi, who, like those über-geeks Steve Jobs and Bill Gates a hundred years later, would change world communication by inventing the internet of his day when he succeeded in receiving the first transatlantic wireless communication from 2,100 miles across the sea. When his turn-of-the-twentieth-century geek buddies in Poldhu, England, tapped out a Morse code message asking how he was doing, local St. John's lore swears that Marconi replied, "If I spend one more night getting hammered on George Street till 4 a.m., I'm putting myself in rehab."

The national park path that traverses the Battery to get up the hill literally crosses the front steps of a person's house. You'd get the cops called on you for doing that in every other Canadian city and shot for it in the States. But not in a city with streets named Merrymeeting Road and Hill o' Chips. Go farther inland and there's Tickle Cove Pond, Joe Batt's Arm, Dildo and Itchy Balls Corner. (I made that last one up.) The elderly owner was sitting on his front porch, smiling into the sun, the day I walked past. He saw me coming, and as ol' timers will do, he threw a non-sequitur in my direction just to see if I was on my toes.

"How much is a case o' beer now, b'y?"

I was quick on the draw, though.

"I don't know, my buddy. Haven't paid much attention to anything since I got back from the war."

My riposte was acknowledged with a twitch of his head, as is the wont of every male over forty living there, and a "What odds, me son? What odds?" (I don't know exactly what the phrase means, but I think it's got something to do with being helpless in the hands of fate, and anyone who's waited two days for a flight out of St. John's thanks to a demonic brew of weather roiling in off the Atlantic has an idea. Plus, it's way better than "Whatever.")

Waving goodbye, I went up and over Signal Hill profuse with blueberries, huckleberries, asters and tiny wildflowers clinging tenaciously to that big lump of Precambrian granite overlooking a humbling body of water.

Newfoundland always had a way of wrapping me in a blanket of belonging to something bigger than the gig that brought me there. It always felt like I was going home to a Halifax lost. Going home to days when Uncle Percy called up tunes from that squeezebox of his on those humid August nights in my mother's kitchen, that was damn near close to bursting at the seams with all that Burgeo-born Foote, Vatcher and James blood as we watched our father tap-dance himself over the hardwood into a state of near transcendence, feet pumping with the ferocity of that runaway train he was imitating, accompanied by a chorus of rum-fuelled, rosy-cheeked laughter and shouts of support from all those Newfoundlanders in exile.

After an October night in old St. John's spent among faces flush with pints aplenty at the Ship's Inn, all singing along with Ron Hynes playing his haunting ode to their hometown harbour, I woke bleary-eyed but happy the following morning for a six-hour drive west to the pulp-mill town of Corner Brook, "The City That Grew from the Forest."

Crossing the Avalon that day, the needles of turning tamarack trees had wrapped the peninsula in an autumn halo gold as a ruler's crown. My father's country was rolling out a welcome mat for me over more than a billion years' worth of bedrock doorstep, that was already old as God in some long-gone Beothuk dawn. Two cars passed me headed east, each carrying either end of a moose on its roof. From the head, its two-foot pink tongue flapped in the breeze at 100 kilometres an hour. *There's* a picture that won't make the tourist brochure! Moose are everywhere in Newfoundland—or, as a hunting guide in Gander confirmed to me, "Lard Jesus, m'son, the woods is maggoty with them."

On that trip I saw a man in his truck beside the road with two dead partridges and three dead rabbits on the hood. I parked, got out, walked over and asked, "Are those dead animals on your hood for sale?" He turned towards me sporting that saucy, sarcastic twinkle behind the eyes they all get before setting you straight, and said, "Well, they're not there for decoration, are they, skipper?" It's that easy for them. I don't know why anyone pays to see a comedian in that province, because most people living there are ten times funnier than half the ones in my profession!

I was headed there years ago on a flight from Toronto when an elderly grandmother going back home to Deer Lake from Mississauga, where she'd been to visit her grandchildren, told me of her life. She was a small, wrinkled matriarch whose weeping family I watched her wave goodbye at Pearson Airport as we passed though security. Soon as we started taxiing up the runway, the grandmother started talking. I put down the book I was reading, knowing there was no sense in cracking the spine for this flight.

She told me the grandson I saw at the airport was one of fourteen, along with two great-grandchildren from five sons and daughters, born to her and her husband, now gone two years.

"I took care of him at 'ome," she said, "'cause he wanted to go looking out the front window at the brook and trees. He got his wish. Cancer is what took him. Leukemia in the lymph nodes was all t'ru him. Before he died, he hadn't had a drink in over seventeen years. I remember the day he stopped, too. I come back from my son's place, taking care of the little ones, and he'd been home by himself, into the bottle all day. Not eating, just drinking and shaking something fierce.

"He says, 'Call the doctor. I'se dying.'

"I says, 'No.'

"He says, 'But I'se dyin'.'

"I says, 'Then if you'se dyin',' stretch out on the couch and die, 'cause I'se tired and going upstairs for a nap. If I wakes up and you'se dead, I'se 'll call the funeral home.'

"When I woke up, there were two men from AA sitting in the kitchen. He never took another drop.

"So now I'se all alone," she said, with quiet resignation. "Got enough potatoes for the winter, lots of corn, turnips and a fridge full of pork. Gets me a piglet in spring. Lets him get to be 110 pounds, then slaughters him. Bacon's right lean. No fat to speak of. I'se got a woodstove. In fact, I'se burning wood me 'usband split two years ago. Every day he was out there, knowing someday soon he wouldn't be. Swinging the axe until he couldn't. A great big pile of wood he chopped me, lined up right nice and neat beside the back door. Now, every time I gets me a load to put on the fire, soon as the heat starts warming the kitchen it's like his arms is wrapped around me giving me a big hug."

"That's poetry," I told her.

"It's not poetry. It's true."

She stared out the window, pensive, then suddenly perked up. "So now I gets to go and see my kids on their flying points they gets from flying back and forth from Fort McMurray!"

"My father went blind at thirty-five from a disease what ran in the family," she continued. "I can still remember the severance pay he got from the pulp mill in Corner Brook: five thousand dollars. No workers' comp. No pension. No nutting. He always said, 'Don't complain, 'cause some has it lots worse.' He couldn't read or write, so Mom signed the cheques for him. After his setback, he bought land and built houses."

I thought, *"Setback"? There's an understatement. The man went blind!*

"Hold on," I said, trying to fathom what resources this man called on to turn his life around, long before motivational memes and self-help books were here to heal our First World problems. "He went *blind* and then built *houses*?"

"Yes, b'y."

I asked whom he built the houses with.

She looked at me like I'd missed the point.

"By himself."

"Like, alone? No help?"

"Yes, b'y."

"Christ," I said, "I can *see* and I'm lucky to get away with all my fingers just sawing the top off a hockey stick!"

"He had no use for a level neither," she assured me.

"No level? Every carpenter needs a level," I said.

She stared right through me, as if I'd entirely missed the point.

"Not if you can't see the bubble you don't."

Not if you can't see the bubble, you don't.

See, it's that easy for them there.

Although the runaway hit musical *Come from Away* beautifully captured the generosity of Newfoundlanders as true ambassadors of the human heart, they *can* be blunt. When my father turned seventy-five, I took him salmon fishing to Haida Gwaii, in British Columbia. We had family friends from Halifax living there and one night were invited to a party with nothing but Newfoundlanders.

So eager was Dad to embrace his tribe, the man practically did a tuck and roll out the passenger-side door onto the road before the car came to a stop. The kitchen was filled with drywall craftsmen, roofers and carpenters whose contracts had expired with whatever they'd been building and who would soon be bound elsewhere, looking for work. Their wives sat together in the living room, smoking cigarettes and laughing, while the men were corralled in the kitchen, making a serious dent in several bottles of rum. Working-class nomads the lot of them, from a birthplace my father had left at the age of six, but to which he was still anchored with a pride bred in the bone.

Entering the house as if it were his own, he ruled the place with the skill of a seasoned road comic, regaling that kitchen with bawdy jokes in his typical machine-gun delivery and bug-eyed animation. His face took on that familiar glow born of a good buzz, as our hosts poured rum after rum for this elfin trickster, whom I'm sure they thought had left a hidden forest kingdom for the night to work his magic amongst mere mortals.

He tap-danced along to buddy whaling away on a squeezebox, got moist and all teary-eyed maudlin when they sang "Let Me Fish Off Cape St. Mary's," and, in his telling of crossing the Cabot Strait at the age of six on the ill-fated *Caribou*, torpedoed by German U-boats during the Battle of the St. Lawrence in 1942, he practically put himself in a lifeboat with survivors, even though he made the crossing three years before it was struck. Never let the truth get in the way of a good story.

I wasn't quite in the kitchen, but standing off to the side, when the wife of one of those men came up, looked me square in the face and said, "I heard you'se a comedian, b'y. Tell us a joke."

That request is the number-one method for getting any comedian I know clamming up faster than a tongueless mute. I tried to be polite and explain the difference between "telling jokes," which my father in his prime could do effortlessly by rote, and my own work as a professional comedian. What I came up with was, hands down, the most pretentious explanation ever to escape this writer's cakehole.

"I don't tell jokes so much as describe the regional idiosyncrasies of Canada, hoping at the end of the day to elevate the virtues of people and place by unifying an audience through laughter."

I watched her nose wrinkle in disdain and her eyes narrow suspiciously, like someone trying to locate the source of rotting food in the fridge.

"You'se not funny at all, b'y." And, pointing to my father, who at this point was holding up a dishtowel he'd turned into what looked exactly like a skinned rabbit, said, "But him? Now *he's* funny!" Then she pushed me hard in the chest and walked away.

Like I said . . . blunt.

Once settled in the room, I sat down to phone Tundra Tom himself. It was still early, so I naturally assumed either he or one of his assistants would be there to take my call and allay any fears I had of the trip going completely south. I phoned five times and let it ring. No answer. *They must be out*, I thought. Four hours later, at almost 7 p.m., I was still phoning and getting no answer.

The following morning, I tried again. The voice that answered was what you'd hear after waking a mountain ogre from a winter's nap: a voice thick with phlegm from a three-pack habit and an attitude so far removed from courteous, it belonged behind the customer complaints counter at a communist department store in a forgotten corner of the Soviet bloc. He growled into the receiver.

"What do you want?!"

Praying to whatever angels watch over lapsed Anglicans, I hoped this wasn't *him*. Hoped this would not be the man I was entrusting with our lives for ten days in the wilderness.

"I'm calling for Tundra Tom."

"You're talkin' to him."

From his esophageal recess, he rolled up a hefty ball of mucus that, when he spat, I heard it hit his wastebasket with the weight of a stone.

Mustering my courage, I soldiered on.

"It's Ron James. You didn't show up at the airport yesterday as promised."

"I fell asleep and forgot."

No apology. No sorry. No "Did you get to the hotel okay?" Nor was there an attempt to cover his tracks with a well-crafted lie, or even a charming fib. I'd even have welcomed flagrant bullshit, because God knows, running an outfitting enterprise in an area as vast as Canada's North certainly lends itself to an imaginative tall tale.

"I couldn't pick you up at the airport because I had flown bear-tagging biologists to some denning sites, but one of them got eaten alive."

I'd have believed that.

"There's a lot of spooky stuff happens up here. We followed a black-ops chopper with no markings until we ran out of gas."

I would have endorsed that explanation, while swearing myself to a lifetime of secrecy.

"I found a perfectly preserved woolly mammoth when I was digging for diamonds, so then I took some skin grafts to a lab—and they're going to clone it and I'm gonna raise it!"

I'd have been on board. I read *National Geographic* and know that because of global warming, creatures from the Ice Age are poking their desiccated snouts out of the permafrost with regularity. Who wouldn't want to raise a cloned woolly mammoth, provided they had the space in their backyard?

But no. Turns out Tundra Tom *just forgot*. Whatever he was, he certainly was not a liar.

"You fell asleep and *forgot*," I repeated with incredulity. "My kid and I are about to go kayaking for a week in the wilderness. That doesn't make me feel very secure."

Although personally motivated to salvage the trip, and out of a greater fear of antagonizing this ogre any further, my last words were conciliatory and understanding. "Well, everyone makes mistakes," I said. "We're all human."

And that's when the inner Vesuvius ruling his lizard brain exploded with such an f-bomb-laced diatribe, it would have made the darkest devils in hell weep.

Let me be clear. I am no stranger to spontaneous, purple-faced rage. The James patriarch was once formidable in this regard and could deliver a door-slamming, foot-stomping blind fury as his Burgeo-born blood hit the boiling point igniting a litany of alliterative profanity that would make Wordsworth himself envious. Oddly enough, Dad's explosive rants at baseboards he'd cut too short, plumbing he didn't understand, spilled paint, the Toronto Maple Leafs blowing a two-goal lead in the third, and a temperamental furnace, were entirely devoid of any f-bombs.

Tundra Tom, on the other hand, opened with that heavy artillery right off the top.

"Then fuck off and go home!" he barked. "Just fuck off! Fuck. Right. Off! The trip is cancelled! Cancelled! I've got forty people strung across three hundred kilometres of territory, and here's some guy from *To*-ronto telling me how to run my fuckin' business ?! Look, buddy. I'm a bush pilot! I save *lives* for a living!"

A sensible person would have hung up, filed a complaint with the Yellowknife Chamber of Commerce, taken the loss of the deposit and gone home. Instead, I said, with my voice cracking, "But we came all this way to see wolves and caribou and stuff. Does this mean we won't see them?"

"How am I supposed to know if you'll see them? They're animals! It's not Disneyland up here!" (That's when I wished we'd gone there instead. We could be on Mr. Toad's Wild Ride right now getting motion sickness.) He uttered a war-weary sigh. Tundra was clearly a man overwhelmed by circumstance.

"Look," he said. "I've got everyone from geologists to German filmmakers dropped all over the tundra. Picking you up at the airport didn't seem like such a priority. But since you're here, be in the hotel lobby in two hours, packed and ready to go."

My daughter had heard the entire conversation and, closing her journal, matter-of-factly offered, "I guess he didn't like it when you called him human."

We sat in the hotel restaurant, enjoying a breakfast of thirteen-dollar bagels. Food all across the North is off-the-charts expensive, and nothing is ever fresh—unless, of course, you're a grunt moiling for diamonds in the Diavik mine.

I had a gig once at their mother ship of an outpost, 225 kilometres south of the Arctic Circle. Employing a thousand people with an airport big enough to accommodate a Boeing 737, the company had a cafeteria at this sprawling complex whose counters were bursting with enough fresh fruit and vegetables to supply a Loblaws store in any southern Canadian city. That's not the case for most people living up north. About the only green you'll see in the grocery stores of Canada's Arctic communities from October to June is on a Gore-Tex jacket. Don't get me wrong: a person can *find* lettuce . . . they just can't afford it.

No wonder people living in our northern communities think Canada's Food Guide, with its emphasis on maintaining a diet of fresh fruit, vegetables and water, is utterly contemptuous of their daily reality. It's all well and good if you're part of the 87 percent of our population strung along the American border, but by the time produce gets to the North in wintertime, it's practically compost. I bought a banana in Inuvik once that was so bruised and beaten, it looked like Chiquita had kicked it there from Brazil!

People who live in the North sometimes tell you things about living up there that rattle your southern perspective. I once flew with a couple of teachers from Fort Simpson who were headed to Florida for a honeymoon, and they told me about Wild Dog Day. The outskirts of towns and reserves across the North are overrun with neglected and abandoned domestic dogs gone feral. "You'd be better off seeing a pack of wolves than wild dogs," they told me, "because wolves still have a fear of man, but a collie who used to sleep at the foot of your bed, not so much."

I imagined fighting for my life in some snowy wood, surrounded by a pack of chihuahuas and pugs, half-crazed with hunger, attacking my Achilles tendon. Getting eaten by wild dogs is a tragedy, but getting eaten alive by pugs and chihuahuas, that's just embarrassing.

"It's true," they insisted. "We have Wild Dog Day. The local butcher dumps a wheelbarrow of meat in the middle of the street just on the outskirts of town. Townspeople wait a couple hundred yards away with their rifles, and when the dogs come for it, they shoot them."

"That's got to rile the SPCA," I said.

"Rile the SPCA? They organize it!"

My daughter's pupils widened as I heard that unmistakable voice from the phone talking at the reception desk.

"I'm here for Ron James."

"That's him," my daughter gasped.

I turned to see a man who easily tipped the scales at three hundred pounds stride into the restaurant. He was of a Cyclopean stature and wearing a filthy sweatsuit so crusty with last week's breakfast, I'm sure it must have doubled as a tablecloth, while on his feet were—wait for it—slippers.

That's right. Slippers. I had no idea something I'd wear around the house on a lazy, rainy Sunday was the preferred footwear of the fabled northern bush pilot. You learn something new every day.

The man's bedhead was an extraordinary arrangement of hair that hadn't seen a shower, I'll wager, since it was patted down by his mother's spit in church on his confirmation day. In one ham hock–sized fist, he clutched three large packs of Player's Light, while in the other were squeezed a mittful of pepperoni sticks. As he stood over our table, I got the unmistakable sour whiff of yesterday's whisky bender.

"I'm Tundra Tom. Let's go."

With a foolish disregard for our own safety, we obediently rose from our chairs and followed the hungover, slipper-wearing ogre.

My daughter, always one with the quick quip, mumbled under her breath, "Just because an outfitter has a great website, Dad, doesn't mean he didn't learn to build it in prison."

People still ask me why I went way up there, let alone take one of my daughters. Well, my youngest was at camp, my wife didn't like to tent and my eldest thought it would be cool to see caribou. Besides, it would be the last August she'd have free before summer jobs and friends monopolized her time, so why not spend it paddling face-first into a thirty-knot headwind on Arctic finger lakes in a tandem kayak with her ol' man, as waves crashed over the bow while he sings "We're Gonna Hang Out the Washing on the Siegfried Line" and other World War II marching songs no fifteen-year-old wants to hear. Scratch that—*anyone* under the age of ninety-three wants to hear.

The other reason I went is because I don't golf. Chasing a little white ball around from dawn to dusk on a beautiful weekend, hoping to blend your short game with your long game in one elusive moment of bourgeois perfection before a five-alarm coronary drops you face-first to the floor of the nineteenth hole, doesn't stoke my mojo.

Let me be clear: I'm not judging those who golf—but as most golfers will agree, it is one of those sports that takes a modicum of proficiency to enjoy. Years ago, I invested a summer's worth of leisure time in the sport and discovered that wrapping a 9-iron round a tree after my twenty-third slice of the day didn't work wonders for my stress level. If I'm going to be humbled, I'd prefer the learning curve be shorter than an entire lifetime.

Tom shuttled us to a loading dock on the shores of Great Slave Lake, where a bush plane sat. It definitely wasn't a new one. I'm sure it was the pride of the North in its day, but this being 2004, I found that flying in a single-prop Beaver that came off the assembly line Rosie the Riveter worked on was reason for worry. It was banged-up and dented from a lifetime of tackling the Arctic and it was made for carrying cargo, not people. Obviously, it could never have taken ground fire from enemy troops but judging by the holes in the fuselage below my seat, it sure looked like it had.

A mechanic in grease-smeared overalls lifted his head from beneath the opened engine bonnet and, holding what looked like a set of distributor caps, turned to Tom and said, "That's why it was stalling on you." Stalling. Hmmm. The thought of stalling in a bush plane with a narcoleptic Tundra nodding off at the controls did not inspire confidence.

Back in 1972, a bush pilot called Marten Hartwell, flying from Cambridge Bay to Yellowknife with a pregnant Inuk woman, an Inuk boy with appendicitis and a nurse on board, crashed in a snowstorm in the uncharted wilderness of Great Bear Lake. The nurse and Inuk woman died on impact. With two broken ankles, Marten survived for thirty-one days, thanks in large part to help from the boy—and the dead nurse, whom he ate. That's correct. *Ate*. Which reinforces a rule of thumb: when flying any distance in a bush plane, always pack a substantial lunch and more Mars bars than you think you'll need, because should you crash and not be found for a while, things could turn ugly as soon as the pilot's jujubes start running low.

Given Tom's impressive girth, his appetite was probably formidable. *Summertime or not*, I thought, *if this plane goes down, that fat bastard will be drooling over us as soon as his pepperoni sticks are gone.*

If you ever have the need to feel small, take a bush plane flight over this corner of the country. The vast glaciated topography of the barren grounds running west from Hudson Bay clear to the Arctic Ocean is twice the size of Alberta. It's an uncompromising hyperborean world of dwarf willow, stunted spruce, birch and alder that cling tenaciously atop eskers of Caribbean-fine sand, formed by the till of subterranean rivers that once ran beneath seven kilometres of ice. During their retreat, these glaciers scraped the Earth's surface clear to its mantle, leaving behind a blanket of moss and lichen where a people beyond our knowing once pulled a living from this primal plain, hunting antlered armies on the hoof with nothing but bone, stone and sinew, a million moons before Romulus and Remus suckled on the She Wolf's nipple. Playing golf just doesn't provide me that level of buzz.

However, when camping in Canada, the mosquitoes will give you far more buzz than you bargained for. Don't hold back when it comes to bug spray, either. Go nuclear and settle for nothing less than Muskol. That is *not* your average fly dope. It's closer to basement bucket slop from the cooling towers of Chernobyl. No need for a Coleman lantern to light your way round camp at night when you're sporting a cloak of radioactive isotopes. Sure, your hair might fall out in a couple weeks, but if you're like me, you at least won't mind losing it off your back.

You need to be smeared in serious levels of DEET when you're on the radar of the *Culicidae* family. There are eighty-seven types of mosquitoes in Canada, but only five that bite: no-see-ums; gnats; blackflies; horseflies; and big bastards I don't know the name of that come humming round your ears, sounding like B-17s on a bombing run over war-torn Berlin. Baptize yourself from head to toe in Muskol, or you'll bleed out before the bacon is done.

Mosquitoes will abate, however, when the wind picks up. And in a place where a six-foot tree can be considered old growth, there's nothing to stop its relentless blitzkrieg. Did you know it's tricky taking number two on the tundra in a windstorm? If you ever have to, here's a tip: don't take your drawers off when you do, because when Mother Nature calls the shots, she connects you to the fundamentally elemental, and nothing knocks the urban cocky from you faster than having to run bare-ass naked, clutching your shrunken junk, while chasing your pants as they're blown across a primal stretch of real estate.

Millions of geese and waterfowl visit to breed during the fleeting summer, and the sky is filled with loons, jaegers and dive-bombing Arctic terns who do not suffer trespassers. Their hatchlings sit in such brilliantly camouflaged nests on the ground, a person could easily step on one and not know it until they felt that sickening, soft squish under their boot. The parents defend their nests from above by diving for your face with a bone-chilling shriek worthy of a Stuka strafing the beaches of Dunkirk. Best to give these winged velociraptors a wide berth. I figure if you're genetically hard-wired to fly from pole to pole from spring to fall every year, *just to sit on an egg*, you deserve respect.

When we headed out kayaking, it wasn't Tom who took us but one of his guides. The kid was a thirty-year-old West Coast Earth cookie who could start a campfire with nothing more than incantations and a handful of dried ptarmigan turds he kept in a bag attached to his belt. One night, he told me to start the fire, so I squirted half a quart of kerosene on the wood, threw a match in and it erupted with a *woof* worthy of Little Boy. Despite the loss of my eyebrows, I highly endorse this method.

We camped on and explored these eskers, home to gyrfalcon, caribou, wolf and fox. Although we never spotted the true landlord of these parts, the barren ground grizzly, it does wonders for the imagination to stumble on their tracks in the sand, knowing full well one could lumber into your campsite unannounced and radically alter the equation.

One evening at sunset, clearly bored with our company and itching for some alone time, our guide disappeared over the hill. He was gone until well after dark, no doubt enjoying a toke while shape-shifting with the Caribou People. Minus any rifle or bear spray for protection, we sat in a dinner tent covered in mosquito netting that Tom had flown in a few days before. The smells of the Hamburger Helper we'd had for dinner must have been tickling the olfactory of whatever member of *Ursus arctos* was within sniffing distance. And knowing how acute a bear's sense of smell is, I imagined a surly gang of bruins making a hungry beeline across the tundra for our camp. In fact, a bear had passed by recently; its scat sat in a pile not far from our tent. When the guide returned two hours or more after leaving, I admonished the high-as-a-kite, squinty-eyed simp for his negligence.

"You left us alone with no gun or bear spray, and there's a pile of bear scat outside the tent!"

"Relax, dude," he said with that condescending confidence we'd grown to hate the past six days. "You've got a better chance of being hit by a car than attacked by a grizzly."

Stretching my arms wide in emphasis, I implored, "Do you see any cars up here?"

What we did see plenty of were caribou, back when a herd of 325,000 moved in mind-boggling migratory numbers across the tundra as it had for millennia. But that was seventeen years ago. From the Torngat Mountains of Labrador to the Rocky Mountains of British Columbia and all across the Canadian north populations of this iconic ungulate are nosediving. A lethal combination of resource development and global warming has reduced the once-thriving herds to dire levels, with neither Conservative nor Liberal governments doing squat to stem the collapse. The feds pass the buck to the provinces and territories, which in turn sweep the issue under the carpet in the name of progress. If the caribou disappear, wolves and bears won't be far behind, nor will the lives of the First Peoples across the North who, since time immemorial, have depended on caribou for sustenance.

By the time we returned to camp, word had gotten out about what I did for a living, and the change in Tundra Tom was unsettling. He'd gone from an apoplectic, piss-and-vinegar-filled, profanity-spitting ogre to an ingratiatingly accommodating host. I missed the former.

"Why didn't you tell me you were on TV?" he said with arms stretched wide in welcome. Now that he realized I was "someone" and not just a run-of-the-mill worrisome client whose head he'd bitten off in a telephone tirade, he was obviously worried I'd use whatever superpower you get from being on television to destroy his reputation. Clearly, he'd never seen my work, or he would have known it amounted to a handful of commercials, a special that aired on CTV's Comedy Network and an ill-fated television series whose handful of viewers were comprised of grade seven history teachers, twelve-year-old boys, War of 1812 re-enactors and shut-ins. I was hardly a player of influence. Still, my fame brought dividends that night when we weren't served canned peas again.

One day, a Dene elder called Joe, whom Tom had flown in from Fort Resolution, came looking to hunt caribou for his people. A middle-aged Indigenous co-owner of the camp named Charlie was guiding him, so I asked to tag along. Leaving my daughter at the camp, who was content to hang out in our Quonset hut, probably writing in her journal about what lapse in judgment made her join her Dad up north in the first place. With a wary nod they agreed, and in the chill of a late-August morning, we headed across the lake for wilder country beyond camp. Pulling the craft ashore, we ascended the hill, careful to keep the wind in our face so that our smell wouldn't give us away. Caribou are peculiar creatures that, provided they don't get a whiff of you, will actually walk towards you with a stunned stare of bovine curiosity . . . and that's when you shoot them.

Cresting the hill, I saw a pair of ravens flying overhead and remembered, as a kid, reading in Farley Mowat's book *Two Against the North* that these birds and wolves actually hunt together, with the raven providing the ears and eyes for the wolf, while the wolf provides the kill. It's even been proven that they communicate with each other—and given the raven's love of language, if you've ever heard them shooting the breeze on telephone wires, a person wouldn't need to be David Attenborough to believe it.

While following those birds in flight, I caught a blur of marshmallow-pure white moving hard across the land. "Wolves," I said, pointing at a pair of them. These were tundra wolves, looking almost spectral in the dawn of a new day whose clouds were broken by sunbeams that bathed their coats of fur in angelic light. I had never seen wolves in the wild before, nor have I since, but watching them move across the land as they have for millennia was as close to a vision of Creation as a fellow can get.

It was a good sign. Where there's wolves, there's caribou.

We dropped our packs and settled behind an erratic dropped twelve thousand years ago by retreating glaciers. (Or, depending on your literal reading of biblical scripture, dropped *six* thousand years ago by Noah from the ark because the pair of elephants in the bow who wouldn't stop mating threw the ballast off. I'm not even going to ask how he fit a pair of blue whales aboard, but I guess that's what they mean when they say, "God works in mysterious ways.")

Sitting with our backs to the boulder, we broke out bologna-and-mustard sandwiches on white bread, washed down with steaming-hot cups of tea, watching weather from one extreme to the next play its way across the firmament—delivering rain and sleet one minute, a Phoenix-in-July level of heat the next. It's not an exaggeration to say a person could get sunburnt on one side of their face and frostbitten on the other. (Okay, it *is* an exaggeration, but an innocent one.)

Charlie was forty-nine—seventeen years ago and a residential school survivor. We sat waiting for the caribou to come. He was smoking a Player's Light and passing one to Joe. Sharing smokes is one thing I miss about the habit. (Not so much the getting of cancer.)

When lunch was finished and the tenth cigarette smoked, Charlie poked his head slightly above the boulder to glass the land. So far in the distance that it was barely visible to the naked eye sat a growth of trees. "All we've got is the moment," said Charlie. "I bring people up here to photograph wolves. You've got to be patient. Don't matter how much high-end gear you've got, unless you can sit and wait, you're not getting nothing."

He took a drag and looked at me.

"So, television, eh?"

"Well, I mostly work live. I'm on the road. A stand-up. Started in the clubs but made the move to theatres a few years back."

"How many years have you been at it?"

"Twenty-three in 'the business,' but just ten in stand-up," I said.

He looked at me hard. Not to see if I'd say something funny, but to see if I was telling the truth.

"I guess that's long enough to know what you're doing."

"I suppose. It's still a mystery, though. As soon as you think you've got it figured out, you're back to point A again."

Charlie agreed with a nod and turned to glass the hillside. Then his story rolled out.

"I studied to be a cinematographer," he said. "Twenty-five years ago, I left my rez north of Sioux Lookout. For two years, I went to Vancouver Film School. Graduated, too. There wasn't a lot of call for an Indian cinematographer back then, so I started driving cab in the Downtown Eastside. Graveyard shift. Nothing but junkies, pimps, killers and whores. That was my clientele. I found them to be more upfront than most people in showbiz. Saw all the great bands. Go down to Seattle. Always bought great seats. It cost peanuts in 1980. We'd get right up front.

"I started using heroin. Been clean for ten years. I blame the residential school. A Jesuit killed me, and a Jesuit resurrected me. Talk about coming full circle, eh? Like you say, it's a mystery.

"I met a great woman," he continued. "She's Cree. She teaches yoga. We moved back to my reserve, three hours north of Kenora, to take care of my parents. Just buried them last year. They died six weeks from each other. Dad was Scottish. A trapper. Mom was an Ojibwa from Fort Frances. They lived to be ninety-one and ninety-three. That's what living off the land does for you.

"We help the kids up there now. There are lots of suicides. It's epidemic. We lost twenty-three kids last year. Twenty-three. If twenty-three kids hung themselves in Toronto, it would be front-page news. They send social workers up from Toronto with all kinds of letters after their names. Some don't last a week. One guy was there less than a month and went home. Came highly recommended. Best in his field, they said. Two kids hung themselves when he was there. We found the first one in the barn. He said, 'I'm not trained for this.' I said, 'I don't care what you're trained for, help me cut this kid down.' He threw up instead.

"I don't blame him. Reality is hard to face. Life is fleeting. All we've got is the moment. Right now. Right here. You've got to make the moments matter, otherwise you're nowhere."

I sat between these men from another world for a good hour or more. Neither spoke. They just sat there, staring across a forever belly of tundra as if willing their quarry into being. Now, I come from people who talk . . . a lot. The Celtic tribe is clinically uncomfortable with silence. Many of us never shut up until we're dead, and even then, we're haunting castles and inns with a ghostly howling only an exorcist can silence.

Sit I did, though, and never said a word. A record for me! The last time I sat still that long without talking was during a grade nine detention at Chebucto School . . . that I *got* for talking!

Charlie turned and raised his binoculars. "Hey, Joe," he said. "You want a moose?"

Joe said, "No, too much meat to carry."

Wondering what moose he was referring to, I raised my binoculars, pointing them towards the very distant patch of spruce, and saw absolutely nothing.

"He's right there," Charlie said without turning around.

I glassed the same trees until my eyes watered, and still I saw absolutely nothing. Twenty minutes later, the sun broke through those bible-picture clouds as that elusive moose rose from a lone thicket a day's walk away—a solitary speck on a vast canvas of tabula rasa. It stood stoic, and then nonchalantly ambled away, one stride at a time, living moment to moment.

"How in the hell did you see that?" I asked.

Charlie looked at me and, pointing to his face with a grin, said, "Indian eyes."

I laughed and said, "You guys have a whole different rhythm to your funny."

"You got that right."

It occurred to me right then, had I turned tail and gone home after my phone call with Tom, this moment of connection would never have been. Sure, the condescending kayaking guide, with his ludicrous self-assurance in bear country, could have ended badly had a bruin got a whiff of the Hamburger Helper leftovers and come scrounging, but sitting against a boulder as old as the world in timeless communion with Charlie was worth the chance I took.

Suddenly, Joe tapped him on the shoulder and the spell was broken. Pointing across the ridge, they saw half a dozen antlers sticking up from shapes on the ground. As if hit by an electric shock, a once-sedentary Joe and Charlie slung their rifles over their shoulders and were up and running full tilt, back to the boat. We followed the lake and beached the boat at the foot of where the reclining caribou would be.

"We want to shoot them sitting down," Charlie told me.

"Why?" I asked.

"Good eatin'," explained Joe.

We scrambled from the boats and up the hill. I was waved back by Charlie, when suddenly five caribou crested the hill from where they'd been lying. The wind was in our favour. I figured Joe would drop one with a bullet between the eyes and kill the other before it even knew his buddy was dead. Joe let loose a fusillade of shots from his semi-automatic Winchester . . . and missed them all!

They turned and bolted, never to be seen again. As Charlie walked past me, he said to Joe, "You can't be shooting like that when the white guy's here."

On the way back to the boat, several more caribou walked in front of us, and without missing a beat, Joe raised his gun and dropped one.

"Perfect," he said. "Right by the boat."

They had it gutted, skinned and quartered in under forty-five minutes, leaving the offal for the ravens and wolves.

Motoring back to camp, we discussed Tundra Tom. I mentioned his meltdown on the phone and his forgetting to pick us up.

"We've barely got eight weeks of summer to make it happen up here in tourism, and he's full-on 24/7. He works too hard, drinks too much, smokes too much, and then he just passes out, falls asleep and forgets where he's supposed to be. Anywhere but here, he'd be out of a job, but the North lets a lot of stuff go. You have to. It's the North."

Chapter Nine

ACROSS THE GREAT DIVIDE

Steve Earle singing "Another Town" carries me over the Rockies to that enchanted land on the other side, where the hand of time is held at bay and everything east of Golden is suspect. Beautiful British Columbia, where "starting over" is the mantra for those laden with the weight of another world, all hoping to score what they're looking for on the other side of the Great Divide.

In 2007, the real estate gold rush for a piece of paradise was on. Every hillside from Selkirks to Courtenay-Comox had an active-lifestyle baby boomer retirement community on it. Talk about great timing! Baby boomers scored all that inheritance money left them by hard-working Depression-era parents who wouldn't know a day spa from a can of Spam. Now their pampered sons and daughters will be dropping dead in a gated retirement community at a sun-punished age of 107 during a loofah-seaweed body scrub, with a Cabernet in one hand and a life coach in the other. Life coach. There's a scam: some New Age knob charging you money for something you should get from a friend for free: advice. "Quit drinking so much. You're an asshole!"

And active? You'd better believe it. In the high, dry desert climate of Osoyoos, people are regularly living well past a hundred. A pair of sun-weathered, mummified elders rode past me on a tandem-bicycle and I thought, *Shouldn't you be under hermetically sealed glass at the museum?*

Everything is extreme in BC. I went for a run in a mountainside conservation area, and just when I thought I was doing all right, keeping the Reaper at bay, some über-woman with cannonball calves blasted past me on the forest path, carrying a deer on her back! (An exaggeration, yes, but not by much.)

Caribou crossing endless miles of tundra for springtime calving grounds have nothing on the migration of Canadian retirees bound for the idyllic, sea-kissed climate of Vancouver Island. Despite the 350 years of built-up seismic energy that's pushing against the Pacific plates, which, when released, will most certainly move the stately homes of Oak Bay, Victoria to a driveway in Honolulu, they keep coming. Prairie people particularly love it out there. Can you blame them? If you were at the mercy of nosediving mercury for seven months of the year, you too would be counting the days till you could bolt for Shangri-La. After all, how many February nights can you spend at the curling rink in Regina before you want to drop the rock on your own head?

Everything exacts a price, and there's not a person I've met who doesn't feel held hostage to the BC ferry service. As a visitor, I find a ferry ride represents the most egalitarian of Canadian virtues, because everyone is literally in the same boat. You've got a Mercedes sedan–driving West Vancouver venture capitalist headed for their multimillion-dollar cedar retreat on Hornby Island, parked beside a '97 Subaru with more holes in the muffler than a JFK assassination conspiracy theory, being driven by a couple of semi-feral hard-core Earth cookies from the forest, who've been living so long off the grid, their ass cracks are turning to compost.

After the hellacious white-knuckler of a drive three winters prior, suffering primal blizzards on avalanche-prone mountain passes, this crossing is a breeze. Spring has arrived and is shirking winter's yoke in a seasonal tsunami of meltwater. Hope rules defiant once more, as slabs of ice slide from cliff faces like body armour dropped after the battle has been won. In the distance, sunbeams catch the prisms hidden in sheer curtains of rain and stretch across the sky in a rainbow so spectacular it would get Noah and Pride parade marshals alike doing cartwheels down Main Street. Snowbanks crumble and dissolve into rushing streams flowing down to the Columbia River in the shadow of the Kootenays. Scruffy bighorn sheep, sporting scraggy winter coats even the homeless would leave on a rack at the Sally Ann, pick at frugal strips of new grass along the Trans-Canada. Yes, indeed, it is *very* different than last time . . .

British Columbia is a province of geographic and climatic extremes. I've been humbled quiet standing small before dwindling old-growth giants in her coastal rainforests, where shadows and sun build pillars of light beneath a canopied cathedral of green. I've caught a fine Cabernet buzz more than once in the fruit-bellied farmlands of the Okanagan, where bourgeois wine snobs live in pseudo–Santa Barbara bliss in their California climate, all but a four-hour drive from the swine-rich Fraser Valley lowlands, where God-fearing Chilliwack and Abbotsford abut Vancouver sprawl.

But woe betide the careless traveller, lulled into complacency while sitting beneath blossoming cherry trees on a Victoria February afternoon, who assumes the weather in the town they're headed to tomorrow will be similar to what they're enjoying today. Because I did, driving a rental car with tires baby ass bald and windshield washer fluid made for far more temperate climes than the subarctic lumber country of Prince George, where I was bound.

The coulees were dusted with snow during the drive into Kamloops, as red-tails and sharp-shinned hawks floated thermals on a blue-sky day, hoping to snatch a groundhog supper for their hungry hatchlings, eagerly waiting in the nest for a mouthful of their mother's regurgitations. (Every time I get to wishing I was a hawk I remember that fact—and the feeling goes away.) I like this high, dry country of rolling grasslands, trout-happy lakes and sweet-smelling sage overlooking the Thompson River.

It's named for David Thompson, hands down the greatest geographer in Canadian history, who mapped ninety *thousand* kilometres of Canada for the HBC—kilometres he'd either canoed or hiked. There's a dude who walked the talk! What's even more impressive, he managed this Herculean feat of wilderness travel without ever once visiting Mountain Equipment Co-Op. (Now, *there's* a gang of hippie capitalists who have redefined the meaning of fleece. You can't help but be overcome by a compulsion to spend money in one of their stores. All you're looking to buy are a couple of propane canisters for your weekend camping trip, but *seven hours later*, you've maxed out the Visa and are loading up the truck with enough water-resistant, sweat-wicking, state-of-the-art down-filled adventure gear to circumnavigate the polar ice cap on foot.)

Unfortunately, I had no time to linger and enjoy the view. There were 476 kilometres left to drive if I was to make Prince George that night and be ready for the radio interview at 6 a.m. the next morning.

That winter of 2003 was my first tour across BC, and I had to sell the show. Doing radio morning shows was a coup my producer worked hard to procure. Going live with Type A DJs who've been mainlining caffeine since rising at 4 a.m. is a serious jolt to the system. You've got to have your game face on. Keep the jokes coming fast and furious. They've no patience for long set-ups. They want laughs *now, funny man!*

The experience of a high-octane early morning radio interview is like sitting in the cockpit with a couple of pilots trying to land a 787 Dreamliner in a thunderstorm while Zeus rattles lightning bolts off the nose cone. Those DJs are remarkably skilled at multi-tasking; flipping buttons, reading charts, delivering their riffs while listening to your answers and trying not to fake-laugh. CBC radio interviewers, on the other hand, have a very different energy. They are just as skilled, but far less effusive. Their radio interviews are so earnest, once they're over, you feel like you've just had a nice chat with a United Church deacon about wallpaper and sourdough.

The sun was going down as I left Kamloops and headed for the Gold Rush Trail. It's one of those historic travel routes families in Winnebagos drive in summer, looking to relive the journey miners took in 1897 on their way to the Klondike with nothing but a mule, forty pounds of flour and a shovel. I, conversely, was travelling it during the winter of 2003, looking for comedy gold instead, wishing

I had a mule instead of a car with Kleenex for tires, which I'd rented in a very rainy and mild Vancouver.

Darkness fell fast as I passed through Cache Creek, where listless packs of ferret-faced townies loped like shadows from a fever dream, stopping occasionally to kick at desiccated roadkill as they watched my car pass by with furtive stares. I'm sure they're a jovial bunch up there come summer, but whenever I mention that town's name onstage one hour south in Kamloops, the entire audience lets out an audible gasp and makes the sign of the cross.

Not salt, but sand is the preferred method of combatting ice on British Columbia's highways, and it's not uncommon for eighteen-wheelers blowing past at an unholy clip to kick up chunks of gravel that whistle into your windshield with the deadly *ting* of 75-millimetre artillery shells hitting a D-Day landing craft from the heights above Normandy. Pushing on, I stopped for gas in 100 Mile House, wrestling with whether or not I should bunk there for the night. Ten minutes outside town, I wished I had.

The snow fell fast, heavy and wet, smothering the windshield in a dough-thick blanket of white. My high beams only exacerbated the blizzard, so I turned the headlights to low and could barely see at all. I slowed from a confident eighty klicks to a ten-kilometre-an-hour crawl. One of those miner's mules would have been faster than me.

I hit the wiper fluid. It wouldn't squirt. It was frozen block-solid as the forehead of Frankenstein's monster. The wipers suddenly stopped, too. They were too burdened by the weight of the wet snow and wouldn't budge. I couldn't see my hands in front of my face—and I was *in* the car.

Easing over to the shoulder, I felt my tires sink with a sickening give, and fearing the vehicle was seconds from sliding over the embankment, I cut the wheel hard to the left, which got me back to solid ground. As I did, the car was filled with a retina-blinding light worthy of a nuclear flash at ground zero, seen seconds before your silhouette is burned into a brick wall. It was a double-trailered twenty-two-wheeler bearing down full throttle with nothing but malignant contempt for whatever unfortunate had the temerity to impede its passage. The big bastard was hell-bent on flattening me into oblivion with the same commitment a Panzer tank would a wounded Russian on the road to Moscow.

Its driver lay hard on the horn, ripping the night open with an eardrum-bursting blare that I will bet good money was a decibel level higher than the opening artillery barrage at the Battle of the Somme. To this day, I'm still impressed my bowels did not liquify.

A scream filled my vehicle with a surround-sound wail, coming from somewhere between my soul and scrotiliac (I made that word up too). The rear end of this rented piece-of-shit Chevy with paper-thin tires slid back and forth on the road with the fluidity of a gelatinous-assed bingo-playing duchess on a church basement chair.

At the last possible second before collision, the driver roared past with all the malevolence of the Great White Whale buffeting Ahab's dory. Once past, its backdraft threw a glutinous wave of slush into my windshield.

I can't see! I cannot fucking well see!

The car was in the middle of the highway at a dead stop. In fact, I wondered if I might already *be* dead. Maybe that truck dinged me into some Nordic Valhalla, and this snowy netherworld was its purgatory? My only route of escape from eternal imprisonment would be a hero's quest through their underworld. If my recall of Nordic myth is correct, that would involve engaging in feats of strength with magical dwarves, fighting a giant sturgeon and *not* succumbing to temptations of sex with a Valkyrie seductress at the crossroads who transforms into a three-headed witch with snakes for pigtails, before ultimately facing a rune-reading dragon full of tricky riddles, seated before the Golden Throne of Asgard. Or something like that.

I didn't dare get out of the truck to clean the windshield for fear I couldn't find my way back to the driver's seat. So, I leaned my head out the window and wiped the snow off with my left hand while I steered with my right. That's when another set of trucker's lights roared out of the night behind me . . .

Compounding this flirtation with death was disappointment at the recent cancellation of my first television series, *Blackfly*. Two years before, I'd sold a premise to Global Television that sought to "satirize current social and political trends in the context of the eighteenth-century fur trade." The cast of characters I'd created were archetypes plucked from the pages of Canadian history. With plenty creative liberties taken, I threw them together in a stockade fort somewhere on the shores of Lake Superior in 1783 and hoped for the best.

Stepping into the fray of my first television series proved a Herculean task—the equivalent of juggling a million moving pieces while strapped to a rocket . . . *blindfolded*. Despite an original premise and great cast (Colin Mochrie, Shauna Black, Cheri Maracle, Lorne Cardinal, Richard Donat and James Kee), the series never got the chance to fulfil its true potential. Global Television's idea of humour was broad-based, hokey-jokey corny slapstick and not the satiric tone I'd envisioned, as exemplified by *Blackadder* and the Monty

Python films, which used historic context to maximum comedic effect. I'm sure they had their own share of battles with the powers that be, but finding yourself contractually bound to follow inane network notes, coupled with the benign neglect of the production company, Salter Street Films, led critics to compare us to the goofy *F Troop* television show from the 1960s. Not the comparison I was hoping for.

When it comes to comedy, having editorial control of your own vision is crucial. I did not have that. Michael Donovan, the regally aloof owner of Salter Street, insisted a laugh track be added to the show, which I fought against but eventually acquiesced to, based on the inordinate number of industry awards lining the walls of his office.

Who was I to argue with a visionary who'd given the country *This Hour Has 22 Minutes* and financed the brilliant award-winning television industry satire *Made in Canada*, and would go on to share an Oscar with Michael Moore for *Bowling for Columbine*?

Judging by the first episode of *Blackfly*, though, it was blatantly clear that whatever skills the man had producing television sure as shooting did *not* apply to laugh tracks. It wasn't "laughter," either, but *cackling*. A wild and unhinged cackling of the kind heard only in asylums for the criminally insane during a total lunar eclipse, rather than the kind of laughter a "regular" audience would make while enjoying a lighthearted comedy set in a fort . . . in the forest.

The experience proved a Faustian bargain. You are forced to answer to powerful people who don't trust your funny, even though they've hired you to *be* funny. The paradox is that the "you" they want you to be . . . isn't you! So, instead of channelling the affably subversive tone of my stand-up act, in *Blackfly* I acquiesced to network demands, accepted a patronizing production company's indifference and became an eighteenth-century Gilligan in a tri-corner hat.

Lesson learned: just because someone has the power, it doesn't make them right.

The silver lining in *Blackfly* was seeing a frontier fort rise from the forest along Nova Scotia's South Shore, where a myriad number of trades such as drivers, carpenters, caterers, editors, writers, directors, cast and crew made a good living for two summers in a row. That an idea whose gestation period had rolled round the amniotic fluid of my brainpan for several years was finally made manifest proved a validation of the imagination. Given the unholy amount of money spent on Spielberg's Hollywood blockbusters, the man must have had daily nerdgasms on the set of *Jurassic Park*!

During twelve-hour days spent on my feet shooting (which, half the time, meant falling down), or in the writing room either breaking story, writing scripts or fixing ones we'd commissioned (that came in either three days late or fifteen pages too long), I'd remember those lean years of struggle in Los Angeles. Just to stay sane in that paradise of non-stop unemployment and ever-mounting personal debt, I threw my name in the hat with thirty other unknowns at local cof-fee-house amateur nights for the privilege of performing a five-min-ute set. The acts were an eclectic collection of poets, comedians, singers and what I swore were the guitar-playing, grown-up illegiti-mate spawn of the Manson clan who wandered in from their sage-brush warrens somewhere north of Chatsworth, looking for the love that Charlie never gave. Remembering those nights reminded me the production demands I experienced were good problems to have, compared to following someone who said they'd been abducted by aliens . . . and had the scars to prove it.

Having a television series is constant creation, negotiation and compromise as you stick-handle your way through production deadlines and network demands 24/7. The fight for your vision gets tiring. You win some and lose some. But you stay the course because the only way you'll ever win is by never ever giving up.

Besides, last I heard, the banks don't accept pride as a mortgage payment.

That's why I love the road. It's just you, a microphone and an audience, all there for the same thing: laughs. On the road, your creative integrity is not at the mercy of powerful network mandarins, but rather a fickle, omnipotent God whose price for allowing you to follow your bliss is to stick you in a primal blizzard straight from the Pleistocene on the way to Prince George!

My car rocked again, but I had an idea: follow his tail lights! Follow them! Follow them to sanctuary!

And I did just that. With my head out the driver's-side window and steering with my right hand, I tailgated that leviathan for twenty-six klicks into Williams Lake. The hotel I was booked into appeared in the distance. Thoughts of the loss of *Blackfly* had fled. After all, nothing lasts forever. And besides, I was alive and no longer stuck in a Nordic purgatory about to wrestle magical dwarves.

The hotel's entranceway illuminated an iron silhouette of a heavily knapsacked voyageur with a musket in his hand, head bent into the wind, making his way to some far point of frontier. The irony was not lost on me.

My phone rang, waking me at 7 a.m. It was the DJ Prince George, sounding half-a-dozen-Red-Bulls-into-the-morning way-too-chipper.

"Heard you were having some trouble on the highway last night. What? No winter storms where you come from? This is how we roll up here! Hope you've got something funny to say about that . . . and we're on!"

After that drive in 2003, I wrote this in my journal: "I know one thing. I'm not going to be out here at sixty, looking for laughs at the far points of frontier, dodging death on killer roads." *Bahahahahaha!* Think again, pilgrim!

I did exactly that not long ago in December 2019. On the way to Fort St. John, the non-winter tires on my Avis rental (because in all provinces but Quebec companies are not legally bound to provide winter tires) flagrantly rebuked my driving skills on a two-lane road glazed with a death-smooth coat of freezing rain. Those tires were forbidden purchase on the icy wet surface, and just as before, my fate was placed in the hands of a fickle Almighty, who thankfully wasn't sleeping on the job that day.

When the temperature rose and began to thaw the ice rink I'd been driving on, fifty-ton goliaths with nuclear waste warning plaques on their grilles blew past in the opposite direction, throwing great tsunamis of a bitumen-rich soup up all over my windshield. Lessons still being learned: life is all about the long haul.

I'm headed for the BC Interior first and make the turn at Revelstoke, where a museum to the infamous Canadian Pacific Railway sits. A mere forty-five kilometres west, in Craigellachie, you can see where, in 1885, after ten daunting years of sweat, death and engineering genius (not to mention graft, kickbacks and an audacious level of political corruption), the actual last spike of the CPR was hammered, linking the new nation of Canada from east to west. It also made a lot of white dudes with the right political connections filthy rich. I guess as much as things change, they stay the same.

Under a sky of cobalt blue, menthol-cool breezes dance down from marshmallow-white mountaintops, tickling the nape of my neck with the softness of a lover's kiss. It is 2007, and spring has returned to the Slocan Valley of Kootenay country in a mighty scream of green. Aspens leaf. Blossoms burst. Trout lilies sprout sentinel-tall from wetlands where beavers, those obsessive-compulsives of the animal kingdom, push the limits of logic with feats of engineering. It's not hard to imagine the domestic chatter in the lodge:

"I've got to build another wall, honey."

To which she responds, "Can we have just one Saturday where you're not doing anything? Just one?"

In aeries high above, eagles are hatching; bears in caves are scratching awake; and sasquatch mothers, perhaps, are suckling their young in secret groves of old-growth forest. On the backs of several cars and trucks, I see bumper decals depicting the shadow of a sasquatch above the statement "I believe." (By the way, if sasquatches are real, why do we never see footage of baby ones? In most simian subgroups, babies are the most curious and least fearful of humans. It's always the babies coming out of the jungle that steal your binoculars, play with your foot or break into the camp's medicine chest. Just sayin'.)

There's always been the myth of magical mountain valley Shangri-Las hidden from the wider world, home to those who live a life of blissful reverie mere mortals like ourselves can never hope to know . . . unless you live in Nelson town, that is. It's wonderfully, warmly welcoming here, with a live-and-let-live vibe, home to fresh-faced, heart-warm neo-hippies, semi-feral vagabonds looking like they've been on the road since Neil Young was in a garage band, and trust-fund ski-bum nomads, come to carve orgasmic Kootenay powder.

This mountain town of heritage buildings is flush with restaurants, cafés, art galleries, indie-hipster coffee shops and sports stores filled with the kind of adventure gear you'd need for that weekend you're looking to spend in a snow cave. There's a sidewalk food truck called Bite that serves salmon burgers named after David Suzuki and lactose-conscious poutine in cups to friendly, smiling people strolling down Baker Street.

For those who enjoy a toke, the town is flush with head shops. For some reason, authorities turned a blind eye to the marijuana trade in Nelson for years, and as a result, the enterprise was well ahead of the curve before legalization, playing a pivotal role in setting a standard look for an industry whose future had yet to arrive.

Every head shop was operating-room antiseptic in a smooth, Zen-clean setting, with engaging staff in starched white lab coats coming across more like professional pharmacists than the tie-dyed Jerry Garcia look-alikes traditionally associated with the selling of dope.

You remember those proprietor stoners of youth? They were always running their illicit businesses from a secret hole in the wall where you needed to know a password to enter. I stopped smoking up years ago because I found the pot grown today far more potent than the innocent, munchie-inducing homegrown ganja of yore. After one toke of the turbocharged weed they were pulling out of hydroponic warrens prior to legalization, you went cross-eyed, had no spit, and in ten minutes were squirrelled away beneath the sink, talking to Jesus.

The pioneers of the Kootenay region's marijuana industry were American draft dodgers who crossed our undefended border in Volkswagen vans during the Vietnam War with fifty bucks in their pockets and Bob Dylan on the eight-track. With close access to a porous border, Nelson became the illicit trade's epicentre, as tons of the wacky-tabacky headed south for a generation.

Twenty years prior to legalization, organized crime had knocked a lot of mom-and-pop operations to the curb, but now that the bud is legal, they've begun to proliferate once again. In fact, several years ago, Mounties raided a grower's operation in the backcountry and discovered the operation was "guarded" by half a dozen docile, non-threatening black bears lounging round the property. (It's been rumoured two were playing backgammon and another was shooting hoops, but this can't be confirmed.) Turns out the bruins were all royally fried. The owner had been feeding them marijuana cookies. You don't hear stories like that in Toronto.

I was enjoying lunch beside the Bite truck, overlooking Kootenay Lake, when a tired woman whose arms were laden with grocery bags sat to rest. She said she was a massage therapist whose husband had moved her to Canada from Germany, where they'd met.

"He took me to Edmonton. It was dark, cold and had no culture. After Europe, can you imagine? I hated it." I remembered those raucous nights playing to two thousand people at a sold-out Winspear Centre and thought she must be talking of a different place.

"Did you know Nelson's built on a crystal mountain that sits below the lake? People find crystals there all the time. The Indians came to fish, hunt and bury their dead, but wouldn't live here. The energy's too intense. The town is criss-crossed by vortex lines, like they have in Sedona."

When I hear stories about vortex lines and energy belts, I start to check out. In fact, I camped in Sedona, Arizona, when driving back to Toronto from LA in '93. High-end spas and too many shops selling everything from T-shirts to dream catchers hadn't turned the town into a cornucopia of New Age commercialism yet. It was still a natural wonder of red rock canyons and pinyon pine with no bumper-to-bumper traffic jams choking the main drag, provoking irate townsfolk in their cars to swear at visitors in *their* cars who'd come to get their chakras cleansed. I set up my tent in a private campground beside a brook—and a couple with clinically desert-dry, cracked skin that I assumed they'd earned from too many days spent staring up at the sun while wandering the canyons high on peyote. These drifters in love told me there were 137 different vortex lines in Sedona, but "the strongest was up behind the Dairy Queen."

The woman continued: "After standing there and buzzing on the energy for an afternoon, we couldn't sleep for a week." I told them they'd most likely been kept awake by the Mr. Mistys they'd been drinking. "That DQ treat is so cold, it freezes the temporal lobes that house the seat of reason in the brain," I said, "making people who believe in the power of a vortex to cure everything from a stutter to a brain tumour even more susceptible to bullshit." I bade them good night and prayed they wouldn't murder me in my sleep.

Vortex lines are supposedly swirling fields of energy emanating from the Earth's surface that are conducive to spiritual healing . . . and other stuff. So, that explains things! Nelson is the *only* place in my twenty years spent criss-crossing Canada where I've seen a six-foot-seven man in a white beard the length of Gandalf's wander through town with a walking staff, telling anyone who'll listen that there's an extraterrestrial landing base north of town . . . and not be considered crazy.

In fact, Gandalf's double could be on to something, because not far from Nelson, the artist's enclave of Kaslo has the most UFO sightings in Canada. Then again, given the potency of the BC bud I bought, you don't need a mother ship to get to another planet. (When I said I no longer smoke up, what I meant was *a lot*. I don't smoke up *a lot*.)

Now a new breed of nomad is showing up: wanderers with money. They arrive with fat portfolios, driving a Lexus, while they listen to Bruce Springsteen on their playlist sing songs about the working man. In a region where gold and silver were once pulled from the Earth in a mad turn-of-the-century scramble for riches, real estate has replaced mining as the predominant industry.

It's the only thing I hear from everyone everywhere. I once stopped for breakfast at the Main Street Diner and struck up a conversation with the manager. I commented on the number of luxury cars I saw in town.

"Now that the land around Fernie's been all bought up," she said, "they're coming here with their oil-patch millions, driving land values through the roof. Pretty soon, none of us will be able to afford to live here." (Mind you, this was thirteen years ago, before oil prices tanked, Alberta's economy took a nosedive and racist yellow-vest rednecks took to looking for scapegoats.)

"There's ghost towns above the Slocan Valley where miners lived before the gold got played out back in the 1900s," she continued. "Been empty for generations, but now people have returned to claim their birthright to that real estate, bequeathed to families long before anybody ever thought it would matter as much as it does today."

Farther south of Nelson and tucked into the rugged East Kootenay country between the Rocky and Purcell Mountain ranges is Cranbrook. It's more Alberta than BC, with an authentically rugged working-class soul. It's far rougher round the edges than the gated communities farther west, where Cabernet-soaked Boomers golf away their golden years. Cranbrook is where Mom and the kids pile into a ram-tough Dodge truck to pick up the groceries at IGA, as opposed to West Vancouver, where a nanny in a Range Rover visits Whole Foods with the children of the mother she's working for, hoping to snag the last half dozen ten-dollar Peruvian mangoes.

Cranbrook is not given to that passive reverie more contemplative souls enjoy on the wild west coast of Vancouver Island. For those who live beside the Pacific Ocean's soothing lullaby, the cacophonous bang and clang of industry is another man's soundtrack. Islanders of the Pacific Rim enjoy the stress-free reverie that comes from living in an enchanted land of fog and fern, where misty mountain forests greet the sea and Green Party officials milk their unicorn herds in the magical meadows of Nevermore. Whereas in Cranbrook, there are no unicorns, but if there were, there'd be a two-bag limit on them during hunting season.

It was in Cranbrook that an old teammate from Halifax minor hockey–playing days said hello post-show. We played on the Bantam B Arrows the year we won our house league championship, after four periods of overtime. His callused handshake told me his life's labour had been different than mine. Raised in public housing by the railway tracks, his world growing up was a give-no-quarter corner of

Halifax. Some who left "the pubs" played a far better hand than the one they were dealt, while others fell hard in a world beyond the familiar that broke them lonesome. Not this dude, though. After going bankrupt with an unreliable partner running a pizza shop in Richmond, he met the woman who would become his wife and they headed for her hometown of Cranbrook.

Although we went to the same high school, we ran with different crowds, and other than a cursory nod in the hallways, our social circles were chasms apart.

In a thumbnail trajectory of his life until now, he said he'd quit school in grade eleven and made for Vancouver. I mentioned I'd gone to university after graduating, and he went quiet. Even growing up, the dude had the wary eye of a warrior about him, accompanied by a permanently tuned bullshit detector ready to deflate the first sign of pomposity. My mention of university turned the air around us tight. He was the one who read the room and broke the tension, though, not me.

"It's good you're funny, 'cause you never had much of a slapshot."

"Cripes, I still don't!" I said, and we laughed.

"Remember how those Civic Arena dressing rooms where we played always smelled like chickens?" I asked. He roared laughing. Suddenly, we were back. A memory shared of a seminal moment in time, teleported us back to an arena's dressing room circa 1972, thanks to the barnyard's worth of poultry kept caged there during the Atlantic Winter Fair.

This agricultural exposition always arrived after Thanksgiving, planting itself on the hallowed grounds of the Halifax Forum. For ten days, anyone who raised, rode or milked livestock came to compete and congregate among their own, while city-dwelling Haligonians

came to watch equestrians jumping, oxen pulling, farmers milking—
and some, I guess, to look at chickens sitting in cages, staring at the
wall, doing nothing at all.

The infamous Bill Lynch carnival tagged along too, setting itself
up in the parking lot to get that one last nickel from your pocket
before winter set in and they pulled out of Dodge. Bill's prime-time
appearance was during the waning days of summer, when August
arrived on swollen grey Atlantic clouds and the nights sat heavy and
still. That's when you'd hear the carny's haunting, nasal twang come
sailing down from Windsor Street for our bedtime ears to catch:

"Come see the Mini Horse! Come see the Mini Horse! The world's
smallest pony!"

Outside a circus tent hung a ten-foot tapestry depicting the star
attraction. This rendering inferred, in no uncertain terms, that the
Mini Horse was a holdout from the dawn of mammals, when ground
sloths weighed two thousand pounds and the equine genus we're
familiar with today could fit in a teacup. It stood Lipizzan stallion–
proud in the tapestry amongst a herd of its own, all grazing content-
edly on an imagined Cenozoic plain.

Bill Lynch's Mini Horse looked every inch the creature Doug
McClure and his band of cowboys chased through a crack in a wall
of rock, leading them to discover *and* capture a Tyrannosaurus rex,
in the film *The Valley of Gwangi*. (Spoiler alert: never lasso a T-Rex
and bring it back to a turn-of-the-century carnival being held in a
Western town, because the Gwangi will break its shackles, gobble
down an elephant, and then run amok and eat a one-eyed witch.)

After paying a full dollar, you stepped inside a dimly lit tent with
a dozen other gullible fools, only to witness a P. T. Barnum–level of
hucksterism whose audacity should have warranted applause—or

imprisonment. The Mini Horse was nothing more than a chihuahua with a little homemade saddle on its back!

"Look! It's prancing just like a horse," I heard someone say.

If it were a horse, I remember thinking, *but it's a chihuahua*!!

It was our own fault for believing the Mini Horse was real and not just an imaginative carny ruse. We should have known, given Bill's reputation for skirting round the rules. His midway flaunted safety standards. The Ferris wheel had bits of flesh and clothing hanging off it. For my money, it was and still is the scariest midway ride. You were seated in nothing more than a bucket that was totally open to the elements, with nothing but a rattling bar across the seats to wrap your fingers round in a death grip, while a million miles below, the controls were being operated by a chain-smoking carny with seven teeth, a grade eight education and a three-pack-a-day habit. They'd leave you at the top forever, too. I remember watching weather patterns change over the Gulf Stream. A family of miscreants excited their dad had finally been paroled would be seated with their felon father in the bucket in front of us, rocking it back and forth.

"You're not supposed to do that," one of us would yell way too loud. Expecting any help from the carny running the ride was futile . . . he was related to the people rocking the bucket!

One summer, the midway also featured a petting zoo. A more accurate description would be a *diseased animal* petting zoo. It was the Devil's menagerie! I saw a child pet a piglet with his bare hand, and it turned black and fell off! Bill advertised a real, live unicorn, too. In actuality, it was a blind pit pony with half a hockey stick taped to its head.

The Forum had a professional-sized ice surface that was removed for the run of the fair. Equestrians— rich girls from the South End in the Bengal Lancers—competed in jumping contests; big Dutch–German hybrids from the South Shore and their Eaton's catalogue "husky"-sized spawn cursed their oxen in feats of strength; dairy cows were milked in competition by meaty-handed, dairy-fresh maidens from farms in the Annapolis Valley; teamsters drove their quarter horses, with skills worthy of the Golden Horde, up the aisles at full speed into the Forum's arena. The Forum featured all the main attractions while the Civic Arena next door, with its smaller ice surface, housed stalls selling sundries, games of chance, miraculous household cleaning agents you couldn't find at Canadian Tire and, of course, chickens, in the dressing rooms.

I suppose the powers that be could justify stuffing avian livestock from floor to ceiling in the Civic's dressing rooms. You most certainly couldn't have that barnyard hum lingering in the dressing rooms of the Forum, because that temple of worship was the home ice of the Montreal Canadiens' Calder Cup–winning American Hockey League farm team, the Nova Scotia Voyageurs. Having future Stanley Cup winners like Yvon Lambert or Larry Robinson complaining their lockers smelled like chicken shit would never do. (Which, given that *chicken shit* in popular vernacular means "lack of courage," would smart even worse for a team's chosen goon, who weekly pulverized the snot out of opponents and even leapt over penalty box Plexiglas in full gear with skates laced to finish the fight they were in there for.)

In September 1970, NHL teams came to the Halifax Forum for an exhibition game. Kids at Chebucto School, where I went, had to attend morning shop class once a week at Bloomfield School, which sat much closer to the Forum than ours. This gave us the opportunity to catch a practice on our way home for lunch. The fancy name for shop class was "industrial arts," a form of gender-specific education where boys learned how to make metal cookie sheets while girls learned how to actually *make* the cookies in "home economics." A far more practical skill than the medieval one of metallurgy. When I moved out on my own at twenty-two, I could barely boil a can of soup without burning it, but give me three sheets of corrugated tin, metal-cutting shears and a can of red paint, and you've got yourself a weather-vane that looks like a lobster.

This particular weekday morning, we were watching the Boston Bruins practise. We had our autograph books out, when around the boards came their tough, scrappy right winger, Johnny McKenzie. I was leaning over as far as I could, yelling, "Johnny! Johnny! Gimme your autograph!" He stopped and turned toward me. It was the first NHL player's face I'd ever seen close up. The hockey card I had of him at home showed a player sporting a warm, welcoming, full-toothed grin from ear to ear. On this day, I learned real life is somewhat different.

Sweet Jesus! He had five teeth, and two of those were broken, sitting in a ferociously frightening visage. It was a face of great contusions, wrinkled folds of skin and lumpy scars earned from a million blueline collisions, high sticks, goal-crease battles and fists in the face. In actuality, Johnny's whole head was closer to a forgotten ball of suet, chewed over the winter by rodents that a spring thaw might reveal.

"Johnny," I pleaded louder, "gimme your autograph." He looked and said, "Piss off, you little red-headed prick." (Because I was once.) Another player skating close by overheard Johnny's rebuke and reprimanded him: "Johnny. Don't talk to the kid like that. He'll remember what you said forever."

And today, may I say, "Thank you, Derek Sanderson."

A week later, we got into the Forum during a Montreal Canadiens practice, when it was empty of onlookers. Even the ubiquitous Gollum-like Lusher, who we swore lived in the subterranean bowels of the building, was nowhere to be seen. Lusher doubled as a janitor and trainer's assistant, scurrying warily from behind the player's bench to the dressing room after every V's game, clutching the team's top-of-the-line Sherwood and Victoriaville hockey sticks, ready to run the gauntlet of kids asking those gods-who-walked-as-men for their game sticks.

Tough older kids, who'd soon be doing a stretch in juvie for pulling lunchtime B & E's, tried to snatch a loose one, but Lusher would give no quarter, for his mitts held a Gorilla Glue–tight grip on his bounty, protecting it with the same level of devotion a Benedictine monk would a Bible written by Saint Paul himself.

The Canadiens had just left the ice, save for defenceman Terry Harper, who was taking slapshots on an empty net. Beside him sat two buckets brimming with hockey pucks. Regina-born Harper would win four Stanley Cups and have a sterling career in the NHL as a solid "stay-at-home defenceman," a term reserved for those who played the position with more concern for protecting their goalie's crease than scoring goals. In fact, the man stayed at home so much, a "Terry Harper hat trick" wasn't scoring three times in a game, but three goals in a season! He was clearly a man not in it for the glory but for the game. Perhaps the morning we saw him taking shots on that empty net, he was daydreaming as to how great it would be to actually pop a few during a real game for a change.

One of us yelled, "Hey, Harper! How about a puck or two?" And I'll be damned if he didn't oblige! With a smile that lit up the Forum, he yelled, "Sure, boys!" and picking pucks from the bucket beside him, began flipping them over the boards to every corner of the stands, even pointing to where they'd be going, like cocky batters will do at home plate to let a stadium of fans know the next ball will soon be over the fence. High into the Forum they went, rattling off the seats and stairwells, as we, in unbridled grade seven Chebucto School rink-rat glee, chased our rubber bullion down, cradling them home in our arms much as Jack would have done those golden-goose eggs he'd stolen from the giant's kitchen.

And today, may I say, "Thank you, Terry Harper."

Life always came full circle during my travels. People from long ago showing up in theatre lobbies, waiting to say hello while I autographed the DVDs of my specials I'd be selling. Some faces who said hello at these signings belonged to those who'd not crossed my mind in forty-five years, save for a fleeting cameo appearance they'd made in a dream I had after eating Camembert cheese too close to bedtime. They'd stare with a knowing look, waiting for me to remember their names. Truth be told, I always did—and do—because I never really left the Maritimes. Do any of us from there? Does the melancholy tickle in our belly for back home ever really disappear? Meeting so many from there was most definitely due to the nomadic gene economic necessity has bred into a Maritimer's bones. After all, even Jesus had to leave home to find work. Yet even though the wind had carried us to different points of the compass, the necessity to regain a sense of "then" was tangible.

On occasion, the meeting was more than a cursory exchange of pleasantries and a wave goodbye with a wish for the best. Instead, it was one anchored to deeper water, held fast by the connective tissue of shared experience the struggle for a foothold in the wider world had not frayed.

Here in Cranbrook, on this pit stop on the road, I saw one man who'd found what he'd been looking for on the other side of the Great Divide. Standing beside his wife in their new home, we looked out through a bay window at a stunning panoramic view of the southern Rockies.

"Not a bad view for a kid from the ghetto, eh, Ronnie?"

"No, buddy. Not bad. Not bad at all."

Chapter Ten

CAR FROM AWAY

I'll never forget that summer a man walked on the moon—partly because I saw it on TV, but mostly because we were camping at the time, camping way at the northeastern tip of the continent, where Cape Breton's pretty green highlands fall to the sea.

As Dad's Plymouth Fury II drove over Cape Smokey, headed for our site in the national park, the scent of spruce, pine, ocean and field wafted through the open windows of that gas-guzzling dreadnaught of the highway. I'm willing to wager that every time we filled it up, Saudi Arabia dropped seven feet! His annual three-week parole from the airless towers of Maritime Telegraph and Telephone meant freedom for all, when we in great numbers of fun sang the night forever through, smothered in sunburnt arms and rum-toddy grins of family and friends, all of us illuminated by the softly hissing Coleman lanterns that cast our shadows into the evening road. Lobsters bound for the pot scratching in a box kept time to a guitar's strumming, while the cadence of a cribbage game danced along on the evening air, teasing its way in and out of conversation like lures in a trout pool.

Fifteen two, fifteen four, the rest don't score and your mother's a whore! (Not *our* mother; it's just the way the cribbage rhyme went. Had to clarify that.)

The drive from our home in Halifax took six hours. That's an eternity when you're eleven. My seven-year-old sister and I sat in the back seat while Mom rode shotgun. She was a traditional stay-at-home mom who, besides raising a family and doing *all* the cooking, lived for one thing: to clean house. It was her calling. She embraced the role as a sinner would the pursuit of salvation, scrubbing every corner, sink and baseboard, never missing a rogue dust bunny buried beneath the bed, or last summer's housefly, dead in a never-used wedding gift teacup relegated to the top shelf at the back of the cupboard.

"You don't have to clean back there, Ma. No one will see it."

"I don't care if someone else doesn't see it. I'll know it's there!"

Even today, her house is still so frighteningly spotless you'd be safer getting an appendectomy on her kitchen floor than in any hospital operating room in the country. A shrink would call it obsessive-compulsive, where she just called it "a clean friggin' house is what it is!" She took pride in what defined her. She enjoyed it. Preparing for three weeks of camping, not so much.

By the time we were ready to pull out of the driveway, she'd open the passenger-side door, exhale that world-weary sigh unique to mothers the world over whose home was their job but were finally scoring some R and R, then collapse in the seat, exhausted. In minutes, she was asleep against the window, her head wobbling in slumber, only to bolt upright an hour down the road screeching, "I forgot the friggin' towels!" We assured her she hadn't, holding them up in our hands—they doubled for pillows. She'd smile, blink and then say, "Anyone want a bologna-and-mustard-pickle sandwich?"

We camped in an Eaton's TruLine tent trailer we towed behind the car. It had a metal body and wooden cover that opened into sleeping platforms attached to the sides of the trailer, supported by rods attached to the lower chassis. A canvas covering acted as a roof and walls, held up by an abstract cat's cradle of aluminum poles that you practically needed a degree from MIT to construct.

The poles never seemed to fit together the same way each year, and the patronizing instructions, featuring an artist's shamelessly fraudulent rendering of a happy, smiling family on the box, was insulting. Our family never looked like the family from the instruction manual setting up their tent trailer . . . *ever*.

Clouds of mosquitoes from hell's fetid fields weren't draining the instruction-manual family dry of blood while the mom rooted frantically for repellent at the bottom of a box she swore she'd put it at the top of. Nor was there a conversation bubble over the dad's head, saying, "Sonofabitch bastard! Where in the name of Joe Jumping Jesus H. Christ on hockey skates is the other goddamn pole?!"

Once the tent trailer was up, there was one rule that had to be obeyed: never, *ever* touch the canvas walls when it was raining, or it would leak.

"But how bad will it leak?" I asked.

"Don't touch the canvas, Ronnie, and we won't find out," Dad said, staring at me like I wasn't his.

"Like, will it be a tidal wave of water?"

"Dad said just don't touch it," my sister put in, splatting another mosquito fat with blood on her arm.

"Or will it be a slow flood, like in the Bible?" I was a curious kid.

"Christ Almighty! Am I speaking Russian? Just don't touch it!"

"*Okayyyyyy . . .*"

No wonder my line of questioning got on his nerves. He didn't ask to be grilled about the consequences of touching wet canvas by his hyperactive kid. He just wanted his three weeks' vacation far from the airless tower where he worked, nostalgic for the days when he was on the road, installing phone systems, instead of shackled to a middle-management desk surrounded by professional engineers.

"Do you know why an engineer wears that iron ring on his finger, Ronnie?"

"No, Dad. Why?"

"It's to balance the lead in his arse."

Mom weighed in on his warning as she slathered calamine lotion on our mosquito bites, covering my sister and me in a chalky residue from tip to tail until we resembled primitive children painted in ceremonial pigment.

"Listen to your father and don't touch the canvas unless you want to wake up drowned," Mom warned.

"Don't be simple," Dad corrected. "You can't *wake up* drowned."

"Well, then, he won't *wake up* drowned, but we'll *see* him drowned when *we* wake up." Mom turned to me. "Don't touch the canvas when it's raining, he said."

That night, it rained. Hard. Dad turned to face me just before bedtime.

"What did I tell you?"

"Don't touch the canvas when it's raining. I heard you."

"So . . . don't."

"I won't."

He didn't believe me, because he kept staring. Did he see hesitation behind my eyes? Did he see a nanosecond of impertinence cross my brow that said, "Like hell I won't touch it"? I say this, because he said it again, only with an alliterative emphasis unique to his Burgeo-born pedigree that lent his profanity a poetic gravitas.

"By the lumped-up, woolly-eyed gentle German Jesus, don't touch the canvas walls when it's raining, or I will guaran-Goddamn-tee, there's gonna be a stranger in hell for breakfast by the Lord-snappin' arseholes!"

"I *heard* you. I'm not mental."

But I also heard the canvas beside my head, slick with moisture, beckoning.

"Over here. That's right, Ronnie. Look here. Touch me. Reach your finger out and touch . . . the . . . walls . . . of . . . the tent trailer. How bad can it be? It's not like it's going to drown you. But I bet you wonder if it will. Touch me."

Temptation began working its weird juju. My index finger was possessed of a will of its own.

I can't help it. Must . . . touch . . . the canvas. And just as my finger reached out, inches from satisfaction, a flashlight beam broke the night.

"Caught you, ya little Christer!"

Today, they call my condition ADHD. Back then they called it "Jesus Christ, there's something wrong with him."

When it did rain that summer, it fell heavily and consistently for several days in a row for a full week. Whatever sepia-toned nostalgia people might nurture of childhood days spent camping with family can be easily vanquished by simply remembering, "Isn't that the summer it poured rain so hard that the campground flooded, and a drunk guy almost drowned after passing out in a puddle beside his tent?"

At least we were off the ground in our tent trailer, and provided I never touched the canvas walls—*again*—it wouldn't leak—*again*—and we would not be forced to pack up and leave, like the tenting families we saw piling into cars headed for home. Their faces looked grateful with relief, like stranded victims of rising floodwaters suddenly plucked from their rooftops by rescue boats. Not us.

"We paid for three Jesus weeks and we'll camp for three Jesus weeks, by the Jesus," Dad said.

One particular morning, Dad decided we were going for a drive, because another family we'd been camping with had done it the day before. Only we'd go . . . "just a little bit farther." The drive was something to take the edge off our waterlogged cabin fever, even though it wasn't a cabin we were in, but a leaky Eaton's TruLine tent trailer I couldn't stop touching the canvas walls of.

Turning left from the campground, we headed north and just kept going. For some reason still unknown to me, Dad steered off the Cabot Trail proper and took, to quote Robert Frost, "the road less travelled." It was a secondary local road running by the small settlement of Dingwall, that went past an even smaller village of Capstick, towards the tip of the island where sat Meat Cove, the most northerly habitation in a destitute corner of a long-ago have-not province.

So bucolic is this knoll of emerald green today, you'd swear it belonged to some enchanted corner of Middle Earth. Besides the dozen perfectly groomed campsites scattered round the property, there's a charming gift shop and snack bar serving gloriously good clam chowder you'd truly go to war for. That's why it's particularly difficult to fathom the barefoot-hillbilly Hobbiton of tarpaper shacks and hillside dugouts we saw that summer when men walked on the moon.

The last time I drove there, twenty-seven years ago, there was still no guardrail to protect the absent-minded motorist from taking a deadly trip over the cliff to a beach of boulders far below. In 1969, the road was far deadlier and but a single dirt track where a shepherd could comfortably lead sheep, but a father could *not* comfortably manoeuvre a monstrous Plymouth Fury II with an engine bonnet "so Jesus big, if I hit a moose in this, you kids won't feel it in the back seat!"

The road ended where the shacks began. Meat Cove was a collection of rudimentary tarpaper hovels built of wood and cinder block. Save for the rusted skeleton of a 1950s-era Chevy sitting in a front yard, the scene was Neolithic.

We sat slack-jawed in our idling Plymouth, gauging the netherworld we'd driven into, when from nowhere and everywhere there suddenly arrived a swarm of filthy, snot-crusted, semi-feral urchins with rink-wide foreheads, clamouring round the car, exhibiting the dangerous curiosity of game farm simians, hell-bent on vandalism. That's when our mom began to curse.

"Jesus Christ! Jesus Christ almighty! Turn the car around, Bernie! Turn it around!"

Dad put the car in reverse and hit the gas. But instead of moving backward, we sank. In fact, we sank up to the wheel rims in a glutinous, thick gumbo that adhered with the conviction of the Krazy Glue that hadn't been invented yet. We were stuck in the muck of Meat Cove!

The pack had circled the vehicle by now, and although the doors were locked, our mother was frozen shell-shock still, her face contorted in primal fear worthy of a marmot trapped in a raptor's shadow, far from the safety of its cozy burrow.

As Dad gunned the gas, I turned to see a rooster tail of mud rising high behind us. Mom was starting to hyperventilate, and her usual voice was replaced by the feverish, high-pitched squeak of the afore-mentioned marmot. With eyes bugged out and loopy, she turned to me and my sister, shouting, "Don't open the fuckin' windows!"

We'd never heard our mom drop an f-bomb before. Ever. By the frenzied look in her eyes, though, we knew a switch had been flipped and she'd slipped into a dangerous valley of crazy all mothers are capable of falling into.

"Why would we open the windows?" we said.

Dad piped up, barking, "You touch the goddamn tent when I tell you not to; why wouldn't you open the goddamn windows, too?"

"But we're not in a tent now," I corrected.

"Don't talk back to your father," said Mom.

"I'm not. I'm just sayin' . . ."

"Then don't *just say* anything."

"I won't," I promised.

"Don't open the windows." The word *windows* became frighten-ingly elongated, ending in a high-pitched screech unique to an OCD-plagued sister whose piercing shriek could be heard in celes-tial orbits if you tracked dirt into her home, which was covered in more plastic than an autopsy table.

"I said I won't."

"Then don't."

"He won't!" My little sister said.

Like a lone prairie schooner crossing a cruel frontier, we sat help-less as the guttural hoots and raucous hollering of Meat Cove's barefoot denizens scurried to the back of our car and began, one at a time, to gleefully run through that rooster tail of spraying muck, as would Kool-Aid–drinking suburban children a backyard sprinkler.

"Ho-leee fuck," Dad muttered under his breath. He knew full well things had taken a bizarre and unsettling turn. Anything could happen now. Their blood was up, and that's when a mob is capable of anything. The car was surrounded by a brood of hilltop wildings of all ages, either half-naked or wearing tattered raiments perhaps pulled from the bodies of drowned sailors washed ashore. Their hair was either shaved to the scalp or a rat's nest of unkempt locks; they looked frighteningly similar to photos of those Rumanian children you'd see in the newspaper on occasion, the accompanying stories saying they'd been raised by wolves in the Carpathian Mountains and suddenly showed up one morning on a farmer's back porch, naked and filthy, chewing on a squirrel.

Perhaps fearing that should he continue revving the engine, the spinning wheels would drill all the way up to the chassis, Dad took his foot off the accelerator. The showering of mud stopped. So did the braying of the pack. They were flummoxed. Smeared in Meat Cove muck from tip to tail, they now looked lost and confused, much like a hyperactive two-year-old who's thrown a kitten against a wall and can't figure why it's not moving anymore. That's when the leader of the pack pressed his proscenium-browed, bucktoothed kisser against the driver's-side window and, scowling, pointed at my father, demanding he hit the gas again.

"We're only going to go deeper into the muck," Dad tried to say, but he couldn't, because he stuttered when he was nervous, and we knew his sentence was now an eternity short of completion. Dad was stuck spinning his own verbal wheels on the word *going*, and the poor man could not unstick them. When you stutter, it's bad enough trying to get a sentence out under pressure in an everyday social setting but having a menagerie of wildings laugh at you while you try does not work wonders in expediting the process. In his efforts to get past the dreaded *g*, his facial contortions tweaked the funny bone of the Meat Cove youngster, and he began to laugh at our father. Hearing this, the entire pack ran from behind the car and joined in—at what, they weren't certain, but their voices soon rose in a cacophonous imitation of their leader's guffaws.

Without warning, the pack backed away from the window and, parting, revealed a woman of fierce countenance. She wore a tattered cotton dress of simple design, and her skinny legs rose from a pair of green gum-rubber boots. In one hand, she clutched a stubby of Ten Penny, while in the other, a smoke dangled from nicotine-stained fingers. A gaunt face, chiselled sharp by the daily assault of the seasons, housed a hollow-eyed, thousand-yard stare born from isolation and God knows how many dark nights of the soul this woman had wrestled with during a lifetime's incarceration on this lonesome hilltop. She began yelling at the children, and although we couldn't hear the exact content, it seemed the eldest was getting the brunt of it. She kept pointing back and forth between him and the car. The woman walked towards us.

Dad rolled the window down, and our mother made that marmot sound again.

"We is gonna give you'se a push."

Dad stuttered a thank you. We stayed seated.

"That one's strong," she said pointing, "but he's not that strong. You'se'll have to get out," she said.

Dad, turning round to us in the back seat, tried to say, "Get out of the car," but judging by the way his eyes were rolling to the back of his head, we knew he'd never get past that troublesome *g* for at least ten minutes, so we just opened the doors and did what the poor man was desperately trying to tell us. Mom sat immovable in the passenger seat, trapped in a state of shell-shocked catatonia and making that weird marmot sound.

Standing outside the safety of our car in our clean-smelling summer clothes facing a pack of mud-covered children in their tattered raiments, we were the ones who suddenly felt dirty. Even though it was nothing but a sense of adventure that had taken us there that day, the woman's baleful stare said we'd come to take vicarious pleasure at the misfortune of others.

The leader barked orders to three of the bigger kids, and bending down, the four of them gripped the front bumper of that car and, with several mighty grunts, heaved it clear of its entrapment.

Our mom began to frantically wave us into the car.

Dad turned to the woman.

"Thank you," he said, and gave her five dollars.

She stared long at the fiver, so he gave her a twenty.

"That's better." And turning on her heel, she disappeared into a house lit only by candlelight, sitting on the edge of forever.

Pulling away, we saw the pack scurrying over the Meat Cove cliff for the beach—where, I assumed, they'd soon be picking the pockets of drowned sailors washed ashore.

We pulled away. The air inside the car felt close. Mom rolled a window down. Dad cleared his throat.

"Next time," he said, "we'll only go as far as Dingwall."

Dad always took his vacation the last week of July and the first two weeks of August, so being cursed with poor weather could scuttle what already was a laughably short summer.

"No harm with a little rain. The ocean's warmest then," Dad assured. I always wondered what measure of warmth he was referring to, because given the park's northern latitude, that stretch of the Atlantic Ocean never, *ever* got warm—and still doesn't in, say, a *Caribbean* sense of the word. Like, when you go to Cancún now, ten minutes after checking into the hotel you're neck deep in the Gulf of Mexico sucking back a tequila Slurpee and splashing in an ocean so tub-water-temperature perfect, you're as good as back in the amniotic yolk sac.

Warm water is not a luxury accorded summertime swimmers in "Canada's Ocean Playground." Other than a random two weeks at the end of August and a few fleeting days in September, taking a dip comes with a price: it stings your feet, softens your teeth and numbs your extremities, while a minion of whatever deity rules the deep squeezes your *cojones* in a vice-tight grip.

There are exceptions to the rule, however. On occasion, hurricanes, which once delivered a glancing blow to Nova Scotia but now come far too close for a homeowner's comfort, happen to come perfectly close for a swimmer's. The storms' tropical air warms the Gulf Stream to a euphoric degree of ideal bathtub temperature, when a week previous it was only tolerable for mackerel, seals and haddock. Three days before a hurricane makes landfall, suffering arthritics lucky enough to spend but a scant twenty minutes splashing about in the healing surf are rewarded such profound redemption from pain, they've been seen sprinting from the ocean and up the beach, doing backflips towards their towels, where they happily open jars of pickles for their family's picnic.

When it comes to that fleeting Maritime summer, the hospitality industry has basically four months to make the money they need to get through winter. Tourists are a course to be run full out, but come October, every grunt who's spent the season slinging trays of food and grog is suffering sore bunions, an aching back and a Tylenol habit, sporting that thousand-yard shell-shocked stare unique to the beaten and bloodied foot soldiers of their industry. They know every tip was a hard-won boon that came at the cost of catering to busloads of waddling, swag-happy travellers who spilled from a Carnival Cruise Line's gangplank for day trips hither and yon, to lay siege to every craft shop from Lunenburg to Corner Brook, where they'll load up on everything from jams and soaps and painted dories, to a replica of Joshua Slocum's johnson in a bell jar.

Anyway, back to my point. There's only so much of that service-with-a-smile a working stiff can take. Waitresses are the shock troops of the industry. They're the ones who take on the full-frontal barrage of surly patrons. I happened to be at a Nova Scotia South Shore restaurant late in the season when two busloads of cruise ship passengers took a diner hostage, and I watched a cranky customer complaining way too loudly for that late in the season that she'd "ordered my refill twenty minutes ago and it's still not here."

The waitress spun on her heel cornered weasel fast.

"You ordered your refill twenty minutes ago and it's still not here? Well, pardon me all to hell, but I was a slim eighteen-year-old queen of the sea twenty minutes ago, and now I'm not. I'm a forty-one-year-old, overworked single mother of two, running my hole off from dawn to double-shift dusk, hoping to scrounge enough from my savings to get four new snow tires on my Dodge Neon before winter comes or I shoot myself first. So, suck it up, buttercup—you'll get the tea when it's good and ready!"

Actually, I stand corrected. I believe she said, "I'm so terribly sorry. Coming right up, you horse-faced cow."

Like any perceived utopia, Nova Scotia does have its dark side. You're just not supposed to mention it. But hang around the wrong tavern on a Saturday night after the summertime postcard smiles are tucked away and replaced by winter's hard grimace. That's when a crusty, skunky-draft-drinkin' local with more attitude than teeth would cut your throat with a scallop shell just for beating him in shuffleboard.

About 150 kilometres outside Halifax, you lost radio contact with CJCH, which played the hits of the day. There'd be no decent reception for another few hours until you caught the signal coming from Antigonish. That radio station loved to play fiddle music. A *lot* of fiddle music. The instrument is fine in small doses, but as a soundtrack for life, it can test the tolerance of most mortal men. Fifteen years earlier, my father had been stationed in Antigonish for six months on a phone company job, and he woke to jigs and reels on the radio in the morning and went to sleep with jigs and reels at night. There are earworms and then there's "fiddle earworms": a pernicious brain invasion of uncompromising persistence. I'm certain that if fiddle music were piped non-stop into a black-ops interrogation cell from dawn till dusk, the most resistant captive would curl up in the corner, praying for a waterboarding session instead. (Note to self: never share this observation with a local audience in Mabou.)

On the other hand, my Cape Breton–born mother took issue with the bagpipes, a Maritime standard. Her justification for taking umbrage with the pipes was concise and to the point: "The sound gives me a headache, and I'm scared the people playing them with their faces turning purple are going to either have a stroke or shit themselves. I don't like them. No, I don't."

Once outside the radius of CJCH, there'd be no more singing along to "Bad Moon Rising," "These Eyes," or, yes, "Snowbird." Because Anne Murray hailed from Springhill, Nova Scotia, "Snowbird" hitting the top ten on Billboard in the US had everyone talking. I was partial to buddy who actually wrote the song, PEI's Gene MacLellan. His brilliant oeuvre includes "Put Your Hand in the Hand," recorded by a dozen artists as diverse as Elvis and Joan Baez, but outside of the Maritimes and musicians familiar with his work, he's largely uncelebrated by the general public. That's proba- bly because he was never feted in the United States, unlike the songstress who made "Snowbird" famous. That American woman casts a long shadow.

"Car from away! Car from away!" I yelled as the licence plates zipped past.

"Don't yell in my ear when I'm driving!" Dad barked.

"But it's a game, Da. It's car from away."

"From away" meant anywhere but Nova Scotia. It especially meant *Americans*.

And there they were, driving road-hogging Oldsmobiles and Cadillacs, headed for the majestic Keltic Lodge that sat in Tudor splendour on a promontory of land jutting into the Atlantic above the town of Ingonish. Built by the provincial government in 1939 on property purchased from an Ohio rubber magnate, the hotel catered to high-rolling Americans come to golf its state-of-the-art eighteen-hole course and escape the summer heat of Florida, South Carolina and other lands of the imagination. Stepping from their Detroit-built land boats, sporting white shoes, Lacoste shirts and plaid pants, their perky blonde wives in tennis skirts bouncing beside them, the men strode with a high-noon swagger befitting those born to the world's post-war beacon of prosperity.

It was in the holy light of a purple gloaming that I first laid eyes on them, entering our national park in an avocado-coloured Oldsmobile and pulling a sixty-foot, chrome-plated, hermetically sealed Airstream living unit.

"Look!" I pointed. "It's the friggin' Jetsons!"

Here was the myth made manifest. Americans were here! In 1969, it was the country where a kid could order a two-man submarine from the back of a DC comic book. "Fires rockets and torpedoes," promised the ad. The claim seemed a stretch, but if it appeared in the back of an issue of *Sgt. Rock*, it must be true. Painful but also true, stamped on the ad was "Order Void in Canada." Did that ever suck, eh? The only thing I could get here in the winter was the flu. Not in America, though. There, you could get anything. Because America was the land of cool stuff!

Standing in the middle of the dirt road staring in slack-jawed wonder, however, was the personification of *un*cool: me, in ankle-high "floodwater" Tee Kay flares, a pair of Zellers-bought two-stripe North Star sneakers, a T-shirt and a too-goofy haircut courtesy of Lester and Earl, the gin-soaked barbers of our neighbourhood.

Lester and Earl's partnership consisted of a big, round, loud man and a soft-spoken thin one, who took turns falling on and off the wagon. When one was steady and drunk, the other was shaky and sober. Scissors whirred and snipped in reckless abandon around your head.

During that summer, long hair was *the* ticket to cool. It said you belonged to the side of history that mattered. The side that was taking the world in the right direction. The side that was fighting "the pigs" in the streets of Chicago, burning their draft cards and playing in bands.

Long hair was the ticket, but repeated pleas to let me grow mine fell on my father's stone-deaf ears. Instead, I was told to get my arse across the street for a sensible trim, or "By the Jesus, I'll chop it off with my garden shears!"

So away I went, peering back over my shoulder, hoping for a last-minute reprieve where I'd hear, "I'm joking! C'mon back. We're all going to be hippies, raise llamas and grow dope on a commune in the Annapolis Valley with Noel Harrison! Let's start by tie-dying my suit jacket!" Instead, I climbed the stairs to the sacrificial altar that belonged to the bastard sons of Sweeney Todd.

Perhaps in a long-ago, the notorious barbers had obliged customer requests for "a little off the top," "square back" or "just a trim" with professionalism and pride, competently wielding the tools of their trade in a two-chair shop redolent with the medicinal smells of Wildroot and Clubman Pinaud, which glowed translucent in iridescent blues and greens from neat rows of bottles. Their Dartmouth Barber Academy graduation certificates hung on the wall beside one of those ubiquitous calendars of a smiling woman in a bathing suit, cradling enormous breasts while standing beside a new Buick.

Lester and Earl formed their partnership not long after Europe fell to Nazi tyranny. With the port city of Halifax soon to be an embarkation point for thousands of troops bound for overseas, it's not hard to imagine Lester's voice booming with optimism: "The war is a gift, Earl! A gift! Sure, it might not be so good for the countries the Germans invaded, and everybody they killed and are still going to kill before they're killed themselves and it's all over, but for barbers . . . it's a gold mine, buddy, a gold mine! Because what do soldiers need most besides a rifle, smokes and a pack of French safes? Haircuts, Earl! Haircuts!"

The future lay plump with promise. After all, it was the beginning of their career, and beginnings are always rife with possibility. They had legitimate reason to be optimistic, what with the strategic location of their shop a few blocks north of a tent city housing hundreds of Allied troops. With army barbers overwhelmed by the sheer number of soldiers, headquarters put out a tender looking for civilian barbers to accommodate the overflow, which Lester bid for and won. All through the war, and for twenty years afterwards, both men were making the kind of living any barber would envy. That all changed forever the fateful day a deer ran into a clothesline full of washing in Earl's backyard.

Earl's wife, Doreen, had been hanging her bedsheets and undergarments out one crisp fall morning. Their house sat at the far end of Purcell's Cove Road, only a thirty-minute drive to the city. Earl preferred to live in what he considered the country. Lester could brag all he wanted about walking to work; Earl enjoyed the forest being so close to the house that "we can see deer in our field every morning after we screw."

As Doreen draped her sheets on the line, perhaps she felt the waning days of a summer sun warming her apple-bright cheeks and the chilly breeze of coming winter tickling the nape of her neck. Perhaps she heard the pounding of deer hooves as well. Did she hear the rifle shot, too? It's all conjecture. What is not, was the ten-point buck who burst from the forest in a blur of wide-eyed fear that made it oblivious to both the clothesline and Doreen.

One can surmise that on any given day other than this, an acuity bred in the bone would have made the buck very aware of any obstruction to its passage. But that day, running for its life, it did not. The deer hit the clothesline full sprint, and Doreen and the creature suddenly found themselves entangled in a bizarre *danse macabre*, feverishly trying to free themselves from the hanging sheets and underwear. Neighbours down the road said they heard a following shot and then quiet. By the time they arrived, there was no hunter to be seen, only poor Doreen and a ten-point buck draped in bedsheets, dead on the grass, a pair of panties hanging lazily on its impressive antlered head as if they'd been nonchalantly tossed there prior to their carnal tryst.

The hunter responsible was never found. It wouldn't have mattered to Earl anyway. No manner of vengeance could have soothed his broken heart, so a bottle of Tanqueray had to do the work instead. Although he arrived at the shop punctually each morning, dressed in his crisply starched barbershop tunic, he did so stewed, as he would be all day, floating half-aware of the world around him on a melancholy river of gin. His rheumy eyes threatened to spill into your lap from liquid sockets as his manicured hands, scrubbed to a waxy formaldehyde sheen, whirred a pair of scissors far too close to your face for comfort.

Earl's pièce de resistance was a truly heathen style of cut. Back when the Cowsills were singing that hair should be "shoulder-length or longer" and "shining, gleaming, streaming, flaxen waxen," mine was not. Earl shaved up the back of your head to the crown and around the sides, while the top was hacked with nicks and gouges to the porcelain smoothness of the skull. It was a Meat Cove trim, not a haircut. When the barber chair spun round to the mirror, mouths fell open with horror, marvelling at the audacity of Earl's butchery. Once you were outside the shop, your ears suddenly felt embarrassingly large and pink as they flapped, exposed and vulnerable to the hungry winds of winter.

Back at your kitchen table, you received nary an ounce of sympathy. Instead, you were told, "Don't worry. You're only eleven. It will grow back. And don't blame poor Earl, either. If your wife and a deer were found shot dead hugging each other with her panties on its head, you'd give bad haircuts, too."

As any good partner would, Lester tried his best to assuage Earl's sadness, offering a shoulder of support each evening after work as they closed Comeau's Beverage Room, their bellies full of skunky draft. Lester hoped Earl's depression would pass, but the hurt went too deep; time would not heal this. Meanwhile, Lester's marriage to Lois, a woman he'd met at a dance in Sambro after the war, ended childless when she left him for a carny who worked for Bill Lynch midways. During Lester's failed attempts to win her a large stuffed poodle at a game of skill, Lester swore he saw the spark of love ignite between his woman and the carny.

The point of the game was to roll wooden balls on what resembled an uphill bowling alley towards holes of ever-decreasing circumference, which increased in monetary value as they got smaller. If enough balls landed in the richest hole, you'd warrant a prize. As Lois stood tapping her feet with impatience, smoking Export As down to the filter, Lester spent a small fortune trying his best, to no avail.

Seeing his opportunity, the carny stepped from behind his booth and, with patronizing ease, effortlessly rolled the balls into holes of all the top denominations. Then, like a knight returning from a grail quest, he handed Lois the stuffed poodle, throwing a smug sideways glance to Lester that let him know his days were numbered.

Sitting with cold indifference at home in their living room, Lois would wistfully stroke the poodle's head reminding Lester of his inadequacy.

"I'm a barber," he'd plead, "not a bowler."

Lois was hearing none of it, and shortly thereafter, with promises of a life of adventure amongst his midway nomads, Lois followed her carny south to the Florida Panhandle, where his tribe whiled the winter away in sunny comfort, when they weren't doing time for petty theft.

That's when Lester started to drink more, and suddenly, Earl had company.

By the time of my visits, the darkest days of their tenure were upon them. Caring little for style or virtue of cut, they mowed into your scalp in a clear-cutting frenzy. Sometimes, your ears would almost be snipped by the tip of the scissors, and you'd jump with a fright, only to be reprimanded by Lester's whisky breath warning you to "stop squirming or I *will* cut ya!"

Time might not have healed Earl's broken heart, but it certainly worked wonders for haircuts. By the time 1975 rolled around, whatever issues had once polarized opinions regarding the length of your hair had disappeared with the last helicopter off the embassy roof in Saigon. The world had moved on. "Get your arse across the street for a trim" was replaced with "If you want my car on Friday night, you'll get your arse outside and shovel the Jesus sidewalk!"

Still, you kept a wide berth between yourself and that barbershop, just in case some malevolent force would magnetically pull you into one of those chairs for some butchery. I saw Lester's bulk from time to time, mowing white heads returned home after passing a winter's worth of kidney stones in Florida. On occasion, you'd see Earl standing on the barbershop steps, having a smoke and looking wraithlike in the sun. I'd pass by and nod, throwing up a "Hello, Earl," but he was elsewhere in thought, floating away on his dreamy river of gin, waiting for yesterday.

Little did I know the Americans' visit to our national park wasn't for basic summertime R and R. A war in Vietnam had forced their only boy to seek sanctuary in Canada. When his draft card arrived the previous year, he joined the legions of tie-dyed, knapsacked sons who threw their thumbs to the merciful hum of the highway. I guess Clyburn Brook in the Cape Breton Highlands had a healthier ring to the ear than the Mekong Delta.

His first winter there, the young man lived on the western side of the park, amongst the Acadians in Chéticamp. They know all too well what exile means, having walked *back* to Nova Scotia from the swamps of Louisiana, after the British gave these peaceful farmers of Norman blood the boot from their bucolic fields of Evangeline in 1755. The lonesome price of exile still haunts Acadian blood, and if anyone knows how to roll the welcome mat out for fellow travellers, it's them.

The American kid spent his year working in the woods and on the water, far from a war he had no faith in fighting, safe amongst a people who had hewn a home from Longfellow's "forest primeval" two centuries prior. Once summer came, he made his way over French Mountain and down to the squatter camps of his fellow draft dodgers, near to where a copper-coloured Black Brook gurgles into the sea. When his parents received the postcard from his home in exile, they too followed the road north from Baltimore, hoping to find him.

The father's change of heart had been a long time coming. I heard his story through the canvas walls of our trailer (on a rare night I wasn't touching them), as he sat with my father at our picnic table, weeping softly for the son he'd struck with his fist as a burning draft card turned to ash on a sidewalk two generations stood their ground on. Minutes later, the young man had walked away, holding his bleeding nose in one hand and his Boy Scout duffle bag in the other.

It was during that very summer that I saw men walk on the moon. The Americans in the Airstream trailer had invited several families over to watch the event on their TV. They gave the children grape Tang, too. *Grape* Tang—I hadn't even seen the orange kind yet! When they emerged from the back of that Airstream, carrying their portable TV, they actually *plugged* it into the side of what I figured was as close to an interstellar spacecraft as I'd ever get. But not only that—their TV was in colour! Colour! We didn't even have a colour TV at home. All we had was a little black-and-white Panasonic that sat on the kitchen counter. Its screen was so small, I think we had the first iPod and didn't know it. Dad got it for free from a stevedore neighbour after one of the Halifax dockyard containers "broke." Sporting a set of grape Tang lips from ear to ear, I sat wide-eyed, watching America take "one small step for man, one giant leap for mankind." How incredibly cool was that? They could plug a colour TV into the side of their trailer, and I wasn't even allowed to touch the walls of ours!

Several days later, bad weather roared in again, wreaking malicious havoc on the campground, blowing tent trailers over, trashing picnic tables and turning Black Brook from a gentle stream into a raging river that overran its banks. This was the very same storm that bereft of conscience, had drowned two local boys my age. They'd stolen a fisherman's dory for a joyride at the onset of the storm, only to disappear into the Atlantic's hungry maw.

Shortly after the storm's passing, we made our way to the beach, past the detritus of campground ruin and flooded sites. The beach was a battle zone of huge driftwood deadfall wound with monofilament nets, jellyfish, seagrass and seaweed ripped from the ocean floor and angrily strewn far inland by the gale's fury. Many campers were at the water's edge, scanning the grey horizon for some sign of the missing boys. Squinting through the drizzle and sea spray, I thought I saw things: a waving hand in a yellow dory, a flash of red baseball cap on the waves, anything other than the foreboding drone of the rescue boat moving back and forth across an empty point.

"There's something," I said too loudly.

A face turned towards us, all pale, streaked in pain and bottomless loss.

"Is he sure?" the man stammered.

I knew it was the father of one of the lost boys. Avoiding his eyes, I shook my head no and headed back to the campground, arms linked round my family. Looking back, I saw the Americans from the Airstream still staring out to sea.

That night in the cookhouse, someone started playing guitar, and before long we were singing again, the sadness of the day having given way to a few brews and good tunes. Requests were going back and forth, until the Americans asked for that Johnny Horton tune "Sink the Bismarck." No one knew the lyrics, so they started in alone: *In May of 1941, the war had just begun . . .* We all stopped cold, except the Americans, who saw nothing wrong with the lyrics. When told the war had started in 1939, they had no idea Canada had been in it for two years, alongside Britain, before the Japanese even knew where

Pearl Harbor *was*. Besides, they said laughing, we'd still be fighting it if they hadn't stepped in.

The guitar playing stopped. The night felt humid and close. People forgot the moon landing. "The astronaut's suits looked green," someone whispered. A guitar player started strumming "Farewell to Nova Scotia," and everyone joined in. Everyone except the Americans. They didn't know the words. After all, they were from away.

Chapter Eleven

VERNE

He was squatting on the asphalt beside the front door of the Petro-Canada station in Airdrie, Alberta, when I pulled in to fill up. Stepping out of my vehicle, I noticed this big fellow stand, cock his head and look my way.

Surrounded by a serpentine river of highways, gas stations are really isolated islands whose safety can be illusory at times. Despite being brightly lit, with strategically placed security cameras covering every angle, they can leave a person feeling somewhat exposed. A target. And I spook easily. It's an instantaneous full-body response, too, one that twists me into a wide-eyed wrestler's stance, hyperalert and ready to launch a litany of spitting profanity at my protagonist with the same religious zeal a Tourette's-suffering Quaker would direct at a spinning weather-vane.

This unfortunate reaction is bred in the bone. Not because I'm a Quaker, but because I'm descended from high-strung, high-blood-pressure-suffering, cholesterol-producing, poetically profane

Newfoundlanders and anxiety-prone Cape Bretoners. We also exhibit an equal predisposition for spontaneity and hospitality . . . provided you don't spook us. Spook us, and if we're holding something sharp, you could bleed.

Filling up the gas tank in my shirt sleeves, I thought how great it was not to be touring during winter for a change. Drifting into a reverie, I happily began butchering the lyrics to that old Seals and Crofts tune "Summer Breeze" and giving thanks that I hadn't suffered through the non-stop run of minus-40 days these flatlanders were still talking about a good month into an idyllic prairie spring.

In every town I'd visited, main streets were choked with strolling locals whose pale faces were lifted towards the warming sun. After six months locked in frigid incarceration, they were enthusiastically embracing a new-found freedom, much like hostages would who'd recently been sprung from some airless, dank dungeon where their captors had played nothing but Nickelback, fed them field mice and forced them to shit in a bucket.

"Summer breeze makes me feel fine," I sang as I turned to put the pump back. That's when a hand grabbed my shoulder . . .

I screeched. The fright had triggered the fight-or-flight response, releasing a tsunami of cortisol throughout my limbic system, trashing all sense of social restraint in its path. In a nanosecond, the happy man pumping gas singing an insipid pop song from the 1970s, was now crouched bug-eyed and frozen in a wrestler's stance that would look right at home on Billy and Eric's rodeo circuit but was oddly incongruous at a set of Petro-Can gas pumps.

"Ronnie James! Holy shit! I've been watching you since I was little."

I couldn't imagine this guy ever being little. He towered over me.

"Little? How old are you?" I asked.

"Fifty-seven."

"I'm sixty-one. You couldn't have been watching me since you were little."

"Whatever."

His dismissive indifference didn't bother me. Why? Because he knew my name!

After all, I'm in *Canadian* show business! No one knows our names. NDP backbenchers have more name recognition than Canadian performers. Oh well, with no star system here, we don't have as far to fall if the career takes a nosedive. We can take solace in knowing we'll never be Chubby Checker, bemoaning his lost mock chicken billions.

Most times when people meet you, it's "Hey! You're that guy from TV. What's your name again?" Then I say, "I'm Paul Gross," and they don't have a clue who he is, either. Name recognition from a stranger assures Canadian performers that we are not bound for obscurity faster than a 1960s child star who was put to pasture by Walt Disney at the onset of puberty.

The recognition also stroked my fragile self-confidence, which regularly vacillates between the existential despair of a forgotten refugee, standing on the beach without a toothbrush, and a delusional sense of destiny, where I envision leading the Israelites from bondage to the fertile valleys of Canaan.

"Are you gonna keep crouching, or what?" he asked.

I realized I was still locked in my wrestler pose.

"Sorry," I said, standing, "but you kinda scared me."

"You're not much taller even when you stand up," he said, and started laughing at his own joke. Everyone's a comedian.

He had a weathered jean jacket slung over one arm and wore a scruffy T-shirt that hung over a pair of torn and soiled grey sweatpants. His arms and knuckles were marked with tattoos. At a glance, some looked as though they'd been legitimately inked by a professional in a parlour with a sterilized needle, while others could have been carved with a hot nail in prison. On his feet were running shoes of two different brands and colours, at which I chose not to stare. His hair was a dusty, matted mess in serious need of attention.

Fists of opponents had clearly built his flattened boxer's nose over the years, and the scars of those battles fought showed on dry, chapped lips he'd sometimes twist into a puckered grimace, while shutting one rheumy eye as he gauged my comments with a suspicion born to those whose trust in the world had long since been broken.

"Ha! Ronnie James! I can't believe Verne Cardinal is talking to a rock 'n' roll star from the radio!"

"I'm not a rock 'n' roll star. I'm a comedian. And I was on TV, not the radio."

"Whatever." There's that dismissive *whatever* again. I thought only teenage girls said this to each other in the hallways of junior high, but apparently not.

"What the hell are you doing here?" he asked.

"I'm headed for a gig in Leduc."

"Leduc? No shit! I'm headed for Leduc, too!"

Ah, Jesus. I saw his face brighten. Dollars to donuts, Verne was going to ask me for a lift. Something had registered behind his eyes— it was hope. My car was his salvation from this Petro-Can purgatory.

All the while, I was thinking, *Sure pal, I'd like nothing more than to share my vehicle for three hours with a stranger who's been sleeping by a dumpster at the back of a gas station for a week in decomposing sweatpants.*

He kept staring, waiting for me to offer a ride. I was cornered.

As mentioned in the first chapter, I'd been employed as an improviser in the Second City organization ten years prior to becoming a stand-up. Time spent in that company may have provided me the rudimentary stage skills needed to entertain suburbanites visiting downtown Toronto for a night of inoffensive satire, but in no way did it nurture the talent I'd need if ever I'd have to negotiate my way out of a tight corner with a casualty of colonialism at a set of gas pumps in Alberta.

Then the request came.

"Can you give me a lift to Leduc?"

The first rule of improvisation is to always "Yes, and—" the offering. Saying no will stall the scene, and the prime directive is to *always* move the scene forward. But this wasn't a scene, it was real life, and real life doesn't come with a script, so I did the next worst thing to saying no and asked a question. "Wha-what?"

How lame of me! It lacked gravitas. Why hadn't I at least come back with "As long as you don't mind travelling with someone being chased by alien bounty hunters, who will stop at nothing to get the Crystal Sphere of Zorlac I stole from the intergalactic warlord Slimy Jerry, during a trip to the Andromeda Galaxy. Hop in."

Another motorist had pulled up and was watching the scene unfold. Damn. An audience. I had to be on my toes. Can't suck in front of a potential reviewer. You never know when those career assassins will suddenly materialize out of the ether, ready to eviscerate you with their poison pen.

"Leduc! I'm headed to Leduc, just like you! My nephew works as a cashier at River Cree Casino and I need a place to crash."

This guy is good! He's furthering the scene by adding more information, and I'm just standing here like a stammering wannabe during a game of freeze tag in the Second City workshops.

(For those readers unfamiliar with the discipline's vernacular, freeze tag, or "switch," is an improv game where two actors start a scene based on an innocuous line of dialogue, while the rest of the cast stands onstage behind them. They watch the actors for body movements that spark inspiration. When one of the actors watching sees a physical position worth capitalizing on, they yell, "Freeze!" and then tap that actor on the shoulder, whereupon the new actor enters the scene, assuming the *exact* position of the one they've replaced. They, in turn, must justify the position they've taken with a line of dialogue, which hopefully takes the scene in an entirely different direction and elicits a big laugh—as opposed to the tedious explanation I've just given.)

"My nephew works as a cashier at River Cree Casino!" yelled Verne. So, in the parlance of my long-gone trade in improvisation, I chose to "Yes, and—" the unfolding scene by moving it forward with "I did stand-up at River Cree Casino! It's a great room!" A blatant repeat of what had already been said, that on a Second City stage would get an audience drifting into delirium looking for the exit sign.

Still, I had added something to the scene with Verne.

River Cree Casino, by the way, is a great gig as far as casinos go. Some of them have barns for theatres that are vast acoustic nightmares, designed more to house armies of gamblers who'd rather be blowing their children's university tuition at the blackjack table than watching you. I stand corrected. The term is no longer *gambling* but *recreating*. You have to love the audacity of that PR spin. If sitting in a diaper from dawn till dusk at a one-armed bandit hoping three lemons will line up so a fortune in nickels might land in your lap is recreating, then scratching your ass on the couch while binge-watching Netflix must be a triathlon.

With outstretched pleading hands and eyes moist with tears, Verne began his lamentation. "I lost the keys to my Kia, and this is where the bus from Worsley dropped me off. Been sitting here for two days. I'm trying to get to my nephew's place in Edmonton. It's true. I'm not shittin' ya."

I hadn't a clue where Worsley was, but judging by the wear on this man, it could have been Pluto and not a hamlet that, according to Wikipedia, is tucked into the western edge of Alberta's high plains Peace River Country, sixty kilometres shy of the BC border. In other words, it's a far point of frontier where one of the major food groups is still moose tongue.

Strange as it may sound, I believed him. The details were too specific to be fictitious. When you live in an urban centre, as I have in Toronto for the past forty years, you run a daily gauntlet of panhandlers. You learn to sort out the legitimately homeless from the junkies and drunks. To my trained urban eye, Verne was telling the truth. Besides, refusing to help the man would just kill the scene, and no one gets anywhere in improv unless they keep moving the scene forward. Kind of like life—and Verne's life at the moment was stuck, not going anywhere, at a Petro-Can station in Airdrie.

"All right, then," I said. "Hop in the back seat."

He stiffened at my suggestion and his tone sharpened.

"Why are you always putting Indians at the back of the bus?"

Pointing to the weeks' worth of potato chip wrappers, apple cores and banana peels on the passenger side, I said, "Because the seat is filthy."

"Filthy?" he said, pointing to his dirty clothes. "Like that's gonna matter. Don't you see what I'm wearing?! I'll be right back. I need to take a leak."

The other motorist had watched our scene unfold. His vehicle had one of those Christian stickers on the back window—the word *Faith* in the shape of a fish—that lets those of us who don't have the sticker know that the people who *do* have it are going to heaven and we're not. The man nodded his approval in much the same way Jesus might have a Good Samaritan whom He'd just seen handing a leper his last spoonful of baba ghanoush.

But I was alone, unlike peace-loving Jesus, who, when strolling the back roads of Galilee, performing miracles and keeping the wine flowing at a wedding, was always flanked by a posse of twelve bearded, sandal-wearing bros who looked like the opening act for the Oak Ridge Boys.

"What else could I do?" I said.

"It's the only thing you could do," the Christian replied, as he drove away with a smile and a wave worthy of Ned Flanders.

No, I thought, *there was another option*. When Verne was in the restroom, I could have called the cops and told them I was being harassed at the gas pumps by a dangerous-looking homeless dude. And what a giant prick move that would have been! The cops would show up and he'd be thrown in the paddy wagon, left to dry out in a cell, only to be swallowed by the penal system, and I'd be haunted by the knowledge I'd handed the poor guy over to the mercy of an institution that's been ridden with racial bias since the Mounties served the Cree Sir John A. Macdonald's eviction notice. Calling the cops just didn't seem right. Besides, shallow showbiz act that I am . . . Verne was a fan!

Another cardinal rule of improv is to always contribute—always offer something up to your fellow performer. It doesn't have to be perfect, so goes the theory, because once you make honest choices, there are no mistakes, only happy accidents. Right. Tell me another one.

Verne returned, grinning widely, and got in.

"I can't believe I'm driving to Leduc with a rock 'n' roll star from the radio," he said, getting into the back seat.

I pulled out of the station.

"I'm not a rock 'n' roll star. I'm a comedian. And it wasn't radio. I was on TV," I corrected . . . again.

"If you say so," he said and settled in for the drive.

It's one thing to know that Canada's Indian Act is a draconian document of colonial oppression responsible for the cultural genocide perpetrated by the paternalistic mandate of successive governments upon generations of Indigenous peoples. It's something else entirely to have a casualty of that patriarchy sitting in the back seat of your car, eating cashews whose chewed bits are hitting the back of your neck as he slaps the sides of his head, yelling, "I fucked up!"

On a canoe trip down the Nahanni River several summers ago, I met an enlightened couple from Pemberton, British Columbia, whose family had farmed eight hundred acres for several generations, not far from the affluent and internationally renowned ski resort of Whistler. The property was also close to a First Nations reserve suffering under squalid conditions, and this farmer employed as many of the residents as he could, making a point to give a lift to any he saw hitchhiking. "It's my contribution to reconciliation. It's every Canadian's moral duty to do what they can if given an opportunity," he said. Maybe giving Verne a lift was mine.

Canada's Truth and Reconciliation Commission has made Canadians aware of the generational impact our nation's unforgivably cruel residential school system has had on Indigenous people. Not many know the civil servant responsible for its implementation, though: Duncan Campbell Scott.

We like to think that the infamous Nazi war criminal Adolf Eichmann was the prototype of the cold-hearted bureaucrat who, with a total lack of conscience but a great degree of diabolical efficiency, orchestrated Hitler's "final solution to the Jewish problem." He personified, in the words of Hannah Arendt, "the banality of evil." Scott, on the other hand, never had that clipped German accent we heard watching every World War II movie growing up. As a kid, no fear was more primal than watching an SS officer demand to see "your papers!" That archetype has conditioned us to believe the Nazi evil was Germany's alone.

Well, Scott, as Canada's deputy superintendent of Indian affairs, had Eichmann beat with a chilling level of foreshadowing by thirty-five years. Ottawa-born Scott may not have performed his duties with an arrogant Prussian accent, but the darkness of the mandate was exactly the same. Check out this quote of Scott's from 1910:

> "It is readily acknowledged that Indian children lose their natural resistance to illness by habituating so closely in the residential schools and that they die at a much higher rate than in their villages. But this alone does not justify a change in the policy of

this Department, which is geared towards a final solution of our Indian Problem."

Gripping the wheel hard, I concentrated my energy on keeping the conversation on an even keel. The man who delivered a plaintive appeal at the service station had been replaced by one racked with confusion, sobs, torment and anger, whose stories veered into the fantastical. I stickhandled my way through our conversation, never knowing what comments might trigger the wrong reaction. Our ride was a high-wire act strung across the cultural divide between different worlds. I tried to find a common denominator.

"How about a few tunes?" I offered.

"Sure. Got any Doors? I played the Doors all the time in my DJ days."

"You were you a DJ?"

"At Brigham Young University," he said. "I was a Sixties Scoop kid. Ever hear of that?" In fact, I had. When Canada began dismantling the residential school system in the late 1950s, the practice of snatching Aboriginal children from their families didn't end with it.

The Canadian Encyclopedia explains:

"[A]mendments to the Indian Act gave the provinces jurisdiction over Indigenous child welfare (Section 88) where none existed federally. By the 1960s, after nearly a century living under draconian and devastating federal policies, such as the Indian Act and residential schools, many Indigenous communities—particularly those living on-reserve—were rampant with poverty, high death rates and socio-economic barriers. With no additional financial resources, provincial agencies in 1951 inherited a litany of issues surrounding children and child welfare in Indigenous communities. With many communities under-serviced, under-resourced and under the control of the Indian Act, provincial child welfare agencies chose to remove children from their homes rather than provide community resources and supports."

Justified on the grounds of child neglect, instead of the true cause—poverty—up to twenty thousand children were taken from their families by government fiat and placed in foster homes to be raised by white people across North America, some of them sent as far away as New Zealand. Verne was one of those taken, and he ended up with a Mormon family in Utah.

"Yes. I was scooped. The Canadian government did that to me."

"I'm sorry."

"Whatever, though, eh? My Mormon father was really nice. So were my brothers and sisters. But they weren't my real family; my Indian family." With a yell, his mood shifted again.

"Hey, buddy, are you gonna play some Doors or what?"

Verne started to cry, filling the car with great, racking sobs that I most definitely did not have the skills to address in a confined space moving at 120 klicks.

"Don't cry, Verne. I'll find the Doors," I said, as I began to frantically scroll through my iPhone, secretly hoping I'd get stopped for distracted driving so the cops I didn't phone at the service station would appear and save me from what I was now thinking was a really stupid decision.

"I can't believe I fucked up! Hugh got me a good job at the community centre and everything. Hugh is a good man. He's my buddy. I gotta get in touch with Hugh to see what happened to my car keys and my wallet. I just can't remember his fuckin' phone number."

As if to loosen the number, Verne smacked his head—and more

cashews shot out of his mouth. Verne's flying cashews were starting to remind me of Uncle Ronald's flying peas, and for a second I wondered if anyone had ever given *him* a lift when he needed one.

Having a change of mind at this juncture of the drive was clearly a moot point. Nevertheless, my faith in the validity of Verne's tale had lapsed when, instead of seeing a vulnerable man down on his luck, I now saw a wily survivor of the mean streets who had cleverly played this gullible tool for a fool.

I found a Doors song: "Riders on the Storm."

Can't have that! No need to be singing along to that catchy lyric about a "killer on the road whose brain is squirming like a toad." I tell myself it's just my imagination working overtime. Verne's not going to whack me; he's just pissed off he can't find his car keys. I've been there. I just wish he'd eat with his mouth closed and stop spitting cashews on the back of my neck.

Indigenous activists, leaders and authors all confirm that the road to reconciliation depends on non-Aboriginals reaching across the racial divide to a people who can rightly claim, as the title of Arthur J. Ray's seminal history of Indigenous habitation in North America says, *I Have Lived Here Since the World Began*. It's a tall order to rectify five hundred years of occupation, but the country has to, or else heartless bastards like Duncan Campbell Scott will have won.

Douglas Knockwood, the revered Mi'kmaq elder and spiritual healer, knew this better than most. After a childhood spent suffering in the Shubenacadie residential school in Nova Scotia, he spent twenty years trying to erase the trauma, first by joining the army and fighting in the Korean War, seeing action on the infamous Hill 677, where seven hundred Canadian and Australian soldiers repelled five thousand Chinese regulars in close hand-to-hand combat. After being discharged, he disappeared into the darkness of Boston's skid row, until the day he stepped into an AA meeting and began wrestling his addiction to submission.

Returning to his Nova Scotia birthplace of Indian Brook, this warrior of the human heart dedicated the rest of his life to leading his people (and whoever else needed help) down the difficult and demanding road to sobriety. By the time he died at eighty-eight years of age, his rehab centres across Canada had helped thousands find freedom from alcohol.

The day I met Knockwood, he was receiving an honorary doctorate from my alma mater, Acadia University. Laugh lines wore deep grooves in his face. Grey hair hung long over his shoulders. His eyes twinkled with a mischievous enthusiasm capable of dissolving the hardest of hearts. I'd never met someone whose joy at being alive was so effusive. This healer of uncontestable achievement hummed with a tangible life force. We shook hands.

"You're that funny guy from TV," he said. "We watch you a lot. Comedy is good medicine."

"You've got to work with what you've been given," I said, "and since my math marks in high school were laughable, I figured I'd stay with what works."

He laughed hard. I congratulated him on his doctorate and the incredible contribution he had made in dedicating his life to helping others. His response was a humble understatement befitting this man of grace and fortitude: "I try and give people a road map to a better life is all, when the one they walk is hard."

"I can't remember my nephew's phone number, either!"

In frustration, Verne punched the headrest of the passenger seat, and I jumped. The car swerved.

"Jesus!"

"Relax," said Verne. "You're too jumpy."

Gripping the wheel harder and pressing my face closer to the dashboard, I thought the next punch, given Verne's agitation, could be upside my head. I was seriously beginning to doubt that the nephew existed. After all, despite only three years' difference in our ages, Verne *did* say he'd been watching me since he was little. Impossible . . . unless I'd guest-starred on *The Friendly Giant* as a three-year-old, which I did not, but that's not to say I didn't want to. It was the CBC's iconic morning show, one that every Canadian-born baby boomer was glued to during their preschool years. For those readers not born to my era (or born to it but raised by wolves who never had a TV), *The Friendly Giant* featured, well, a giant. He wasn't a real giant, though, just a guy in a costume who played a recorder and conversed with Jerome, a talking giraffe whose buddy, Rusty the Rooster, lived in a bag nailed to the castle wall. And they wondered why my generation did mind-altering drugs!

Right now, I was wishing I'd played a shrink on TV so I could use some second-hand psychology skills I might have picked up in the role to calm Verne down. Unfortunately, all I had to work with were very dormant improv skills. Comedy has its limitations in the real world. I realized I hadn't been breathing. That would help.

"When I can't remember a phone number, I start doing something else and eventually it pops in my head," I suggested.

"Do something else?" said Verne. "I'm sitting in a car. What else can I do? I was doing something when I was eating cashews, but they're all gone."

Not all *gone*, I thought. *Half the bag is still stuck to the back of my neck.*

Then I made a choice—a strong choice, I figured. One that would move the scene forward and hopefully take Verne to a calmer place where he didn't want to punch things. So, on this sunny spring day, surrounded by a waking Earth freed from winter's grip, I decided to extol the virtues of the country I've had the good fortune to embrace, while stringing my trapline from coast to coast across the peaceable kingdom whose benevolent ways and standard of living are the envy of the world.

"What a day we're having, Verne! God, I love touring Canada!"

"Love Canada? *Love Canada?!*" And that's when Verne, his lips twisted in a hateful grimace, launched half his body over the back seat and growled in my ear, "Have you ever woken up an Indian?"

Not the reaction I'd been hoping for.

I wished Viola Spolin had been in the car with me now. So much for improvisational theatre and its bogus promise that there's no such thing as a bad choice, only happy accidents. Happy accident, my ass! Given the head-on collision that was Verne's reaction to my choice, it's a wonder the car's airbag didn't explode.

In improv, a location, a situation, an emotion and a profession are the only components you're given to construct a reality. In the current scene that I was trying to orchestrate to its happy conclusion, a lone cast member might introduce it to the audience by saying something like, "Based on your suggestions, we now take you to a very scared comedian's rental car on a highway in Alberta."

Have you ever woken up an Indian?

How could I answer that? That one question contained the full weight of Canada's treatment of Verne's people and our complicity in it. The systemic racism; the never-ending battle over land claims; the hundreds of places like Grassy Narrows, where the only ones who ever pay for the corporate malfeasance are the poisoned; the 1,400 cases of missing and murdered Indigenous women our government promised to solve and hasn't; the high rate of teenage suicide in dead-end boreal gulags strung along the treeline, where clean drinking water is a rumour and tuberculosis is not. You can bet that if brown water were coming out of the taps in some tony corner of Canada, like Westmount, Rosedale, Tuxedo Park or Kitsilano, it would be fixed faster than a horny horse in the Mounties' Musical Ride.

No, I thought, *I've never woken up an Indian and I never will.* I've enjoyed a white man's privilege in a white man's nation. No priest flanked by a couple of Mounties ever snatched me from my mother's arms when I was watching *The Friendly Giant*.

Have you ever woken up an Indian?

The question sat between us with the dead weight of history. How could I ever answer that to his satisfaction without coming off as a patronizing prick? Then I did what every comedian does to defuse a bomb when things get tense. I took a chance and went for the laugh.

"Have I ever woken up an Indian?" I replied. "No. But I *have* given one a lift to Leduc."

Verne's face pulled back. He got that look I spoke of earlier. The one where he squinted one eye and twisted his lips the way you do when you're trying to solve a math problem—or figure out whether the person who just made a joke has done it at your expense, and if they have, where in their face you'll be punching them. The quiet was broken by a thunderclap worthy of heavenly intervention.

"*Ah-hahahahahaha!*" he roared. "That's fuckin' funny! *Bahahahaha!* 'But I *have* given one a lift to Leduc!' Good one! I can't believe I'm driving in a car with a rock 'n' roll star from the radio! This is my lucky day!"

No, Verne, I thought as my sphincter unclenched and I began to breathe again, *it's* my *lucky day, buddy.*

With the music blaring, two men crossed a cultural divide in an Avis rental car, singing "Break on Through (to the Other Side)" while hitting the kind of odious notes that guaranteed neither of us would ever be the front man for a Doors tribute band.

"There's a service station," Verne pointed out. "I gotta take another piss."

We pulled in, and he went inside. I got out of the car to stretch my legs. *I could leave right now*, I thought. *Just pull away.* Anyone would. Things had gotten scary back there. The dude is bent out of shape. He's carrying the kind of weight no amount of singing along to the Doors can lift. Just pull away and leave. But what a douchebag move that would be! Gutless. It would be the height of cruelty. I was embarrassed for even entertaining the thought. Imagining Verne walking out of that pit stop and not seeing my car was a thought I just could not entertain. Besides, if I learned one thing during my days at Second City, it's that you never, *ever* bail on a scene.

Verne ran from the station, shouting. "I remembered my nephew's phone number! Let's go!"

"That's fantastic, Verne," I said, wondering why he was in such a rush.

"It just came to me in there," he said, smiling and ripping into a package of beef jerky sticks.

"I thought you lost your wallet?" I said.

Verne bit into a stick.

"I did," he said with a wink. "Want some jerky?"

I punched into my phone the number Verne gave me. A recording answered.

"Hi. It's me. Eric Buffalo. Leave a message."

With a good three hours left until showtime in Leduc, I decided to drive Verne thirty minutes farther, to his nephew's house in Edmonton. He was lucid now. Happier. Things had turned around. I had a reasonable suspicion he'd been drinking prior to our meeting at the Petro-Can station, but it appeared the drive had sobered him up somewhat. An enthusiasm had lifted his dark spirit. He bobbed around in the back seat, looking out the windows at familiar landmarks.

"See that hospital there? It's where we had our daughter. She's so beautiful. So is her mother. She's a Navajo. Have you ever met a Navajo woman?"

"No," I said.

"You should. And if you marry her, don't fuck it up like I did."

Having forsaken the woman who had my back during many lean years of struggle, I knew what he meant.

"I'm just gonna drink a lot of water and sleep for two days. Did I tell you my brother runs a sweat lodge? He keeps it too hot, though. You're supposed to heal in there, not drop dead," he said laughing.

His life began to spill from him now. All the years estranged from his three children. A passing reference to prison time he waved off with an obvious reluctance for detail. His buddy Hugh, who hired him to work at the community centre way up in Worsley. He remembered *that* phone number, too.

We dialed it. A voice came on the line—a recording sounding measured and sure. Verne's story was true. Like Douglas Knockwood said, some people just need a road map.

As we pulled up beside his nephew's house, a teenage kid on rollerblades was busy stickhandling an orange ball up and down the driveway. Vern got out.

"Hey."

The kid stopped.

"Hey, Uncle."

"Where's Eric?"

"Working at the casino."

"Oh."

I got out of the car. Verne pointed at me.

"Do you know who this is?"

The kid looked at me as if he was supposed to.

"No."

"He's Ron James. A rock 'n' roll star from the radio."

"I'm not a rock 'n' roll star, Verne. I'm a comedian, and I was on TV, not the radio."

"If you say so."

And with that, Verne turned and headed for the house.

Chapter Twelve

WHAT NIETZSCHE SAID

For a comedian used to performing in an intimate club setting, nothing could've prepared me for the first time I stepped on the flagship stage of Just for Laughs International Comedy Festival: the intimidating 1,700-seat Théâtre St-Denis. This was the setting for the televised gala performances the country would be seeing on the CBC the following winter. Your set had to come in at a tight eight minutes, which I always found daunting. Given my long-winded runs, it took me that long just to set up the joke! I guess that's why it took me six failed showcases to make their cut.

My problem was, I always tried to fit in *way* too much content. I was always too far down the road before the words got out. The performance was too frenetic. Marry my overtly Canadian content to that kind of energy, and it's clear why a critic once called me "Stephen Leacock on Benzedrine." Bull's eye! You'll get no argument here.

Watching some of those earlier sets, it's a wonder I didn't self-combust. I never gave myself time to enjoy the moment. It took until

2009, after a substantial ten-year learning curve, to deliver a set at the Théâtre St-Denis that pleased me as much as the audience. Being comfortable in my own skin on *their* stage had everything to do with learning to be comfortable in *mine*.

Every comedian has their own way of getting in the zone. Lining up the night's script from end to end on three banquet tables in my dressing room helped me. Touring with Shantero Productions provided this luxury, allowing me the time alone backstage to visualize the performance to come without interruption. Getting your pre-show game face on right is imperative. But no such luxury existed at comedy festivals. Whether Montreal, Winnipeg or Halifax, during those pressure-packed nights you'd be in the company of a dozen other comedians strung tripwire taut, pacing a backstage electric with tension. It was absolutely necessary to do time in those trenches, but once I found a way of working that suited me, I stayed with it. Performing back-to-back dates nurtured a confidence that allowed me to deliver the kind of show I'd been trying to grow into: one where the rhythm of words and respect for language painted a picture that worked in tandem with the joke. Eventually, my previously frenetic stage energy was replaced with a comfort level onstage which allowed for pauses and the content that I'd worked so hard to craft to finally breathe.

The first five CBC specials helped tremendously as well. Having to deliver a new one-hour special each year, along with the subsequent shooting and editing of them, provided an exponential leap in my learning curve. During the shooting of *Quest for the West* (the second, and my favourite, of the first five regionally themed specials) at the Jack Singer Concert Hall in Calgary, I received this note from network executive Anton Leo: "Don't forget to have fun. Even if you're not, look like you are." That advice was a definitive turning point. Prior to that special, I approached every live performance with the aggressive energy of a boxer about to enter the ring. With seven cameras, a packed house and eighty pages of script memorized, I was literally going from the page to the stage. Thanks to that note, I did have fun that night, and it changed my approach forever.

Anything worth doing well takes time, and in this particular craft, as George Carlin once said, it's "stage time, stage time, stage time." *That* is fundamental. Becoming competent in anything demands repetition. Just as the first hammer a carpenter picks up doesn't build him a mansion, neither does a comedian's first great set land him a television special. You have to fail first . . . and fail repeatedly.

The adage "That which does not kill us makes us stronger" comes from the pen of the nineteenth-century German philosopher Friedrich Nietzsche. He also said, "These shoes feel too tight in the toe, Herr Klinghoffer," but that quote never stuck. It clearly lacked the gravitas to warrant a place in the zeitgeist.

Why? Because innocuous comments have a short shelf life. To last, a comment has to *say* something. On the other hand, sage wisdom, with its Windexed clarity into the human soul, never has a best-before date. (I'm pretty sure "Windexed" is not a verb but as I've said before, "What odds?" It's my book.)

A good joke lacks an expiry date, too. Certain ones stand the test of time. "They smoke in Quebec like it's a cure for cancer" happens to be one of mine.

Sometimes you work hard for a good joke. Its gestation period can be as long as a blue whale's, rolling and lolling in the amniotic fluid of your brainpan until its eventual birth. At other times, a joke is born standing up, with strong legs that will last a lifetime. It will also provide, for its creator, a definitive memory of the moment it stepped into this world.

For instance, while driving back to Nova Scotia one summer, I happened to miss the turn-off to the Champlain Bridge in Montreal and decided I'd stay in Old Quebec, three hours farther east instead. I remember feeling fine about my oversight and not bothered in the least. After all, it was July and I was bound for Canada's Ocean Playground, whose waters wouldn't warm up enough for a five-minute swim until the last Saturday in August anyway, so why rush?

I imagined waking to the smell of fresh croissants in a charming eighteenth-century hotel overlooking the Plains of Abraham, where General Wolfe met his maker, General Montcalm met his match *and* his maker, France got the boot, and Britain got the continent. Once up and about, I'd pick up a copy of *Le Devoir*, then kick myself for never having learned French beyond *ouvre la porte*, grab a cappuccino to go and hit the road.

And it would have been nice, had I not missed the turnoff to Quebec City as well. That's because I was listening to an audiobook read by a Buddhist scholar who was telling me how to "stay in the moment," and I forgot to . . . but mostly because I have a PhD in ADHD that hadn't been diagnosed yet.

Pushing well past a reasonable hour to still be at the wheel, I drove onward and stopped for the night in Sainte-Anne-de-Beaupré. This corner of La Belle Province is home to an infamous Roman Catholic basilica named for St. Anne, grandmother of Jesus and patron saint of sailors, that attracts devout pilgrims from all over the world who come to worship at this place of recorded miracles. Had I known back then I'd drawn a genetic card for ADHD, I could have dropped some coin in the plate, lit a candle and prayed for some divine deliverance— but I'm a lapsed Anglican, and saints don't smile on the heathen.

The original recipient of St. Anne's benevolence was an arthritic local stonemason, Louis Guimond, in 1658. (I'm not sure why the stonemason received St. Anne's first miracle when it's sailors she's fond of, but such points are lost to history.) Apparently, after laying three stones for the foundation, Louis was miraculously cured of his affliction, and immediately went from walking with the posture of a peddler carrying a kingdom's worth of bricks on his back to exhibiting the agile grace of a man who just scarfed a mittful of extra-strength Robaxacet and downed a couple tequila shooters.

That's not why I stopped in Sainte-Anne, though. I stopped because, after ten straight hours on the road, my eyes wouldn't stay open, and I've heard that's bad for driving.

There was only one motel with a vacancy sign, and when I entered the lobby, it was clear why. It was a hole. This wasn't a chain motel. No lucky franchisee had a piece of this action. I felt sticky just standing there.

A bell sat on the counter. I rang it. Five minutes later, the proprietor appeared, rubbing his sleep-crusted eyes. He was a short troll of a man wearing boxer shorts and a wifebeater undershirt who grunted at me in a surly Gaspé patois known only to him and three Franciscan friars from Opus Dei. You'd get a warmer welcome at a halfway house. Thankfully, he had manners enough to scratch his nuts with his left hand as he passed me the room key with his right.

I turned on my heel and headed across the parking lot. Opening the door to my room, I entered a twenty-by-twenty-foot hovel, rank with the smell of stale tobacco and carnal sin, where truck-stop hookers no doubt turned their tricks and Rock Machine enforcers broke thumbs of opponents. In this tiny room sat seven ashtrays. *Seven!* On the bureau, on the nightstand beside the bed, on the toilet, beside the broken TV, the sink and even the tub. That's when I wrote the joke, "They smoke in Quebec like it's a cure for cancer."

Where was I? Right. My trip to Edinburgh in 1996.

After a short but successful run in Toronto and a national CBC radio broadcast of that one-man show I'd written, I naively decided to perform at the most competitive fringe festival in the world.

The minute my feet hit Scottish soil, I started to doubt the intelligence of my choice. The flight attendant had graciously given me a full bottle of Scotch on the plane, saying, "I've seen you many times at the Laugh Resort in Toronto. You always kill! You'll do great over here. Great!"

(In its prime, the Laugh Resort was a great comedy club. With a seating capacity of 175, it catered to a wide demographic and was home to an accomplished and supportive community of comedians. Each brought to their craft a definitive point of view and a style that was all their own. Along with the pugnacious Tim Steeves, comedy lifer Simon Rakoff, LGBTQ trailblazer Elvira Kurt, the indomitable Harry Doupe, thrice-published novelist and former fighter pilot Barry Kennedy, multiple-award–winning writer Mark Farrell, and the irascible Irish rebel, stalwart friend and creative collaborator, Ottawa-born Chris Finn—who, like Tim and Mark, would write for *This Hour Has 22 Minutes* and *Rick Mercer Report*—the club also hosted the likes of Ray Romano, Louis C.K., Rich Hall, Kevin James and Ellen DeGeneres. This club was instrumental in revitalizing my comedic mojo. After hitting the wall in Los Angeles and souring on the fleeting rewards of improvisational theatre, at thirty-six I'd finally found the place I felt I belonged. People say improv and stand-up are similar. Not. At. All. An improvisational comedy troupe is closer to half a dozen Bolsheviks trying to decide the colour of a tractor on a communist farm, while stand-up is an enlightened dictatorship.)

A full bottle of Scotch! Bonus! Great Scotch, too, it was. Scotch distilled in the sacred, peat-sweet waters of Islay that Merlin the Wizard was baptized in.

For some reason lost to time, we disembarked not by the usual walkway leading directly into the airport, the one that ground crews attach to the plane upon landing, but the old-fashioned way, down a set of stairs they'd rolled to the door of the plane, leading to the tarmac. Soon as the doors opened, I thought we'd landed in Ecuador. Scotland was in the throes of an unholy heat wave, and a country synonymous with flushed faces and short tempers was living up to the stereotype. I saw two baggage handlers arguing in the guttural tongue of my forefathers and thought, *I bet this is what Robbie Burns sounded like drunk.*

As I turned to look, the bottle of Scotch I'd irresponsibly tucked between my chest and right arm slipped from its grip and, falling to the ground in slow motion, violently exploded at my feet. The baggage handlers saw it too, and for a moment a look of pity crossed their clinically sunburned faces, then they turned back to poking each other in the chest and cursing.

First step I took on Scottish soil and my free bottle of single malt was bleeding out in a puddle of amber liquid on the hot tarmac. This was the kind of omen that would have turned an Iron Age army back. Not me. I was here for a three-week run.

The opportunity to play the fest had arrived in a roundabout way. The artistic director of a small theatre in Toronto (where I'd originally performed *Up and Down in Shaky Town)* offered me a 50 percent discount on a performance space in Edinburgh after a cancellation by a troupe of actors who'd placed a $5,000 down payment. They'd cancelled because they couldn't afford flights for their cast of twenty-five. That's right: *twenty-five* actors. Not sure what kind of scratch those thespians would pull down from a night's performance, but I'm willing to wager none was eating pheasant under glass after the gig. I understand that suffering for your art is noble, but starving for it was never in my wheelhouse, especially with my squirrelly metabolism. (If I don't eat every two hours, my blood sugar goes squirrelly and I'm taking hostages.)

Scrounging up a rogue five thousand dollars, I matched what was already deposited, bought a plane ticket and, like the architects of the ill-fated landing at Dieppe in 1942, girded myself for battle, blind to the possibility of failure. Plus, along with the theatre space came the troupe's substitute stage manager. I assumed he'd be a professional— say, someone who could co-ordinate elementary lighting and sound cues. Simple. Not advanced calculus. Not transplanting the living brain of an ocelot into a rhesus monkey. It turned out, though, that he was slumming in the theatre as a hobby.

A *hobby*? A hobby involves airplane glue and a model kit, doesn't it? Or singing in a barbershop quartet. Hunting. Gardening. Train sets. Needlepoint. *Those* are hobbies. Stage managing is *not* a hobby.

Maybe he saw it as an opportunity for employment after graduating with a PhD in his chosen field of folklore. *There's* money well spent. What do you do with a degree in folklore? Unless there's a paying gig somewhere for a translator fluent in the Elvin tongues of

Tolkien, I expect the best option with a folklore degree *is* stage-managing for a twenty-five-person cast who aren't making a living, either.

Someone in charge of the University of Edinburgh's real estate department saw an opportunity for a quick cash grab by renting mothballed study halls to festival productions. The troupe had rented an ancient study hall with seventy-five seats that reeked of the gloom of the tomb. I'll wager good money the last time the doors were opened John Locke was in there, writing a mid-term.

However, over on the other side of town it was another story. There, the brightly lit flagship theatres such as Assembly Hall and the Gilded Balloon were festooned with banners of beer sponsors that catered to round-the-block lineups for sold-out performances every single night. No ghostly stench of eighteenth-century cholera victims in those theatres. No, sir. They were filled with joyful, chortling patrons come to laugh the night away, happily quaffing pints of Stella Artois while nibbling bags of haggis-flavoured crisps.

These beautiful venues were featured in the glossy tome of a program that provided biographies, places, dates and times for all performances. Every festival patron carried a copy under their arm. Those programs stood in stacks at every newsstand, restaurant and bar. It was the bible of the festival. Every performer needed to be in *this* program in order to be seen. I was not in it. I was in another one. I was in the program nobody saw, and if they did, never used.

My contact in Edinburgh, the person who'd been hired by the troupe to ensure the details of my show made it into the main program, was a small, ferret-faced grifter who, I would later learn, had done time for petty fraud. I mailed him all my materials from Toronto well ahead of the deadline, but he missed it. Perhaps he had to meet his parole officer that day? Maybe he was at the greyhound races, or forging old ladies' signatures on stolen cheques? His former criminal status was revealed well into the run and at least went some way toward explaining his trouble with deadlines.

As a result of not being in the real program, my show rarely had more than five paying customers at a time. Sometimes none. Sometimes three. Actually, the average *was* three. It's difficult to get an audience on a roll of laughter when there are barely enough people in the house for a game of backgammon. The presence of a rare dozen paying customers stoked my hope that sales had picked up momentum but I found myself the following evening staring into an empty theatre space looking for laughs but instead hearing echoes.

I recall a particular matinee when the theatre held only a pair of exhausted Fringe-goers, collapsed in their front-row seats. One was asleep, while the other wasn't paying attention. They'd come to see *Waiting for Godot* performed by a Bangladeshi puppet troupe but got the wrong address. Suffering from that thousand-yard stare unique to exhausted festivalgoers, once in my space they stayed put, optimistic that they were about to witness that diamond in the rough everyone hopes to discover among 1,500 Fringe acts. Instead, they were stuck watching a Canadian man's monologue about three years of struggle in Los Angeles, whose words didn't sound remotely close to anything ever written by Samuel Beckett.

The comedy gods had it in for me, and their contempt was righteous. The first morning of rehearsals I'd placed a poster on a sandwich board outside the theatre. Besides featuring the title, it had three different photos of my face each representing a different phase of my three-year sojourn in LA: happy, hair-pulling insanity, and resignation. After two frustrating hours spent trying to co-ordinate lighting cues with someone who should have been back in the folklore faculty club discussing the mating rituals of Rivendell over a pitcher of mead with Bilbo Baggins look-alikes, I stepped outside for some fresh air before I suffered an aneurysm.

Standing beside the poster were a couple of Scottish stagehands having a smoke. One of them pointed his cigarette, and in a brogue thick with matter-of-fact understatement, said, "Aye. Someone's puked on your poster." And indeed, sliding down my middle face was a softball-sized dollop of human honk. The other stagehand looked closer at the poster just to be sure. "Aye. That's puke, all right."

Some wandering inebriant had not the decency to duck into an alleyway for their noontime hurl and decided to aim for my poster instead. Lovely. I wouldn't need to see the Oracle of Delphi to know this run was going to suck.

After the first week I wanted to bolt for home. But quitting was for losers . . . and people who had more money than me. See, I'd arrived on a charter flight, and to buy another ticket at full fare would have exhausted a meagre bank account *and* next month's rent in Toronto. Then why did I even go you ask? All these years later, I know exactly why: I thought I was better than I actually was.

In retrospect, my impetuous decision was clearly due to the conceit of a rookie, not to mention a display of glaring disrespect for a craft that takes a lifetime to master, if one ever does. I'd heard stories about Canadian comedians breaking into Britain and doing well, so why not me? After all, I'd had three good reviews for my one-man show and had served two years in the clubs. Twenty-five years and a thousand gigs later, I find it hard to fathom what bade me hop the pond for Edinburgh. A day of reckoning was due, and mine had started with the busted bottle of free Scotch the day before.

I convinced myself the lack of attendance had nothing to do with my show, but more to do with the inordinate number of attractions in Edinburgh that summer. Besides the monster of a fringe festival which featured everything from a Swahili-speaking Shakespeare company to the sold-out-for-their-entire-run-in-minutes Tokyo Shock Boys, an X-rated acrobatic troupe from Japan that twisted and tumbled from trapeze to trampoline—naked—while shooting lit firecrackers out of their asses, there was a military tattoo in the imposing medieval castle on the hill, an international book fair and a film festival catering to the thousands of tourists choking the cobblestone streets of Old Town, which doubled as the summertime home for every balloon-twisting, stilt-walking, juggling busker from Belgium to Tangmalangaloo. Every street corner was filled with one of them doing something. I watched a rummy take a shit in a hat before I realized it wasn't a show!

Compounding it all was the heat: the insufferable, oppressive, stultifying heat. Air conditioning was non-existent in most places, and chain-smoking was still embraced with enthusiasm in every bar.

One morning after celebrating a three-out-of-five-star review from a national newspaper, *The Independent*, that did nothing to increase my sales, I woke with a five-star hangover. It was one of those head-pounding assaults on the system that gets you making pacts with Jesus. My head felt hydrocephalic and so clinically large, it rivalled a gigantic balloon in the Macy's Thanksgiving Day parade, in need of being held down by metal guy wires.

I've always found the best cure for a hangover (besides not drinking in the first place) is to stretch your legs and walk it off. So, I headed out very gingerly for a saunter downtown on a blistering-hot Sunday afternoon, knowing that beneath my feet were ancient catacombs where befouled and semi-conscious junkies lay in cool repose . . . the lucky bastards. I hoped I might find some shade and rest beneath the branches of a healing willow, but there was nary a tree to be found. The last one in Old Town was chopped down in 1310 to burn a witch.

What there were plenty of on that day the mercury was busy breaking records across Great Britain were bagpipers. In fact, Old Town was choked—from the city square and all the way to the Orkney Islands, I'll bet—with the largest gathering of pipe bands in the free world. Did I mention the bands were tuning up their instruments? We are all familiar with the sound of one bagpipe being played. Given my Maritime upbringing, it was hard to attend any function when I was growing up without hearing "the pipes." From funerals to weddings to hockey games, there was always a kilted piper playing some melancholy lament or goosebump–raising battle hymn written for long-gone rebels marching to slaughter on the fields of Culloden that could stir the hardest of Scottish hearts to pudding. Perhaps you yourself have heard their haunting notes echoing over the hills while summering in the countryside when some local kid but six weeks into lessons decides to break out his pipes and play a whining dirge at close of day? *I hope he's only playing one song*, you think, *because cats screwing on a winter's night sound better than that.*

I think it's one of those instruments that takes quite a bit of time to master.

On the cobblestones of Edinburgh that day, scarlet-faced pipers sweating like the damned swayed in the draconian heat. Every one of them was bedecked in a mind-boggling array of tribal finery and tartan kilts, whose matching sashes were held in place by tribal crests, buckles, pins and sporrans. Some even had the skins of leopards and lion manes draped over their shoulders—peeled, no doubt, from the backs of the big cats during a long-gone empire's supremacy, when Africa was ripe for the plunder.

Some held sceptres and sported daggers stuck in woollen socks, rising knee high from spit-polished boots. The ones who weren't constantly adjusting their bags (their *pipe* bags, that is) were strapped into gigantic drums from chin to crotch and wore on their heads fur hats whose chinstraps were yanked tight as a tourniquet, pinching their volcanically purple heads into stroke-inducing, lock-jawed grimaces. Surely there's a better way to spend a sweltering Sunday afternoon than standing in woollen tartan, laden with forty pounds of tradition, under a blistering sun, watching your buddies take a face plant to the pavement?

Recreation during a summertime heat wave in Canada means cracking a cold one and then jumping in the lake—unless you're in a pipe band, of course. Then, I expect, you're marching under a hellacious hot sun at some meeting-of-the-clans just one B-flat away from heatstroke wishing you'd studied piano.

Struggle provides its own unique epiphanies, and in Edinburgh, I had mine. Besides ripping the guts from the show daily, reworking the running order, punching up jokes, writing new ones and trying my best not to buckle under the soul-sucking weight of rejection, it was imperative that I showcase at whatever open-mike venues existed in town. I hoped the sterling response to the five minutes allotted every performer would have the doors of my venue swinging off the hinges with cheerful crowds of festivalgoers, tired of seeing Japanese acrobats fart exploding firecrackers. One space in particular stood out. Its name was synonymous with that quaint European medieval pastime of turning hungry hounds on baited omnivores: the Bear Pit.

Its stage sat floor-level to the audience and was leered over by a balcony packed to the rafters with drunken revellers who'd come to satiate their blood lust in an arena where bedlam ruled. It had a reputation of being, in the parlance of our trade, "an unforgiving room." That's not to say I hadn't been warned. When I signed up, the festival organizers in charge of booking the place did everything short of draping themselves in garlic before uttering the venue's name, as if protecting their souls from a curse. "The room is very cruel," they whispered. I remember thinking, *It can't be any crueller than someone puking on my poster.*

Yes, it could.

On the evening of the performance I stood at the back of the room, feeling a bad case of amateur-night tongue take hold. Biochemical secretions in the hypothalamus had sent raiding parties of cortisol and adrenalin to hijack my nervous system, sucking my mouth so clean of moisture, I'd have sold my soul for a thimble of spit. The fight-or-flight response had been activated. This early-warning system evolved in the human brain countless millennia ago, when bands of early *Homo sapiens* roamed a cruel and harsh savannah, falling prey to hungry carnivores who stalked, ate and then shat this prey in steaming heaps of scat on lonesome hills beneath the eye of a nameless god. Back in a day when we were dinner, it was best to be aware of your surroundings when you were out picking berries.

My heart was beating deer-in-the-headlights fast as I watched each act ascend the stage and get chewed up alive by that meat-grinder of a crowd. From singers to poets to actors to clowns, each did their time to an accompaniment of catcalls, boos and profanities yelled from the room's dark recesses, until a real warrior of my calling took the stage. He strode through the crowd, and as soon as he hit the spotlight, grabbed that microphone, stared those piss tanks square in the eye and delivered . . . in spades.

It was a Canadian comedian by the name of Mike Wilmot, who has since become a household name in Britain but was an unknown on that sweltering Edinburgh night twenty-five years ago. Watching him *own* that room of ornery, raucous liquor pigs stood as a shining example of what I was not: fearless.

It would take several years before I'd be able to work a room with the level of confidence I'd just witnessed in Wilmot. Breaking the imaginary fourth wall, so sacred in theatre, is paramount in stand-up. Separation is not the goal; integration is. Moving fluidly from scripted set to spontaneous, off-the-cuff improvisation creates a symbiotic—and, most importantly, *personal*—relationship between the act and an audience. Harold Pinter didn't work his pauses into a play so an actor could randomly go off script and start riffing with the room. Stand-up, on the other hand, encourages that. It's why it's such an unusual art form. Stand-up is a metaphysical tennis match, where the serve is the joke, and its return the laughter. Each cannot exist without the other. A play can exist whether or not the audience is entertained. Stand-up comedy, on the other hand, exists only *with* laughter; otherwise, you're Rupert Pupkin in his mother's basement.

Following Wilmot is something few seasoned veterans would willingly do even today, but that night, I was next. Never one to tolerate the pretensions of the one-man show with its musical cues and lighting effects, this battle-hardened hit man of the smoke-choked club circuit uttered nary a word as he left the stage to explosive applause. He walked past, wearing the war face of a comedian who's just killed, knowing he's left nothing but slippery viscera on that stage.

Still held captive to the script, and not yet skilled enough on my feet to link the best jokes from the show into a litany of one-liners, get my laughs and get off, I opened with the first paragraph of *Shaky Town*. In a one-person show, you set the tone for the story to come, but here, in this asylum, that decision merely stirred the rage of the inmates.

I began with the earnest delivery Toronto critics had praised me for: "Three years ago with family in tow, I hopped a 747 Conestoga wagon to follow well-worn trails of the jet stream west, like so many other beaming pilgrims before me . . ."

I heard a rustling from the balcony, as though grumpy trolls were waking from an afternoon nap.

". . . we settled on the Western edge of a vast and mythic valley in the City of Angels whose inhabitants felt immune from the ravages of time. It was a pistol-packing Brigadoon . . ."

And then it came, a bellow from the balcony's recess: "Who gives a fuck?!"

Soldiers in a firefight see the world around them move in slow motion. So it was for me as I watched a can of beer sail from the balcony over the audience's heads some and land on that small stage, where it splashed its contents all over my feet. I'd barely had enough time to admire the thrower's accuracy when a loud voice worthy of Luciano Pavarotti bellowed, "You suck!" The crowd took its cue, and in unison began their chant: "You suck! You suck! You suck!" I remember thinking, *Sweet Jesus. I'm here for three weeks.*

Nietzsche definitely had a point.

If you're questioning whether or not Canada is still two solitudes as literary lion Hugh MacLennan so aptly depicted it in his classic 1951 novel of the same name, a night spent watching French comedy at Just for Laughs (*Juste pour rire*) will allay those doubts for good. Québécois comedy is orchestrated insanity. Traditional joke structure is thrown out the window. The French like their comedy loud, zany, prop-heavy and verging on bedlam.

I followed one of the more famous French prop acts once during a corporate show in a convention centre ballroom filled with every Toyota dealer in Canada. About a dozen Japanese executives who'd flown in from Kyoto were seated in the front row, wearing headphones for translation purposes. For the French act they were about to see none were needed, because that act could be universally appreciated from Uzbekistan to Kuala Lumpur: a man wearing a fluorescent orange flight suit *covered* in fifty-seven old-fashioned bicycle horns, on which he played Tchaikovsky's *1812 Overture* . . . while riding a unicycle. How do you follow that?

I didn't have to worry because . . . it wasn't his closer! For that *coup de grâce*, he wriggled into a giant yellow prophylactic, inflated it with an air pump, held the neck closed from inside, then bounced around the stage in his balloon. I watched hopelessly from the wings as the Toyota executives were overcome with laughter, providing him with a level of tectonic applause a comedian following a prop act never wants to hear. By the time I finished my act, they were still laughing . . . at him.

The late, great comedian Mike MacDonald used to tell a story about opening for West Coast militant vegan and musician Bryan Adams. Mike had booked the gig six months prior, when Adams was an unknown. Standing backstage the night of the gig, hearing fifteen thousand people chanting, "We want *Bry*-an! We want *Bry*-an!" made it very clear to Mike that Bryan was now most definitely very *much* known. As the chanting rose to a deafening roar, a grizzled old janitor who'd seen it all tapped Mike on the arm and said, "I hope Bryan's *your* name."

I crossed paths with this trail-blazing icon one Winnipeg winter's night at Rumor's Comedy Club. Mike's two-week headlining run was starting just as mine was wrapping up. I'd first seen this comedian of legendary prowess in 1980, during his incendiary prime, at the original Yuk Yuk's location on Bay Street in Toronto. I was struck by his conviction and confidence standing alone in the spotlight, watching him channel the anger that fuels our funny into a cohesive piece of killer comedy.

That was around the first time I'd ever signed up for an amateur night. I was doing a nerd character at the time, born during those heenie-headed hot-knife sessions in the shadow of Blomidon, when brothers from another day inspired a faith that my funny might one day pay. Playing a character covers you in a sheath of armour that straight stand-up never does. After eight minutes, I stepped off that stage to enthusiastic applause. I was invited to a local diner with Mike and several other comics afterwards and made the mistake of making a joke. No one laughed.

Mike turned to me and said, "You have to be here a year before you're allowed to make a joke." By the reaction of those other comedians, he meant it. About to take a bite of his sandwich, he caught himself in mid-thought, turned back to me and said, "By the way. What I just saw you do was the birth of the Beatles." Then he went back to eating his sandwich and never said another word.

I went back the next week and bombed. Miserably. Then a few more Mondays in a row after that and bombed some more. I never had the guts to suffer the quiet that the learning curve calls for at that stage of a career. Folding up my tent after six weeks' effort, I headed for Second City's improv classes, never going near a stand-up stage again for another fifteen years.

I didn't see Mike again until I had a few years under my belt in the clubs. I mustered the guts to ask this battle-hardened veteran if he'd watch and critique my set. He obliged. I'd hear his unmistakable laugh from the back of the room. More a caw than a guffaw, and it seemed to escape reluctantly from his chest despite himself. But when it did, I knew I was on to something real and right.

When my set was over and the audience gone, we sat at a table in the empty club. With the owner, Ross Rumberg, perched gargoyle-silent beside us, this supposedly hard-headed taskmaster who did not suffer fools—this stellar comedian of ferocious talent, bedevilled by clinical haunts compounded by an American dream unrealized, who, at the peak of his powers, delivered such room-destroying, incendiary sets they're burned into the retinas of every comic who witnessed them—patiently delivered what were, hands down, two hours of the best notes I've ever received. Don't get me wrong: it's not like the Mormon Tabernacle Choir backed them up with stirring harmonies. When that obsidian-sharp comedic mind of his got down to business, I was bleeding! With a reformed addict's respect for a higher power, Mike fought the black dog with GlaxoSmithKline as his wingman, continuing to mine the terrain where comedy gold might lie while marshalling an iron will in pursuit of it.

The fact this skilled road warrior of exemplary pedigree and perseverance took the time to show a greenhorn during his first foray in-country where to ford the river, stands as testimony to his generosity. In an arena the uninitiated consider cutthroat, Mike personified everything but.

He passed far too soon and remains, for me, a totemic figure in Canada's comedic pantheon.

When it comes to giants, the biggest reward of performing at JFL was, hands down, being in the company of them. The card I drew for that boon was the "Merchant of Venom" himself, Don Rickles.

"Mr. Warmth" hosted the Théâtre St-Denis gala I took part in along with half a dozen other acts in 2003. With that jovial bulldog of a noggin poking out of a tailored tuxedo, Rickles entered the theatre to a host of trumpets playing theme music worthy of a matador's entrance to the bull ring, and with his arms spread wide, he drank in the spontaneous, rapturous applause.

This comic god, World War II navy veteran, pal of Sinatra, bang-the-table, funny-as-hell Dean Martin roast guest and Johnny Carson favourite, who honed his craft in the clubs of 1960s Las Vegas playing to pug-nosed wise guys come looking for laughs after dumping a body in the desert, was seventy-five years old at the time and absolutely *owning* that room . . . and he hadn't yet said a word.

Gathered round the monitors backstage with the other comics, I stood slack-jawed with admiration. My mind drifted back to that night on the ninth floor of Crowell Tower at Acadia University in 1976, when half a dozen of us were losing our minds watching this free-form wizard put Frank Sinatra in stitches on Carson's *Tonight Show*.

It's a classic bit. On those days when gravity seems to be pulling harder than usual and the mid-winter blues have your spirit pinned to the mat, do yourself a favour and Google this clip: "Rickles/ Sinatra/Carson 1976."

Rickles walks onto Johnny's set unannounced, surprising Frank. He takes his applause, crosses to the Chairman of the Board, takes a knee—as one would in front of any mafia don—then . . . kisses his ring. That's the set-up. Frank yanks his hand away, laughing. Taking a seat beside a man whose underworld connections were never a secret, Rickles leans in and says, "Marco Mongonanzo was hurt. Fumbino Bombatso . . ."—he puts a finger against his temple—"two bullets in the head . . . Thursday."

Sinatra loses it with laughter, just like we did that night in university and again in Montreal, standing round the TV monitors backstage, watching Rickles claim his place.

When it was our turn to work, he gave everyone an excellent off-the-cuff introduction, and although I don't remember the content of it, I certainly remember his reaction after my set was finished. I'd done a bit about camping beside some Germans: "Camping's fun . . . in the daytime. But soon as the sun goes down, everything that eats meat wakes up. I was pretty safe, though. I camped beside some Germans. God love 'em, but their accent will scare off anything." Then I launched into shamelessly stereotypical World War II–movie German, building into a crescendo worthy of the Führer wrapping up a tight set at Nuremberg. Then I tagged the bit with "and they were only trying to set the tent up." Rickles came right up to me, grinning that trademark grin, and said, "Great set, kid."

I was stunned. *Stunned.* My hero had just complimented my work. He grabbed me by the shoulders and stared me square in the eyes, comic to comic. "I never got my first break in show business until I was thirty-eight." I assumed he was insinuating we shared the same trajectory, and it was only a matter of time before I, too, would have my breakout role as he did with *Kelly's Heroes.*

"How old are ya?" he asked.

"Forty-two."

Without missing a beat, his smile morphed into a face you'd use to greet a widow at a closed casket. With eyes full of pity, he gently slapped the side of my cheek, saying, "You're finished," and then walked away.

Eh? Complimented *and* burned by Don Rickles in under thirty seconds. Pretty sweet.

That night, he generously signed my Just for Laughs poster and wrote, "Funny is as funny does, and you are." That's what I remember the most about JFL. Being able to see and sometimes meet the best acts of our generation. Whenever the road got old, and it certainly did, I reminded myself that Don Rickles let me know I chose the right one to roam.

Even though most professional comedians have been performing stand-up for a lifetime, there's still the occasional set that sends you right back to amateur night. We owe that experience to the Faustian bargain of the much-wanted, well-paying 'corporate gig.'

Ninety-five percent of the time, the suits are a great audience. Having made a company or organization laugh, you were in and out in an hour with five times the scratch in your pocket that you were normally paid. Oh, and it always helped if the clients weren't too rich. Rich people hate to give up status, and the comedian needs that investment in order to get laughs. A recognition of your own imperfections helps, too, but no one ever got rich thinking they weren't the smartest one in the room.

Certain professions are tough. Lawyers are the worst. I once did a benefit at Osgoode Hall in an ornate room full of high-rolling Toronto barristers, raising money for cystic fibrosis. Never took a dime for the gig, and in forty minutes, I never got a laugh, either. A $750-an-hour legal assassin came up to me afterwards and said, "You were funny, but we're lawyers. We laugh on the inside." I bet. Especially when you're crucifying some poor bastard for every nickel they're worth.

Lesson learned: no good deed goes unpunished.

Once you sign on the dotted line, they've got you. Corporate gigs have simple rules: no political content, no religious material and no sex jokes. So, you follow the rules, play it safe and pay the mortgage, just like people do in the real world, even though not wanting to toe the company line in the real world is what made you become a stand-up in the first place. In my experience, the sweeter-sounding the corporate booking, the higher the price that is paid in self-worth. And when corporate gigs go south, they do so in spectacular fashion.

I once had a gig in Cancún, where a company had flown their five hundred managers. You rarely get the opportunity to do the same quality of act for a corporate crowd that real fans pay to see in theatres, because the businesspeople you're performing for never dropped a penny to see you—their entertainment committee did, hoping the same performance they might have seen on TV or in a packed thousand-seater will be effortlessly replicated. In Cancún, though, it proved hard to recreate that magic in a cement-walled echo chamber on a night sticky with humidity, in which I fought to be heard over the eight gigantic fans blaring inside and the Yucatán surf crashing outside.

Over half a dozen planeloads of audience, who'd come from different towns and cities all across Canada, had suffered a fierce bitch-slapping at thirty thousand feet, battling stratospheric winter storms trying to get there and by now were punchy, hungry, exhausted and cranky. Not the ideal conditions for comedy. All they wanted was a tequila-fused cocktail, and sleep. The last thing they wanted was to sit through an hour of stand-up.

Besides being funny, a comedian needs a few simple things to succeed. Steve Martin noted in his stellar autobiography, *Born Standing Up: A Comedian's Life*, that "distraction is the death of comedy." The man must have done a few corporate gigs. All you want is an audience to see and hear you with no interruptions. Simple. It's hard to accomplish that when there's a five-foot ice sculpture of a prancing unicorn blocking the view of the stage you're standing on, and a microphone from a karaoke machine plugged into a scratchy sound system.

Getting laughs from a corporate crowd hasn't changed since the Middle Ages. That's when someone in authority saw the local Fool standing on his stool during market day, doing a tight ten minutes on the price of turnips, and whisked him up from the muddy street to perform for the lord and lady of the manor. If he killed, he'd get a bath, be fed cabbage soup and kept as a halfwit stable pet for their amusement during dinner parties. A definite perk, considering his life up to that point amounted to sleeping in a dry corner of the moat on a bed of urine-soaked straw.

Stepping onstage, I knew the night would be a challenge when I noticed everyone in the first two rows had their backs to me, while the remainder of the room were walking around, chatting. The first few opening jokes dropped stone-dead fast to the floor. I launched quickly into the heavy artillery and surefire road-honed gold that had been killing in every venue I'd just played on tour, that I naturally assumed would surely win them over in the vast cinderblock warehouse of a room I couldn't stop imagining as a temporary morgue during a natural disaster. Much to my surprise, the material elicited the same reaction I'd have received *were* the floor actually covered in corpses. There was absolutely no way to corral this audience into a cohesive whole, where they'd laugh en masse as one living, breathing entity—the way people do when they actually *want* to see you.

All the moisture in my mouth fled to my palms. The professional act I prided myself on delivering to paying audiences was dangerously close to taking a dark turn. I was but a synapse away from turning on the audience, the stage, the company and even the country of Mexico itself by launching into a profane and unprofessional tirade that would have made the darkest devils in the bullring of Hell blush.

But I didn't. Why? Because no matter the vicissitudes of a room filled with an audience who did not give a rat's ass whether I did my act or set my balls on fire, I "screwed my courage to the sticking-place," to quote the Bard, and as every comedian does who is getting paid, *I . . . did . . . my . . . time.*

When I was done, there was no applause. I heard a woman say, "Thank God he's done."

I couldn't agree more.

Then there's a once-in-a-lifetime gig that places you in the middle of a maelstrom.

One day in 2008, I emceed a party for the 99th Grey Cup and the Canadian Football League Alumni Association. That was the event where ex–BC Lions quarterback Joe "The Toughest Chicano" Kapp decided to settle a score for a dirty hit on his wide receiver, Willie "Will o' the Wisp" Fleming, by Angelo "King Kong" Mosca . . . in 1963.

That's right. *Forty-five* years before.

Angie, as he was known (an affectionate but incongruous moniker for a 245-pound bruising assassin) had delivered that career-ending hit after the play was whistled down, and incredibly, it was not seen by the referee.

(Perhaps the guy was related to Kerry "I Didn't See It" Fraser, the NHL referee who missed Wayne Gretzky's infamous high stick that opened up Doug Gilmour's face like a sardine can during the 1993 play off series against the Los Angeles Kings and Toronto Maple Leafs. With blood running down Gilmour's face but no penalty called, the Great One went on to score the winning goal in overtime for LA, eliminating the Leafs from playing the Montreal Canadiens for the Stanley Cup and forever guaranteeing that Fraser's name, if spoken at all by those who bleed blue, would be done so only in the company of blistering profanities.)

Angie's hit knocked Willie out of the game, causing Joe's Lions to lose the Grey Cup to Angie's Hamilton Tiger-Cats. Once again—that would be forty-five years previous, when these titans were in their mid-twenties. Do the math. And you thought the Israelis and Palestinians could hold a grudge?

The intention was for me to interview these CFL Hall of Famers onstage after my stand-up set. Clearly, the organizers hoped these icons would reinforce faith in a league given its last rites far too often, and that, softened by the wisdom of age, the former combatants would reminisce fondly about battles won and lost, soothing old wounds as old warriors should, letting bygones be bygones. Think again.

The Delta Hotel ballroom was packed with CFL fans, drinking beer and happily eating rubbery hotel chicken, their faces flush and eager with expectation, all of them sporting jerseys of their favourite teams. There were assorted CFL alumni of good standing, lifetime achievers, local dignitaries, families, feted guests and armed forces personnel on hand to piggyback our patriotism onto the last bastion of professional sports that is still exclusively ours.

There were also a couple of threatening-looking army tanks parked out front. Vancouver had just experienced a Stanley Cup playoff riot, so, given its recent orgy of liquor-fuelled anarchy, perhaps they stood as a warning to the first drunk punk from Surrey who might want to chuck a beer bottle at a cop car: try it, and you'll wake up with a shaved head in Kandahar, cleaning latrines.

I finished my set, which had been rife with Canadiana . . . surprise me . . . and everyone was in a good mood. Mosca was seated at a table in the front row, stage left. He was the biggest human being I'd ever seen. This mountain of meat and muscle who once wielded a fierce and frightening rage on the field, was now a seventy-one-year-old gentleman seated quietly amongst family members and clutching a cane.

After my lengthy introduction which lauded a lifetime of accomplishments on the gridiron and in wrestling arenas across North America, this Goliath carefully rose and, on wobbly knees, ascended the stage. When we shook hands, my small, freckled paw was swallowed by a Neanderthal-sized mitt belonging less to a twenty-first-century human, than a time when men sat around a feeble campfire in a chilly cave snapping mammoth bones in two at suppertime. It was a monstrous appendage of bone, gristle and callused skin, once used to serious effect in turning strong men in cleats into useless puddles of floppy cartilage.

Kapp, on the other hand, was still a lean, mean, lithe competitor with the coiled energy and athletic grace of a predatory cat. After an equally long introduction by me, in which I touted him as the only man to quarterback in the Rose Bowl, Super Bowl and Grey Cup, he rose from his seat and spontaneously picked a sprig of what looked like heather from the centrepiece on his table and joined me onstage. I said hello, and although he acknowledged me, he never really *saw* me. His eyes were fixed instead on that stolen victory of 1963, when poor Willie hobbled off the field, lost and incoherent after Angie's two-ton hit.

They stood at opposite ends of the stage as a screen lowered and archival footage of the 1963 Grey Cup began to play. It was a grainy black-and-white film of football players wearing helmets so lame in their protective capability, they seemed made of papier mâché. We saw Willie, with the football, get tackled by a linebacker. He was down when from nowhere came the six-foot-six, 245-pound Mosca, who plowed into him with the fury of a runaway train. Standing just to my left was Joe. I heard him whisper between clenched teeth the words he had no doubt barked from restless sleep these past forty-five years: "Dirty prick." I thought, *This can't be good.* Once the pin was pulled on that live grenade of this septuagenarian Chicano, it was primed for maximum impact.

I'm sure the result would have been just as explosive had German and Russian World War II veterans standing on the same stage been entertained with scenes from the Battle of Berlin. Doors to darker days that should have stayed closed forever would open, old haunt-ings would stir, and like reveille echoing down the halls of time, the room would erupt in a spontaneous contagion of grievance, with ancient scores being settled as the former Russian commando, an eighty-three-year-old Yuri planted a fork in the temple of Helmut the former German commando.

With the benefit of hindsight, I suppose it would have been best for all involved if the CFL alumni had shown a Looney Tunes cartoon instead.

It's been said that one can feel the barometric pressure drop before a battle, that the quiet is all-encompassing. After my introduction, the CFL fans who'd been laughing along to my set only moments earlier fell silent. Their eyes were glued to the stage. Carrying the bulk of age, Angie tentatively ascended the three steps to the stage, cane in hand. Joe was standing onstage, looking every inch a spring-loaded weapon of war. His coal-black eyes, furious with memory, stared Mosca down, while his left hand absent-mindedly fingered the heather in his right.

Three chairs sat empty onstage, waiting for their occupants: a pair of former grid-iron titans weighing in collectively at over 400 pounds, carrying an Old Testament level of hate for an ancient grievance, and a non-sportscaster comedian whose premonition of pending doom had his "Spidey sense" tingling.

Instinct is peculiar. It's hard to quantify. It's something that lives in the realm of the supernatural. Nevertheless, it's something one learns to trust after thirty-five years onstage—like when it's telling you to get *off* it. Then again, sometimes I can't shut up, especially when it's imperative that you follow the unwritten rule of the calling and, despite the response to your funny, always do your time!

There was one last chance to turn down the temperature in the room. Turning to face Kapp, I acknowledged the heather in his hand and said, "I see you're bringing a peace offering to Angelo, Joe."

He seemed to hear me, if just vaguely. Perhaps my remark echoed down the halls of time where he was standing, staring across the field at that clueless referee who missed a notorious late hit half a century ago.

"What?" he grunted.

"The heather in your hand," I repeated. "A peace offering to Angie?"

That's when I saw my statement find purchase. He looked at the heather, then back at me, and with a predatory twinkle in his eye reserved for a puma stalking a meal—not a septuagenarian stalking another septuagenarian with a cane—hissed, "Exactly." He had a plan, and I saw it formulating behind a malevolent smirk.

An arthritic Angie lumbered towards his chair and sat down, holding a corded microphone in his right hand and a cane in his left. Joe, on the other hand, strode to centre stage with the determined confidence of an avenger and, looking his nemesis in the eye, flicked the heather he was holding in Angie's face. Angie, taken aback, growled, "Shove it up your ass." Seventy years old or not, if you've been raised in a Boston ghetto, as the big man had, those street skills never leave you.

Joe flicked Angie's face with the heather again, and this time, Angie swung the microphone, barely missing Joe's face. That's when things moved fast. Joe shot the sprig of heather out a second time, and Angie, his ire up despite being a millennium away from the reflexes he once had, lashed out with his cane. Instead of connecting with the hand holding the heather, the cane connected with Joe's head, sending his glasses flying across the stage. (It's not every day you see a septuagenarian behemoth go all Jack Sparrow on another septuagenarian's noggin with a walking stick.)

Joe, in turn, doubled up his street-fighting fist and delivered three rabbit punches to Angie's face. Angelo "King Kong" Mosca, taking the blows full on the beak, teetered backward and toppled downstage right in a plaster-cracking collapse to the floor. I'm sure tectonic plates in the deepest Pacific took a seismic shift that day, for when he dropped, the structure shook.

Although not seen in the video that went viral on YouTube, the bottom half of Angie lay prostrate on the floor, while his massive dome and shoulders hung behind the stage curtain. Only half of him was visible, which was an apt enough encapsulation of the former King Kong Mosca, victim to the ravages of time.

Just because Angie was down for the count didn't mean the fight was over. Remember, this was happening in a matter of seconds. It's already taken me ten times longer to tell this story than the time it took me to witness it. Sure, there was a collective gasp from the room when Mosca fell, and I'm sure whoever might have been choking on a piece of the hotel's poultry was quietly turning blue, but no one had moved.

They were transfixed, particularly the half dozen hard-core veterans of the Afghanistan conflict seated in the front row, sporting jarhead haircuts, stone-cold stares and chests festooned with medals. Perhaps, like the men we'd come to honour, they too were trapped in the past and still in the fray somewhere up in the Panjwayi, chasing the Taliban down some dusty arroyo.

Joe cleared the stage in two determined strides and, as if punting a pigskin for the end zone, wound his leg back and laid three vicious boots to Angie's midsection, barking, "And stay down, you piece of shit!"

Soon as Angie fell, that instinct I spoke of earlier kicked in . . . and I bolted from the stage. In the video clip, there's a short man in a suit making a beeline for the exit, looking more like a circus performer escaping a fire in the Big Top than an emcee. That's me. What else could I do? If I'd got between those angry bulls, the only way I'd have walked away with my life would've been with rodeo clown training.

Truth be told, watching Angie topple over struck me as the saddest thing I'd ever seen. He looked so confused, as if gravity itself had conspired with his assailant and pulled him to the mat. Rushing from their seats, the soldiers helped Angie to his feet. Joe, too, looked lost, standing in the middle of the stage, holding his now-broken glasses while appealing to the audience with outstretched arms, his left hand still holding the heather.

"Sportsmanship!" he said, as he looked back and forth from the audience to Angie. "Sportsmanship."

Clearly, the suppurating wound of grievance had not healed over time. Whatever atonement was expected—and quite frankly, needed—went AWOL that afternoon.

A woman's voice rose from the silent crowd, sounding tired and sad, saying, "Let it go, Joe. Let it go."

Writing this book twelve years later, after what feels like three lifetime's worth of battles won and lost in the comedy trenches, that woman's words resonate with a wisdom worth embracing. Let. It. Go.

Those of us who stand in the solo spot know that anger fuels the funny, and we have all worn the shoes of Joe and Angie one time or another. Haunted by lost moments in the sun. Burdened by professional jealousies and trivial resentments. Personal wounds incurred a thousand lifetimes ago still suppurate. Holding grudges is like holding a thousand-pound bag of bricks: it cripples whoever carries it.

It's best to lighten your load on the road, not add another brick to your back, especially at a point in the journey where mortality is no longer just another man's worry.

By the way, while we're talking mortality, I don't want to go out strapped to a machine in the sepulchral gloom of the hospital room. I want to go standing up, with a take-no-prisoners final charge of adrenalin. If you have the luxury of knowing *when* you go, it's *how* you go that matters most. So, chopper me to the Barrenlands and drop me near the treeline buck naked, smeared in bacon fat . . . just to facilitate predator interest. As the whine of helicopter blades recedes in the distance, you stand alone and exposed, feeling nothing but nature's frigid kiss. Alone you came into this world, and alone you will leave it, *but* you're going to have some company first.

From the forest, there comes a howling. *Wolves! Wolves!* If you want to live, you'd better run, you old bugger! *Run! Run for the life that's left in you.* Clutch your shrunken junk and run!

A burst of fur from the treeline, and Pow!—out across the wasteland the pack sweeps, pink tongues lolling, canines shiny in the morning sun with hungry eyes the colour of a blue, cruel moon.

Your spindly legs, which once moved when you wanted them to, are now taking umbrage with the brain's directions. Still, you do your best to stretch those alabaster pins free of Earth's gravitational pull . . . and will you look at that! You. Are. Running!

With a quick glance over your shoulder, you see the pack moving full tilt towards their prey and think, *Boy, are they ever pretty!* And that's when *Canis lupus*, with jaws agape, flies perpendicular for your jugular and, in a rat-tat-tat of final heartbeats, you step into the eternal. In minutes, what's left of your mortal coil lays on the lap of Mother Earth, where ravens and whisky jacks will come to tug on spare scraps of flesh, the wind your only witness.

One thing's for certain, you'll be the talk round the shuffleboard game at the old folks' home.

"Hey, Earl, did you hear what happened to ol' Ron?"

"No, Archie. What?"

"He got eaten by wolves."

"For the love of God, he *what*?!"

"Got eaten by a pack of wolves. On the tundra. Smeared buck-naked from tip to tail in bacon fat, too."

Earl, holding his shuffleboard stone, will pause in quiet contemplation as the totality of Archie's statement sinks in. He will gauge his surroundings and see this generic, sterile and antiseptic purgatory, ruled by a repetition of soul-sucking sameness that will be his life until the Reaper makes a house call.

That's when Earl will turn to Archie and ask, "Out of curiosity Archie, what do you think a trip like Ron's cost?"

ACKNOWLEDGEMENTS

Thanks to Scott Sellers, associate publisher, Penguin Random House Canada, and Tim Rostron, senior editor, Doubleday Canada, for their patience and encouragement. Thanks to freelance copy editor Lloyd Davis for his gimlet eye. Thanks also to my eldest daughter and old soul Cayley, whose enlightened and thorough suggestions on content throughout the rewrite were very helpful and to my youngest, the irrepressibly irreverent red-haired force of nature Gracie, whose progressive vision keeps her father moving to the right side of history. Much praise for my parents, Bernie 'n' Joyce James, a pair of sterling originals from the Greatest Generation, who gave my sister and me a work ethic, unconditional love and a sense of humour in a home that, once upon a time, was forever filled to bursting with a pantheon of friends and family during good times and bad. A big high-five to all those theatres, both big and small, in every province across the Dominion, whose stage doors have opened with a welcome for my producer and me these past twenty years and whose perseverance during the dark days of the pandemic stands as testimony to their resilience and commitment in maintaining the cultural health of our nation. Finally, I'd like to express my deep gratitude to those Canadian audiences whose faith in my funny has been feeding me and mine for a lifetime. A person telling jokes to a room full of people is a comedian. A person telling jokes to no one is just talking to themselves. We need each other.

The Reform Impulse, 1825–1850

The Reform Impulse, 1825-1850

Edited by

WALTER HUGINS

UNIVERSITY OF SOUTH CAROLINA PRESS

Columbia, South Carolina

THE REFORM IMPULSE, 1825–1850

Introduction, editorial notes and compilation © 1972 by
Walter Hugins.

First HARPER PAPERBACK edition published 1972.

This edition published by the UNIVERSITY OF SOUTH CAROLINA PRESS, *Columbia, S. C.,*
1972, by arrangement with HARPER PAPERBACKS, from whom a paperback edition is
available.

International Standard Book Number: 0-87249-264-8
Library of Congress Catalog Card Number: 76-187905

Suggested Library of Congress classification furnished by McKissick Memorial Library
of the University of South Carolina:
HN64.H

Manufactured in the United States of America

For Jo ann

Contents

Introduction

Reform. *n*. The amendment of some faulty state of things; the removal of some abuse or wrong. *v.t.* To convert, bring back, or restore to the original form or state, or to a previous condition; to convert into another and better form; to free from previous faults or imperfections; to amend or improve by removal of faults or abuses; to put a stop or end to by enforcing or introducing a better procedure or conduct; to bring, lead, or force to abandon a wrong or evil course of life, conduct, etc., and adopt a right one. *v.i.* To abandon wrong-doing or error; to free oneself from misconduct or fault.

The Shorter Oxford English Dictionary on Historical Principles

THE SECOND quarter of the nineteenth century saw the earliest flowering of "universal reform" in the United States, characterized by a humanitarian belief that society could be improved by human effort and that the individual was capable of moral redemption and ultimate perfection. These social and humanitarian movements were wholly American—reformist rather than revolutionary, liberating rather than radical—yet they drew support and often inspiration from Europe. The effort to abolish Negro slavery, the best known of these movements, was only one of a multitude of activities which engaged the energies of Americans during the Jacksonian era. Temperance, women's rights, public education and penal reform all had their advocates. Humanitarians made a beginning in ameliorating the lot of the insane, the mentally retarded and the physically handicapped. Skilled workers organized a labor movement in eastern cities, while a few agitators recognized and deplored the plight of the unskilled in an increasingly industrialized society. Some Americans strove to attain the dream of universal and permanent peace. Others established utopian communities as models of the good society.

Reformers and reform societies during this period produced a tremendous volume of reports, resolutions, pamphlets, speeches and sermons from which a selection has been made to demonstrate the variety and complexity of this movement, as well as its essential homogeneity. While many reformers were active in several movements, some disagreed vehemently on tactics or objectives. Rationalists distrusted the "church and state oligarchy," while evangelical reformers feared the growing influence of "infidelity." The Concord circle, hostile to most of the economic and political changes ushered in by Jacksonian democracy, reassured themselves that American materialism could be humanized through their influence. Despite their differences, the objective of all reformers was basically identical: the liberation and perfection of the individual in order to attain a truly democratic society. Although they did not always offer solutions, they recognized fundamental social problems and urged the necessity of creating a social environment in which the individual could fully realize his capabilities and potentialities without the handicap of man-made obstacles. In emphasizing individual liberty over social equality (like Tocqueville, most of them feared the "tyranny of the majority"), these antebellum reformers were endeavoring to quicken the American conscience in order to accomplish the American dream.

The roots of early nineteenth-century reform can be found in the traditions of the preceding two hundred years of the American experience. Emigrants from seventeenth-century Europe had come to America in search of an environment which would provide the matrix of a new society, a "city upon a hill," and thus a new opportunity for the individual. While European, mainly English, institutions, ideas and attitudes were transplanted to the New World, sensitive colonial leaders became convinced from the very beginning that the new climate would produce a new and improved species as well as a new and improved society. The Puritans who created a "Wilderness Zion" and the Quakers who undertook a "Holy Experiment" were especially conscious of this opportunity to re-form human society, but the promise of America was equally part of the consciousness of settlers with more secular interests. Every colonist who assisted in moving the line of settlement westward was attempting to bring to fruition his own version of the utopian dream. In the process of creating a civilization in the wilderness, Americans have from the outset shown a willingness to experiment and a refusal to be bound by traditional ways of ordering society. Looking to the future instead of the past, the American, "this new man" as Crèvecoeur described him in the late eighteenth century, came to believe in inevitable progress and to reject the concept of inherent depravity. If man by his own efforts could change his environment, Americans argued, he could mold this environment to produce an improvement in both human nature and the human condition, since both individual and social evils were but the result of an imperfect society.

An undercurrent of social criticism has been a constant in the American intellectual climate, bursting forth into the national consciousness only at intervals. The first instance of this was an outgrowth of the Enlightenment and the Great Awakening in the mid-eighteenth century. These contradictory, yet complementary, currents converged in the founding of Georgia as a philanthropic colony, a product of British benevolent altruism. The fact that a number of prominent Englishmen were involved in this and associated endeavors reveals much about the attitudes and interests of orthodox Christianity during the Age of Enlightenment and helps to explain the revival of enthusiastic religion shown by the Great Awakening in America and the rise of Methodism in England. The evangelical movement focused upon the individual and his regeneration, while the movement for "practical benevolence" aimed to improve society; when these two tendencies, reinforced by faith in natural law and natural rights, converged, a revolutionary situation was created in the American colonies. The concern for individual salvation, religious humanitarianism or "moral stewardship," and a belief in the inherent and inalienable rights of man not only contributed to the coming of the American Revolution, but produced a climate of social reform as its aftermath.

Even though the Revolution and the principles of the Declaration of Independence were ideologically significant in stimulating the reform impulse, actual accomplishments were comparatively minor. The institution of indentured servitude was criticized, but few ameliorative measures were passed by state legislatures. Improvements in the status of the Negro were largely limited to states where the slave population was infinitesimal, though steps were taken to halt the international slave trade. Abolitionist societies flourished in the northern states as well as in Maryland and Virginia, and within two decades after the Revolution most state legislatures north of Mason and Dixon's Line had provided for the emancipation of their slaves. Other societies proliferated in the post-Revolutionary years, more being organized between 1776 and 1789 than in the entire colonial period; one of the notable developments of the 1780s was the growth of societies organized for charitable purposes, primarily to alleviate the lot of the urban poor. Immigrant aid societies emerged to care for fellow nationals, library and marine societies flourished in seaboard towns, temperance societies were organized in New England, and "humane societies" were founded in Boston and Philadelphia. The problems of crime and the criminal were increasingly a matter of concern, and here Quaker Philadelphia took the lead as it had in poor relief and the abolition of slavery. However, Quaker humanitarianism was less a product of the ideology of the Declaration than of their belief in the brotherhood of man and the equality of all men before God—and even in enlightened Pennsylvania humanitarianism often stumbled against the obstacle of economy and practicality.

Many members of the Revolutionary generation, notably Thomas Jefferson, dreamed of establishing an "empire for liberty" in America, a utopian society that would serve as an example to the rest of the world. But as survival became the principal concern during the first quarter-century of the Republic, the United States being unable to escape involvement in the Napoleonic Wars, social reform had to be postponed until after the War of 1812. From 1815 to the Civil War Americans continually invoked the principles of the great Declaration in calling for reforms in the social and political fabric. With a feeling of relief that the nation had avoided contamination from Europe, they insisted that the full promise of American life be realized. Within a decade most states had liberalized the suffrage to eliminate property qualifications, and efforts were underway to democratize economic opportunity as well; the fruition of these endeavors was the election of Andrew Jackson in 1828. An increasing number of Americans were also endeavoring to further social democracy through a multitude of reform movements. The repeated invocation of the principles of the Declaration of Independence to support abolition of slavery, temperance, women's rights—to name only the most obvious examples—demonstrates the viability of these Enlightenment ideas in early nineteenth-century America. Moreover, the United States had become a "beacon of freedom" to western European liberals and radicals who were endeavoring to create an egalitarian society in the Old World in the image of that across the Atlantic; British and French reformers especially looked to the United States as the model of a new society which would liberate all mankind.

During this time Americans developed a self-confident and self-conscious nationalism, a conviction that Providence had blessed the American nation and destined it for a successful future. The belief in inevitable progress, a heritage of the Enlightenment, was now more soundly established, most Americans looking forward to a future of unexampled peace, prosperity and progress. This feeling was reinforced by the Second Great Awakening, beginning shortly after 1800 and reaching its climax in the 1820s and 1830s. This evangelical upsurge was more than a recapitulation of mid-eighteenth century revivalism; emphasizing the possibility of salvation rather than the certainty of damnation, it called upon all Americans to repent their sins in order to share in the coming of the Kingdom of God. Led by Charles Grandison Finney, the revivalists argued that both the mission and the methods of the evangelical crusade were unique to America and worked to stimulate individual conversions in order to create a Godly society in the United States. The religious enthusiasm that permeated the "burnt-over district" of western New York during this period led to reformist enthusiasms based upon the evangelical spirit, affecting both the aims and the methods of several reform movements.

This evangelical strain was anti-rational and anti-Enlightenment, yet it was complementary to the Revolutionary heritage. Both viewed the American past and future in utopian terms: the United States was destined to establish a new society, based upon the dignity and brotherhood of man and the fatherhood of God, an example to the rest of the world. Another significant strain in the reform impulse, the Transcendentalist temper, reaffirmed the assumptions of the older, more traditional movements. The Transcendentalists assumed the existence of great moral truths that transcended sensational proof, and urged individual self-reliance and the removal of all impediments to the full realization of the individual and the consequent perfection of society. They rejected Unitarianism as too cold and formal, and evangelism as too emotional, stressing intuition and experience as the basis of faith and knowledge, a means for the regeneration of the individual in an increasingly anonymous mass society. Like the evangelicals, they strove to bring about social reform as a by-product of individual conversion.

Transcendentalism influenced only a small but significant group of New England reformers. More characteristic were the "common men" who followed Andrew Jackson and his political supporters in search of greater political and economic equality. While few leading Democrats were prominent in furthering the reform movements of the antebellum period, their struggle against privilege and their commitment to egalitarianism contributed to the climate that produced the reform impulse. In the course of the struggles against monopoly and the "Monster Bank," an increasing number of Americans came to realize that political democracy was meaningless unless it was accompanied by social and economic reforms. The egalitarian revolution could not, therefore, be limited to the accomplishment of universal white male suffrage and greater equality of economic opportunity. A number of Jacksonians, notably Richard M. Johnson, came to realize this in calling for the eradication of social and economic disabilities.

Even though Americans tended to look down upon decadent Europeans, they were also influenced by the reform ferment in England and France following the Napoleonic period. British utilitarianism and the revival of the French revolutionary tradition in the 1830s had an impact upon American reform. Furthermore, the principles of British and French socialism, emphasizing cooperation rather than competition, became well known in the United States. Not only were European treatises read and discussed in America, but influential European socialists traveled to the New World to gain converts. They formed only a small part of the European migration to the United States after 1815, but they contributed immeasurably to the reform agitation which characterized the period. In addition, many Americans traveled to Europe or corresponded with Europeans; they thus benefited from the European experience while at the same time reinforcing their feeling of superiority toward Old World society. Ideas of European reformers were easily adopted for American experiments, and on occasion (particularly in the case of British emancipation of slavery) European advances stimulated American reform movements.

Converging in the second quarter of the nineteenth century, all these influences contributed to the American reform movement.

Yet they do not really explain the reform impulse of this period. The cycles of American reform can be understood only in relation to the national psyche, and even in such an analysis much must be taken as given. Any movement that enlists a large number of intellectuals, always a minority in American society, is difficult to explain objectively, and its influence and accomplishments are sometimes doubtful. Comparatively few Americans have ever been concerned beyond their own personal future, altruism having been regarded as a luxury which pragmatists can ill afford.

The resurgence of religious benevolence in the decades following the War of 1812 was both a product of the Second Great Awakening and an endeavor by a conservative elite to use morality as a means of social control over the population in a changing America. Determined to take the lead in molding a Christian nation, thcsc heirs of the Puritan and Federalist traditions, principally laymen like the Tappan brothers of New York, established a group of interlocking organizations to carry out their aims: the American Bible Society, the American Tract Society, the American Home Missionary Society, the American Sunday School Union, and the American Education Society. In the mid-1820s some of them strove to organize a "Christian party in politics," but most chose to carry on their activities outside the political realm. Sincerely concerned with saving both conscious and unconscious sinners, they considered it their obligation to seek out sin, persuade the sinner to repent, and thus regenerate the nation. The principal arenas for their contests with Satan were the uncivilized Western frontier and the festering Eastern cities; they brought the written and spoken Word of God to the West and organized societies to assist and redeem the urban disinherited. Convinced that the continued existence of the Republic depended upon the triumph of evangelical Protestantism, these zealous humanitarians contributed to the development of organized philanthropy in the United States, as well as to the morbid American predilection for moral legislation and self-righteous judgment of others. During the antebellum period these men joined most productively in furthering the temperance and antislavery movements, but they also shared the anti-Catholic and anti-immigrant sentiments demonstrated in the Know Nothingism of the 1850s.

Other strands than evangelical do-goodism were woven into the pattern of humanitarian benevolence of the period. Even before the Revolution Philadelphia Quakers had established institutions for poor relief and prison reform, providing a precedent for the early nineteenth century. Pennsylvania, influenced by prominent Friends, was the first state to modify its penal system in an effort to reform rather than punish the criminal, her example being followed by other states. The concern over prison conditions in antebellum America was partially the result of a liberalization of the criminal code, which had changed prisons from way-stations to the gallows to places of detention and correction. To most reformers incarceration should provide an opportunity for the redemption and reformation of the criminal, rather than serving as a school for crime. Solitary confinement, reflection, Bible reading, productive labor and exercise comprised the formula adopted to regenerate the criminal disinherited. Different patterns of penology were developed in Pennsylvania and New York, spreading throughout the nation with local variations, but the assumptions, the means and the objectives were essentially the same. Tocqueville and Beaumont were not the only Europeans who crossed the Atlantic to inspect American prisons, all visitors remarking that the young Republic was far in advance of even the most enlightened European nations. Just as evangelical Presbyterians had hoped to eradicate prostitution by redeeming the prostitute, Quakers, evangelical New Englanders and non-sectarian rationalists joined forces to eliminate crime in America by regenerating the criminal.

Imprisonment for debt, a colonial remnant, was another instance in which mutually antagonistic groups were able to cooperate. Friends were the first to question this system, and in the early decades of the nineteenth century debtor relief societies sprang up in most of the seaboard cities. The Panic of 1819 served as an impetus to reform; Kentucky in 1821, under the leadership of Richard M. Johnson, became the first state to abolish all imprisonment for debt as an anachronism which punished the unfortunate rather than the guilty. Johnson and his supporters used rational rather than religious or moralistic arguments, instituting an eventually successful campaign in Congress for abolition of debtor imprisonment—which furthered reform efforts on the state level. Another example of the rationalist critique was the movement for abolition of capital punishment: although originated by the Quakers, it was largely supported by those like John L. O'Sullivan who invoked the principles of the Enlightenment rather than the tenets of evangelical Christianity.

Advances in the care and treatment of the mentally and physically handicapped were slow in coming, in spite of the efforts of Dr. Benjamin Rush and others at the turn of the century. As late as 1840 the majority of the insane were still confined under private care or were lodged in jails and poorhouses. The greatest influence for change was the propagandizing activity of Dorothea Dix, who successfully enlisted a number of male reformers in the effort to obtain increased state appropriations for the establishment and improvement of asylums. Meanwhile, Thomas Gallaudet and Samuel Gridley Howe developed schools for the education of the deaf, the blind and the mentally retarded. While all these pioneers were orthodox Christians in the evangelical tradition, their accomplishments were primarily those of selfless and devoted humanitarians, without reference to creed or dogma. A problem existed, it was recognized, and a means was found to alleviate it; it was less a question of religious salvation than an effort to salvage the disinherited in order to further the American dream.

Many of these problems resulted in part from urbanization, a phenomenon that affected a relatively small minority of the American populace. Similarly, the impact of industrialization during this period, although limited in terms of the total American experience, caused dislocations which were emphasized by a number of reformers. Two problems were involved here. In the first place, European immigration, principally from the British Isles, was renewed following the Napoleonic Wars, while the burgeoning seaboard cities served as a magnet to discontented and ambitious rural and small-town Americans. Most of the immigrants, foreign and domestic, who flooded into Boston, New York, Philadelphia and Baltimore had only rudimentary skills, forming an urban "social scum" which Mathew Carey and other philanthropists cited as a worthwhile target of benevolence. The second problem concerned the skilled artisan. Until after the War of 1812 master and journeyman mechanics had many interests in common: the maintenance of prices, quality of work and requirements for apprenticeship. To achieve these ends, as well as to provide sickness and death benefits, they had organized various "mutual benefit societies." But changes in the social and economic environment soon produced tensions. The transportation revolution was widening markets, the greater availability of credit was inducing a new type of entrepreneur to enter industrial pursuits, technological improvements were introduced into some mechanical trades, and the factory system was being established in some areas of the Northeast. All these factors changed or threatened to change the status of the journeyman mechanic; skilled artisans feared not only that they might never become masters in their own right, but that under the impact of the Industrial Revolution their craft was in danger of being degraded to an unskilled occupation. In response, skilled craftsmen of the eastern cities during the late 1820s and 1830s strengthened and reorganized existing journeymen's societies, formed city-wide unions of trades for unified action, and endeavored to use their newly won power at the polls to attain their objectives. Some, like Ely Moore, called for an economic and political union of "the producing classes," while others, like George Henry Evans, saw the ultimate salvation of the American laboring man on the frontier.

European visitors waxed enthusiastic at the paternalistic atmosphere surrounding the Lowell girls without investigating the working conditions or the extent of female and child labor in other New England textile mills. American artisans, on the other hand, generally ignored the situation of the factory worker, as they did the plight of seamstresses and female shoebinders in Manhattan lofts, except to protest against the competition of "slop-shops" turning out mass-produced inferior goods at low prices. Seth Luther was one of the few who denounced the effect of the new industrialism upon the bodies and minds of the workers. The Panic of 1837 and the resultant economic depression brought unemployment and acute distress especially to the working population and killed the flourishing labor movement for a decade or more. During this period critics of industrial capitalism like Orestes Brownson and John C. Calhoun foreshadowed Marx by predicting an imminent proletarian revolution unless significant social and economic changes were made (obviously, Calhoun's prescription differed from that of Brownson). However, the return of prosperity, the appeal of manifest destiny, the discovery of gold in California and the growing concern with the slavery question rendered their doleful predictions irrelevant until after the Civil War.

Many fair-minded Americans admitted that the prostitute, the felon, the imprisoned debtor, the slum dweller, and even the journeyman mechanic were suffering under various economic, social and moral disabilities, yet few were willing to concede that American women formed a disinherited or degraded group. Foreign visitors continually remarked on the unusual amount of freedom and the lack of chaperonage for young unmarried females; furthermore, American wives and mothers seemed to be standing upon a higher pedestal than their European sisters—all agreed that they excelled in modesty, humility, piety and chastity. Nevertheless, to some women the pedestal was an unsatisfactory substitute for their legal and social inferiority; by law a husband had control of his wife's property, had exclusive use of her person, and could inflict "moderate correction" by whipping or locking her up. Woman's place in society was justified by her physical disabilities: smaller and weaker than man, she was obviously mentally as well as physically inferior to her male counterpart. Her only comfort was the recognition that she was morally superior to man, but this superiority would unquestionably be endangered if she were permitted to participate in the hurly-burly of the marketplace or the political arena; she must, therefore, never appear on a public platform except before an audience of her own sex.

As the nineteenth century progressed, more and more women began to rebel against their status, refusing to accept sex as a badge of inferiority. Some remained chaste, but most continued to bear children while deploring the limitation of their role to childbearing and child-nurture. None of them dared to urge or even consider birth control as a means either to improve their own status as middle- or upper-class females, or as a solution to some of the problems of their poorer sisters who seldom had a pedestal upon which to stand. It was a man, Robert Dale Owen, who wrote the first birth-control manual published in the United States. This was primarily an effort to answer the Malthusian argument rather than a contribution to the women's rights movement, although Owen was sympathetic to the needs and desires of American females. His treatise was probably most significant in its insistence that women were human beings whose concerns and fears should be given equal, if not superior, weight to those of men.

Most crusaders for women's rights came to the movement because of their participation in other reform activities, such as antislavery and temperance. Finding their contributions limited to action behind the scenes, these women attacked what they regarded as absurd social conventions; a typical example is the reaction of the Grimké sisters to efforts to restrict their activities in the abolition movement. Contrary to the popular view, feminists were not all unsexed and frustrated spinsters, even though Frances Wright and Margaret Fuller were often cited as flagrant examples of the iconoclastic female reformer. Both women remained militantly unmarried while they developed and publicized their views, but both eventually succumbed to matrimony while maintaining their independence as human beings. Miss Fuller, a Transcendentalist associate of Emerson and Channing, wrote what has been called "the first considered statement of feminism in this country"; she was mainly concerned with explaining the dilemma of the intelligent and cultured woman in a male-dominated society.

American middle-class women were usually repelled by Fanny Wright's notoriety and radicalism, nor did they share Margaret Fuller's intellectual pretensions. They were much more likely to identify themselves with Susan B. Anthony or Elizabeth Cady Stanton, both of whom were not only as uncompromising and logically rigorous as the Misses Wright and Fuller, but were considerably more influential for nearly a half-century in the cause of women's rights. Mrs. Stanton, happily married and a devoted mother, became a feminist largely because of the humiliation and frustration she and other women had suffered by being barred from equal participation in the abolition and temperance movements, yet she quickly became a fervid and radical advocate of female emancipation in all areas. Together with Lucretia Mott, she planned and organized the first Women's Rights Convention in 1848. The themes she sounded there were to dominate the movement down to the twentieth century and the ultimate achievement of women's suffrage. The realization that those who labored under the disability of both sex and race had a double burden was seldom verbalized in the nineteenth century except by Sojourner Truth, who linked the causes of abolition and women's rights. Some white feminists saw the connection, though after the Civil War most of them tended to regard emancipation as the ultimate solution of the black problem while resenting the refusal of white males to recognize, let alone free them from their bondage.

One of the factors behind the feminist revolt was the psychic discomfort of many middle-class American women resulting from their status in the Victorian conjugal family, yet there is little evidence to suggest that the younger generation, third-class citizens at best in this nuclear unit, rebelled against the dominance of their elders. Children were expected to learn morality at their mother's, and occasionally over their father's, knee, the family being regarded as the principal civilizing institution of society. Formal education was therefore viewed as a necessary extension of familial nurture, reinforcing the morality of hearth and home, developing a few basic literary and mathematical skills, and providing exposure to the classics. Children were regarded as savages who must be curbed, cowed and civilized, so discipline was strict and rote recitation the rule. A few progressive educators, like Bronson Alcott, Robert Owen and Frances Wright, disagreed with the prevailing view and attempted to introduce the educational ideas of Pestalozzi and other European reformers into American schools. Focusing upon the individual child, whom he regarded as unspoiled by prejudice or traditional misconceptions, Alcott hoped to develop intuition and the reasoning faculty so that each child could learn self-reliance and grasp transcendental truths.

The situation was different with residents of urban slums, New England factory villages and frontier settlements. Here the family was both more closely knit because of the interdependence of its members and more diversified because of its division of labor. Not only wives but children were expected to contribute to the group by their labor; in many cases the family unit might not survive unless all made their contribution. Child labor, except on the farm, was never as prevalent in antebellum America as in Victorian England, but many Americans became convinced that a common-school system was a necessity in a republic that depended for its success upon an educated citizenry. With the widening of suffrage to all free white males in the early nineteenth century, this demand for public education became more vocal. Spokesmen for skilled workers agitated for free public education for their children as a means of improving their status. Others like Horace Mann in Massachusetts viewed education as the only hope for the preservation of democratic institutions, providing not only the most effective means for ensuring equality of opportunity and social mobility, but a method of social control, mitigating the distress and dissatisfaction inherent in an increasingly industrial society. During this same period colleges were multiplying, though most were small denominational institutions which served only a small fraction of the population, even a secondary school education being the exception for most Americans. Yet a beginning was made in state-supported higher education in this period; the plea for a liberal arts curriculum by Thaddeus Stevens, the champion of common schools in Pennsylvania, was somewhat atypical in an era when the professions and the ministry were regarded as the principal occupations of the educated elite.

If the concern for education could be faulted for ignoring the desires and needs of American children, the antislavery movement tended to deal with the Negro as an abstraction. The plight of another ethnic minority in the United States, the American Indian, was virtually ignored by reformers, only a few New England intellectuals protesting against the Jacksonian policy of Indian removal. Similarly, only a handful of abolitionists seemed knowledgeable or concerned about the lot of the black American, free or slave; it was slavery as an institution that was denounced as a moral anachronism in a democratic society. A few sensitive European visitors like Beaumont and Tocqueville and self-appointed Negro spokesmen like David Walker were virtually the only ones who attempted to deal with the black experience in human terms. Negrophobia in both free and slave states led to the support of colonization schemes which, while deploring slavery, saw forced emigration as the only solution to the problem of the relation of the races, applying the same remedy to the black problem that had seemingly resolved the Indian question. In the 1830s a number of agitators emerged who denounced colonization as a solution and demonstrated a serious concern about the lot of a subjugated minority.

William Jay was the most logical, with a legal brief refuting the colonizationists, but William Lloyd Garrison was the most eloquent, his diatribes from press and platform making him the best-known American abolitionist. He scorned the necessity of planning or organization; his paper, the *Liberator*, had only a handful of subscribers, mostly free Negroes—but he continued to agitate against the moral blot of slavery, refusing to compromise with his colleagues who sought to develop a plan for emancipation and a movement that could bring it to fruition. Garrison probably had greater rapport with blacks, both Northern free Negroes and escaped slaves, than any other white abolitionist, but it is questionable whether he was more concerned with their welfare than with eradicating a moral excrescence that was blighting American democratic society. The most effective organizer and propagandist of the movement was Theodore Dwight Weld, a disciple of Finney, who in a few short years successfully applied the evangelical techniques of his master in the effort to abolish slavery. His speeches and writings had their share of emotional rhetoric, but he was mainly concerned with gathering facts which would indict the "peculiar institution." Others like William Leggett, originally opposed to abolitionism for its fanaticism, were gradually drawn into the movement, as they saw the apologists of slavery calling for an abridgment of civil liberties; probably the most respected of such proselytes was John Quincy Adams, whose long struggle against the Congressional "gag rule" eventually made him an adherent of abolitionism.

Most of the above reformers were utopians in the sense that they were convinced that the adoption or implementation of their particular demand would contribute to the inevitable progress of mankind and the success of the American experiment. The first example of pervasive utopianism keyed to a single reform was probably the temperance movement. Many humanitarian evangelists came to believe that the primary cause of poverty, crime and other social evils was intemperance. It was viewed not only as a sin of the individual but as a crime against society, its toleration making every citizen a party to the evil. The temperance movement went through two phases: an effort by a declining social and religious elite to regain control over the "common man" by imposing its moral code upon him, and the later effort of native Americans to consolidate their middle-class respectability by distinguishing between their life style and that of the immigrant and lower-class native.

In the first stage the leading figures in the movement were clergymen and pious laymen, male and female, many of whom were active in other reform movements of the period. Increasingly convinced that this reform was the key to the regeneration of America, these spokesmen demonstrated an evangelical concern for the souls of drunkards, exemplified by their efforts to induce their congregations to take the pledge. As shown by Heman Humphrey and the National Circular, it was assumed that alcoholism could not be cured, but only prevented; the stereotyped case histories of inebriates were used to persuade the abstinent to forego the dubious pleasures of the bottle. Similarly, the efforts to organize "juvenile friends of temperance" and "cold-water armies" was an attempt to prevent rather than redeem sin. In spite of their unanimity on objectives the temperance movement split into factions; conservatives opposed the pledge and advocated a "temperate" use of wine and beer, while radicals insisted upon a pledge of total abstention and condemned the producer and retailer of "ardent spirits" as well as the consumer. This schism led to the decline of the movement in the late 1830s. But in 1840 the crusade was reborn with a new focus and new leadership as a result of the efforts of the Washingtonians, a group of reformed drunkards. Recruiting their members from frequenters of grog shops, the new organization made effective use of revivalist techniques such as the sawdust trail and the mourners' bench. The popular and democratic nature of the movement was shown by the songs, poetry and fiction published under its auspices—*Ten Nights in a Bar Room* was probably the most famous. Even a pragmatic politician like Abraham Lincoln could support this movement. Immigrants, particularly the Irish, and intemperate natives in the urban lower class were special targets; by the 1850s temperance had joined forces with nativism and, to an extent, with antislavery, serving as a means of defining a middle-class white Anglo-Saxon Protestant life style which provided the foundation of the Republican party.

America, utopia incarnate, became the mecca for idealistic experiments both native and imported. At the opposite pole from the individualistic reformers were the utopians, those who were convinced that real and permanent reform depended upon reorganizing society on a cooperative basis. Some religious groups practiced communism as a revival of primitive Christianity, while others undertook similar social experiments in an effort to build a new social order based upon rational principles. Religious communism, with its roots in European pietism, had first come to America in the eighteenth century; in most cases communism was not part of the basic creed, but lack of capital and the necessity of pooling resources made communal cooperation the only practical form of enterprise. Religious sanctions for communal sharing were easily found in the Bible, as was celibacy, an important practice in many of these early communal experiments. The Shakers, probably the most successful and influential religious communitarian society, established themselves in the United States during the Revolution and spread throughout the Northeast during the ensuing half-century. Many Americans were attracted by the simple Shaker life, and the community had an inordinate influence upon the development of communal utopianism in this period.

One of the most long-lived religiously-oriented native utopias was the perfectionist community established by John Humphrey Noyes, first in Vermont and then in Oneida, New York. It was not only in many ways the most radical of the utopian experiments, rejecting private property as well as traditional marriage and family arrangements, but it was the only community that for four decades consistently adhered to principles that were largely a product of the American rather than the European experience. After being converted by Finney's revivalistic preaching, Noyes gave up the ministry in favor of social engineering; convinced that socialism without religion was impossible, he attempted to create a society that would abolish sin, marriage, work and death. "Bible Communism," based upon community of property and "complex marriage," was the solution he offered. The society flourished until the 1880s, when Oneida joined the capitalistic society it had earlier denounced.

Non-religious utopias also flourished in the United States, the most famous of which, in spite of its short life, was Robert Owen's New Harmony. Established to solve the problems of industrial capitalism, the community was intended to become a model for all mankind, proving that the competitive instinct could be eliminated and that human nature could be improved in a cooperative society. Frances Wright, a young disciple of Owen, attempted to apply his theories in establishing a colony of free Negroes in Tennessee as a means of solving the problem of slavery and race relations. The same secular approach to utopia was demonstrated by Brook Farm, first a Transcendentalist experiment and later a Fourierist phalanx. Longer lasting than New Harmony and Nashoba, it was probably no more successful in attaining its objectives. While many of its members looked back upon their experience as a bucolic adventure, it failed to provide a viable model for American society. Even in its later phase, influenced by the theories propounded by Charles Fourier and his American disciple Albert Brisbane, it failed to demonstrate that small communal societies could survive within the larger society.

These were only a few of the multitude of utopian experiments which were born, and then gradually died, in antebellum America. In spite of some harassment, their existence demonstrates an early American tolerance toward eccentricity and experimentation which has largely disappeared in the twentieth century. On the other hand, their failure, not only to survive but to provide the pattern for modern American society, indicates that the competitive capitalist society which came to characterize the post–Civil War period was destined to prevail. American economic and political individualism, working in tandem with the American egalitarian tradition, came to dominate the American character. At the same time a general distrust of government and a belief that it should be limited both in scope and power served to make the activities of private associations reputable. The pervasiveness of this feeling helps to explain both Jeffersonian and Jacksonian democracy: true liberty and equality were to be attained only if the government refrained from dispensing favors or privileges to special groups. Some Americans in the antebellum period expressed a more extreme position. Garrison and Thoreau, for example, distrusted all government, urging passive disobedience of all laws that infringed upon the individual conscience. In contrast to most of the Founding Fathers they believed that man was basically good and hence required no curbing by any superior power. In this conviction they adhered to the philosophy expressed by the leading Democratic paper in the nation, the *Washington Globe*, whose masthead declared: "the world is governed too much." True happiness, it seemed, could be attained only if the state were encouraged to wither away.

Supporters of the peace movement were normally not philosophical anarchists like Garrison and Thoreau, but they strove to limit the power and sovereignty of the state by establishing an international organization to prevent war. Building on the pacifist sentiments of eighteenth-century Quakers, several reformers worked for the cause of perpetual peace. Elihu Burritt, who advocated the creation of a Congress of Nations and was the first to urge a strike against war, was a leading figure. Yet the movement had difficulty gaining support. Foreign affairs seemed to be of slight significance to America in the years after 1815, and the possibility of war seemed far away. The two traumatic experiences of this generation were the Mexican War and the Civil War; the first was widely opposed on moral principles, while the second was hailed by abolitionists and their sympathizers as the only solution to a moral question. As a result of this ambiguity, pacifism was forgotten or rationalized away. Nevertheless, the pacifist movement of the early nineteenth century, even though it engaged only a small minority of the American people, was important in stating the arguments in favor of peace and in devising systems to provide for the peaceful settlement of international disputes upon which twentieth-century pacifists have been able to build.

Criticism of reform and reformers, their objectives and the means they used to attain them, was widespread. Abolitionists were especially castigated, but other reformers were also subjected to a measure of vituperation. The "benevolent empire" was seen as a revival of puritanical meddling and a conspiracy of "church-and-state oligarchs" to subvert American democratic institutions. The fledgling labor movement was depicted as a European-influenced threat to American enterprise, a conscious effort to tarnish the reality of the American dream. Both the women's rights movement and efforts toward educational reform were viewed as subversive activities designed to undermine the very foundations of the American family. Utopian experiments were seldom taken seriously, often being described in the tone of skeptical amusement normally reserved for accounts of the manners and customs of primitive tribes. Reform in antebellum America, while enlisting legions of devotees, was a minority movement, and hence in contradiction to the majoritarian temper of the time. The mass of Americans during the Jacksonian era had a more optimistic and less critical vision of America's future. Followers of Jackson or Clay, seekers after economic opportunity, they generally had little sympathy for intellectuals who seemed unduly critical of the materialistic mainstream of American life. On the other hand, "nay-sayers," men like Hawthorne, Melville and the later Brownson, constituted another group of critics who rejected the optimistic view of human nature and the belief in inevitable progress that characterized most reformers; they emphasized man's irrationality, the tragic element in human life and the organic nature of human society. These men were not representative and had little impact in their own time. Yet the criticisms of these sensitive writers, who had at one time been part of the movement or at least on its fringes, were more fundamental than those of their more mundane contemporaries.

Increasingly self-conscious spokesmen for the South formed another group in opposition to the reform impulse. In the early decades of the nineteenth century reformers, even abolitionists, were to be found in these states, particularly the upper South, but by the 1830s defensiveness about slavery, fear of slave revolts and hysteria regarding abolitionist propaganda had produced a closed Southern mind. Because of their antagonism towards abolitionism they opposed any and all reform movements originating in the North, viewing them as an entering wedge which might subvert or call into question their "peculiar institution." Moreover, most Southern intellectuals by this time had a static view of their section's future: the South had achieved the best possible society, a Greek democracy based upon a benevolent slave system. The agrarian dream of Jefferson, in a somewhat perverted form, was utilized again to attack the industrial and mercantile North. If evils existed in American society, they were obviously products of urbanism and industrialism; both John Calhoun and George Fitzhugh predicted a bloody class war in the North, while asserting that revolution and social chaos would be avoided in the placid South where agitation and social change were unnecessary. Further progress need not be sought, for utopia had been attained. It is not surprising, then, that reformism had little impact in the Southern states.

Most antebellum reform movements had only limited success in attaining their objectives, so in the final analysis the reform impulse must be deemed a failure. A possible exception can be made for abolitionism, yet it is questionable whether this movement was primarily responsible for the coming of the Civil War or for the emancipation of the slaves which followed it. Certainly the status and condition of black Americans was not markedly improved as a result of abolitionist agitation. The situation of other disinherited members of society was improved in some cases, although their problems were not really solved. Moreover, in the late nineteenth century, poverty increased along with wealth, and the condition of the laboring classes deteriorated. Women gradually gained their emancipation from some of their disabilities, but their hard-won equality has proved both deceptive and illusory. While common-school and secondary-school education spread throughout the land, it has failed in many ways to fulfill the visionary hopes of early educational reformers. Furthermore, when the temperance movement finally attained its objective of legally enforced total abstinence, it discovered that it had created a monster instead of a utopia. The model societies designed by utopians as alternatives to competitive capitalism soon succumbed to the inexorable march of industrialization and urbanization. Likewise, the efforts of anarchists and pacifists to reduce the power of the state proved fruitless, as developments in twentieth-century American history will testify.

The American Civil War brought an end to a quarter-century of reform activity. The Gilded Age saw a revival of some humanitarian activities, but much of the uncompromising, often fanatical and dogmatic, social criticism that had characterized antebellum reformers had virtually disappeared, degenerating into the fastidious and alarmed distaste of the Mugwumps. True, new social critics emerged, culminating in the reform activities of Populists, Progressives and New Dealers. The emphasis, however, was different: whereas antebellum reform emphasized regenerating the individual in order to reform society, these later movements sought to reform society primarily through governmental action, an approach that would have been suspect to earlier reformers. Most twentieth-century reform has been more pragmatic and political, focusing more upon the "art of the possible" than upon transcendental truth; reforms have been brought about, but they have been piecemeal, generally failing to cope successfully with fundamental social problems.

The fact that innumerable social evils still exist in the second half of the twentieth century in America makes the concern of the antebellum reformers more than a historical curiosity, for most of the evils that they denounced and strove to eradicate are with us yet. The reformist, even revolutionary, agitation which has characterized the 1960s and 1970s demonstrates that gradual and pragmatic change, which has become an American tradition, is no longer sufficiently satisfying to an increasing number of Americans. Many in the current generation have revived another American tradition, epitomized by the antebellum reformers, in demanding that the equal rights of all Americans be made an immediate reality, that poverty be eliminated in the world's most affluent society, that all individuals be given full opportunity for self-realization, that both the social and the natural environment be protected against human selfishness—in sum, that the utopian hopes and dreams of past generations finally be realized. If those who are currently attacking the establishment familiarize themselves with the thrust of the early nineteenth-century reform impulse, they will find that much of what they are saying now has been said before. Perhaps they will succeed where their predecessors failed.

I

Roots of the Reform Impulse

1. Utopianism

A New System of Society. Robert Owen

EARLY *in 1825 the British reformer and industrialist Robert Owen
(1771–1858) fired the opening salvo in behalf of utopian socialism
when he delivered this address in the chamber of the House of Representatives before an assemblage of American dignitaries, including President James Monroe. Internationally famous because of his success in
improving the living and working conditions of his employees, Owen had
arrived in the United States a few months earlier to take possession of
a settlement in southern Indiana, where his utopian dream could become a reality. He had become convinced that the spirit of cooperation
must supplant competition as the motive force in society; since human
nature was a product of the environment, man could be improved only
as a result of fundamental changes in social institutions. New Harmony,
his projected cooperative community, was designed to embody these
ideas. Two years later, after spending nearly four-fifths of his fortune,
Owen was forced to admit that the experiment had failed; personality
conflicts among the colonists and his inability to devote full attention
to the community were largely responsible. Despite this failure, he inspired other antebellum reformers who accepted his belief in the perfectibility of man through social engineering.*

. . . It is . . . no light duty that is about to devolve on those who
are to direct the affairs of this extensive Empire. For the time is
come when they will have to decide, whether ignorance and
poverty, and disunion and counteraction, and deception and im-
becility, shall continue to inflict their miseries upon its subjects; or
whether affluence and intelligence, and union and good feeling,
and the most open sincerity in all things, shall change the condition of this population, and give continually increasing prosperity
to all the states, and secure happiness to every individual within
them. And this is but a part, and a small part, of the responsibility
with which they cannot avoid being invested: for it is not merely
the ten or twelve millions who are now in these states who will be

SOURCE: Robert Owen, *The First Discourse on A New System
of Society, as Delivered in the Hall of Representatives, at Washington on the 25th of February, 1825* (Manchester and London:
F. Looney, n.d. [1825]), pp. 3–5, 9, 11–15.

injured or essentially benefitted by their decisions, but their neighbors in the Canadas, in the West Indies, and over the whole
continent of South America, will be almost immediately affected
by the measures that shall be adopted here. Nor will their responsibility be limited within this new Western world; the influence of
their proceedings will speedily operate most powerfully upon the
Governments and people of the old world.

If, upon a fair and full examination of the principles which I am
to present to you, they shall be found true and most beneficial for
practice, those who are appointed to administer the general affairs
of the Union, and of the respective states of which it is composed,
will have to decide upon the adoption of measures to enable the
people of this continent to enjoy the advantages which those principles and practices can secure to them and to their posterity. . . .

The result of . . . [my] reading, reflection, experiments, and
personal communication, has been to leave an irresistible impression on my mind, that society is in error; that the notions on which
all its institutions are founded are not true; that they necessarily
generate deception and vice; and that the practices which proceed
from them are destructive of the happiness of human life.

The reflections which I am enabled to make upon the facts
which the history of our race presented to me, led me to conclude
that the great object intended to be attained, by the various institutions of every age and country, was, or ought to be, to secure
happiness for the greatest number of human beings. That this
object could be obtained only, first, by a proper training and
education from birth, of the physical and mental powers of *each*
individual; second, by arrangements to enable *each* individual to
procure in the best manner at all times, a full supply of those
things which are necessary and the most beneficial for human
nature; and third, that *all* individuals should be so united and
combined in a social system, as to give to each the greatest benefit
from society. . . .

Man, through ignorance, has been, hitherto, the tormentor of
man.

He is *here*, in a nation deeming itself possessed of more privileges than all other nations, and which pretensions, in many
respects, must be admitted to be true. Yet, even *here*, where the
laws are the most mild, and consequently the least unjust and

irrational, individuals are punished even to death, for actions which are the natural and necessary effects arising from the injurious circumstances which the government and society, to which they belong, unwisely permit to exist; while other individuals are almost as much injured by being as unjustly rewarded for performing actions for which, as soon as they shall become rational beings, they must be conscious they cannot be entitled to a particle of merit. . . .

Vast numbers of men, and more particularly women, in all countries have been forced, from generation to generation, to receive in infancy, as true, various imaginary notions, long prevalent in those countries, and they have been taught that their happiness or misery depended upon their belief or disbelief in the truth of those notions. . . . In this manner, every imaginable bad feeling that can be implanted in human nature, is generated and fostered. National, sectarian, and individual antipathies necessarily follow; division and counteraction of every description succeed, and the world is thus forced to become a chaotic scene of confusion, disorder, and misery. . . .

My desire now is to introduce into these States, and through them to the world at large, a new social system, formed in practice of an entire new combination of circumstances, all of them having a direct moral, intellectual, and beneficial tendency, fully adequate to effect the most important improvements throughout society. This system has been solely derived from the facts relative to our common nature, which I have previously explained.

In this new social arrangement, a much more perfect system of liberty and equality will be introduced than has yet any where existed, or been deemed attainable in practice. Within it there will be no privileged thoughts or belief; every one will be at full liberty to express the genuine impressions which the circumstances around them have made on their minds as well as all their own undisguised reflections thereon, and then no motive will exist for deception or insincerity of any kind. . . .

The degrading and pernicious practices in which we are now trained, of buying cheap and selling dear, will be rendered wholly unnecessary; for so long as this principle shall govern the transactions of men, nothing really great or noble can be expected from mankind. . . .

In the new system, union and co-operation will supersede individual interest, and the universal counteraction of each other's
objects; and, by the change, the powers of one man will obtain for
him the advantages of many, and all will become as rich as they
will desire. The very imperfect experiments of the Moravians,
Shakers, and Harmonites, give sure proof of the gigantic superiority
of union over division, for the creation of wealth. But these associations have been hitherto subject to many disadvantages, and their
progress and success have been materially counteracted by many
obstacles which will not exist under a system, founded on a correct
knowledge of the constitution of our nature. . . .

Under this system, real wealth will be too easily obtained in
perpetuity and full security to be much longer valued as it is now
by society, for the distinctions which it makes between the poor
and rich. For, when the new arrangements shall be regularly organized and completed, a few hours daily, of healthy and desirable
employment, chiefly applied to direct modern mechanical and
other scientific improvements, will be amply sufficient to create a
full supply, at all times, of the best of every thing for every one,
and then all things will be valued according to their intrinsic
worth, will be used beneficially, and nothing will be wasted or
abused. . . .

This is a revolution from a system in which individual reward
and punishment has been the universal practice, to one, in which
individual reward and punishment will be unpracticed and unknown, except as a grievous error of a past wretched system. On
this account, my belief has long been, that wherever society should
be fully prepared to admit of one experiment on the new system, it
could not fail to be also prepared to admit the principle from
which it has been derived, and to be ready for all the practice
which must emanate from the principle; and, in consequence, that
the change could not be one of slow progression, but it must take
place at once, and make an immediate, and almost instantaneous
resolution in the minds and manners of the society in which it shall
be introduced—unless we can imagine that there are human beings
who prefer sin and misery to virtue and happiness. . . .

It is to effect this change that I am here this night; that, if
possible, a mortal blow shall be now given to the fundamental
error which, till now, has governed this wretched world, and in-

flicted unnumbered cruelties and miseries upon its inhabitants. The time has passed, within the present hour, when this subject can be no longer mentioned or hidden from the public mind of this country. It must now be open to the most free discussion, and I well know what will be the result. . . .

2. Evangelism

The Great Work of Salvation. *Charles Grandison Finney*

In 1821 a young lawyer in western New York, an area which came to be called the "burned-over district" because of the religious and reformist enthusiasms that swept over it, had an intense conversion experience. Like Paul on the road to Damascus, Charles Grandison Finney (1792–1875) became conscious of his own past sinfulness and determined to devote the rest of his life to the salvation of others. Following his ordination as a Presbyterian clergyman three years later, he embarked upon a career of evangelical revivalism which was the most significant phenomenon of the Second Great Awakening, his successful techniques and allegedly heretical theology bringing him into conflict with orthodox Calvinists. Though sympathetic with reform movements of the time, especially temperance and abolition, Finney subordinated social reform to individual spiritual regeneration, and therefore took an increasingly conservative position on social issues. His most radical pronouncements are to be found in his Lectures on Revivals, first published in 1835, which had a noteworthy influence upon his disciples throughout the United States. Finney's revivalistic techniques proved successful in many of the antebellum reform movements, and his call for individual moral reform was a theme continually invoked by the evangelical reformers.

. . . It has always been the case, whenever any of the servants of God do any thing in his cause, and there appears to be a *probability* that they will succeed, that Satan by his agents regularly attempts to divert their minds and nullify their labors. So it has been during the last ten years, in which there have been such remarkable revivals through the length and breadth of the land. These revivals have been very great and powerful, and extensive. It has been estimated that not less than TWO HUNDRED THOUSAND persons have been converted to God in that time.

And the devil has been busy in his devices to divert and distract

SOURCE: "Hindrances to Revivals," in Charles Grandison Finney, *Lectures on Revivals of Religion*, ed. William G. McLoughlin (Cambridge: The Belknap Press of Harvard University Press, 1960), pp. 277–278, 286–288, 301–302, 304–306, reprinted by permission of the publishers. Copyright © 1960 by the President and Fellows of Harvard College.

the people of God, and turn off their energies from pushing forward the great work of salvation. . . .

Resistance to the Temperance Reformation will put a stop to revivals in a church. The time has come that it can no longer be innocent in a church to stand aloof from this glorious reformation. The time was, when this could be done ignorantly. The time has been when ministers and Christians could enjoy revivals, notwithstanding ardent spirit was used among them. But since light has been thrown upon the subject, and it has been found that the use is only injurious, no church member or minister can be innocent and stand neutral in the cause. They must speak out and take sides. And if they do not take ground on one side, their influence is on the other. . . .

Revivals are hindered when ministers and *churches take wrong ground in regard to any question involving human rights.* Take the subject of SLAVERY for instance. The time was when this subject was not before the public mind. . . . But recently, the subject has come up for discussion, and the providence of God has brought it distinctly before the eyes of all men. Light is now shed upon this subject as it has been upon the cause of temperance. Facts are exhibited, and principles established, and light thrown in upon the minds of men, and this monster is dragged from his horrid den, and exhibited before the church, and it is demanded of them, "IS THIS SIN?" Their testimony *must* be given on this subject. . . . Their silence can no longer be accounted for upon the principle of ignorance, and that they have never had their attention turned to the subject. Consequently, the silence of Christians upon the subject is virtually saying *that they do not* consider slavery as a sin. The truth is, it is a subject upon which they cannot be silent without guilt. . . . The church cannot turn away from this question. It is a question for the church and for the nation to decide, and God will push it to a decision.

. . . Christians can no more take neutral ground on this subject, since it has come up for discussion, than they can take neutral ground on the subject of the sanctification of the Sabbath. It is a great national sin. It is a sin of the church. The churches by their silence, and by permitting slaveholders to belong to their communion, have been consenting to it. All denominations have been more or less guilty, although the Quakers have of late years washed their hands of it. It is in vain for the churches to pretend it is merely a political sin. I repeat it, it is the sin of the church, to which all denominations have consented. . . . While she tolerates slaveholders in her communion SHE JUSTIFIES THE PRAC-TICE. And as well might an enemy of God pretend that he was neither saint nor sinner, that he was going to take neutral ground, and pray "good Lord and good devil," because he did not know which side would be the most popular. . . .

I believe the time has come, and although I am no prophet, I believe it will be found to have come, that the revival in the United States will continue and prevail, no farther and faster than the church take right ground upon this subject. The church are God's witnesses. The fact is that slavery is, pre-eminently, the *sin of the church*. It is the very fact that ministers and professors of religion of different denominations hold slaves which sanctifies the whole abomination, in the eyes of ungodly men. Who does not know that on the subject of temperance, every drunkard in the land, will skulk behind some rum-selling deacon, or wine-drinking minister? It is the most common objection and refuge of the intemperate, and of moderate drinkers, that it is practised by pro-fessors of religion. It is *this* that creates the imperious necessity for excluding traffickers in ardent spirit, and rum-drinkers from the communion. Let the churches of all denominations speak out on the subject of temperance, let them close their doors against all who have anything to do with the death-dealing abomination, and the cause of temperance is triumphant. A few years would annihi-late the traffic. Just so with slavery.

It is the church that mainly supports this sin. Her united testi-mony upon this subject would settle the question. Let Christians of all denominations meekly but firmly come forth, and pronounce their verdict, let them clear their communions, and wash their hands of this thing, let them give forth and write on the head and front of this great abomination, SIN! and in three years, a public sentiment would be formed that would carry all before it, and there would not be a shackled slave, nor a bristling, cruel slave-driver in this land. . . .

There are those in the churches who are standing aloof from the subject of Moral Reform, and who are as much afraid to have any thing said in the pulpit against lewdness, as if a thousand devils had got up into the pulpit. On this subject, the church need not expect to be permitted to take neutral ground. In the providence of

God, it is up for discussion. The evils have been exhibited, the call has been made for reform. And what is to reform mankind but the truth? And who shall present the truth if not the church and the ministry? Away with the idea, that Christians can remain neutral and keep still, and yet enjoy the approbation and blessing of God. . . .

There must be more done for all the great objects of Christian benevolence. There must be much greater efforts for the cause of missions, and education, and the Bible, and all the other branches of religious enterprise, or the church will displease God. Look at it. Think of the mercies we have received, of the wealth, numbers and prosperity of the church. Have we rendered unto God according to the benefits we have received, so as to show that the church is bountiful and willing to give their money and to work for God? No. Far from it. Have we multiplied our means and enlarged our plans, in proportion as the church has increased? Is God satisfied with what has been done, or has he reason to be? Such a revival as has been enjoyed by the churches of America for the last ten years! We ought to have done ten times as much as we have for missions, Bibles, education, tracts, free churches, and in all the ways designed to promote religion and save souls. If the churches do not wake up on this subject, and lay themselves out on a larger scale, they may expect the revival in the United States will cease.

. . . If the whole church as a body had gone to work ten years ago, and continued it as a few individuals, whom I could name, have done, there would not now have been an impenitent sinner in the land. The millennium would have fully come in the United States before this day. . . . I do not deny that there are many things which are wrong done in revivals. But is that the way to correct them, brethren? So did not Paul. He corrected his brethren by telling them kindly that he would show them a more excellent way. Let our brethren take hold and go forward. Let us hear the cry from all their pulpits. To THE WORK. Let them lead on, where the Lord will go with them and make bare his arm, and I, for one, will follow. Only let them GO ON, and let us have the United States converted to God, and let all minor questions cease. . . .

3. Transcendentalism

Man the Reformer. *Ralph Waldo Emerson*

WHEN he resigned his pastorate in the Unitarian Church in 1832 because of serious and growing theological reservations, Ralph Waldo Emerson (1803–1882) embarked upon a new and ultimately more significant career. Henceforth devoting his life to writing and lecturing, he became the center of a circle of like-minded New England intellectuals and reformers. Yet Emerson was neither a systematic philosopher nor a confident leader of a coterie. With his fellow Transcendentalists he emphasized the correspondence between man and nature, inveighing against materialism and selfishness while urging each individual to remove the impediments to natural perfection within himself. He supported and encouraged the reform impulse of the period, but at the same time severely criticized individual reforms and reformers and avoided involvement in causes (see Document 40). To Emerson, the necessary first step towards remaking society was individual regeneration and reform in accordance with a secular gospel of love. The following lecture, delivered before the Mechanics' Apprentices' Library Association of Boston in 1841, demonstrates his characteristic ambivalence toward the reform movement.

I wish to offer to your consideration some thoughts on the particular and general relations of man as a reformer. I shall assume that the aim of each young man in this association is the very highest that belongs to a rational mind. Let it be granted, that our life as we lead it, is common and mean; that some of those offices and functions for which we were mainly created are grown so rare in society, that the memory of them is only kept alive in old books and in dim traditions; that prophets and poets, that beautiful and perfect men, we are not now, no, nor have even seen such; that some sources of human instruction are almost unnamed and unknown among us; that the community in which we live will hardly bear to be told that every man should be open to ecstasy or a divine illumination, and his daily walk elevated by intercourse with the spiritual world. Grant all this, as we must, yet I suppose none of

SOURCE: R. W. Emerson, "Man the Reformer," *The Dial* (Boston: Weeks, Jordan & Co., 1841), no. 4 (April 1841), pp. 523, 525–526, 531–534, 536–538.

my auditors,—no honest and intelligent soul will deny that we ought to seek to establish ourselves in such disciplines and courses as will deserve that guidance and clearer communication with the spiritual nature. And further, I will not dissemble my hope, that each person whom I address has felt his own call to cast aside all evil customs, timidities, and limitations, and to be in his place a free and helpful man, a reformer, a benefactor, not content to slip along through the world like a footman or a spy, escaping by his nimbleness and apologies as many knocks as he can, but a brave and upright man, who must find or cut a straight road to everything excellent in the earth, and not only go honorably himself, but make it easier for all who follow him, to go in honor, and with benefit. . . .

It cannot be wondered at that this general inquest into abuses should arise in the bosom of society, when one considers the practical impediments that stand in the way of virtuous young men. The young man on entering life finds the ways to lucrative employments blocked with abuses. The ways of trade are grown selfish to the borders of theft, and supple to the borders (if not beyond the borders) of fraud. . . .

But by coming out of trade you have not cleared yourself. The trail of the serpent reaches into all the lucrative professions and practices of man. Each has its own wrongs. Each finds a tender and very intelligent conscience a disqualification for success. Each requires of the practitioner a certain shutting of the eyes, a certain dapperness and compliance, an acceptance of customs, a sequestration from the sentiments of generosity and love, a compromise of private opinion and lofty integrity. Nay, the evil custom reaches into the whole institution of property, until our laws which establish and protect it seem not to be the issue of love and reason, but of selfishness. . . .

The duty that every man should assume his own vows, should call the institutions of society to account, and examine their fitness to him, gains in emphasis, if we look now at our modes of living. Is our housekeeping sacred and honorable? Does it raise and inspire us, or does it cripple us instead? . . . We spend our incomes for paint and paper, for a hundred trifles, I know not what, and not for the things of a man. Our expense is almost all for conformity. It is for cake that we run in debt; 't is not the intellect, nor the heart, not beauty, not worship, that costs so much. Why needs any man be rich? Why must he have horses, and fine garments, and hand-some apartments, and access to public houses, and places of amusement? Only for want of thought. Once waken in him a divine thought, and he flees into a solitary garden or garret to enjoy it, and is richer with that dream, than the fee of a county could make him. But we are first thoughtless, and then find that we are moneyless. We are first sensual, and then must be rich. We dare not trust our wit for making our house pleasant to our friends, and so we buy ice-creams. He is accustomed to carpets, and we have not sufficient character to put floorcloths out of his mind whilst he stays in the house, and so we pile the floor with carpets. . . .

I do not wish to be absurd and pedantic in reform. I do not wish to push my criticism on the state of things around me to that extravagant mark, that shall compel me to suicide, or to an abso-lute isolation from the advantages of civil society. . . . we must clear ourselves each one by the interrogation, whether we have earned our bread to-day by the hearty contribution of our energies to the common benefit? and we must not cease to tend to the correction of these flagrant wrongs, by laying one stone aright every day.

But the idea which now begins to agitate society has a wider scope than our daily employments, our households, and the institu-tions of property. We are to revise the whole of our social struc-ture, the state, the school, religion, marriage, trade, science, and explore their foundations in our own nature; we are to see that the world not only fitted the former men, but fits us, and to clear ourselves of every usage which has not its roots in our own mind. What is a man born for but to be a Reformer, a Re-maker of what man has made; a renouncer of lies; a restorer of truth and good, imitating that great Nature which embosoms us all, and which sleeps no moment on an old past, but every hour repairs herself, yielding us every morning a new day, and with every pulsation a new life? Let him renounce everything which is not true to him, and put all his practices back on their first thoughts, and do noth-ing for which he has not the whole world for his reason. If there are inconveniences, and what is called ruin in the way, because we have so enervated and maimed ourselves, yet it would be like dying of perfumes to sink in the effort to reattach the deeds of every day to the holy and mysterious recesses of life.

The power which is at once spring and regulator in all efforts of reform, is faith in Man, the conviction that there is an infinite worthiness in him which will appear at the call of worth, and that all particular reforms are the removing of some impediment. . . .

. . . I see what one brave man, what one great thought executed might effect. I see that the reason of the distrust of the practical man in all theory, is his inability to perceive the means whereby we work. Look, he says, at the tools with which this world of yours is to be built. As we cannot make a planet, with atmosphere, rivers, and forests, by means of the best carpenters' or engineers' tools, with chemist's laboratory and smith's forge to boot,—so neither can we ever construct that heavenly society you prate of, out of foolish, sick, selfish men and women, such as we know them to be. But the believer not only beholds his heaven to be possible, but already to begin to exist,— . . .

. . . We must be lovers, and instantly the impossible becomes possible. Our age and history, for these thousand years, has not been the history of kindness, but of selfishness. Our distrust is very expensive. The money we spend for courts and prisons is very ill laid out. We make by distrust the thief, and burglar, and incendiary, and by our court and jail we keep him so. An acceptance of the sentiment of love throughout Christendom for a season, would bring the felon and the outcast to our side in tears, with the devotion of his faculties to our service. See this wide society of laboring men and women. We allow ourselves to be served by them, we live apart from them, and meet them without a salute in the streets. We do not greet their talents, nor rejoice in their good fortune, nor foster their hopes, nor in the assembly of the people vote for what is dear to them. . . . In every knot of laborers, the rich man does not feel himself among his friends,—and at the polls he finds them arrayed in a mass in distinct opposition to him. We complain that the politics of masses of the people are so often controlled by designing men, and led in opposition to manifest justice and the common weal, and to their own interest. But the people do not wish to be represented or ruled by the ignorant and base. They only vote for these because they were asked with the voice and semblance of kindness. . . . Let our affection flow out to our fellows; it would operate in a day the greatest of all revolutions. . . . The state must consider the poor man, and all voices must speak for him. Every child that is born must have a just chance for his bread. Let the amelioration in our laws of property proceed from the concession of the rich, not from the grasping of the poor. . . . Let us understand that the equitable rule is, that no one should take more than his share, let him be ever so rich. Let me feel that I am to be a lover. I am to see to it that the world is the better for me, and to find my reward in the act. Love would put a new face on this weary old world in which we dwell as pagans and enemies too long, and it would warm the heart to see how fast the vain diplomacy of statesmen, the impotence of armies, and navies, and lines of defence, would be superseded by this unarmed child. . . . one day all men will be lovers; and every calamity will be dissolved in the universal sunshine. . . .

II

Aims of the Reform Impulse

4. Prevent the Progress of Prostitution
New York Magdalen Society

FOLLOWING the War of 1812 a "benevolent empire" spread throughout the nation. Clergymen and pious laymen, epitomized by Arthur Tappan (1786–1865), a wealthy New York merchant of New England ancestry, established interlocking societies whose objective was to convert the United States to Christian righteousness. Tappan's commitment to "moral stewardship" was exemplified when he and others instituted the New York Magdalen Society in 1830 to end prostitution by appealing to the innate purity of fallen females. John R. McDowall, a Presbyterian seminarian from Princeton, was recruited as agent of the society to rescue and regenerate these unfortunate creatures. This report, written largely by McDowall, was published in order to obtain support for the cause by a sensational exposé of the problem. The reaction was hysterical: an Anti-Magdalen meeting, attended by leading figures in New York politics and society, condemned the report as exaggerated and irresponsible, a "printed dictionary to all the bad houses in town." Although few prostitutes were permanently converted, McDowall continued his activities for nearly a decade, conducting a journal which stimulated the organization of similar societies in other areas of the Northeast. Tappan, meanwhile, moved on to the antislavery movement.

. . . The extent of prostitution in this city, as shown by facts already developed during our labors, and the alarming increase of the unhappy victims of seduction among us, of which we have attained the most demonstrative evidence, so far exceed all our previous calculations that we are prepared to anticipate scepticism and incredulity in others. Indeed enough is in our possession to cause a thrill of horror to be felt by every virtuous man and woman in the community, such as was never produced by any expose of vice which has ever met the public eye. Did not prudence and delicacy forbid the disgusting detail of what has been brought to our knowledge . . . , every parent would tremble for the safety of

SOURCE: Magdalen Report: First Annual Report of the Executive Committee of the N.Y. Magdalen Society, Instituted, January 1, 1830, With Remarks, By a Layman. (New York: 1831), pp. 7–11, 16.

his sons as well as his daughters, and we could a tale disclose which would cause the blood to "chill within the veins, and each particular hair to stand erect, like quills upon the fretful porcupine." . . .

First then we would present the fact, that we have satisfactorily ascertained that the number of females in this city, who abandon themselves to prostitution is not less than TEN THOUSAND!! . . .

. . . Besides these we have the clearest evidence that there are hundreds of private harlots and kept misses, many of whom keep up a show of industry as domestics, seamstresses, nurses, &c., in the most respectable families, and throng the houses of assignation every night. Although we have no means of ascertaining the number of these, yet enough has been learned from the facts already developed to convince us that the aggregate of these is alarmingly great, perhaps little behind the proportion of the city of London, whose police reports assert, on the authority of accurate researches, that the number of private prostitutes in that city, is fully equal to the number of public harlots. . . .

. . . many of them are the daughters of the wealthy, respectable and pious citizens of our own and other states, seduced from their homes by the villains who infest the community, preying upon female innocence, and succeeding in their diabolical purpose, either by promises of marriage; or, after deceiving them in a brothel, by the commission of rape; often first depriving the victims of their lust, of their reason, by stupefying drugs kept in these dens of iniquity for the purpose. . . .

But we will not affect to conceal that hundreds, perhaps thousands of them, are the daughters of the ignorant, depraved and vicious part of our population, trained up without culture of any kind, amidst the contagion of evil example, and enter upon a life of prostitution for the gratification of their unbridled passions, and become harlots altogether by choice. These have a short career, generally dying of the effects of intemperance and pollution soon after entering upon this road to ruin.

Without attempting to protract these loathsome details, or offering comment which we deem unnecessary, we would here present the result of our observation, in reference to the effects of this course of life upon the wretched females themselves. Soon after they begin their vicious indulgence, in a drunken frolic, at the dance house, or the theatre, or in the street, they become involved in riotous conduct, are arrested and sent to the watch house, whence they are committed to the Penitentiary for sixty days. This penance is most generally unproductive, for on their discharge they are eagerly sought for by the former companions of their guilt, and return to their crimes. Soon they are overtaken by that disease, the judicial visitation of heaven for the sin of uncleanness, and are presently found in the Alms House Hospital, where for weeks together the deaths among them are said to average nearly one every day. Indeed, it is evident in this city as elsewhere long since shown, that among those who commence a life of prostitution early, from three to five years is the average period of their existence, for intemperance and pollution rapidly hurry them into the grave, a signal proof of the declaration, that "the wicked shall not outlive half their days."

. . . It is a lamentable fact that men are the original cause of the evil complained of; yet it is but too true that women take their revenge an hundred fold. Seductions of females among us are often attended with peculiar aggravations, and the abandoned of both sexes are reciprocally the tempters of the virtuous. But it is clearly ascertained that bad women multiply the seduction of heedless youth, more rapidly than bad men seduce modest women. A few of these courtesans suffice to corrupt whole cities, and there can be no doubt that some insinuating prostitutes have initiated more young men into these destructive ways than the most abandoned rakes have debauched virgins during their whole lives. So that though the latter deserve execration and great severity, yet the grand effort of those who would promote reformation, should be directed to arresting, and if possible reclaiming, those wretched females, who are the pest and nuisance of society, though equally the objects of our compassion and abhorrence.

What then is to be done? To this question we are aware many answers may be given, but without presenting the pretexts on which many contend that nothing can be done, or, even glancing at the views of those who say nothing ought to be done, we shall briefly set forth what we propose to do. . . .

The object is declared to be "to reclaim such females as have strayed from the paths of virtue, and to take measures to prevent the progress of prostitution." It is, therefore, to withdraw from society a fallen and injurious member, who by her guilt has become an outcast, but is desirous to reform; to train her to habits of diligence, order, and industry—to teach her the truth and duties of Christianity, and then to place her in a situation, where by the exertion of her abilities, she may obtain an honest livelihood. . . . It is, therefore, required that the applicant be in *good health, not pregnant, not afflicted with any contagious distemper,* and that she be *really desirous to reform* and *wholly to forsake* her former ways of iniquity. Our object, in short, is to restore to society those who had not only ceased to benefit it by useful labor, but were a burden upon it by their idleness, and a nuisance by their debaucheries—it is to diminish the number of temptations to the young and thoughtless—to pour consolation into the hearts of parents, mourning the ruin of beloved and once hopeful children—to save souls from death, and to hide a multitude of sins.

All this we propose to accomplish not barely by *rescuing* but *reforming* them; not merely by affording a *refuge from misery* but by providing a *school of virtue;* not simply to destroy the habits of idleness and vice, but to substitute those of honorable and profitable industry, thus *benefiting society,* while the *individual is reclaimed.* And all this we believe to be practicable by the single weapon of the Gospel of God, our Saviour; hence the preaching of this Gospel is this grand efficient agency on which we rely for success.—This is the means which God has appointed to lead sinners to repentance, and we as Christians are bound to cause the "chief of sinners" to hear the Gospel. . . . To the shame of Christendom be it spoken, that while she has in obedience to God been sending the Gospel to the ends of the earth, and causing joy in the presence of the angels over sinners who have there repented; she has had at the same time hundreds of thousands of sinners equally abandoned, congregated in her populous cities, doing vastly more mischief, and ripening for unspeakably more dreadful condemnation, to many of whom in direct disobedience to the command of God, she has never to this day preached the Gospel. . . .

These are the hopes indulged by the founders of the "New-York Magdalen Society," and thus early they have been favored with the clearest evidence of the smiles and benedictions of Heaven. One of the earliest inmates of the Asylum, after affording unequivocal evidence of genuine repentance and saving faith, has already died in peace, and left the encouraging assurance that she now rests from her sorrows and sufferings in the paradise of God. She was not eighteen years of age, of poor but respectable parents who were dead, but had relatives in this city. We witnessed the depth of her contrition, the hatred of her sins, and the fervency of her supplications for Divine mercy, after she had received religious instruction, and been taught to believe that there was yet hope of her salvation. . . . We were at last permitted to witness the strength of her faith, and hear her testimony of the consolation she had found in Christ. Truly her peace flowed like a river, and prayer and praise became her constant delight. She had been tenderly brought up, was of a delicate constitution, and shortly after began to sink in a state of debility from which she never recovered. As she drew near her end, her relatives in this city, male and female, were informed of her wish to see them. They visited her in the Asylum, were present in her last hours, and heard her dying testimony to the truth of the holy religion, requesting us to sing

> "Were not the sinful Mary's tears
> An off'ring worthy heav'n
> While o'er the crimes of former years
> She wept and was forgiven,"

and she breathed her last in full hope of a blessed immortality. . . .

We will now conclude our report by making our appeal to the *virtuous females* of our city, the wives and daughters of our citizens, the mothers of the rising and future generation. . . . We see you . . . animated by benevolence, and glowing with zeal, step forward to save these perishing daughters of sorrow and affliction. We see the tear of sympathy and compassion glistening in your eye, and your liberal hands attesting the generous emotions of your souls. We hear you in the native eloquence of the heart, pleading the cause of suffering humanity, awakening the insensible, stimulating the inactive, exciting liberality in the selfish, and imparting to the benevolent mind a more ardent zeal, and a more active energy. We behold you in short employing all the peculiar influence of your sex . . . in promoting the interest and success of an institution which . . . is founded for the relief of the miserable of your own sex, *exclusively*.

5. This Unmerciful Practice, Imprisonment for Debt
Richard M. Johnson

MANY Americans in the early nineteenth century viewed imprisonment for debt as an anachronism in a democratic society, but Senator Richard M. Johnson (1780–1850) of Kentucky was determined to do something about it. Elected to Congress as a War Hawk in 1807, and serving with distinction in the War of 1812, he played a major role in the passage of a law in 1821 abolishing imprisonment for debt in Kentucky. Responsive to the demands of his constituents and supporters in other states following the Panic of 1819, he repeatedly introduced a bill in the United States Senate to abolish this practice in federal courts, finally succeeding in 1832; of greater significance, his national agitation was instrumental in furthering this reform on the state level. Later he gained both fame and notoriety from his 1830 report to Congress, denouncing the efforts of the "Christian party in politics" to prohibit the transportation of mail on Sundays, and in 1836 he was elected Vice President of the United States.

. . . The power of a creditor to imprison his debtor, is the only case in the United States, where, among free men, one citizen has legal authority to deprive his co-equal fellow citizen, at discretion, of the right of personal liberty. It constitutes an awful exception, both in our civil and criminal code, which, in my humble opinion, is repugnant to the spirit of the Constitution. In the case of minors, it is true, the parent has a limited control over the child— the guardian over his ward—and the master over his apprentice; but this power is necessarily given only on account of the minority of the subject.

When the years of infancy are past, and man attains to the age of freedom, our laws regard his personal liberty too sacred to be annihilated by his own voluntary act. If a man by solemn contract binds himself to serve another, even if the reward of that service is

SOURCE: Richard M. Johnson in the Senate, January 14, 1823, *Annals of the Congress of the United States*, 17th Congress, 2nd Session (Washington, D.C.: Gales & Seaton, 1855), pp. 107–111, 124–125.

paid at its commencement, the contract is void in law, and cannot be enforced. . . . however strong your claim may be to his personal service, the principle is deemed too dangerous to be tolerated in a free government, to permit a man, for any pecuniary consideration, to dispose of the liberty of his equal. But, in cases of debt, our present law, regardless of the honesty or the misfortunes of the debtor, gives to the creditor this sovereign power over his person, a power too sacred to be abridged by his own act, to lodge him in prison at discretion. You vest the creditor with the prerogative of Heaven, without imparting to him its attributes of righteousness or mercy: the power to execute vengeance where there is no crime, and to inflict punishment without trial or proof of guilt.

Let us examine, whether there is any solid foundation on which this barbarous practice, this anomaly in our laws, can find support. I will advance it as an incontrovertible principle, that poverty is no crime; nor is a failure to fulfil a pecuniary engagement, when prevented by misfortune, in any degree associated with guilt. The victim of penury is a proper object of sympathy and benevolence. If there is a spark of divinity remaining in fallen man, it inspires this sentiment; and the revelation of God's will to his creatures confirms it. A striking illustration of this is given us in the miraculous interference of heaven on behalf of a poor widow, recorded in the Old Testament. Her husband had been a righteous man, though reduced to insolvency. After his death, an unrelenting creditor, like those for whose malicious pleasure this law exists, was threatening to sell her two sons into bondage to pay the debt of their deceased father. She cried to a prophet for advice. Moved with divine compassion, he raised a cry to heaven in her behalf; and the Almighty interposed, by increasing her only remaining store, a solitary cruse of oil, into an abundance equal to the relief which her necessity demanded. Had poverty been a crime in the sight of God, she would not have been rescued from its consequences by a miracle.

Riches carry influence into every society. Wealth is power. But analize merit, and it is found to consist in virtue—in honour—in benevolence. It is a fundamental principle in our institutions, and a uniform sentiment in social life, that the worth of every man depends alone on his mental endowments and his moral qualities; and I believe there never has been a criminal code, either in ancient or modern times, which denounced poverty as a crime. . . . But here we punish misfortune and fraud indiscriminately.

Our laws make no distinction betwixt the honest and dishonest debtor. The honest victim of disappointment, when all his fair prospects are blasted by the unforeseen accident which rends from him in a moment the honest gains of many industrious years, must at this unpropitious moment be torn from the embraces of his family and dragged to the felon's den, where nothing but a wall of stone or brick separates him from the murderer. His poverty is made a crime of so deep a hue as to transcend the pardoning power of the government; and neither the tears of his wife, nor the cries of his helpless children, can restore him to them, nor his industry to their support, till the vengeance of an incensed creditor shall be satiated. . . .

My object is to protect the innocent and punish the guilty; and to effect both of these purposes, guilt must be made manifest by conviction on an impartial trial; and not presumed against every appearance of fact. As the law now exists, guilt is presumed, but not proved; and though we admit the fact that a debtor may be guilty of fraud by concealment, or conveyance of property without a valuable consideration, we do also know that he may be unfortunate and yet honest. . . .

. . . inability to meet pecuniary engagements does not furnish *prima facie* evidence of fraud. It may be received as the evidence of misfortune—of the want of foresight—or of indiscretion; but our present system regards it in the light of conviction of fraud, and delivers over the body to the arbitrary decision of the creditor. This is the essence of tyranny. It is a violent outrage upon the humane maxim of the law, which presumes every person innocent till his guilt is established upon certain evidence; and we have a grievous sin to answer for in permitting a principle so sacred to be thus violated.

But it is said that no honourable man will abuse this power. If this were the fact, and if all men were truly honourable, my feeble efforts today would be worse than useless. But sad experience tells us, that even honourable men, so called, when lured by the love of wealth and made judges in their own cause, are not always entitled to confidence. . . . But admit that no honourable man will mis-use this power: are all creditors honourable? They are not; and we arm the dishonourable with the tyrant's rod to scourge the innocent.

Millennial days have not yet commenced. Satan is not yet

bound; and man is not restored to his pristine purity. The history of the world shows us, that depraved man, savage or civilized, is the same in every country and in every age, when placed under the same circumstances; and that arbitrary power cannot be safely confided to any human being. He will abuse it. For this reason the constitution of the United States has wisely imposed limitations upon the powers of Congress. We cannot abridge the freedom of speech, nor restrict the rights of conscience. Why this limitation upon our power? Because it is liable to abuse. The wisdom and virtue of the whole nation concentrated, are not sufficient to guard against the misuse of power without restriction; and it should never be imparted unless indispensable. Necessity requires that powers . . . should be vested in the government; but they should be confined to the government, and not transferred to citizens in their individual character.

It is far from my desire to limit the power of the creditor over the property of his debtor. It is the sacred duty of government to protect every individual in the quiet and absolute enjoyment of his honest acquisitions; and it is perfectly clear, in my mind, that our laws should recognize an interest of the creditor in the possessions of his debtor. If, in case of debt, the remedy against the property is too limited, let it be extended: give it the greatest latitude; but confine its operation to that object, and do not carry it to personal liberty. . . . The whole property of the debtor is subject to execution, except the tools of the mechanic, the utensils of the farmer and perhaps, in some instances, a bed for the wife and children to lie down and mourn, when all their dependance is gone, and the prison door is barred upon the husband, and the father. . . . Strip the debtor of every thing that can benefit the creditor; but do not take that which will degrade the man, reduce his wife to unnatural widowhood, the children to untimely orphanage, and inflict the keenest wound upon the whole family, without one solitary advantage to the creditor, except the infernal pleasure of gratifying the most diabolical of all human passions, the revenge of a vindictive spirit. . . .

From the remotest period of antiquity to the present day, there never was a time when so many individuals were exerting themselves to improve the intellectual and moral condition of man. The good and the virtuous throughout Christendom, are employing all their energies: and Christians, of every denomination, are united in the mighty effort. Benevolent societies are established in every region of the civilized world. The deaf and the dumb, the male and the female orphan, the pagan and the savage, are all embraced in those moral exertions. Missionaries of our holy religion are penetrating every country. Burmah and Hindostan are receiving lessons of Christian morality, and the worshippers of Juggernaut are learning the knowledge of the true God. Jerusalem is again becoming the field of gospel labour. Divine light begins to beam on Persia, where the sun has long been the idol of their devotion. The savages of our own country are recipients of the same benevolent efforts, and the wilderness of America begins to wear the aspect of gladness. It is not expected that we, as a government, should become members of these societies, and make appropriations of money to carry on their designs; but, while we witness these interesting scenes, which, on every hand, are calculated to rejoice the heart of the philanthropist, it is our duty, and I trust we shall find it our pleasure, to remove every obstacle to the happiness of the human race, and to take from the hand of tyranny the rod of oppression. . . .

. . . there is a general coincidence of sentiment and concurrence of action throughout the nation to increase the happiness of man. Nothing escapes the vigilance of those who are the appointed guardians of public liberty and political prosperity. Commerce and Manufactures, Agriculture and Internal Improvement, Education and Moral Refinement, all occupy the attention of the first statesmen: and now the denunciation of this unmerciful practice, imprisonment for debt, finds its way into executive recommendations and legislative discussions; and as certain as that moral light is irresistible, so sure is the rapid approach of that day, when personal liberty, sacred to every American bosom, shall be held paramount to every pecuniary obligation, and no longer made the sport of misfortune and a prey of despotism. . . .

6. The Radical Reformation of a Depraved Person
Alexis de Tocqueville and Gustave de Beaumont

Two young French aristocrats, Alexis de Tocqueville (1805–1859) and Gustave de Beaumont (1802–1866), arrived in New York in 1831 to study American methods of penal reform. For nearly a year they traveled throughout the United States, recording their observations in journals which were to serve as raw materials for their report to the French government. Because American prisons, especially those in New York and Pennsylvania, had long been a topic of enlightened interest in Europe, the report of the two French travelers produced reforms in the Old World, European officials coming to agree with American reformers that penal institutions should be concerned more with reform and rehabilitation than with punishment of the criminal. The most important byproduct of Tocqueville's visit was his writing of Democracy in America, unquestionably the most perceptive analysis of American society to be published in the nineteenth century. Beaumont, on the other hand, wrote a novel Marie about racial problems in America (Document 25).

. . . There are in America as well as in Europe, estimable men whose minds feed upon philosophical reveries, and whose extreme sensibility feels the want of some illusion. These men, for whom philanthropy has become a matter of necessity, find in the penitentiary system a nourishment for this generous passion. . . . they consider man, however far advanced in crime, as still susceptible of being brought back to virtue. . . .

Others, perhaps without so profound a conviction, pursue nevertheless the same course; they occupy themselves continually with prisons; it is the subject to which all the labours of their life bear reference. Philanthropy has become for them a kind of profession; . . . the penitentiary system . . . to them seems the remedy for all the evils of society.

SOURCE: Alexis de Tocqueville and Gustave de Beaumont, On the Penitentiary System in the United States, and Its Application in France, translation, introduction, notes and additions by Francis Lieber (Philadelphia: Carey, Lea and Blanchard, 1833), pp. 48–60, abridged.

We believe that both overrate the good to be expected from this institution, of which the real benefit can be acknowledged without attributing to it imaginary effects.

There is, first, an incontestable advantage inherent in a penitentiary system of which isolation forms the principal basis. It is that the criminals do not become worse in the prison than they were when they entered it. On this point this system differs essentially from that pursued in our prisons, which not only render the prisoner no better, but corrupt him still more. . . . Such is the fatal influence of the wicked upon each other, that one finished rogue in a prison suffices as a model for all who see and hear him to fashion their vices and immorality upon his.

Nothing, certainly, is more fatal to society than this course of mutual evil instruction in prisons. . . . It is an evil which the penitentiary system of the United States cures completely.

It is evident that all moral contagion among the imprisoned is impossible, particularly in Philadelphia, where thick walls separate the prisoners day and night. . . . The new penitentiaries, in which this contagious influence is avoided, have therefore gained a signal advantage; and as long as that prison has not yet been found whose discipline is completely regenerating in its effects, perhaps we may be permitted to say that the best prison is that which does not corrupt.

It is nevertheless clear, that this result, however weighty, does not satisfy the authors of the system; and it is natural that having preserved the prisoner from the corruption with which he was threatened, they aspire at reforming him. . . .

In Philadelphia, the moral situation in which the convicts are placed, is eminently calculated to facilitate their regeneration. . . .

Nothing distracts . . . the mind of the convicts from their meditations; and as they are always isolated, the presence of a person who comes to converse with them is the greatest benefit, and one which they appreciate in its whole extent. When we visited this penitentiary, one of the prisoners said to us: "it is with joy that I perceive the figure of the keepers, who visit my cell. This summer a cricket came into my yard; it looked like a companion. When a butterfly or any other animal happens to enter my cell, I never do it any harm." If the soul is thus disposed, it is easy to conceive what value the prisoners must attach to moral communications, and how great must be the influence of wise advice and pious exhortations on their minds.

The superintendent visits each of them at least once a day. The inspectors visit them at least twice a week, and a chaplain has the special charge of their moral reformation. Before and after these visits, they are not entirely alone. The books which are at their disposal, are in some measure companions who never leave them. The Bible, and sometimes tracts containing edifying anecdotes, form their library. If they do not work, they read, and several of them seem to find in it a great consolation. . . .

Can there be a combination more powerful for reformation than that of a prison which hands over the prisoner to all the trials of solitude, leads him through reflection to remorse, through religion to hope; makes him industrious by the burden of idleness, and which, whilst it inflicts the torment of solitude, makes him find a charm in the converse of pious men, whom otherwise he would have seen with indifference, and heard without pleasure?

The impression made by such a system on the criminal, certainly is deep; experience alone can show whether the impression is durable. . . .

In the prisons of Auburn, Wethersfield, Sing-Sing, and Boston, the system of reformation does not rest upon so philosophical a theory as at Philadelphia. . . .

The Auburn plan, which permits the prisoners to assemble during the day, seems, indeed, less calculated than that of Philadelphia to produce reflection and repentance; but it is more favourable to the instruction of the prisoners; in all prisons subject to the same discipline, the instructor and the chaplain can address all the prisoners at once. . . . After the school, and the service of Sunday, the prisoners return to their solitary cells, where the chaplain visits them; he visits them in a similar way on the other days of the week; and strives to touch their hearts by enlightening their conscience; the prisoners feel pleasure when they see him enter their cell. He is the only friend who is left to them; they confide in him all their sentiments; if they have any complaint against the officers of the prison, or if they have a favour to sue for, it is he who is intrusted with their wishes. By showing the interest which he takes in them, he gains more and more their confidence. He soon becomes initiated into all the secrets of their previous life, and, knowing the moral state of all, he endeavours to apply to each the proper remedy for his evil. . . .

Now, to what point is this reformation actually effected by the different systems which we have examined?

Before we answer this question, it will be necessary to settle the meaning attached to the word *reformation.*

Do we mean by this expression the radical change of a wicked person into an honest man—a change which produces virtues in the place of vices?

A similar regeneration, if it ever take place, must be very rare. What would it be in fact? To give back its primitive purity to a soul which crime has polluted. But here the difficulty is immense. It would have been much easier for the guilty individual to remain honest, than it is to rise again after his fall. It is in vain that society pardons him; his conscience does not. Whatever may be his efforts, he never will regain that delicacy of honour, which alone supports a spotless life. Even when he resolves to live honestly, he cannot forget that he *has been* a criminal; and this remembrance, which deprives him of self-esteem, deprives also his virtue of its reward and its guaranty.

Yet if we consider all the means employed in the prisons of the United States, in order to obtain this complete regeneration of the wicked, it is difficult to believe that it should not be sometimes the reward of so many efforts. It may be the work of pious men who devote their time, their cares, and their whole life to this important object. If society be incapable of calming the conscience, religion has the power. If society pardon, it restores liberty to the prisoner's person—this is all. When God pardons, he pardons the soul. With this moral pardon, the criminal regains his self-esteem, without which honesty is impossible. This is a result which society never can attain, because human institutions, however powerful over the actions and the will of men, have none over their consciences. . . .

But if it be true that the radical reformation of a depraved person is only an accidental instead of being a natural consequence of the penitentiary system, it is nevertheless true that there is another kind of reformation, less thorough than the former, but yet useful for society, and which the system we treat of seems to produce in a natural way.

We have no doubt, but that the habits of order to which the

prisoner is subjected for several years, influence very considerably his moral conduct after his return to society.

The necessity of labour which overcomes his disposition to idleness; the obligation of silence which makes him reflect; the isolation which places him alone in presence of his crime and his suffering; the religious instruction which enlightens and comforts him; the obedience of every moment to inflexible rules; the regularity of a uniform life; in a word, all the circumstances belonging to this severe system, are calculated to produce a deep impression upon his mind.

Perhaps, leaving the prison he is not an honest man; but he has contracted honest habits. He was an idler; now he knows how to work. His ignorance prevented him from pursuing a useful occupation; now he knows how to read and to write; and the trade which he has learnt in the prison, furnishes him the means of existence which formerly he had not. Without loving virtue, he may detest the crime of which he has suffered the cruel consequences; and if he is not more virtuous he has become at least more judicious; his morality is not honour, but interest. . . . if he has not become in truth better, he is at least more obedient to the laws, and that is all which society has the right to demand. . . .

The advantages of the penitentiary system of the United States may then be classed in the following manner.

First, Impossibility of the mutual corruption of the prisoners.

Secondly, Great probability of their contracting habits of obedience and industry, which render them useful citizens.

Thirdly, Possibility of a radical reformation.

Though each of the establishments which we have examined aims at these three results, there are nevertheless, in this respect, some shades of difference, which distinguish the Auburn system from that of Philadelphia.

Philadelphia has, as we have already observed, the advantage over Auburn in respect to the first point. Indeed, the prisoners, separated by thick walls, can communicate with each other still less than those who are separated by silence only. The Auburn discipline guaranties the certainty that silence shall not be violated, but it is a mere moral certainty, subject to contradiction; whilst at Philadelphia, communications among the convicts is physically impossible.

The Philadelphia system being also that which produces the deepest impressions on the soul of the convict, must effect more reformation than that of Auburn. The latter, however, is perhaps more conformable to the habits of men in society, and on this account effects a greater number of reformations, which might be called "legal," inasmuch as they produce the external fulfilment of social obligations.

If it be so, the Philadelphia system produces more honest men, and that of New York more obedient citizens.

7. Inviolability of the Life of Man
John L. O'Sullivan

FEW Americans who urged prison reform in the early nineteenth century also advocated abolition of capital punishment, for the list of capital crimes had been reduced to a mere handful during the preceding half-century. After Louisiana and Massachusetts had discussed and rejected such a proposal during the 1830's, a committee headed by John L. O'Sullivan (1813–1895) presented a report to the New York legislature; in spite of the eloquence of its arguments this effort too was defeated. O'Sullivan, a descendant of a prominent Irish family in New York, graduated from Columbia College and practiced law before entering Democratic politics. In 1837 he established The United States Magazine and Democratic Review which for a decade was the chief Party exponent of exuberant nationalism and "manifest destiny." After serving in the legislature, O'Sullivan held minor diplomatic posts for a time. Because of Southern sympathies he lived abroad during the Civil War, returning to New York in 1879, where he lived until his death. Throughout his life O'Sullivan was both a champion of lost causes and a spokesman for humanitarian ideals and aspirations.

. . . The question . . . is nothing more nor less than that of the expediency of the total abolition of the punishment of death by law. . . .

It may be conceded, . . . in the abstract, that society does possess the public right of inflicting the punishment of death for the crime of murder, as an extension of the natural private right of self-defence which resides in the hand of every individual. The wilful murderer, says the argument, has proved by his one crime the danger to which the community would be liable of its repetition, if he is ever placed in a position of liberty again to gratify the sanguinary impulses which he has already manifested. It is lawful therefore to put him to death, as the only sure and safe guarantee against his ever being placed in that position. And again, the threat held out by the law, of death as the penalty of murder, of blood as

SOURCE: *Report in Favor of the Abolition of Capital Punishment made to the Legislature of the State of New York, April 14, 1841* (Albany: New York Senate Documents, 1841), vol. 6, no. 249, pp. 2–139, abridged.

the retribution of blood, is calculated to operate as the most powerful restraint possible against the commission of that crime; therefore society has the right to hold out that threat, and with it, that to make it effectual to the end proposed, by carrying it into execution.

The first branch of the argument is not entitled to much consideration. . . . In countries and in times in which the science of the construction and discipline of penitentiaries, which in ours has been so highly cultivated, was almost or wholly unknown . . . — the reasoning of this part of the argument would not be without weight. . . .

The strongholds that we build, are not those in which iron-handed crime may find an inaccessible impunity for the past, and license for the future; they are the prisons in which the stern but enlightened penal justice of the society grasps and compresses the former with a skilfully directed power which equally crushes all resistance, and baffles all evasion. . . .

. . . With us, therefore, the execution of the criminal is never necessary as the fulfilment of the condition above stated, as legalizing the practice of capital punishment, namely, as an act of self-defence against a repetition, by the criminal, of the offence of which its first commission has proved him capable. . . .

How dangerous and doubtful a principle, then, this is, on which the right of capital punishment by society rests—how liable to abuse and misuse—how fruitful a source it has been of tyranny the most monstrous . . . [by] governments, and . . . of suffering the most appalling—it cannot be necessary here to point out. And if this right is to be recognized at all, on this last and sole ground remaining to it, of *social expediency*, to sacrifice that life which the worst criminal cannot forfeit—to extinguish that "vital spark of heavenly flame" which we have no Promethean reed to rekindle—it cannot at least be denied that it is one of the applications the most to be distrusted, and the most carefully to be guarded, of that old principle from which have proceeded so much of human wretchedness and wrong, *the principle of doing an evil that a good may come.* This principle it is that has in all ages heretofore made the very rivers of the earth to flow with blood and tears. This it is that has many a time buried the massacred bodies of a whole population, in indiscriminate confusion, of age, sex and condition, beneath the ashes of their homes—that has mowed down, as with a huge scythe of destruction, all the life, human, brute and vegetable, which had before gladdened the face of provinces—when war has swept through them, with his torch and his sword and his merciless heart. This it is that has ground millions of mankind to the dust, beneath the oppression of countless false social and civil institutions, which have been founded on narrow and partial views of political expediency, in disregard of the essential and unalienable equal rights of humanity. This it is that has chained to the flaming stake tens and hundreds of thousands of the martyrs to great truths which have been deemed in their day, by society, to portend danger to the leading institutions and interests of its existing organization. . . .

. . . Therefore, while the committee will not now any further discuss or question the principle, in its abstraction— . . . that society may lawfully inflict the doom decreed by it of blood for blood, if necessary, to the end of preventing, by the terror of the example, the future perpetration of other murders by other murderers—they will content themselves with urging the truth which no voice will be raised to controvert, that it is only in a *clearly established* case of such *absolute necessity*, that the right, if it exists at all, can rightfully be exercised. . . .

In opposition to the proposed reform it must therefore be clearly shown, that the punishment of death for the crime of murder is necessary as the most effectual preventive possible of the frequency of that crime; and also . . . that it is not accompanied with other evil consequences, upon the general well-being of society, sufficient to neutralize the amount of advantage which it may be supposed to possess in this respect over all other modes of preventive punishment. . . .

The substitute proposed by the committee, for the punishment of death, is, as will appear more fully below, *solitary imprisonment for life, with labor, placed beyond the reach of either Executive or Legislative clemency.* It may safely be left to the mind of every hearer of the mere mention of so dreadful a doom, to decide which of the two, in prospective, as the alternative penalties of crime, would exert, upon the mind of the man who might be brooding over the idea of such a temptation, the strongest influence to arrest the incipient purpose; or its execution, even after decision.

The truth is undoubtedly, . . . that to those passions, and those motives, from which proceed the great crimes visited by us with the penalty of death, the anticipation of such an imprisonment—perpetual, hopeless and laborious—involving civil death, with the total severance of all the social ties that bound the convicted culprit to the world—under a brand of ignominy and a ban of excommunication from his race, than which alone it is difficult to imagine a more fearful doom—would operate as a far more powerful control and check, than the fear of a hundred deaths. . . .

The committee hope that they will not be here met with the objection, sometimes heard from those "tender mercies" which prefer to hang a criminal for very love and kindness, that the punishment they propose would be, as Cain exclaimed, "greater than man can bear"—though the objection itself would be fatal to the whole doctrine of capital punishment. . . . the distinction between the two may be thus stated, that while the one (death) is cruel without being sufficiently severe, the other would be severe without being unnecessarily cruel. It would spare, at least, the soul, and leave to it all of Time allowed by its Maker himself for its preparation for the Eternity that awaits it. The internal arrangements of the establishment should afford and require the exercise in the open air, proper for the preservation of health. And hard as would be the life and dreadful the doom, yet labor would afford to every hour its needful occupation, and occasional indulgences of books, etc., might perhaps be usefully allowed, as convenient aids to the means and methods of the prison discipline; while the minister of religion would have free scope for the application of all the resources of that mighty and benignant spiritual power of which he is the organ, to reform and to renew the fallen nature of the guilty and miserable wretch, who, though irrevocably under the ban of man's violated law, can never be cast beyond the reach of the pardoning love and the consoling mercy of that of God. . . .

The practice of capital punishment by society, for the purpose of exciting a moral influence on the minds of men to deter them from the crime of murder, is in truth a suicidal one—its direct tendency being clearly subversive of its own object. The Voice of God has issued the perpetual and universal mandate to the race of his creation, "Thou shalt not kill!" From the inmost depths of man's own nature, where reside all those instincts and sympathies that bid him revolt with horror from the thought of murder, the same Voice still forever repeats to him the high and holy law. "Thou shalt not kill!" It should be the policy of all social government to maintain and magnify by every means in its power this great idea of the inviolability of the life of man. . . . That blood should never be shed—that union should never be severed—whether by public or private hand, "*for in the image of God made He man!*" This sacrosanctity of human life should never be violated. Though he should be crimsoned thrice over with the blood of the most deliberate and malignant crime, still in the murderer's own person should the holiness of this high principle be always recognized and respected. . . .

Now, on the contrary, we ourselves directly attack the idea of the sacred inviolability of life. We hold up high aloft in the view of the whole community, amid all the most solemn formalities of public deliberation and public judgment, the sanction of our own example, in the infliction of death as the fitting and lawful punishment for human crime. We justify it, we suggest it, we teach it; and the trains of thought which we ourselves thus start and prompt, in many a mind already, perhaps, more or less disordered by physical or moral derangement, by an excited passion under a pressure of suffering, or resentment under a sense of wrong, whether just or imaginary—who can say where they may end? . . . what can be more dangerous than the example which society does thus hold out, of the punishment that may rightfully be inflicted by man upon man? . . . In the opinion of the committee it cannot be doubted that many a murder has its origin in this source. . . .

The history of all human progress is but a record of the slow and successive conquests of reason over error. . . . All civilizations have had their birth in barbarism; and hence the long and obstinate retention by the former of many of the habits and ideas which were a disgrace even to the latter. It is not in this country—happily for us a thousand ways—that such an argument as this will avail much, to turn back our hand from any good work of reform to which we are prompted, alike by that Christianity which brings us a direct revelation of the will of the great Author of our being, and by that Reason which interprets to us that same will from the evidences of experience and the philosophy of our own wonderful nature. . . .

8. Flogging in the Navy Is Immutably Wrong
Herman Melville

LIFE in the United States Navy in the 1840s was neither easy nor pleasant, young Herman Melville (1819–1891) discovered. At the age of twenty-one he sailed on a whaling expedition to the Pacific, returning to Boston nearly four years later as a seaman on an American frigate. During this period he had successively deserted from the whaler, lived with cannibals in the Marquesas Islands, and voyaged throughout the South Seas. His adventures provided material for four novels, including Moby Dick, which he wrote in the succeeding seven years. Yet it was his experience aboard the man-of-war United States from Honolulu to Boston which called forth his greatest indignation. White-jacket, first published in 1850, is not his greatest novel, but it was instrumental in bringing humanitarian reform to the Navy; after copies of the book had been placed on the desk of every member of Congress, a law was passed abolishing flogging as a form of punishment. In some ways Melville's plea for this reform was uncharacteristic: his pessimistic view of human nature was not conducive to a belief in the efficacy of reform, either of man or of society.

'All hands witness punishment, ahoy!'

To the sensitive seaman that summons sounds like a doom. He knows that the same law which impels it—the same law by which the culprits of the day must suffer; that by that very law he also is liable at any time to be judged and condemned. And the inevitableness of his own presence at the scene: the strong arm that drags him in view of the scourge, and holds him there till all is over: forcing upon his loathing eye and soul the sufferings and groans of men who have familiarly consorted with him, eaten with him, battled out watches with him—men of his own type and badge—all this conveys a terrible hint of the omnipotent authority under which he lives. Indeed, to such a man the naval summons to witness punishment carries a thrill, somewhat akin to what we may impute to the quick and the dead, when they shall hear the Last Trump, that is to bid them all arise in their ranks, and behold the final penalties inflicted upon the sinners of our race. . . .

SOURCE: Herman Melville, White-jacket; or The World in a Man-of-war (New York: Harper & Brothers, 1850), chapters XXXIII–XXXVI, abridged.

As if in sympathy with the scene to be enacted, the sun . . . was now setting over the dreary waters, veiling itself in vapours. The wind blew hoarsely in the cordage; the seas broke heavily against the bows; and the frigate, staggering under whole topsails, strained as in agony on her way.

'*All hands witness punishment, ahoy!*'

At the summons the crew crowded round the mainmast; multitudes eager to obtain a good place on the booms, to overlook the scene; many laughing and chatting, others canvassing the case of the culprits; some maintaining sad, anxious countenances, or carrying a suppressed indignation in their eyes; a few purposely keeping behind to avoid looking on; in short, among five hundred men there was every possible shade of character. . . .

Presently the captain came forward from his cabin, and stood in the centre of this solemn group, with a small paper in his hand. That paper was the daily report of offences, regularly laid upon his table every morning or evening, like the day's journal placed by a bachelor's napkin at breakfast.

'Master-at-arms, bring up the prisoners,' he said. . . .

'You John, you Peter, you Mark, you Antone,' said the captain, 'were yesterday found fighting on the gun-deck. Have you anything to say?'

Mark and Antone, two steady, middle-aged men, whom I had often admired for their sobriety, replied that they did not strike the first blow; that they had submitted to much before they had yielded to their passions; but as they acknowledged that they had at last defended themselves, their excuse was overruled.

John—a brutal bully, who, it seems, was the real author of the disturbance—was about entering into long extenuation, when he was cut short by being made to confess, irrespective of circumstances, that he had been in the fray.

Peter, a handsome lad about nineteen years old, belonging to the mizen-top, looked pale and tremulous. . . . To all his supplications the captain turned a deaf ear. Peter declared that he had been struck twice before he had returned a blow. 'No matter,' said the captain, 'you struck at last, instead of reporting the case to an officer. I allow no man to fight on board here but myself. *I* do the fighting.'

'Now, men,' he added, 'you all admit the charge; you know the penalty. Strip! Quarter-masters, are the gratings rigged?' . . .

At a sign from the captain, John, with a shameless leer, advanced, and stood passively upon the grating, while the bare-headed old quarter-master, with grey hair streaming in the wind, bound his feet to the crossbars, and stretching out his arms over his head, secured them to the hammock-nettings above. He then retreated a little space, standing silent. . . .

The captain's finger was now lifted, and the first boatswain's mate advanced, combing out the nine tails of his *cat* with his hand, and then, sweeping them round his neck, brought them with the whole force of his body upon the mark. Again, and again, and again; and at every blow higher and higher rose the long, purple bars on the prisoner's back. But he only bowed over his head, and stood still. . . . One dozen lashes being applied, the man was taken down, and went among the crew with a smile, saying, 'D--n me! it's nothing when you're used to it! Who wants to fight?'

The next was Antone, the Portuguese. At every blow he surged from side to side, pouring out a torrent of involuntary blasphemies. Never before had he been heard to curse. When cut down, he went among the men, swearing to have the life of the captain. Of course, this was unheard by the officers.

Mark, the third prisoner, only cringed and coughed under his punishment. He had some pulmonary complaint. He was off duty for several days after the flogging; but this was partly to be imputed to his extreme mental misery. It was his first scourging, and he felt the insult more than the injury. He became silent and sullen for the rest of the cruise.

The fourth and last was Peter, the mizen-top lad. . . . The fourth boatswain's mate advanced, and at the first blow the boy, shouting 'My God! Oh! my God!' writhed and leaped so as to displace the gratings, and scatter the nine tails of the scourge all over his person. At the next blow he howled, leaped, and raged in unendurable torture.

'What are you stopping for, boatswain's mate?' cried the captain. 'Lay on!' and the whole dozen was applied.

'I don't care what happens to me now!' wept Peter, going among the crew, with blood-shot eyes, as he put on his shirt. 'I have been flogged once, and they may do it again if they will. Let them look out for me now!'

'Pipe down!' cried the captain; and the crew slowly dispersed.

Let us have the charity to believe them—as we do—when some

captains in the Navy say, that the thing of all others most repulsive to them, in the routine of what they consider their duty, is the administration of corporal punishment upon the crew; for, surely, not to be scarified to the quick at these scenes would argue a man but a beast.

You see a human being, stripped like a slave; scourged worse than a hound. And for what? For things not essentially criminal, but only made so by arbitrary laws. . . .

One of the arguments advanced by officers of the Navy in favour of corporal punishment is this: it can be inflicted in a moment; it consumes no valuable time; and when the prisoner's shirt is put on, *that* is the last of it. Whereas, if another punishment were substituted, it would probably occasion a great waste of time and trouble, besides thereby begetting in the sailor an undue idea of his importance.

. . . But in accordance with this principle, captains in the Navy, to a certain extent, inflict the scourge—which is ever at hand—for nearly all degrees of transgression. In offences not cognisable by a court-martial, little, if any, discrimination is shown. . . .

. . . though the captain of an English armed ship is authorised to inflict, at his own discretion, more than a dozen lashes (I think three dozen), yet it is to be doubted whether, upon the whole, there is as much flogging at present in the English Navy as in the American. The chivalric Virginian, John Randolph of Roanoke, declared, in his place in Congress, that on board of the American man-of-war that carried him out Ambassador to Russia he had witnessed more flogging than had taken place on his own plantation of five hundred African slaves in ten years. Certain it is, from what I have personally seen, that the English officers, as a general thing, seem to be less disliked by their crews than the American officers by theirs. The reason probably is, that many of them, from their station in life, have been more accustomed to social command; hence, quarter-deck authority sits more naturally on them. A coarse, vulgar man, who happens to rise to high naval rank by the exhibition of talents not incompatible with vulgarity, invariably proves a tyrant to his crew. It is a thing that American man-of-war's men have often observed, that the lieutenants from the Southern States, the descendants of the old Virginians, are much less severe, and much more gentle and gentlemanly in command, than the Northern officers, as a class. . . .

. . . Are we not justified in immeasurably denouncing this thing? Join hands with me, then; and, in the name of that Being in whose image the flogged sailor is made, let us demand of legislators, by what right they dare profane what God Himself accounts sacred. . . .

It is to no purpose that you apologetically appeal to the general depravity of the man-of-war's man. Depravity in the oppressed is no apology for the oppressor; but rather an additional stigma to him, as being, in a large degree, the effect, and not the cause and justification of oppression. . . .

If there are any three things opposed to the genius of the American Constitution, they are these: irresponsibility in a judge, unlimited discretionary authority in an executive, and the union of an irresponsible judge and an unlimited executive in one person.

Yet by virtue of an enactment of Congress, all the commodores in the American Navy are obnoxious to these three charges, so far as concerns the punishment of the sailor for alleged misdemeanours not particularly set forth in the Articles of War. . . .

Certainly the necessities of navies warrant a code for its government more stringent than the law that governs the land; but that code should conform to the spirit of the political institutions of the country that ordains it. It should not convert into slaves some of the citizens of a nation of freemen. . . .

. . . Irrespective of incidental considerations, we assert that flogging in the Navy is opposed to the essential dignity of man, which no legislator has a right to violate; that it is oppressive, and glaringly unequal in its operations; that it is utterly repugnant to the spirit of our democratic institutions; indeed, that it involves a lingering trait of the worst times of a barbarous feudal aristocracy; in a word, we denounce it as religiously, morally, and immutably wrong.

No matter, then, what may be the consequences of its abolition; no matter if we have to dismantle our fleets, and our unprotected commerce should fall a prey to the spoiler; the awful admonitions of justice and humanity demand that abolition without procrastination; in a voice that is not to be mistaken, demand that abolition to-day. It is not a dollar-and-cent question of expediency; it is a matter of *right and wrong*. . . .

. . . The world has arrived at a period which renders it the part of Wisdom to pay homage to the prospective precedents of the

Future in preference to those of the Past. The Past is dead, and has no resurrection; but the Future is endowed with such a life, that it lives to us even in anticipation. The Past is, in many things, the foe of mankind; the future is both hope and fruition. The Past is the text-book of tyrants; the Future the Bible of the Free. Those who are solely governed by the Past stand like Lot's wife, crystallised in the act of looking backward, and forever incapable of looking before. . . .

. . . we Americans are driven to a rejection of the maxims of the Past, seeing that, ere long, the van of the nations must, of right, belong to ourselves. There are occasions when it is for America to make precedents, and not to obey them. We should, if possible, prove a teacher to posterity, instead of being the pupil of bygone generations. More shall come after us than have gone before; the world is not yet middle-aged.

Escaped from the house of bondage, Israel of old did not follow after the ways of the Egyptians. To her was given an express dispensation; to her were given new things under the sun. And we Americans are the peculiar, chosen people—the Israel of our time; we bear the ark of the liberties of the world. Seventy years ago we escaped from thrall; and, besides our first birthright—embracing one continent of earth—God has given to us, for a future inheritance, the broad domains of the political pagans, that shall yet come and lie down under the shade of our ark, without bloody hands being lifted. God has predestinated, mankind expects, great things from our race; and great things we feel in our souls. The rest of the nations must soon be in our rear. We are the pioneers of the world; the advance-guard, sent on through the wilderness of untried things, to break a new path in the New World that is ours. In our youth is our strength; in our inexperience, our wisdom. At a period when other nations have but lisped, our deep voice is heard afar. Long enough have we been sceptics with regard to ourselves, and doubted whether, indeed, the political Messiah had come. But he has come in us, if we would but give utterance to his promptings. And let us always remember that with ourselves, almost for the first time in the history of earth, national selfishness is unbounded philanthropy; for we cannot do a good to America, but we give alms to the world.

9. The Strong Claims of Suffering Humanity
Dorothea L. Dix

IN 1841 a former teacher struggling against incipient tuberculosis volunteered to give religious instruction to women incarcerated in the House of Correction near Boston. There, Dorothea Lynde Dix (1802–1887) first became conscious of the plight of the insane. With the support of prominent legislators and reformers such as Charles Sumner, Samuel Gridley Howe and Horace Mann, she launched a crusade to arouse the public conscience and stimulate reform. During the next two years the indefatigable Miss Dix, overcoming physical infirmities, visited every jail and almshouse in Massachusetts, presenting her findings in the following memorial. She worked behind the scenes, and by enlisting the aid of leading male citizens to push her proposals avoided much of the disapprobation usually visited upon feminist reformers. Following her success in Massachusetts with a nationwide campaign for state-supported asylums, Miss Dix traveled more than thirty thousand miles in ten years. After serving as Superintendent of Nurses for the Union Army during the Civil War, she resumed her crusade until her eighty-fifth year when she died at the New Jersey State Asylum where she had retired to conclude her work.

Gentlemen,—I respectfully ask to present this Memorial, believing that the cause, which actuates to and sanctions so unusual a movement, presents no equivocal claim to public consideration and sympathy. Surrendering to calm and deep convictions of duty my habitual views of what is womanly and becoming, I proceed briefly to explain what has conducted me before you unsolicited and unsustained, trusting, while I do so, that the memorialist will be speedily forgotten in the memorial.

About two years since leisure afforded opportunity and duty prompted me to visit several prisons and almshouses in the vicinity of this metropolis. I found, near Boston, in the jails and asylums for the poor, a numerous class brought into unsuitable connection with criminals and the general mass of paupers. I refer to idiots and insane persons, dwelling in circumstances not only adverse to their

SOURCE: D. L. Dix, "Memorial to the Legislature of Massachusetts, 1843," Old South Leaflets (Boston: The Directors of the Old South Work, n.d. [1904]), vol. VI, no. 14, pp. 489–491, 493, 497–501, 503–505, 513–514, 519.

own physical and moral improvement, but productive of extreme disadvantages to all other persons brought into association with them. I applied myself diligently to trace the causes of these evils, and sought to supply remedies. As one obstacle was surmounted, fresh difficulties appeared. Every new investigation has given depth to the conviction that it is only by decided, prompt, and vigorous legislation the evils to which I refer, and which I shall proceed more fully to illustrate, can be remedied. I shall be obliged to speak with great plainness, and to reveal many things revolting to the taste, and from which my woman's nature shrinks with peculiar sensitiveness. But truth is the highest consideration. *I tell what I have seen*—painful and shocking as the details often are—that from them you may feel more deeply the imperative obligation which lies upon you to prevent the possibility of a repetition or continuance of such outrages upon humanity. If I inflict pain upon you, and move you to horror, it is to acquaint you with sufferings which you have the power to alleviate, and make you hasten to the relief of the victims of legalized barbarity.

I come to present the strong claims of suffering humanity. I come to place before the Legislature of Massachusetts the condition of the miserable, the desolate, the outcast. I come as the advocate of helpless, forgotten, insane, and idiotic men and women; of beings sunk to a condition from which the most unconcerned would start with real horror; of beings wretched in our prisons, and more wretched in our almshouses. . . .

I proceed, gentlemen, briefly to call your attention to the *present* state of insane persons, confined within this Commonwealth, in *cages, closets, cellars, stalls, pens! Chained, naked, beaten with rods, and lashed* into obedience.

As I state cold, severe *facts*, I feel obliged to refer to persons, and definitely to indicate localities. But it is upon my subject, not upon localities or individuals, I desire to fix attention; and I would speak as kindly as possible of all wardens, keepers, and other responsible officers, believing that *most* of these have erred not through hardness of heart and wilful cruelty so much as want of skill and knowledge, and want of consideration. . . . Prisons are not constructed in view of being converted into county hospitals, and almshouses are not founded as receptacles for the insane. And yet, in the face of justice and common sense, wardens are by law compelled to receive, and the masters of almshouses not to refuse, insane and idiotic subjects in all stages of mental disease and privation.

It is the Commonwealth, not its integral parts, that is accountable for most of the abuses which have lately and do still exist. I repeat it, it is defective legislation which perpetuates and multiplies these abuses. . . .

. . . In traversing the State, I have found hundreds of insane persons in every variety of circumstance and condition, many whose situation could not and need not be improved; a less number, but that very large, whose lives are the saddest pictures of human suffering and degradation. I give a few illustrations; but description fades before reality.

Danvers. November. Visited the almshouse. A large building, much out of repair. Understand a new one is in contemplation. Here are from fifty-six to sixty inmates, one idiotic, three insane; one of the latter in close confinement at all times.

Long before reaching the house, wild shouts, snatches of rude songs, imprecations and obscene language, fell upon the ear, proceeding from the occupant of a low building, rather remote from the principal building to which my course was directed. Found the mistress, and was conducted to the place which was called *"the home"* of the *forlorn* maniac, a young woman, exhibiting a condition of neglect and misery blotting out the faintest idea of comfort, and outraging every sentiment of decency. . . . There she stood, clinging to or beating upon the bars of her caged apartment, the contracted size of which afforded space only for increasing accumulations of filth, a *foul* spectacle. There she stood with naked arms and dishevelled hair, the unwashed frame invested with fragments of unclean garments, the air so extremely offensive, though ventilation was afforded on all sides save one, that it was not possible to remain beyond a few moments without retreating for recovery to the outward air. . . .

Ipswich. Have visited the prison there several times; visited the almshouse once. In the latter are several cases of insanity; three especially distressing, situated in a miserable outbuilding, detached from the family-house, and confined in stalls or pens; three individuals, one of whom is apparently very insensible to the deplorable circumstances which surround him, and perhaps not likely to comprehend privations or benefits. Not so the person directly opposite to him, who looks up wildly, anxiously by turns, through those strong bars. Cheerless sight! strange companionship for the mind flitting and coming by turns to some perception of persons and things. He, too, is one of the returned incurables. . . .

Violence and severity do but exasperate the insane: the only availing influence is kindness and firmness. It is amazing what these will produce. How many examples might illustrate this position! I refer to one recently exhibited in Barre. The town paupers are disposed of annually to some family who, for a stipulated sum, agree to take charge of them. One of them, a young woman, was shown to me well clothed, neat, quiet, and employed at needlework. Is it possible that this is the same being who, but last year, was a raving mad woman, exhibiting every degree of violence in action and speech; a very tigress wrought to fury; caged, chained, beaten, loaded with injuries, and exhibiting the passions which an iron rule might be expected to stimulate and sustain. It is the same person. Another family hold her in charge who better understand human nature and human influences. She is no longer chained, caged, and beaten; but, if excited, a pair of mittens drawn over the hands secures from mischief. Where will she be next year after the annual sale? . . .

. . . I have . . . stated facts of personal history, in order that a judgment may be formed from few of many examples as to the justness of incarcerating lunatics in all and every stage of insanity, for an indefinite period or for life, in dreary prison, and in connection with every class of criminals who may be lodged successively under the same roof, and in the same apartments. I have shown . . . to what condition men may be brought, not through crime, but misfortune, and that misfortune embracing the heaviest calamity to which human nature is exposed. . . .

Westford. Not many miles from Wayland is a sad spectacle; was told by the family who kept the poorhouse that they had twenty-six paupers, one idiot, one simple, and one insane, an incurable case from Worcester Hospital. I requested to see her, but was answered that she "wasn't fit to be seen. She was naked, and made so much trouble they did not know how to get along." I hesitated but a moment. I must see her, I said. I cannot adopt descriptions of the condition of the insane secondarily. What I assert for fact, I must see for myself. On this I was conducted above stairs. . . . A young woman, whose person was partially covered with portions of a blanket, sat upon the floor; her hair dishevelled; her naked arms crossed languidly over the breast; a distracted, unsteady eye and low murmuring voice betraying both mental and physical disquiet. *About the waist was a chain*, the extremity of which was fastened into the wall of the house. . . .

I have been asked if I have investigated the causes of insanity. I have not; but I have been told that this most calamitous overthrow of reason often is the result of a life of sin: it is sometimes, but rarely, added, they must take the consequences; they deserve no better care. Shall man be more just than God, he who causes his sun and refreshing rains and life-giving influence to fall alike on the good and the evil? Is not the total wreck of reason, a state of distraction, and the loss of all that makes life cherished a retribution sufficiently heavy, without adding to consequences so appalling every indignity that can bring still lower the wretched sufferer? Have pity upon those who, while they were supposed to lie hid in secret sins, "have been scattered under a *dark veil of forgetfulness*, over whom is spread a heavy night, and who unto themselves are more grievous than the darkness." . . .

The master of one of the best-regulated almshouses, namely, that of Plymouth, where every arrangement shows that the comfort of the sick, the aged, and the infirm, is suitably cared for, and the amendment of the unworthy is studied and advanced, said, as we stood opposite a latticed stall where was confined a madman, that the hours of the day were few when the whole household was not distracted from employment by screams and turbulent stampings, and every form of violence which the voice or muscular force could produce. . . . It was morally impossible to do justice to the sane and insane in such improper vicinity to each other. The conviction is continually deepened that hospitals are the only places where insane persons can be at once humanely and properly controlled. Poorhouses converted into madhouses cease to effect the purposes for which they were established, and instead of being asylums for the aged, the homeless, and the friendless, and places of refuge for orphaned or neglected childhood, are transformed into perpetual bedlams.

This crying evil and abuse of institutions is not confined to our almshouses. The warden of a populous prison near this metropolis, populous not with criminals only, but with the insane in almost every stage of insanity, and the idiotic in descending states from silly and simple, to helpless and speechless, has declared that . . .

"the prison has often more resembled the infernal regions than any place on earth!" . . .

It is not few, but many, it is not a part, but the whole, who bear unqualified testimony to this evil. A voice strong and deep comes up from every almshouse and prison in Massachusetts where the insane are or have been protesting against such evils as have been illustrated in the preceding pages. . . .

10. The Darkened Mind of the Blind
Samuel Gridley Howe and Charles Dickens

THE lot of the physically and mentally handicapped in the United States was first significantly alleviated through the efforts of Dr. Samuel Gridley Howe (1801–1876). Following graduation from Harvard Medical School, and an eight-year romantic interlude fighting for Greek and Polish independence, he determined to devote his life to the improvement of the human condition. The first objective which seized his interest was education of the blind and deaf; after surveying European educational programs, he began his work at the Perkins Institution in Boston in 1832. Howe's success with blind, deaf and dumb Laura Bridgman was widely publicized, and in 1842 Charles Dickens, on a lecture tour of the United States, visited his school; the British novelist's American Notes, while severely critical of American manners and morals in general, praised his activities. The final decades of Howe's life were devoted to abolitionism, in which he was ably supported by his wife Julia Ward Howe, author of "The Battle Hymn of the Republic." Like most New England reformers, Howe was involved in a multitude of reform activities, but unlike many of them his life was a record of concrete accomplishments.

The Perkins Institution and Massachusetts Asylum for the Blind, at Boston, is superintended by a body of trustees. . . . The indigent blind of that state are admitted gratuitously. . . . Those who prove unable to earn their own livelihood will not be retained; as it is not desirable to convert the establishment into an almshouse, or to retain any but working bees in the hive. . . .

I went to see this place one very fine winter morning; an Italian sky above, and the air so clear and bright on every side, that even my eyes, which are none of the best, could follow the minute lines and scraps of tracery in distant buildings. . . . When I paused for a moment at the door, and marked how fresh and free the whole scene was— . . . and, turning, saw a blind boy with his sightless face addressed that way, as though he too had some sense within him of the glorious distance: I felt a kind of sorrow that the place should be so very light, and a strange wish that for his sake it were darker. It was but momentary, of course, and a mere fancy, but I felt it keenly for all that. . . .

SOURCE: Charles Dickens, American Notes for General Circulation (New York: Harper & Brothers, 1842), chap. III, abridged.

It is strange to watch the faces of the blind, and see how free they are from all concealment of what is passing in their thoughts; observing which, a man with eyes may blush to contemplate the mask he wears. . . . every idea, as it rises within them, is expressed with the lightning's speed, and nature's truth. If the company at a rout, or drawing-room at a court, could only for one time be as unconscious of the eyes upon them as blind men and women are, what secrets would come out, and what a worker of hypocrisy this sight, the loss of which we so much pity, would appear to be!

The thought occurred to me as I sat down in another room, before a girl, blind, deaf, and dumb; destitute of smell; and nearly so, of taste: before a fair young creature with every human faculty, and hope, and power of goodness and affection, inclosed within her delicate frame, and but one outward sense—the sense of touch. There she was, before me; built up, as it were, in a marble cell, impervious to any ray of light, or particle of sound; with her poor white hand peeping through a chink in the wall, beckoning to some good man for help, that an Immortal soul might be awakened.

Long before I looked upon her, the help had come. Her face was radiant with intelligence and pleasure. . . . From the mournful ruin of such bereavement, there had slowly risen up this gentle, tender, guileless, grateful-hearted being.

Like other inmates of that house, she had a green ribbon bound round her eyelids. A doll she had dressed lay near upon the ground. I took it up, and saw that she had made a green fillet such as she wore herself, and fastened it about its mimic eyes. . . .

I have extracted a few disjointed fragments of her history, from an account, written by that one man who has made her what she is. It is a very beautiful and touching narrative; and I wish I could present it entire.

Her name is Laura Bridgman. "She was born in Hanover, New Hampshire, on the twenty-first of December, 1829. She is described as having been a very sprightly and pretty infant, with bright blue eyes. She was, however, so puny and feeble until she was a year and a-half old, that her parents hardly hoped to rear her. . . . but when a year and a-half old, she seemed to rally; the dangerous symptoms subsided; and at twenty months old, she was perfectly well. . . .

"But suddenly she sickened again; her disease raged with great violence during five weeks, when her eyes and ears were inflamed, suppurated, and their contents were discharged. But though sight and hearing were gone for ever, the poor child's sufferings were not ended. . . . It was now observed that her sense of smell was almost entirely destroyed; and, consequently, that her taste was much blunted.

"It was not until four years of age that the poor child's bodily health seemed restored, and she was able to enter upon her apprenticeship of life and the world. . . .

"At this time, I was so fortunate as to hear of the child, and immediately hastened to Hanover to see her. . . . The parents were easily induced to consent to her coming to Boston, and on the 4th of October, 1837, they brought her to the Institution.

"For a while, she was much bewildered; and after waiting about two weeks, until she became acquainted with her new locality, and somewhat familiar with the inmates, the attempt was made to give her knowledge of arbitrary signs, by which she could interchange thoughts with others.

"There was one of two ways to be adopted: either to go on to build up a language of signs on the basis of the natural language which she had already commenced herself, or to teach her the purely arbitrary language in common use: that is, to give her a sign for every individual thing, or to give her a knowledge of letters by combination of which she might express her idea of the existence, and the mode and condition of existence, of any thing. The former would have been easy, but very ineffectual; the latter seemed very difficult, but, if accomplished, very effectual. I determined therefore to try the latter.

"The first experiments were made by taking articles in common use, such as knives, forks, spoons, keys, &c., and pasting upon them labels with their names printed in raised letters. These she felt very carefully, and soon, of course, distinguished that the crooked lines s p o o n, differed as much from the crooked lines k e y, as the spoon differed from the key in form.

"Then small detached labels, with the same words printed upon them, were put into her hands; and she soon observed that they were similar to the ones pasted on the articles. She showed her perception of this similarity by laying the label k e y upon the key, and the label s p o o n upon the spoon. She was encouraged here by the natural sign of approbation, patting on the head. . . .

"Hitherto, the process had been mechanical, and the success about as great as teaching a very knowing dog a variety of tricks. The poor child had sat in mute amazement, and patiently imitated everything her teacher did; but now the truth began to flash upon her: her intellect began to work: she perceived that here was a way by which she could herself make up a sign of anything that was in her own mind, and show it to another mind; and at once her countenance lighted up with a human expression: it was no longer a dog, or parrot: it was an immortal spirit, eagerly seizing upon a new link of union with other spirits! I could almost fix upon the moment when this truth dawned upon her mind, and spread its light to her countenance; I saw that the great obstacle was overcome; and that henceforward nothing but patient and persevering, but plain and straightforward, efforts were to be used. . . .

"The whole of the succeeding year was passed in gratifying her eager inquiries for the names of every object which she could possibly handle; in exercising her in the use of the manual alphabet; in extending in every possible way her knowledge of the physical relations of things; and in proper care of her health.

"At the end of the year a report of her case was made, from which the following is an extract.

" 'It has been ascertained beyond the possibility of doubt, that she cannot see a ray of light, cannot hear the least sound, and never exercises her sense of smell, if she have any. Thus her mind dwells in darkness and stillness, as profound as that of a closed tomb at midnight. Of beautiful sights, and sweet sounds, and pleasant odors, she has no conception; nevertheless, she seems as happy and playful as a bird or a lamb; and the employment of her intellectual faculties, or the acquirement of a new idea, gives her a vivid pleasure, which is plainly marked in her expressive features. . . .

" 'During the year she has attained great dexterity in the use of the manual alphabet of the deaf mutes; and she spells out the words and sentences which she knows, so fast and so deftly, that only those accustomed to this language can follow with the eye the rapid motions of her fingers.

" 'But wonderful as is the rapidity with which she writes her thoughts upon the air, still more so is the ease and accuracy with which she reads the words thus written by another; grasping their hands in hers, and following every movement of their fingers, as letter after letter conveys their meaning to her mind. It is in this way that she converses with her blind playmates, and nothing can more forcibly show the power of mind in forcing matter to its purpose than a meeting between them. For if great talent and skill are necessary for two pantomimes to paint their thoughts and feelings by the movements of the body, and the expression of the countenance, how much greater the difficulty when darkness shrouds them both, and the one can hear no sound! . . .'

"In her intellectual character it is pleasing to observe an insatiable thirst for knowledge, and a quick perception of the relations of things. In her moral character, it is beautiful to behold her continual gladness, her keen enjoyment of existence, her expansive love, her unhesitating confidence, her sympathy with suffering, her conscientiousness, truthfulness, and hopefulness."

Such are a few fragments from the simple but most interesting and instructive history of Laura Bridgman. The name of her great benefactor and friend, who writes it, is Doctor Howe. There are not many persons, I hope and believe, who, after reading these passages, can ever hear that name with indifference. . . .

The affection that exists between these two—the master and the pupil—is as far removed from all ordinary care and regard, as the circumstances in which it has had its growth, are apart from the common occurrences of life. He is occupied now, in devising means of imparting to her higher knowledge, and of conveying to her some adequate idea of the Great Creator of that universe in which, dark and silent and scentless though it be to her she has such deep delight and glad enjoyment.

Ye who have eyes and see not, and have ears and hear not; ye who are as the hypocrites of sad countenances, and disfigure your faces that ye may seem unto men to fast; learn healthy cheerfulness, and mild contentment, from the deaf, and dumb, and blind! Self-elected saints with gloomy brows, this sightless, earless, voiceless child may teach you lessons you will do well to follow. Let that poor hand of hers lie gently on your hearts; for there may be something in its healing touch akin to that of the Great Master whose precepts you misconstrue, whose lessons you pervert, of whose charity and sympathy with all the world, not one among you in his daily practice knows as much as many of the worst among those fallen sinners, to whom you are liberal in nothing but the preachment of perdition! . . .

11. Appeal to the Wealthy of the Land
Mathew Carey

CHARITABLE benevolence had been accepted as a social as well as a Christian duty in the eighteenth century, but the rise of industrial society saw this concept challenged in Europe and America by proponents of the "dismal science" of political economy. Arguing that the natural and inevitable tendency of the economic system was to force wages down to the subsistence level, David Ricardo, Thomas Malthus and their American disciples maintained that charity to the poor and indigent was wasteful, wicked and self-defeating. The most eloquent American critic of this view was Mathew Carey (1760–1839), a relic of the Enlightenment who flourished as a Philadelphia journalist, publisher and philanthropist for more than a half-century. In his youth Carey's pamphleteering activities in his native Ireland and in pre-revolutionary France had sent him to jail, until he came to the attention of Franklin and Lafayette, who encouraged him to emigrate to the United States in 1785. Success and influence affected neither the humanitarian fervor nor the charitable activities of this pious Catholic, who a few years before his death published several pamphlets reiterating the rational justification for "moral stewardship."

I PROPOSE in these essays to consider, and attempt to refute, certain pernicious errors which too generally prevail respecting the situation, the conduct, the characters, and the prospects of those whose sole dependence is on the labour of their hands—who comprise, throughout the world, two-thirds, perhaps three-fourths, of the human race—and on whose services the other third or fourth depend for their necessaries, their comforts, their enjoyments, and their luxuries.

According to these calculations, the number of persons in the United States depending on wages for their support must be eight of nine millions. . . . Whatever concerns their comfort or happi-

SOURCE: M. Carey, *Appeal to the Wealthy of the Land, Ladies as well as Gentlemen, on the Character, Conduct, Situation, and Prospects of Those Whose Sole Dependence for Subsistence is on the Labour of Their Hands.* Third Edition, Improved (Philadelphia: L. Johnson, 1833), pp. 5–12.

ness—whatever tends to increase or decrease their comforts—to improve or deteriorate their morals, demands the most serious attention of the friends of humanity, of all whose views extend beyond their own narrow selfish concerns, and who, without the services of this class, would be forlorn and helpless.

The class in question is susceptible of two great subdivisions—those who are so well remunerated for their labours, as to be able, not merely to provide, when employed, for seasons of stagnation and sickness, but by industry, prudence, and economy, to save enough in the course of a few years, to commence business on a small scale on their own account. With this fortunate description, which is numerous and respectable, I have no concern at present. My object is to consider the case of those whose services are so inadequately remunerated, owing to the excess of labour beyond the demand for it, that they can barely support themselves while in good health and fully employed; and, of course, when sick or unemployed, must perish, unless relieved by charitable individuals, benevolent societies, or the guardians of the poor. . . .

The erroneous opinions to which I have alluded are—

1. That every man, woman, and grown child, able and willing to work may find employment.

2. That the poor, by industry, prudence, and economy, may at all times support themselves comfortably, without depending on eleemosynary aid—and, as a corollary from these positions,

3. That their sufferings and distresses chiefly, if not wholly, arise from their idleness, their dissipation, and their extravagance.

4. That taxes for the support of the poor, and aid afforded them by charitable individuals, or benevolent societies, are pernicious, as, by encouraging the poor to depend on them, they foster their idleness and improvidence, and thus produce, or at least increase, the poverty and distress they are intended to relieve.

These opinions, so far as they have operated—and, through the mischievous zeal and industry of the school of political economists by which they have been promulgated, they have spread widely—have been pernicious to the rich and the poor. They tend to harden the hearts of the former against the sufferings and distresses of the latter,—and of course prolong those sufferings and distresses. . . .

Many wealthy individuals, benevolent and liberal, apprehensive lest by charitable aid to persons in distress, they might produce evil to society, are, by these pernicious and cold-blooded doctrines, prevented from indulging the feelings of their hearts, and employing a portion of their superfluous wealth for the best purpose to which it can be appropriated—that purpose which, at the hour of death, will afford the most solid comfort on retrospection—that is, "to feed the hungry; to give drink to the thirsty; to clothe the naked; to comfort the comfortless." The economists in question, when they are implored by the starving poor for "bread," tender them "a stone." To the unfeeling and uncharitable of the rich (and such unhappily there are), these doctrines afford a plausible pretext, of which they are not slow to avail themselves, for withholding their aid from the poor. They have moreover tended to attach a sort of disrepute to those admirable associations of ladies and gentlemen, for the relief of the poor, on which Heaven looks down with complacence, and which form a delightful oasis in the midst of the arid deserts of sordid selfishness which on all sides present themselves to the afflicted view of the contemplative observer. . . .

Far from being surprised that among the poor there are to be found many worthless persons, it appears, that the surprise, all things considered, ought to be, that there are so few. In the first place, it is well known that we are the creatures of education and example; and how lamentably deficient the mass of the poor are in point of education and example, we all know. No small proportion have had no education; others only a mere smattering: and the examples which they are to copy, are, alas! too generally ill qualified to form them as useful or estimable members of society. . . .

The first position on which I propose to animadvert is—

"That every man, woman, and child, able and willing to work, may find employment."

So far is this from being true, that a very cursory reflection would satisfy any candid person, that in the most prosperous times and countries, there are certain occupations, which, by the influence of fashion or other causes, suffer occasional stagnations. There are other occupations, at which employment is at all times precarious—and others, again, which furnish little or no employment at certain seasons of the year. . . .

It is frequently said, as a panacea for the distresses of those people—"Let them go into the country; there they will find employment enough." To say nothing of the utter unfitness of most of those persons for country labour, this is taking for granted what remains to be proved. The country rarely affords employment for extra hands, except for a few weeks at harvest time. Farmers are generally supplied with steady hands at all other seasons. But were it otherwise, take the case of a man of a delicate constitution, with a wife and three or four small children; what a miserable chance would he stand of support by country labour! . . .

The second position which I propose to controvert is—

"That the poor, by industry, prudence, and economy, may at all times support themselves comfortably, without depending on eleemosynary aid: and, as a corollary from this,

"That their sufferings and distresses chiefly, if not wholly, arise from their idleness, their dissipation, and their extravagance."

A primary element in this discussion is a consideration of the wages ordinarily paid to the class of persons whose case I attempt to develope, and whose cause I have undertaken to plead—and first, of the very numerous class, labourers on canals and turnpikes.

. . . it appears that the average wages of this class, in common times, are from ten to twelve dollars per month and found; that in winter they may be had for five dollars; and that sometimes, in that season, when labour is scarce, they work for their board alone. . . .

I HAVE too good an opinion of human nature, although by no means a believer in its perfection or perfectibility, to doubt that those speculative citizens, who have for years employed their time and their talents in denouncing the idleness, the worthlessness, and the improvidence of the poor, will, on a cool examination of the subject here presented to view, be filled with astonishment and deep regret at the infatuation, whereby they have attempted to dry up the sources of charity and benevolence in the breasts of the rich, and, as far as in them lay, doomed the poor to remediless pauperism—an unholy and ungodly employment. . . .

I might extend these views to a greater length, and embrace various other occupations, which stand on nearly the same ground as those I have specified: but I presume it cannot be necessary; and hope I have established a point of infinite importance to the poor, and highly interesting to the rich—that is, that even among the occupations of males, there are some which are so indifferently remunerated, that no industry, no economy, no providence, in times when the parties are fully employed, will enable them to save wherewith to support themselves and families in times of stagnation, and during severe seasons; and that of course they must rely, on those occasions, upon the overseers of the poor, or benevolent societies, or charitable individuals, or on such extraordinary aid, as, to the honour of our citizens, the late (1830) distressing scenes called forth. If I succeed in deeply imprinting this important truth on the public mind, so that it may produce the proper effect, by removing the injurious prejudices that prevail on the conduct and character of the labouring poor, on the effects of benevolent societies, and on the claims of those societies for extensive support, I shall regard myself as signally fortunate. . . .

Let it not be for a moment supposed, that I carry my defence of the poor to such an extravagant and ill-judged length, as to contend that all their distresses and sufferings arise from inadequate wages, or that they are all faultless: far from it. I know there are among them, as among all other classes, worthless persons—and some supremely worthless. Among the heavy sins of this class are intemperance, and desertion by some of them, of their wives and children, or, what is at least as bad, living in a state of idleness on the earnings of their wives. Indeed, so far as regards their ill-fated partners, the latter course is the worse. In the one case, the husband only withdraws his aid: in the other, he not only commits that offence, but adds to the burdens of his wife. . . .

But while I freely admit that there are among the poor many worthless, I am fully satisfied, from the most attentive examination of the subject, that the worthless of both sexes bear but a very small proportion to those who are industrious and meritorious. Unfortunately, the worthless occupy a more prominent space in the public eye, and with many are unceasing objects of animadversion and reprobation; their numbers and their follies and vices are magnified: whereas the industrious and meritorious are, I repeat, generally in the background, out of view. . . .

12. A General Union of the
Various Trades and Arts
Ely Moore

AN important development of the 1830s was the organization of unions
by skilled workers in several Eastern cities. As inflationary pressures
mounted, strikes or "turnouts" demonstrated labor militancy; separate
crafts formed loose city-wide alliances, and in 1834 the first national labor
organization in American history came into being, drawing its member-
ship from a half-dozen cities. Ely Moore (1798–1860), a former printer
who had recently become active in New York City Democratic politics,
was elected first president of the General Trades' Union of New York in
1833, and a year later presided over the first convention of the National
Trades' Union. Within a few months New York Democrats had nomi-
nated and elected him to Congress. Surviving periodic accusations of
political opportunism, he served two terms, notable mainly for his
reiterated defense of the right of labor to organize to defend its rights
and improve its status. A labor spokesman rather than a labor leader,
Moore in later years primarily devoted his energies to the pursuit of
political office. The following address was given at the first annual celebration of the General Trades' Union; although its rhetoric frightened
conservatives, it demonstrates his moderation regarding the aims and
methods of labor agitation and organization.

We have assembled, on the present occasion, for the purpose of
publicly proclaiming the motives which induced us to organize a
general union of the various trades and arts in this city and its
vicinity, as well as to defend the course and to vindicate the
measures we deign to pursue. This is required of us by a due regard
to the opinions of our fellow men.

. . . man, by nature, is selfish and aristocratic. *Self-love* is constitutional with man, and is displayed in every stage and in all the
diversities of life; in youth and in manhood, in prosperity and in
adversity. . . . This prevailing disposition of the human heart, so
far from being an evil in itself, is one of the elements of life and

SOURCE: Ely Moore, *Address delivered before the General trades'
union of the city of New-York, at the Chatham-street chapel,
Monday, December 2, 1833* (New York: J. Ormond, n.d.
[1833]), pp. 7–14, 19–20, 32.

essential to the welfare of society. The *selfish* generate the social feelings. It is only pernicious in its tendency and operation, therefore, when it passes its true and natural bounds and urges man to encroach upon the rights and immunities of man. . . .

. . . Wherever man exists, under whatever form of government, or whatever be the structure or organization of society, this principle of his nature, selfishness, will appear, operating either for evil or for good. To curb it sufficiently by legislative enactments is impossible. Much can be done, however, towards restraining it within proper limits by unity of purpose and concert of action on the part of the *producing* classes. To contribute toward the achievement of this great end is one of the objects of the "General Trades' Union." Wealth, we all know, constitutes the aristocracy of this country. Happily no distinctions are known among us save what wealth and worth confer. . . . The greatest danger, therefore, which threatens the stability of our Government and the liberty of the people is an undue accumulation and distribution of wealth. And I do conceive that real danger is to be apprehended from this source, notwithstanding that tendency to distribution which naturally grows out of the character of our statutes of conveyance, of inheritance, and descent of property; but by securing to the producing classes a fair, certain, and equitable compensation for their toil and skill, we insure a more just and equal distribution of wealth than can ever be effected by statutory law.

. . . We ask . . . what better means can be devised for promoting a more equal distribution of wealth than for the producing classes to *claim*, and by virtue of union and concert, *secure their claims* to their respective portions? And why should not those who have the toil have the enjoyment also? Or why should the sweat that flows from the brow of the laborer be converted into a source of revenue for the support of the crafty or indolent?

It has been averred, with great truth, that all governments become cruel and aristocratical in their character and bearing in proportion as one part of the community is elevated and the other depressed, and that misery and degradation to the many is the inevitable result of such a state of society. And we regard it to be equally true that, in proportion as the line of distinction between the employer and employed is *widened*, the condition of the latter inevitably verges toward a state of vassalage, while that of the former as certainly approximates toward supremacy; and that whatever system is calculated to make the many dependent upon or subject to the few not only tends to the subversion of the natural rights of man, but is hostile to the best interests of the community, as well as to the spirit and genius of our Government. Fully persuaded that the foregoing positions are incontrovertible, we, in order to guard against the encroachments of aristocracy, to preserve our natural and political rights, to elevate our moral and intellectual condition, to promote our pecuniary interests, to narrow the line of distinction between the journeyman and employer, to establish the honor and safety of our respective vocations upon a more secure and permanent basis, and to alleviate the distresses of those suffering from want of employment have deemed it expedient to form ourselves into a "General Trades' Union."

It may be asked, how these desirable objects are to be achieved by a general union of trades? How the encroachments of aristocracy, for example, are to be arrested by our plan? We answer, by enabling the producer to enjoy the full benefit of his productions, and thus diffuse the streams of wealth more generally and, consequently, more equally throughout all the ramifications of society. . . .

There are, doubtless, many individuals who are resolved, right or wrong, to misrepresent our principles, impeach our measures, and impugn our motives. Be it so. They can harm us not. . . . We have the consolation of knowing that all good men, all who love their country, and rejoice in the improvement of the condition of their fellow men, will acknowledge the policy of our views and the purity of our motives. . . . And why, let me ask, should the character of our Union be obnoxious to censure? Wherefore is it wrong in principle? Which of its avowed objects reprehensible? What feature of it opposed to the public good? I defy the ingenuity of man to point to a single measure which it recognizes that is wrong in itself or in its tendency. What, is it wrong for men to unite for the purpose of resisting the encroachments of aristocracy? Wrong to restrict the principle of selfishness to its proper and legitimate bounds and objects? Wrong to oppose monopoly and mercenary ambition? Wrong to consult the interests and seek the welfare of the producing classes? Wrong to attempt the elevation of our moral and intellectual standing? Wrong to establish the honor and safety of our respective vocations upon a more secure and permanent basis? I ask—in the name of heaven I ask—can it be wrong for men to attempt the melioration of their condition and the preservation of their natural and political rights?

I am aware that the charge of "illegal combination" is raised against us. The cry is as senseless as 'tis stale and unprofitable. Why, I would inquire, have not journeymen the same right to ask their own price for their own property or services that employers have? or that merchants, physicians, and lawyers have? Is that equal justice which makes it an offense for journeymen to combine for the purpose of maintaining their present prices or raising their wages, while employers may combine with impunity for the purpose of lowering them? I admit that such is the common law. All will agree, however, that it is neither wise, just, nor politic, and that it is directly opposed to the spirit and genius of our free institutions and ought therefore, to be abrogated.

It is further alleged that the General Trades' Union is calculated to encourage *strikes* and *turnouts*. Now, the truth lies in the converse. Our constitution sets forth that "Each trade or art may represent to the Convention, through their delegates, their grievances, who shall take cognizance thereof, and decide upon the same." And further, that "No trade or art shall strike for higher wages than they at present receive, without the sanction of the Convention." True, if the Convention shall, after due deliberation, decide that the members of any trade or art there represented are aggrieved and that their demands are warrantable, then the Convention is pledged to sustain the members of such trade or art to the uttermost. Hence, employers will discover that it is idle, altogether idle, to prolong a contest with journeymen when they are backed by the Convention. And journeymen will perceive that in order to obtain assistance from the Convention, in the event of a strike or turnout that their claims must be founded in justice, and all their measures be so taken as not to invade the rights or sacrifice the welfare of employers. So far, then, from the Union encouraging strikes or turnouts, it is destined, we conceive, to allay the jealousies and abate the asperities which now unhappily exist between employers and the employed. . . .

Again, it is alleged that it is setting a dangerous precedent for journeymen to combine for the purpose of coercing a compliance with their terms. It may, indeed, be dangerous to aristocracy, dangerous to monopoly, dangerous to oppression, but not to the general good or the public tranquillity. Internal danger to a state is not to be apprehended from a general effort on the part of the people to improve and exalt their condition, but from an alliance of the crafty, designing, and intriguing few. What! tell us, in this enlightened age, that the welfare of the people will be endangered by a voluntary act of the people themselves? That the people will wantonly seek their own destruction? That the safety of the state will be plotted against by three-fourths of the members comprising the state! O how worthless, how poor and pitiful, are all such arguments and objections! . . .

My object in inviting you to a consideration of this subject at the present time is to impress upon your minds the importance of the situation which you, in reality, ought to occupy in society. This you seem to have lost sight of in a very great degree; and, from some cause or other, have relinquished your claims to that consideration to which, as mechanics and as men, you are entitled. You have, most unfortunately for yourselves and for the respectability of your vocations, become apparently unconscious of your own worth, and been led to regard your callings as humble and inferior, and your stations as too subordinate in life. And why? why is it so? Why should the producer consider himself inferior to the consumer? Or why should the mechanic, who builds a house, consider himself less important than the owner or occupant? It is strange, indeed, and to me perfectly unaccountable that the artificer, who prepares the accommodations, the comforts, and embellishments of life, should consider himself of less consequence than those to whose pleasure and convenience he ministers. . . .

. . . Pursue knowledge with a diligence that never tires and with a perseverance that never falters; and honor and glory and happiness will be your reward! You have no longer an excuse why you should not prosper and flourish, both as a body and as individuals. You know your rights and, consequently, feel your strength. If mortification and defeat should attend you, blame not your fellowmen; the cause will be found within yourselves. Neither blame your country; the fault will not be hers! No, Land of Genius, Land of Refuge, Land of the Brave and Free! thy sons have no cause to reproach thee! All thy deserving children find favor in thine eyes, support on thy arm, and protection in thy bosom!

13. Right of the People to the Soil
George Henry Evans

BEGINNING in 1828 a political movement of "mechanics and working-men" challenged the dominant parties in the principal northeastern cities. George Henry Evans (1805–1856), a young British emigrant, was the chief journalistic spokesman of the New York Workingmen's Party. For six years he edited and published a series of newspapers, most notably the Working Man's Advocate and the Man, expressing the reformist aspirations of this militant group and supporting the growing trade-union movement. In 1835 Evans, disillusioned with the failure of the political party and facing personal financial problems, left the city for a New Jersey farm, where he eked out a living for nearly ten years. This experience led him to embrace a new program for the salvation of the laboring classes: "vote yourself a farm." He returned to New York to publish a new Working Man's Advocate and to organize the National Reform Association to agitate for land reform. Supported by former associates in the Workingmen's Party and recruits from the Hudson Valley anti-rent wars, Evans dedicated himself to this panacea until his death. Six years later his campaign finally bore fruit with the enactment of the Homestead Act.

Having made due inquiry into the facts, the Committee are satisfied that there is a much larger number of laboring people congregated in the seaboard towns, than can find constant and profitable employment. Your committee do not think it necessary to enter into statistical details in order to prove a fact that is not disputed by anybody. The result of this over-supply of labor is a competition among the laborers, tending to reduce wages, even where employment is obtained, to a scale greatly below what is necessary for the comfortable subsistence of the working man, and the education of his family. It appears to your Committee, that as long as the supply of labor exceeds the demand, the natural laws which regulate prices, will render it very difficult, if not altogether impossible, to permanently improve the condition of the working people. . . .

. . . we find in our cities, and Factory Stations, an increasing population, the great majority of whom depend for a subsistence

SOURCE: "To the People of the United States" [Report of the National Reform Union of the City of New York], Working Man's Advocate (New York), July 6, 1844.

on Mechanical labor; and secondly we find the new born power of machinery throwing itself into the labor-market, with the most astounding effects—withering up all human competition with a sudden decisiveness that leaves no hope for the future. Indeed, if we judge of the next half century by the half century just past, there will be, by the end of that time, little mechanical labor performed by human hands. . . .

This result—this triumph of machine labor, and ultimate prostration of human labor, cannot in the opinion of your committee, be averted. We may wrestle with the monster, as the toilers of England wrestle, till myriads of us perish in the unequal strife. But your Committee are of the opinion that all this will be only so much strife, and so much suffering, wasted in vain. As well might we interfere with the career of the heavenly bodies, or attempt to alter any of Nature's fixed laws, as hope to arrest the onward march of science and machinery.

The question then recurs—the momentous question: "Where lies our remedy? How shall we escape from an evil which it is impossible to avert?"

This question admits of an answer at once simple, satisfactory, and conclusive. Nature is not unjust. The Power who called forth those mechanical forces did not call them forth for our destruction. Our refuge is upon the soil, in all its freshness and fertility—our heritage is on the Public Domain, in all its boundless wealth and infinite variety. This heritage once secured to us, the evil we complain of will become our greatest good. Machinery, from the formidable rival, will sink into the obedient instrument of our will—the master shall become our servant—the tyrant shall become our slave.

If we were circumstanced like the inhabitants of Europe, there would seem to be little hope of getting the laboring population out of the difficulties, and distress, in which they are at present involved. There, every field, of God's inheritance to man, is fenced in, and appropriated by the Aristocracy. There, the working man has nothing to fall back upon. . . .

But in this Republic, all that the Creator designed for man's use, is ours—belongs, not to the Aristocracy, but to the People. The deep and interminable forest; the fertile and boundless prairie; the rich and inexhaustible mine—all—all belong to the People, or are held by the Government in trust for them. Here, indeed, is the natural and healthful field for man's labor. Let him apply to his

Mother Earth, and she will not refuse to give him employment—neither will she withhold from him in due season the fulness of his reward. We are the inhabitants of a country which for boundless extent of territory, fertility of soil, and exhaustless resources of mineral wealth, stands unequalled by any nation, either of ancient or modern times. We live under a Constitution, so just and so equal, that it may well lay claim to a divine origin. As a People we are second to none, in enterprize, industry, and skill. Thus it is clear, that we are in possession of all the elements of individual and national prosperity. And, yet, we allow those elements to lie dormant, that labor which ought to be employed in calling forth the fruitfulness of Nature, is to be found seeking employment in the barren lanes of a city, of course, seeking it in vain. . . .

. . . We regard the Public Lands as a Capital Stock, which belongs, not to us only, but also to posterity. The profits of that stock are ours, and the profits only. The moment Congress, or any other power, attempts to alienate the stock itself to speculators, that moment do they attempt a cruel, and cowardly, fraud upon posterity, against which, as citizens and as honest men, we enter our most solemn protest. It is enough for us to eat our own bread—what right have we to sit down and consume the bread of our children?

The evil of permitting speculators to monopolize the public lands, is already severely felt in all the new states. When the Emigrant reaches the remote borders of civilization he naturally desires to stop there, and fix his home within the pale of civilized society. But the lands lying for many miles around belong to the speculator, and the unfortunate Emigrant must either pay an exorbitant price, which he is generally unable to do, or move off into the desert, and trust himself to the mercy of the wild Indian far beyond the aid of civilized man.

But what is this evil compared with the distress and misery that is in store for our children should we permit the evil of land monopoly to take firm root in this Republic? Go to Europe. Mark the toil, the rags, the hunger, and the despair which is the sole inheritance of its countless millions, while a few thousands run into the opposite extreme of luxury, excess, and guilt unspeakable. Look at this horrible state of things, and whilst you do so, remember that the same fate awaits our own Republic, if we permit a Landed Aristocracy to grow up among us. . . .

The first great object, then, is to assert and establish the right of the people to the soil; to be used by them in their own day, and transmitted—an inalienable heritage—to their posterity. The principles of justice, and the voice of expediency, or rather of necessity, demand that this fundamental principle shall be established as the paramount law, with the least possible delay.

That once effected, let an outlet be formed that will carry off our superabundant labor to the salubrious and fertile West. In those regions thousands, and tens of thousands, who are now languishing in hopeless poverty, will find a certain and a speedy independence. The labor market will be thus eased of the present distressing competition; and those who remain, as well as those who emigrate, will have the opportunity of realizing a comfortable living. . . .

Your Committee can perceive but one way of accomplishing those objects, and that is by combination—by a determined and brotherly union of all citizens who believe the principles set forth to be just, in themselves, and necessary to the public welfare. We propose, therefore, that such Union be organized at once. It is our opinion that all citizens who desire to join the ranks of the National Reformers shall have an opportunity of doing so without delay. . . . we are unanimously of opinion that nothing can be effected without putting the National Reform Test to every candidate for legislative office, State and National. Any man who would oppose the measure of justice for which we contend is not a Republican at all—he is a Monarchist, in soul, and we should treat him as such at the Ballot Box.

. . . if the working men lead the way, manfully, in this reform, they will be immediately joined by a great majority of the non-producing classes. Various motives of a personal nature will induce them to join us—not to say a word about that patriotism and love of justice which, we trust, belong to every class in this Republican Community.

14. The Bodies and Minds
of the Producing Classes
Seth Luther

MOST American labor leaders in this period of increasing industrialization endeavored to improve or maintain the status of the skilled craftsman, barely acknowledging the plight of the unskilled worker; his poverty and degradation were recognized, but his condition was seldom seen to be a consequence of the industrial process. An exception was Seth Luther (1795–c. 1846), who became a spokesman for this submerged class. Despite his training as a skilled carpenter, he labored in New England cotton mills and agitated for improvements in the lot of the factory worker. Even though he had little formal schooling, he expressed faith in education as the bulwark of the Republic. He traveled as an itinerant laborer throughout the West and South, where he acquired a vision of America's democratic promise, capping his career by joining the abortive effort of "Governor" Thomas Dorr to democratize the government of Rhode Island by revolutionary action. Trial and imprisonment affected his mind, and he ended his days in an asylum. The details of Luther's life are obscure, but it is clear from his speeches that he expressed the aspirations of the unskilled—women, children and immigrants—a growing but still silent minority in American society.

. . . In pursuing the proposed subject, on the state of education and condition of the Producing Classes in Europe and America, we assume the following positions, viz. "In a free government, education, which elevates the mind, diffuses intelligence, and leads to virtue, is the only sure foundation of freedom and public safety. Without education a portion of the community is cast into the shade, and oftentimes intellect of the first order is lost to its possessor and to the world. Children of the poor, as well as the rich, ought to be instructed both in letters and morals, and NO STATE

SOURCE: Seth Luther, *An Address to the Working Men of New England, on the State of Education, and on the Condition of the Producing Classes in Europe and America. With Particular Reference to the Effect of Manufacturing (As Now Conducted) on the Health and Happiness of the Poor, and on the Safety of Our Republic*, 3rd ed. (Philadelphia: published by the Author, 1836), pp 6–7, 16–20, 24–29, 31–32.

OF SOCIETY CAN EXCUSE THE NEGLECT OF IT. If we wish to live in a community, peaceably, orderly, free from excess, outrage, and crime, we must use our exertions for the general diffusion of education, of intelligence, among every class of our citizens. In this course, we shall find our interest and happiness. In looking over the catalogue of offenders, we shall find, that vice of every kind and degree most generally springs from ignorance. The want of learning and moral instruction leads to idleness, dissipation, and crime, and often ends in ruin."

. . . A "STATE OF SOCIETY" exists in this country, which prevents the producing classes from a participation in the fountains of knowledge, and the benefits equally designed for all. This state of things is produced and sustained by *Avarice*. . . . Avarice manufactures drunkards, chains and lashes the slave, and crowds down and oppresses the poor, the friendless, and the destitute: it is the father of *all crime* from the days of Adam until the present time. . . .

To hide existing, or anticipated and *inevitable* evils, . . . our ears are constantly filled with the cry of *National* wealth, National glory, *American* System, and American industry. We are told that operatives are happy in our mills, and that they want no change in their regulations, and that they are getting great wages. . . . This stuff is retailed by owners, and agents, and sold wholesale . . . in the capitol at Washington. This cry is kept up by men who are endeavoring *by all the means in their power* to cut down the wages of *our own people*, and who send agents to Europe, to *induce foreigners* to come here, to underwork *American* citizens, to support *American* industry, and the *American* System.

The whole concern (as now conducted) is as great a humbug as ever deceived any people. We see the system of manufacturing lauded to the skies; senators, representatives, owners, and agents of cotton mills using all means to keep out of sight the evils growing up under it. Cotton mills, where cruelties are practised, excessive labor required, education neglected, and vice, as a matter of course, on the increase, are denominated "the principalities of the destitute, the palaces of the poor." . . . A member of the United States Senate [Henry Clay] seems to be *extremely* pleased with cotton mills; he says in the senate, "Who has not been delighted with the clockwork movements of a large cotton manufactory; he had visited them often, and *always* with increased delight." He says the women work in large airy apartments, well warmed; they are neatly dressed, with ruddy complexions, and happy countenances, . . . and at stated periods they go to and return from their meals with a light and cheerful step. . . . And the grand climax is, that at the end of the week, after working like slaves for 13 or 14 hours every day, "they enter the temples of God on the Sabbath, and thank him for all his benefits,"—and the American System above all requires a peculiar outpouring of gratitude. . . .

We would respectfully advise the honorable senator to travel *incognito*, when he visits cotton mills. If he wishes to come at the *truth*, he must not be known. Let him put on a *short jacket and trowsers*, and join the "LOWER ORDERS" for a short time; then let him go into a factory counting room, and pull off his hat, which he will be told to do in some of our "*republican institutions*," called Cotton Mills; then let him attempt to get work for 75 cents or $1.00 for 14 hours per day, . . . and he will then discover some of the *intrinsic beauties* of factory "clockwork." In that case we could show him in some of the prisons in New England, called cotton mills, instead of rosy cheeks, the *pale, sickly, haggard* countenance of the ragged child, haggard from the *worse* than *slavish* confinement in the cotton mill. He might see that child driven up to the "clockwork" by the cowskin, in some cases; he might see, in some instances, the child taken from his bed at four in the morning, and plunged into cold water to drive away his slumbers and prepare him for the labors in the mill. After all this, he might see that child *robbed*, yes, *robbed* of a part of his time allowed for meals, by moving the hands of the clock backwards, or forwards, as would best accomplish that purpose. . . .

We shall . . . omit entering more largely into detail for the present, respecting the cruelties practised in some of the American mills. Our wish is to show that education is neglected . . . ; because if 13 hours actual labor is required each day, it is *impossible* to attend to education among children, or to improvement among adults. . . .

. . . the owners of mills oppose all reduction in the hours of labor, for the purposes of mental culture. Not that they care about hours of labor in cities, but they fear the "contagion" will reach their SLAVE MILLS. Hence they go into the shop of the carpenter, and others who carry on business, and actually *forbid* them to employ what they sneeringly call "*ten hours* men," telling the employers, you shall not have our work unless you do as we say. We have appealed to their sense of justice, their sense of humanity, their love of country, to consider the evils they are bringing on the poor, through ignorance. What has been the reply? One says, "if a man offers to work for me ten hours, I will kick him off my premises;" another says, "I will shut down my gates, and you will starve in a week, and rather than do that, you will work on our terms." Another says, "O, they can't stand it more than a day or two, and they will soon come back and BEG to go to work." . . . Now when these same men want the votes of the Working Men, they will say, "in strains as sweet as angels use," "Fellow Citizens, we want your assistance, give us 'your voices, your voices, your sweet voices.'" But if you want time to improve your minds, take care of your families, and educate your children, you are called "Disturbers of the peace," "Agitators," "An unholy alliance," "Disorganizers," a "Dangerous Combination" against the higher ORDERS. . . .

The situation of the producing classes in New England is at present very unfavorable to the acquisition of mental improvement. That "the manufacturing establishments are extinguishing the flame of knowledge," we think has been abundantly proved. It is true that there is a great cry about the schools, and lyceums, and books of "sentiment, and taste, and science." . . . But of what use is it to be like Tantalus, up to the chin in water, if we cannot drink? . . . It seems the owners of mills wish to control their men in all things; to enslave their bodies and souls, make them think, act, vote, preach, pray, and worship, as it may suit "We the Owners." That the influence of manufacturing (as now conducted) is detrimental to the public, is beyond dispute. The whole system of labour in New England, more especially in cotton mills, is a cruel system of exaction on the bodies and minds of the producing classes, destroying the energies of both, and for no other object than to enable the "rich" to "take care of themselves," while "the poor must work or starve." The rich do take care of themselves, in one sense, both in this country and Europe. While the daughters of these Nabobs are "taking care of themselves," while they are gracefully sitting at their harp or piano, in their splendid dwellings, while music floats from quivering strings through perfumed and adorned apartments, and dies with gentle cadence on the delicate ear of the rich, the nerves of the poor woman and child in the cotton mill are quivering with almost dying agony, from excessive labour, to support this splendour; and after all this, if that woman or child should lose five minutes time out of 13 hours, she is docked a quarter of a day. . . . If these things are so, and we challenge contradiction, are we not justified in making an "excitement," and in forming a "combination," to check these growing evils? Unless these evils can be remedied, are we not justified in "denouncing these sources of present wealth, however overflowing and abundant, while the enriching stream is undermining and contaminating the best interests of man? "Education and intelligence in the *only sure* FOUNDATION of public safety," and if we are convinced that there are causes in active operation sapping and mining that foundation, can any man say "It is nothing to me?" "If the children of the poor ought to be instructed as well as the rich," ought we not to see that it is done? If it depends on education whether we "live in a peaceable, orderly community, free from excess, outrage, and crime, can we say it is nothing to us?" . . . If "without the assistance of the common people a free government cannot exist," and we find that the capability to govern depends on intelligence and learning; is it not a fearful reflection that so many thousands of children are deprived of education, and so many adults of every opportunity for mental improvement? Let us no longer be deceived. Let us not think we are free until working men no longer trust their affairs in the hands of designing demagogues. . . .

. . . If what we have stated be true, and we challenge denial, what must be done? Must we fold our arms and say, It always was so, and always will be. If we did so, would it not almost rouse from their graves the heroes of our revolution? . . . We know the difficulties are great, and the obstacles many; but, as yet, we "know our rights, and knowing, dare maintain." We wish to injure no man, and we are determined not to be injured as we have been; we wish nothing but those equal rights which were designed for us all. And although wealth, and prejudice, and slander, and abuse, are all brought to bear on us, we have one consolation—"We are the Majority." . . .

Fellow citizens of New England, farmers, mechanics, and labourers, we have borne these evils by far too long; we have been deceived by all parties; we must take our business into our own hands. Let us awake. Our cause is the cause of truth—of justice and humanity. *It must prevail.* Let us be determined no longer to be deceived by the cry of those who produce *nothing* and who enjoy *all*, and who *insultingly* term us—the *farmers*, the *mechanics, and labourers*—the LOWER ORDERS, and *exultingly* claim our homage for themselves, as the *Higher* ORDERS—*while the* DECLARATION OF INDEPENDENCE asserts that "ALL MEN ARE CREATED EQUAL."

15. Emancipate the Proletaries
Orestes A. Brownson

ORESTES AUGUSTUS BROWNSON (1803–1876) embodied the contradictory tendencies of the antebellum reform movement, moving continually between the poles of evangelism and rationalism. As a young man he rejected the Presbyterian creed of his family for the more optimistic tenets of Universalism. Under the influence of Frances Wright, Robert Dale Owen and William Ellery Channing, he next gravitated to militant agnosticism and then to Unitarianism. At the same time he flirted with both Transcendentalism and the workingmen's movement, editing the Boston Quarterly Review as an organ of universal reform. Depressed by the Panic of 1837 and the success of the Whig "log-cabin campaign" of 1840, Brownson developed a radical ideology which, though less rigorous than that of Marx, foreshadowed aspects of the apocalyptic vision of the 1848 Communist Manifesto. While his article on "The Laboring Classes" brought him notoriety, he had reached an intellectual dead end. Increasingly critical of majoritarian democracy, Brownson for a time endorsed Calhoun's defense of minority rights and in 1844 was converted to Catholicism, welcoming the authority and discipline of the Church while embracing a mystical religious faith. His intellectual career thus moved from evangelism to rationalism to Transcendentalism, and from reformism to anti-reformism (see Document 45).

. . . No one can observe the signs of the times with much care, without perceiving that a crisis as to the relation of wealth and labor is approaching. It is useless to shut our eyes to the fact, and like the ostrich fancy ourselves secure because we have so concealed our heads that we see not the danger. We or our children will have to meet this crisis. The old war between the King and the Barons is well nigh ended, and so is that between the Barons and the Merchants and Manufacturers,—landed capital and commercial capital. The business man has become the peer of my Lord. And now commences the new struggle between the operative and his employer, between wealth and labor. Every day does this struggle extend further and wax stronger and fiercer; what or when the end will be God only knows. . . .

SOURCE: O. A. Brownson, The Laboring Classes, an Article from the Boston Quarterly Review, 4th ed. (Boston: Benjamin H. Greene, 1840), pp. 9–14, 16, 18–19, 21–22, 24.

What we would ask is, throughout the Christian world, the actual condition of the laboring classes, viewed simply and exclusively in their capacity of laborers? They constitute at least a moiety of the human race. . . .

. . . All over the world this fact stares us in the face, the workingman is poor and depressed, while a large portion of the nonworkingmen, in the sense we now use the term, are wealthy. It may be laid down as a general rule, with but few exceptions, that men are rewarded in an inverse ratio to the amount of actual service they perform. . . . Now here is the system which prevails, and here is its result. The whole class of simple laborers are poor, and in general unable to procure any thing beyond the bare necessaries of life.

In regard to labor two systems obtain; one that of slave labor, the other that of free labor. Of the two, the first is, in our judgement, except so far as the feelings are concerned, decidedly the least oppressive. If the slave has never been a free man, we think, as a general rule, his sufferings are less than those of the free laborer at wages. As to actual freedom one has just about as much as the other. The laborer at wages has all the disadvantages of freedom and none of its blessings, while the slave, if denied the blessings, is freed from the disadvantages. We are no advocates of slavery, we are as heartily opposed to it as any modern abolitionist can be; but we say frankly that, if there must always be a laboring population distinct from proprietors and employers, we regard the slave system as decidedly preferable to the system at wages. It is no pleasant thing to go days without food, to lie idle for weeks, seeking work and finding none, to rise in the morning with a wife and children you love, and know not where to procure them a breakfast, and to see constantly before you no brighter prospect than the almshouse. Yet these are no unfrequent incidents in the lives of our laboring population. Even in seasons of general prosperity, when there was only the ordinary cry of "hard times," we have seen hundreds of people in a not very populous village, in a wealthy portion of our common country, suffering for the want of the necessaries of life, willing to work, and yet finding no work to do. . . .

One thing is certain; that of the amount actually produced by the operative, he retains a less proportion than it costs the master to feed, clothe, and lodge his slave. Wages is a cunning device of the devil, for the benefit of tender consciences, who would retain all the advantages of the slave system, without the expense, trouble, and odium of being slave-holders. . . .

Now, what is the prospect of those who fall under the operation of this system? We ask, is there a reasonable chance that any considerable portion of the present generation of laborers, shall ever become owners of a sufficient portion of the funds of production, to be able to sustain themselves by laboring on their own capital, that is, as independent laborers? We need not ask this question, for everybody knows there is not. . . .

. . . The actual condition of the working-man to-day, viewed in all its bearings, is not so good as it was fifty years ago. If we have not been altogether misinformed, fifty years ago, health and industrious habits, constituted no mean stock in trade, and with them almost any man might aspire to competence and independence. But it is so no longer. The wilderness has receded, and already the new lands are beyond the reach of the mere laborer, and the employer has him at his mercy. If the present relation subsist, we see nothing better for him in reserve than what he now possesses, but something altogether worse. . . .

Now the great work for this age and the coming, is to raise up the laborer, and to realize in our own social arrangements and in the actual condition of all men, that equality between man and man, which God has established between the rights of one and those of another. In other words, our business is to emancipate the proletaries, as the past has emancipated the slaves. This is our work. There must be no class of our fellow men doomed to toil through life as mere workmen at wages. If wages are tolerated it must be, in the case of the individual operative, only under such conditions that by the time he is of a proper age to settle in life, he shall have accumulated enough to be an independent laborer on his own capital,—on his own farm, or in his own shop. Here is our work. How is it to be done?

Reformers in general answer this question, or what they deem its equivalent, in a manner which we cannot but regard as very unsatisfactory. They would have all men wise, good, and happy; but in order to make them so, they tell us that we want not external changes, but internal; and therefore instead of declaiming against society and seeking to disturb existing social arrangements, we should confine ourselves to the individual reason and conscience; seek merely to lead the individual to repentance, and to reformation of life; make the individual a practical, a truly religious man, and all evils will either disappear, or be sanctified to the spiritual growth of the soul. . . .

This theory, however, is exposed to one slight objection, that of being condemned by something like six thousand years' experience. For six thousand years its beauty has been extolled, its praises sung and its blessings sought, under every advantage which learning, fashion, wealth, and power can secure; and yet under its practical operations, we are assured, that mankind, though totally depraved at first, have been growing worse and worse ever since. . . .

The truth is, the evil we have pointed out is not merely individual in its character. . . . the evil we speak of is inherent in all our social arrangements, and cannot be cured without a radical change of those arrangements. . . . The only way to get rid of its evils is to change the system, not its managers. The evils of slavery do not result from the personal characters of slave masters. They are inseparable from the system, let who will be masters. Make all your rich men good Christians, and you have lessened not the evils of existing inequality in wealth. The mischievous effects of this inequality do not result from the personal characters of either rich or poor, but from itself, and they will continue, just so long as there are rich men and poor men in the same community. You must abolish the system or accept its consequences. No man can serve both God and Mammon. If you will serve the devil, you must look to the devil for your wages, we know no other way.

. . . For our part we are disposed to seek the cause of the inequality of conditions of which we speak, in religion, and to charge it to the priesthood. . . .

Mankind came out of the savage state by means of the priests. Priests are the first civilizers of the race. For the wild freedom of the savage, they substitute the iron despotism of the theocrat. This is the first step in civilization, in man's career of progress. . . .

But, having traced the inequality we complain of to its origin, we proceed to ask again what is the remedy? The remedy is first to be sought in the destruction of the priest. . . .

The next step in this work of elevating the working classes will be to resuscitate the Christianity of Christ. The Christianity of the Church has done its work. We have had enough of that Christianity. It is powerless for good, but by no means powerless for evil. It now unmans us and hinders the growth of God's kingdom. . . .

. . . No man can be a Christian who does not refrain from all practices by which the rich grow richer and the poor poorer, and who does not do all in his power to elevate the laboring classes, so that one man shall not be doomed to toil while another enjoys the fruits; so that each man shall be free and independent, sitting under "his own vine and figtree with none to molest or to make afraid." . . . Preach the Gospel of Jesus, and that will turn every man's attention to the crying evil we have designated, and will arm every Christian with power to effect those changes in social arrangements, which shall secure to all men the equality of position and condition, which it is already acknowledged they possess in relation to their rights. . . .

Having, by breaking down the power of the priesthood and the Christianity of the priests, obtained an open field and freedom for our operations, and by preaching the true Gospel of Jesus, directed all minds to the great social reform needed, and quickened in all souls the moral power to live for it or to die for it; our next resort must be to government, to legislative enactments. Government is instituted to be the agent of society, or more properly the organ through which society may perform its legitimate functions. . . .

. . . as we have abolished hereditary monarchy and hereditary nobility, we must complete the work by abolishing hereditary property. A man shall have all he honestly acquires, so long as he himself belongs to the world in which he acquired it. But his power over his property must cease with his life, and his property must then become the property of the state, to be disposed of by some equitable law for the use of the generation which takes his place. Here is the principle without any of its details, and this is the grand legislative measure to which we look forward. We see no means of elevating the laboring classes which can be effectual without this. . . . The rich, the business community, will never voluntarily consent to it, and we think we know too much of human nature to believe that it will ever be effected peaceably. It will be effected only by the strong arm of physical force. It will come, if it ever comes at all, only at the conclusion of war, the like of which the world as yet has never witnessed, and from which, however inevitable it may seem to the eye of philosophy, the heart of Humanity recoils with horror. . . .

16. Control Over the Instinct of Reproduction
Robert Dale Owen

THE primary function of women in male-dominated nineteenth-century America was the production and nurture of children, yet an annual pregnancy was often a tragedy, especially for a poor family. Thomas Malthus, the British economist, had preached sexual restraint as the only preventative of a population explosion among the poor, who were, after all, the authors of their own misery. In 1831 Robert Dale Owen (1801–1877) rejected the Malthusian argument by writing the first American guide to birth control in order to liberate women from the burden of continual pregnancy. The eldest son of the British reformer (see Document 1), he had arrived in the United States with his father in 1825, remaining to teach school and edit the community newspaper at New Harmony. Forming a close association with the dynamic young Scotswoman Frances Wright (Document 39) and adopting some of her radical ideas, he moved to New York after the collapse of the utopian community; he opened a Hall of Science as a forum for religious skepticism and published the Free Enquirer. Owen soon became active in support of the Workingmen's Party, but with the failure of this movement, he settled in Indiana and embarked upon a political career, while continuing to demonstrate an active interest in philanthropy and social reform.

Among the various instincts which contribute to man's preservation and well-being, the instinct of reproduction holds a distinguished rank. It peoples the earth; it perpetuates the species. Controlled by reason and chastened by good feeling, it gives to social intercourse much of its charm and zest. Directed by selfishness or governed by force, it is prolific of misery and degradation. . . .

. . . Like other instincts, it may assume a selfish, mercenary or brutal character. But, in itself, it appears to me the most social and least selfish of all our instincts. It fits us to give, even while receiving, pleasure; and, among cultivated beings, the former power is

SOURCE: Robert Dale Owen, *Moral Physiology; or A Brief and Plain Treatise on the Population Question* (London: F. Farrah, n.d. [1831]), pp. 9–10, 12, 14, 17–18, 20, 22, 24, 26–27, 30–31, 36, 41–42.

ever more highly valued than the latter. Not one of our instincts affords larger scope for the exercise of disinterestedness, and the best moral sentiments of our race. . . .

It is a serious question—and surely an exceedingly proper and important one—whether man can obtain, and whether he is benefited by obtaining control over this instinct. Is IT DESIRABLE, THAT IT SHOULD NEVER BE GRATIFIED WITHOUT AN INCREASE TO POPULATION? OR, IS IT DESIRABLE, THAT, IN GRATIFYING IT, MAN SHALL BE ABLE TO SAY WHETHER OFFSPRING SHALL BE THE RESULT OR NOT? . . .

The population question has of late years occupied much attention, especially in Great Britain. It was first prominently brought forward and discussed, in 1798, by Malthus, an English clergyman. . . .

. . . He asserts, that in most countries population at this moment presses against the means of subsistence; and that, in all countries, it has a tendency so to do. He recommends, as a preventive of the growing evil, celibacy till a late age, say thirty years; and he asserts, that unless this "moral restraint" is exerted, vice, poverty, and misery, will and must remain as checks to population. . . .

. . . The most enlightened observers of mankind are agreed, that nothing contributes so positively and immediately to demoralize a nation, as when its youth refrain, until a late period, from forming disinterested connections with those of the other sex. The frightful increase of prostitutes, the destruction of health, the rapid spread of intemperance, the ruin of moral feelings, are, to the mass, the *certain* consequences. Individuals there are who escape the contagion; individuals whose better feelings revolt, under *any* temptation, from the mercenary embrace, or the Circean cup of intoxication; but these are exceptions only. The mass will have their pleasures: the pleasures of intellectual intercourse, of unbought affection, and of good taste and good feeling, if they can; but if they cannot, then such pleasures (alas! that language should be perverted to entitle them to the name!) as the sacrifice of money and the ruin of body and mind can purchase.

But this is not all. Not only is Malthus' proposition fraught with immorality, in that it discountenances to a late age those disinterested sexual connections which can alone save youth from vice; but it is *impracticable*. Men and women will scarcely pause to calculate the chances they have of affording support to the children ere they become parents: how, then, should they stop to calculate the chances of the world's being overpeopled? Mr. Malthus may say what he pleases, they never will make any such calculation; and it is folly to expect they should.

Let us observe, then: *unless some more ascetic and more practicable species of "moral restraint" be introduced*, vice and misery will *ultimately* become the inevitable lot of man. He can no more escape them, than he can the light of the sun, or the stroke of death. . . .

What would be the probable effect, in social life, if mankind obtained and exercised a control over the instinct of reproduction?

My settled conviction is—and I am prepared to defend it—that the effect would be salutary, moral, civilizing; that it would prevent many crimes, and more unhappiness; that it would lessen intemperance and profligacy; that it would polish the manners and improve the moral feelings; that it would relieve the burden of the poor, and the cares of the rich; that it would most essentially benefit the rising generation, by enabling parents generally more carefully to educate, and more comfortably to provide for, their offspring. . . .

. . . Is it not notorious, that the families of the married often increase beyond what a regard for the young beings coming into the world, or the happiness of those who give them birth, would dictate? In how many instances does the hard-working father, and more especially the mother of a poor family, remain slaves throughout their lives, tugging at the oar of incessant labour, toiling to live, and living only to die; when, if their offspring had been limited to two or three only, they might have enjoyed comfort and comparative affluence! How often is the health of the mother—giving birth, every year, perchance, to an infant—happy, if it be not twins!—and compelled to toil on, even at those times when nature imperiously calls for some relief from daily drudgery —how often is the mother's comfort, health, nay, her life, thus sacrificed! Or when care and toil have weighed down the spirit, and at last broken the health of the father, how often is the widow left, unable with the most virtuous intentions to save her fatherless offspring from becoming degraded objects of charity, or profligate votaries of vice! . . .

. . . is it not most plainly, clearly, incontrovertibly *desirable*, that parents *should have the power* to limit their offspring, whether they choose to exercise it or not? Who can lose by their having this power? and how many may gain!—may gain competency for themselves, and the opportunity carefully to educate and provide for their children? . . .

If the moral feelings were carefully cultivated—if we were taught to consult, in everything, rather the welfare of those we love than our own, how strongly would these arguments be felt! No man ought even to desire that a woman should become the mother of his children, unless it was her express wish, and unless he knew it to be for her welfare, that she should. Her feelings, her interests, should be for him in this matter *an imperative law.* She it is who bears the burden, and therefore with her also should the decision rest. Surely it may well be a question whether it be desirable, or whether any man ought to ask, that the whole life of an intellectual, cultivated woman, should be spent in bearing a family of twelve or fifteen children—to the ruin, perhaps, of her constitution, if not to the overstocking of the world. No man ought to require or expect it. . . .

Thus, inasmuch as the scruple of incurring heavy responsibilities deters from forming moral connections, and encourages intemperance and prostitution, the knowledge which enables man to limit his offspring would, in the present state of things, save much unhappiness and prevent many crimes. Young persons sincerely attached to each other, and who might wish to marry, would marry early; merely resolving not to become parents until prudence permitted it. The young man, instead of solitary toil or vulgar dissipation, would enjoy the society and the assistance of her he has chosen as his companion; and the best years of life, whose pleasures never return, would not be squandered in riot, or lost through mortification. . . .

But there are other cases, it will be said, where the knowledge of such a check would be mischievous. If young women, it will be argued, were absolved from the fear of consequences, they would rarely preserve their chastity. Unlegalized connections would be common and seldom detected. Seduction would be facilitated. . . .

That chastity which is worth preserving is not the chastity that owes its birth to fear and ignorance. If to enlighten a woman regarding a simple physiological fact will make her a prostitute, she must be especially predisposed to profligacy. But it is a libel on the sex. Few, indeed, there are, who would continue so miserable and degrading a calling, could they escape from it. For one prostitute that is made by inclination, ten are made by necessity. Reform the laws—equalize the comforts of society, and you need withhold no knowledge from wives and daughters. It is want, not knowledge, that leads to prostitution. . . .

I know that parents often think it right and proper to withhold from their children—especially from their daughters—facts the most influential on their future lives, and the knowledge of which is essential to every man and woman's well-being. Such a course has ever appeared to me ill-judged and productive of very injurious effects. A girl is surely no whit better for believing, until her marriage night, that children are found among the cabbage-leaves in the garden. . . .

Among the modes of preventing conception which may have prevailed in various countries, that which has been adopted, and is now practised by the cultivated classes on the continent of Europe, by the French, the Italians, and, I believe, by the Germans and Spaniards, consists of complete withdrawal, on the part of the man, immediately previous to emission. *This is, in all cases, effectual.* It may be objected, that the practice requires a mental effort and a partial sacrifice. I reply, that, in France, where men consider this (as it ought ever to be considered, when the interests of the other sex require it,) a *point of honour*, all young men learn to make the necessary effort; and custom renders it easy, and a matter of course. As for the sacrifice, shall a trifling, . . . diminution of physical enjoyment be suffered to outweigh the most important considerations connected with the permanent welfare of those who are the nearest and dearest to us? Shall it be suffered to outweigh a regard for the comfort, the well-being—in some cases, the *life* of those whom we profess to love?—The most selfish will hesitate deliberately to reply in the affirmative to such questions as these. . . .

The most practical of philosophers, Franklin, interprets chastity to mean, *the regulated and strictly temperate satisfaction, without injury to others, of those desires which are natural to all healthy adult beings.* . . .

The promotion of such chastity is the chief object of the present work. It is all-important for the welfare of our race, that the reproductive instinct should never be selfishly indulged; never gratified at the expense of the well-being of our companions. A man who, in this matter, will not consult, with scrupulous deference, the slightest wishes of the other sex; a man who will ever put his desires in competition with theirs, and who will prize more highly the pleasure he receives than that he may be capable of bestowing —such a man appears to me, in the essentials of character, a brute. . . .

Human beings of whatever sex or class! examine dispassionately and narrowly the influence which the control here recommended will produce throughout society. Reflect whether it will not lighten the burdens of one sex, while it affords scope for the exercise of the best feelings of the other. Consider whether its tendency be not benignant and elevating; conducive to the exercise of practical virtue, and to the permanent welfare of the human.

17. My Womanhood Is Insulted
Angelina Grimké, Theodore D. Weld
and John G. Whittier

In the 1830s the Grimké sisters from South Carolina became a major attraction on the abolitionist lecture circuit. Members of an aristocratic, slave-owning Charleston family, they had moved north largely because of their revulsion against slavery, and in 1836 joined the crusade led by the American Anti-Slavery Society. An Appeal to the Christian Women of the South by the younger sister Angelina (1805–1879), widely circulated in the North and suppressed in the South, brought invitations to the sisters for speaking engagements before women's groups throughout the Northeast. More effective as a speaker than her shy elder sister Sarah, Angelina soon attracted men to these female gatherings, resulting in attacks by the clergy against "promiscuous assemblies." Sarah responded with the publication of The Equality of the Sexes and the Condition of Women and Angelina began interjecting a defense of women's rights into her speeches on the evils of slavery. The abolitionist organizer and lecturer Theodore Dwight Weld (Document 30) and Quaker poet John Greenleaf Whittier remonstrated with the outspoken Angelina, who in the following correspondence gave an eloquent defense of her position. Chastened but not cowed, she married Weld a year later; soon they both retired from active participation in the movement.

[Angelina Grimké to Theodore D. Weld]

[August 12, 1837]

My Dear Brother

No doubt thou hast heard by this time of all the fuss that is now making in this region about our stepping so far out of bounds of female propriety as to lecture to promiscuous assemblies. My auditors literally sit some times with "mouths agape and eyes astare," so that I cannot help smiling in the midst of "rhetorical flourishes" to witness their perfect amazement at hearing a woman speak in the churches. . . . we are placed very unexpectedly in a very trying situation, in the forefront of an entirely new contest—a contest for the rights of woman as a moral, intelligent and responsible being.

SOURCE: Letters of Theodore Dwight Weld, Angelina Grimké Weld and Sarah Grimké, ed. Gilbert H. Barnes and Dwight L. Dumond (New York: D. Appleton-Century Co., 1934), vol. I, pp. 414–416, 418, 423–427, 429–431, 434–436, 450, 452.

. . . I cannot help feeling some regret that this sh'ld have come up *before* the Anti Slavery question was settled, so fearful am I that it may injure that blessed cause, and then again I think this must be the Lord's time and therefore the *best* time, for it seems to have been brought about by a concatenation of circumstances over which we had no control. The fact is it involves the interests of every minister in our land and therefore they will stand almost in a solid phalanx against women's rights . . . ; it will also touch every man's interests at home, in the tenderest relation of life; it will go down into the very depths of his soul and cause great searchings of heart. . . . I must confess my womanhood is insulted, my moral feelings outraged when I reflect on these things, and I am sure *I know just* how the free colored people feel towards the whites when they pay them more than common attention; it is *not paid as a* RIGHT, but *given as a* BOUNTY on a *little* more than *ordinary* sense. There is not one man in 500 who really understands what kind of attention is alone acceptable to a woman of pure and exalted moral and intellectual worth. . . . That a wife is *not* to be subject to her husband in any other sense than I am to her or she to me, seems to be strange and *alarming* doctrine indeed, but how can it be otherwise unless *she surrenders her moral responsibility,* which *no woman has a right* to do? . . .

. . . I have no doubt that posterity will read withal *women* were *not* permitted to preach the gospel, with as much amazement and indignation as we do that no *colored* man in No. Ca. is allowed this *holy right.* Now we want thee to sustain us on the high ground of MORAL RIGHT, *not* of Quaker peculiarity. This question must be met *now;* let us do it as *moral* beings, and not try to turn a SECTARIAN *peculiarity* to the best account for the benefit of Abolitionism. WE do not stand on Quaker ground, but on Bible ground and *moral right.* What we claim for ourselves, we claim for *every* woman whom God has called and qualified with gifts and graces. Can't *thou* stand *just here* side by side with us? . . .

[John Greenleaf Whittier to Sarah and Angelina Grimké]

[August 14, 1837]

My Dear Sisters.—

. . . you are now doing much and nobly to vindicate and assert the rights of woman. Your lectures to crowded and promiscuous audiences are a subject manifestly, in many of its aspects, *political,* interwoven with the framework of the government, are practical and powerful assertions of the right and duty of woman to labor side by side with her brother for the welfare and redemption of the world. Why, then, let me ask, is it necessary for you to enter the lists as controversial writers in this question? Does it not *look*, dear sisters, like abandoning in some degree the cause of the poor and miserable slave, sighing from the cotton plantation of the Mississippi, and whose cries and groans are forever sounding in our ears, for the purpose of arguing and disputing about some trifling oppression, political or social, which we may ourselves suffer? Is it not forgetting the great and dreadful wrongs of the slave in a selfish crusade against some paltry grievance of our own? Forgive me if I have stated the case too strongly. I would not for the world interfere with you in matters of conscientious duty, but I wish you would weigh candidly the whole subject, and see if it does not *seem* an abandonment of your first love. Oh let us try to forget everything but our duty to God and our fellow beings; to dethrone the selfish principle, and to strive to win over the hard heart of the oppressor by truth kindly spoken. . . .

[Weld to Sarah and Angelina Grimké]

[August 15, 1837]

My dear sisters

. . . As to the *rights* and *wrongs* of women, it is an old theme with me. It was the *first* subject I ever *discussed*. In a little debating society when a boy, I took the ground that *sex* neither *qualified* nor *disqualified* for the discharge of any functions mental, moral or spiritual. . . . Further, that the proposition of marriage may with just the same propriety be made by the *woman* as the *man*, and that the *existing usage* on that subject, pronouncing it *alone* the province of the *man*, and *indelicacy* and almost, if not quite *immoral* for *woman* to make the first advances, overlooks or rather *perverts* the sacred design of the institution and debases it into the mire of earthliness and gross sensuality, smothering the spirit under the flesh. Now as I have never found man, woman or child who agreed with me in the "ultraism" of womans rights, I take it for granted even *you* will cry out "oh shocking"!! at the *courting* part of the doctrine. Very well, let that pass. What I advocated in boyhood I advocate now, that woman in EVERY *particular* shares equally with man rights and responsibilities. . . . Now notwithstanding this, I do most deeply regret that you have begun a series of articles in the Papers on the rights of woman. Why, my dear sisters, the best possible advocacy which you can make is just what you are making day by day. Thousands hear you every week who have all their lives held that woman must not speak in public. Such a practical refutation of the dogma as your speaking furnishes has already converted multitudes. . . . Besides you are *Southerners*, have been slaveholders; your dearest friends are all in the sin and shame and peril. All these things give you great access to northern mind, great sway over it. . . . Now this peculiar advantage you *lose* the moment you take *another* subject. You come down from your vantage ground. *Any* women of your powers will produce as much effect as you on the north in advocating the rights of free women (I mean in contradistinction to *slave* women). . . . Now can't you leave the *lesser* work to others who can do it *better* than you, and devote, consecrate your whole bodies, souls and spirits to the *greater* work which you can do far better and to far better purpose than any body else. . . . Let us all *first* wake up the nation to lift millions of slaves of both sexes from the dust, and turn them into MEN and then when we all have our hand in, it will be an easy matter to take millions of females from their knees and set them on their feet, or in other words transform them from *babies* into *women*. . . .

[Angelina Grimké to Weld and Whittier]
[August 20, 1837]

Brethren beloved in the Lord.

As your letters came to hand at the same time and both are devoted mainly to the same subject we have concluded to answer them on one sheet and jointly. You seem greatly alarmed at the idea of our advocating the *rights of woman*. . . .

And can you not see that women *could* do, and *would* do a hundred times more for the slave if she were not fettered? Why! we are gravely told that we are out of our sphere even when we circulate petitions; out of our "appropriate sphere" when we speak to women only; and out of them when we *sing* in the churches. Silence is *our* province, submission *our* duty. If then we "give *no reason* for the hope that is in us," that we have *equal rights* with our brethren, how can we expect to be permitted *much longer* to exercise *those rights*? . . . O that you were here that we might have a good long, *long* talk over matters and things, then I could explain myself far better. And I think we could convince you that we cannot push Abolitionism forward with all our might *until* we take up the stumbling block out of the road. . . . If we dare to stand upright and do our duty according to the dictates of *our own* consciences, why then we are compared to Fanny Wright and so on. . . . we shall *very* soon be compelled to retreat for we shall have *no* ground to stand on. If we surrender the right to *speak* to the public this year, we must surrender the right to petition next year and the right to *write* the year after and so on. What *then* can *woman* do for the slave when she is herself under the feet of man and shamed into *silence?* Now we entreat you to weigh candidly the *whole subject,* and then we are sure you will see, this is no more than an abandonment of our first love than the effort made by Anti Slavery men to establish the *right* of free discussion.

With regard to brother Welds ultraism on the subject of marriage, he is quite mistaken if he fancies he has got far *ahead of us* in the human rights reform. We do *not* think his doctrine at all shocking: it is *altogether right.* But I am afraid I am *too proud* ever to exercise the right. The fact is we are living in such an artificial state of society that there are some things about which we dare not speak out, or act out the most natural and best feelings of our hearts. . . .

Anti Slavery men are trying very hard to separate what God hath joined together. I fully believe that so far from keeping different moral reformations entirely distinct that no such attempt can ever be successful. They are bound together in a circle like the sciences; they blend with each other like the colors of the rain bow; they are the parts only of our glorious whole and that whole is Christianity, pure *practical* christianity. . . .

[Weld to Sarah and Angelina Grimké]

[August 26, 1837]

. . . Since the world began, Moral Reform has been successfully advanced only in *one* way, and that has been by uplifting a great *self evident central* principle before all eyes. . . . No moral enterprise when prosecuted with ability and any sort of energy EVER failed under heaven so long as its conductors pushed the *main* principle and did not strike off until they got to the summit level.

On the other hand every reform that ever foundered in mid sea was capsized by one of these gusty side winds. . . .

. . . Now what is plainer than that the grand primitive principle for which we struggle is HUMAN rights, and that the rights of *woman* is a principle purely *derivative* from the other? *Human* rights HUMAN rights—analyze, sift, explain, trace, enforce; show their origin, responsibilities, sacredness; perforate the indurated mind of the church all over with *them*, and you have done nine tenths of the work necessary to bring over the community to womans rights. . . . Your womans rights! You put the cart before the horse; you drag the tree by the top in attempting to push your *womans* rights, until human rights have gone ahead and broken the path. . . .

[Angelina Grimké to Weld]

[September 20, 1837]

Sister seems very much afraid that my pen will be transformed into a venomous serpent when it is employed in addressing thee, my Dear Brother, and no wonder, for I like to pay my debts, and as I received $10's worth of scolding I should be guilty of injustice did I not return the favor. Well—*such* a lecture, I never before received. What is the matter with thee? One would really suppose that we had actually abandoned the A. Sl'y cause and were scouring the country preaching *nothing* but *women's rights*, when in fact I can truly say that whenever I lecture I forget *every thing but the* SLAVE. HE is all in all for the time being. . . .—thine for the poor stricken slave—

18. Inward and Outward Freedom of Woman
Margaret Fuller

MARGARET FULLER (1810–1850) was the epitome of the American female intellectual. Self-educated under the tutelage of a tyrannical father, she taught school for a time before joining Emerson's circle in 1840, editing and contributing articles to the Transcendentalist journal The Dial for the next four years. Her essay "The Great Lawsuit," appearing there in 1843, was later expanded into a book, Woman in the Nineteenth Century, a feminist Bible for a half-century. Late in 1844 Miss Fuller left Boston for New York to write for Horace Greeley's Tribune; this was regarded as near treason by the Concord intelligentsia, who never fully forgave her. After two years she left for Europe, visiting prominent British and French writers and becoming involved in the Italian struggle for freedom and national identity led by Mazzini. Her romantic enthusiasm led to marriage to an Italian revolutionist, the Marquis d'Ossoli, and the birth of their son. With Mazzini's failure she and her new family sailed for the United States, but perished in a shipwreck off Long Island. Margaret Fuller, both admired and deplored by her male competitors, was not really active in the women's rights movement, but she voiced the frustration of the intelligent woman in a masculine society.

. . . It should be remarked that as the principle of liberty is better understood, and more nobly interpreted, a broader protest is made in behalf of Woman. As men become aware that few men have had a fair chance, they are inclined to say that no women have had a fair chance. . . .

Yet by men in this country, as by the Jews when Moses was leading them to the promised land, everything has been done that inherited depravity could do to hinder the promise of Heaven from its fulfillment. The cross, here as elsewhere, has been planted only to be blasphemed by cruelty and fraud. The name of the Prince of Peace has been profaned by all kinds of injustice toward the Gentile whom he said he came to save. But I need not speak of what has been done toward the Red Man, the Black Man. Those deeds are the scoff of the world; and they have been accompanied

SOURCE: S. Margaret Fuller, Woman in the Nineteenth Century (New York: Greeley & McElrath, 1845), pp. 14–15, 23–28, 52–54.

by such pious words that the gentlest would not dare to intercede with, "Father, forgive them, for they know not what they do."

Here as elsewhere the gain of creation consists always in the growth of individual minds, which live and aspire as flowers bloom and birds sing in the midst of morasses; and in the continual development of that thought, the thought of human destiny, which is given to eternity adequately to express, and which ages of failure only seemingly impede. Only seemingly; and whatever seems to the contrary, this country is as surely destined to elucidate a great moral law as Europe was to promote the mental culture of Man. . . .

But to return to the historical progress of this matter. Knowing that there exists in the minds of men a tone of feeling toward women as toward slaves, such as is expressed in the common phrase, "Tell that to women and children"; that the infinite soul can only work through them in already ascertained limits; that the gift of reason, Man's highest prerogative, is allotted to them in much lower degree; that they must be kept from mischief and melancholy by being constantly engaged in active labor, which is to be furnished and directed by those better able to think, &c., &c.— we need not multiply instances, for who can review the experience of last week without recalling words which imply, whether in jest or earnest, these views or views like these—knowing this, can we wonder that many reformers think that measures are not likely to be taken in behalf of women, unless their wishes could be publicly represented by women?

"That can never be necessary," cry the other side. "All men are privately influenced by women; each has his wife, sister, or female friends, and is too much biased by these relations to fail of representing their interests; and if this is not enough, let them propose and enforce their wishes with the pen. The beauty of home would be destroyed, the delicacy of the sex be violated, the dignity of halls of legislation degraded by an attempt to introduce them there. Such duties are inconsistent with those of a mother"; and then we have ludicrous pictures of ladies in hysterics at the polls, and senate chambers filled with cradles.

But if in reply we admit as truth that Woman seems destined by nature rather for the inner circle, we must add that the arrangements of civilized life have not been as yet such as to secure it to her. Her circle, if the duller, is not the quieter. If kept from "excitement," she is not from drudgery. Not only the Indian squaw carries the burdens of the camp, but the favorites of Louis XIV accompany him in his journeys, and the washerwoman stands at her tub and carries home her work at all seasons and in all states of health. Those who think the physical circumstances of Woman would make a part in the affairs of national government unsuitable are by no means those who think it impossible for Negresses to endure field work even during pregnancy, or for seamstresses to go through their killing labors. . . .

As to men's representing women fairly at present, while we hear from men who owe to their wives not only all that is comfortable or graceful but all that is wise in the arrangement of their lives the frequent remark, "You cannot reason with a woman"—when from those of delicacy, nobleness, and poetic culture falls the contemptuous phrase "women and children," and that in no light sally of the hour, but in works intended to give a permanent statement of the best experiences—when not one man in the million, shall I say? no, not in the hundred million, can rise above the belief that Woman was made for Man—when such traits as these are daily forced upon the attention, can we feel that Man will always do justice to the interests of Woman? Can we think that he takes a sufficiently discerning and religious view of her office and destiny ever to do her justice, except when prompted by sentiment—accidentally or transiently, that is, for the sentiment will vary according to the relations in which he is placed? The lover, the poet, the artist are likely to view her nobly. The father and the philosopher have some chance of liberality; the man of the world, the legislator for expediency none.

Under these circumstances, without attaching importance in themselves to the changes demanded by the champions of Woman, we hail them as signs of the times. We would have every arbitrary barrier thrown down. We would have every path laid open to Woman as freely as to Man. Were this done and a slight temporary fermentation allowed to subside, we should see crystallizations more pure and of more various beauty. We believe the divine energy would pervade nature to a degree unknown in the history of former ages, and that no discordant collision but a ravishing harmony of the spheres would ensue.

Yet then and only then will mankind be ripe for this, when inward and outward freedom for Woman as much as for Man shall be acknowledged as a *right*, not yielded as a concession. As the friend of the Negro assumes that one man cannot by right hold another in bondage, so should the friend of Woman assume that Man cannot by right lay even well-meant restrictions on Woman. If the Negro be a soul, if the woman be a soul, appareled in flesh, to one Master only are they accountable. There is but one law for souls, and if there is to be an interpreter of it, he must come not as man or son of man, but as son of God.

Were thought and feeling once so far elevated that Man should esteem himself the brother and friend, but nowise the lord and tutor, of Woman—were he really bound with her in equal worship—arrangements as to function and employment would be of no consequence. What Woman needs is not as a woman to act or rule, but as a nature to grow, as an intellect to discern, as a soul to live freely and unimpeded to unfold such powers as were given her when we left our common home. If fewer talents were given her, yet if allowed the free and full employment of these, so that she may render back to the giver his own with usury, she will not complain; nay, I dare to say she will bless and rejoice in her earthly birthplace, her earthly lot. . . .

It is not the transient breath of poetic incense that women want; each can receive that from a lover. It is not lifelong sway; it needs but to become a coquette, a shrew, or a good cook to be sure of that. It is not money nor notoriety nor the badges of authority which men have appropriated to themselves. If demands made in their behalf lay stress on any of these particulars, those who make them have not searched deeply into the need. The want is for that which at once includes these and precludes them; which would not be forbidden power, lest there be temptation to steal and misuse it; which would not have the mind perverted by flattery from a worthiness of esteem; it is for that which is the birthright of every being capable of receiving it—the freedom, the religious, the intelligent freedom of the universe to use its means, to learn its secret as far as Nature has enabled them, with God alone for their guide and their judge.

Ye cannot believe it, men; but the only reason why women ever assume what is more appropriate to you, is because you prevent them from finding out what is fit for themselves. Were they free, were they wise fully to develop the strength and beauty of Woman; they would never wish to be men or manlike. The well-instructed moon flies not from her orbit to seize on the glories of her partner. No, for she knows that one law rules, one heaven contains, one universe replies to them alike. . . .

In slavery, acknowledged slavery, women are on a par with men. Each is a worktool, an article of property—no more! In perfect freedom, such as is painted in Olympus, . . . in the heaven where there is no marrying nor giving in marriage, each is a purified intelligence, an enfranchised soul—no less. . . .

19. The Degraded and Inferior Position of Women
Elizabeth Cady Stanton

THE first women's rights convention, held in Seneca Falls, New York, in 1848, provided the movement with leadership and a program. Eight years earlier in London Mrs. Lucretia Mott and Mrs. Elizabeth Cady Stanton, two American delegates to the World Anti-Slavery Convention, were denied seats on the floor because of their sex. The 1848 convention, attended by some three hundred men and women, marked the culmination of their determination to emancipate women from male domination; a few months earlier the two women had worked successfully for the passage of the New York Married Women's Property Act. Mrs. Stanton (1815–1902), daughter of a prominent New York judge and graduate of Emma Willard's pioneering Troy Female Seminary, had married an active abolitionist, but soon became discontented with her role as housewife and mother. Her experience and the intellectual stimulation she received from Mrs. Mott convinced her to strive to free her sex from their burden of political, social and economic inferiority. She drafted the Declaration of Sentiments adopted by the convention, a paraphrase of the Declaration of Independence, and delivered the following eloquent address, both of which received wide circulation. Following the convention she joined forces with Susan B. Anthony, a partnership which was to survive more than half a century.

I should feel exceedingly diffident to appear before you at this time, having never before spoken in public, . . . did I not believe that woman herself must do this work; for woman alone can understand the height, the depth, the length, and the breadth of her own degradation. Man cannot speak for her, because he has been educated to believe that she differs from him so materially, that he cannot judge of her thoughts, feelings, and opinions by his own. . . .

. . . Every allusion to the degraded and inferior position occupied by women all over the world has been met by scorn and abuse. From the man of highest mental cultivation to the most degraded

SOURCE: *Address of Mrs. Elizabeth Cady Stanton, Delivered at Seneca Falls & Rochester, N.Y., July 19th & August 2d, 1848* (New York: Robert J. Johnston, 1870), pp. 3–11, 13, 18–19.

wretch who staggers in the streets do we meet ridicule, and coarse jests, freely bestowed upon those who dare assert that woman stands by the side of man, his equal, placed here by her God, to enjoy with him the beautiful earth, which is her home as it is his, having the same sense of right and wrong, and looking to the same Being for guidance and support. So long has man exercised tyranny over her, injurious to himself and benumbing to her faculties, that few can nerve themselves to meet the storm; and so long has the chain been about her that she knows not there is a remedy. . . .

Man's intellectual superiority cannot be a question until woman has had a fair trial. When we shall have had our freedom to find out our own sphere, when we shall have had our colleges, our professions, our trades, for a century, a comparison then may be justly instituted. When woman . . . shall first educate herself, when she shall be just to herself before she is generous to others; improving the talents God has given her, and leaving her neighbor to do the same for himself, we shall not then hear so much about this boasted superiority. How often, now, we see young men carelessly throwing away the intellectual food their sisters crave. A little music, that she may while an hour away pleasantly, a little French, a smattering of the sciences, and in rare instances, some slight classical knowledge, and woman is considered highly educated. She leaves her books and studies just as a young man is entering thoroughly into his. Then comes the gay routine of fashionable life, courtship and marriage, the perplexities of house and children, and she knows nothing beside. Her sphere is home. And whatever yearning her spirit may have felt for a higher existence, whatever may have been the capacity she well knew she possessed for more elevated enjoyments, enjoyments which would not conflict with those holy duties, but add new lustre to them, all, all is buried beneath the weight of these undivided cares.

Men, bless their innocence, are fond of representing themselves as beings of reason, of intellect, while women are mere creatures of the affections. . . . But so far as we can observe, it is pretty much now-a-days as it was with Adam of old. No doubt you all recollect the account we have given us. A man and a woman were placed in a beautiful garden, with everything about them that could contribute to their enjoyment. Trees and shrubs, fruits and flowers, and gently murmuring streams made glad their hearts. Zephyrs freighted with delicious odors fanned their brows, and the serene stars looked down upon them with eyes of love. The Evil One saw their happiness, and it troubled him, and he set his wits to work to know how he should destroy it. He thought that man could be easily conquered through his affection for the woman, but the woman would require more management, she could be reached only through her intellectual nature. So he promised her the knowledge of good and evil. He told her the sphere of her reason should be enlarged. He promised to gratify the desires she felt for intellectual improvement. So he prevailed and she did eat. Did the Evil One judge rightly in regard to man? Eve took the apple, went to Adam, and said; "Dear Adam, taste this apple. If you love me, eat." Adam stopped not so much as to ask if the apple were sweet or sour. He knew he was doing wrong, but his love for Eve prevailed, and he did eat. Which, I ask you, was the creature of the affections?

In consideration of man's claim to moral superiority, glance now at our theological seminaries. . . . Is the moral and religious life of this class what we might expect from minds said to be fixed on such mighty themes? By no means. Not a year passes but we hear of some sad, soul-sickening deed, perpetrated by some of this class. If such be the state of the most holy, we need not pause now to consider those classes who claim of us less reverence and respect. The lamentable want of principle among our lawyers, generally, is too well known to need comment. The everlasting backbiting and bickering of our physicians is proverbial. The disgraceful riots at our polls, where man, in performing the highest duty of citizenship, and ought surely to be sober-minded, the perfect rowdyism that now characterizes the debates in our national Congress,—all these are great facts which rise up against man's claim for moral superiority. In my opinion, he is infinitely woman's inferior in every moral quality, not by nature, but made so by a false education. In carrying out his own selfishness, man has greatly improved woman's moral nature, but by an almost total shipwreck of his own. Woman has now the noble virtues of the martyr. She is early schooled to self-denial and suffering. But man is not so wholly buried in selfishness that he does not sometimes get a glimpse of the narrowness of his soul, as compared with woman. Then he says, by way of an excuse for his degradation, "God made woman more self-denying than man. It is her nature. It does not cost her as much to give up her wishes, her will, her life, even, as it does him. He is naturally selfish. God made him so."

. . . No! God's commands rest upon man as well as woman. It is as much his duty to be kind, self-denying and full of good works, as it is hers. . . . I would not have woman less pure, but I would have man more so. I would have the same code of morals for both. Delinquencies which exclude woman from the society of the true and the good, should assign to man the same place. Our laxity towards him has been the fruitful source of dissipation, drunkenness, debauchery and immorality of all kinds. . . . It has destroyed the nobility of his character, the transparency of his soul, and all those finer qualities of our nature which raise us above the earth and give us a foretaste of the refined enjoyments of the world to come. . . .

We have met here to-day to discuss our rights and wrongs, civil and political, and not, as some have supposed, to go into the detail of social life alone. We do not propose to petition the legislature to make our husbands just, generous and courteous, to seat every man at the head of a cradle, and to clothe every woman in male attire. . . . But we are assembled to protest against a form of government, existing without the consent of the governed—to declare our right to be free as man is free, to be represented in the government which we are taxed to support, to have such disgraceful laws as give man the power to chastise and imprison his wife, to take the wages which she earns, the property which she inherits, and, in case of separation, the children of her love; laws which make her the mere dependent on his bounty. . . . And, strange as it may seem to many, we now demand our right to vote according to the declaration of the government under which we live. This right no one pretends to deny. We need not prove ourselves equal to Daniel Webster to enjoy this privilege, for the ignorant Irishman in the ditch has all the civil rights he has. We need not prove our muscular power equal to this same Irishman to enjoy this privilege, for the most tiny, weak, ill-shaped stripling of twenty-one, has all the civil rights of the Irishman. . . . All white men in this country have the same rights, however they may differ in mind, body or estate. The right is ours. The question now is, how shall we get possession of what rightfully belongs to us. . . . to have drunkards, idiots, horse-racing, rumselling rowdies, ignorant foreigners and silly boys fully recognized, while we ourselves are thrust out from all the rights that belong to citizens, it is too grossly insulting to the dignity of woman to be longer quietly submitted to. The right is ours. Have it, we must. Use it, we will. The pens, the tongues, the fortunes, the indomitable wills of many women are already pledged to secure this right. The great truth, that no just government can be formed without the consent of the governed, we shall echo and re-echo in the ears of the unjust judge, until by continual coming we shall weary him. . . .

Let woman live as she should. Let her feel her accountability to her Maker. Let her know that her spirit is fitted for as high a sphere as man's, and that her soul requires food as pure and exalted as his. Let her live *first* for God, and she will not make imperfect man an object of reverence and awe. Teach her her responsibility as a being of conscience and reason, that all earthly support is weak and unstable, that her only safe dependence is the arm of omnipotence, and that true happiness springs from duty accomplished. Thus will she learn the lesson of individual responsibility for time and eternity. That neither father, husband, brother or son, however willing they may be, can discharge her high duties of life, or stand in her stead when called in the presence of the great Searcher of Hearts at the last day. . . .

. . . There seems now to be a kind of moral stagnation in our midst. Philanthropists have done their utmost to rouse the nation to a sense of its sins. War, slavery, drunkenness, licentiousness, gluttony, have been dragged naked before the people, and all their abominations and deformities fully brought to light, yet with idiotic laugh we hug those monsters to our breasts and rush on to destruction. . . . Verily, the world waits the coming of some new element, some purifying power, some spirit of mercy and love. The voice of woman has been silenced in the state, the church, and the home, but man cannot fulfill his destiny alone, he cannot redeem his race unaided. There are deep and tender chords of sympathy and love in the hearts of the downfallen and oppressed that woman can touch more skillfully than man. The world has never yet seen a truly great and virtuous nation, because in the degradation of woman the very fountains of life are poisoned at their source. . . . We do not expect our path will be strewn with the flowers of popular applause, but over the thorns of bigotry and prejudice will be our way, and on our banners will beat the dark storm-clouds of opposition from those who have entrenched themselves behind the stormy bulwarks of custom and authority, and who have fortified their position by every means, holy and unholy. But we will steadfastly abide the result. Unmoved we will bear it aloft. Undauntedly we will unfurl it to the gale, for we know that the storm cannot rend from it a shred, that the electric flash will but more clearly show to us the glorious words inscribed upon it, "Equality of Rights." . . .

20. Ain't I a Woman?
Sojourner Truth

THE connection between emancipation of the Negro and the equality of all women was dramatized by the appearance of Sojourner Truth (c. 1797–1883) at the 1851 Woman's Rights Convention in Akron, Ohio. Born a slave named Isabella on a Dutch estate in New York, she was freed by the state emancipation law of 1827. Separated from her husband, she moved to New York City where she took the name Sojourner Truth and worked as a domestic servant to support her children, all of whom left her as they grew up. For a time she was a disciple of a religious fanatic, but in 1843 began to travel throughout the country, speaking at camp meetings, abolitionist congregations and women's rights conventions. She remained illiterate, but sold the Narrative of her life, written by her friend Olive Gilbert, at these meetings to raise money for the cause. Praised by Harriet Beecher Stowe as the "Libyan Sybil," she visited President Lincoln during the Civil War and devoted the last fifteen years of her life to assisting the freedmen. This account of her appearance at the Akron convention was written by Mrs. Frances Dana Gage, an Ohio abolitionist and writer of children's stories, who received her baptism of fire as convention chairman on this occasion.

The leaders of the movement trembled on seeing a tall, gaunt black woman in a gray dress and white turban, surmounted with an uncouth sun-bonnet, march deliberately into the church, walk with the air of a queen up the aisle, and take her seat upon the pulpit steps. A buzz of disapprobation was heard all over the house, and there fell on the listening ear, "An abolition affair!" "Woman's rights and niggers!" "I told you so!" "Go it, darkey!"

I chanced on that occasion to wear my first laurels in public life as president of the meeting. At my request order was restored, and the business of the Convention went on. Morning, afternoon, and evening exercises came and went. Through all these sessions old Sojourner, quiet and reticent as the "Lybian Statue," sat crouched against the wall on the corner of the pulpit stairs, her sun-bonnet shading her eyes, her elbows on her knees, her chin resting upon

SOURCE: "Reminiscences by Frances D. Gage," in Elizabeth Cady Stanton, Susan B. Anthony and Matilda Joslyn Gage, History of Woman Suffrage (New York: Fowler & Wells, 1881), vol. I, pp. 115–117.

her broad, hard palms. At intermission she was busy selling the "Life of Sojourner Truth," a narrative of her own strange and adventurous life. Again and again, timorous and trembling ones came to me and said, with earnestness, "Don't let her speak, Mrs. Gage, it will ruin us. Every newspaper in the land will have our cause mixed up with abolition and niggers, and we shall be utterly denounced." My only answer was, "We shall see when the time comes."

The second day the work waxed warm. Methodist, Baptist, Episcopal, Presbyterian, and Universalist ministers came in to hear and discuss the resolutions presented. One claimed superior rights and privileges for man, on the ground of "superior intellect"; another, because of the "manhood of Christ; if God had desired the equality of woman, He would have given some token of His will through the birth, life, and death of the Saviour." Another gave us a theological view of the "sin of our first mother."

There were very few women in those days who dared to "speak in meeting"; and the august teachers of the people were seemingly getting the better of us, while the boys in the galleries, and the sneerers among the pews, were hugely enjoying the discomfiture, as they supposed, of the "strong-minded." Some of the tender-skinned friends were on the point of losing dignity, and the atmosphere betokened a storm. When, slowly from her seat in the corner rose Sojourner Truth, who, till now, had scarcely lifted her head. "Don't let her speak!" gasped half a dozen in my ear. She moved slowly and solemnly to the front, laid her old bonnet at her feet, and turned her great speaking eyes to me. There was a hissing sound of disapprobation above and below. I rose and announced "Sojourner Truth," and begged the audience to keep silence for a few moments.

The tumult subsided at once, and every eye was fixed on this almost Amazon form, which stood nearly six feet high, head erect, and eyes piercing the upper air like one in a dream. At her first word there was a profound hush. She spoke in deep tones, which, though not loud, reached every ear in the house, and away through the throng at the doors and windows.

"Wall, chilern, whar dar is so much racket dar must be somethin' out o' kilter. I tink dat 'twixt de niggers of de Souf and de womin at de Norf, all talkin' 'bout rights, de white men will be in a fix pretty soon. But what's all dis here talkin' 'bout?

"Dat man ober dar say dat womin needs to be helped into carriages, and lifted ober ditches, and to hab de best place everywhar. Nobody eber helps me into carriages, or ober mud-puddles, or gibs me any best place!" And raising herself to her full height, and her voice to a pitch like rolling thunder, she asked, "And a'n't I a woman? Look at me! Look at my arm! (and she bared her right arm to the shoulder, showing her tremendous muscular power). I have ploughed, and planted, and gathered into barns, and no man could head me! And a'n't I a woman? I could work as much and eat as much as a man—when I could get it—and bear de lash as well! And a'n't I a woman? I have borne thirteen chilern, and seen 'em mos' all sold off to slavery, and when I cried out with my mother's grief, none but Jesus heard me! And a'n't I a woman?

"Den dey talks 'bout dis ting in de head; what dis dey call it?" ("Intellect," whispered some one near.) "Dat's it, honey. What's dat got to do wid womin's rights or nigger's rights? If my cup won't hold but a pint, and yourn holds a quart, wouldn't ye be mean not to let me have my little half-measure full?" And she pointed her significant finger, and sent a keen glance at the minister who had made the argument. The cheering was long and loud.

"Den dat little man in black dar, he say women can't have as much rights as men, 'cause Christ wan't a woman! Whar did your Christ come from?" Rolling thunder couldn't have stilled that crowd, as did those deep, wonderful tones, as she stood there with outstretched arms and eyes of fire. Raising her voice still louder, she repeated, "Whar did your Christ come from? From God and a woman! Man had nothin' to do wid Him." Oh, what a rebuke that was to that little man.

. . . "If de fust woman God ever made was strong enough to turn de world upside down all alone, dese women togedder (and she glanced her eye over the platform) ought to be able to turn it back, and get it right side up again! And now dey is asking to do it, de men better let 'em." Long-continued cheering greeted this. "Bleeged to ye for hearin' on me, and now ole Sojourner han't got nothin' more to say." . . .

21. The Moral Response
from the Heart of the Child
A. Bronson Alcott and Elizabeth Peabody

Education as a means to liberate rather than discipline the child had been advocated by European reformers from Rousseau to Pestalozzi. Yet most American educators, like Amos Bronson Alcott (1799–1888) and Elizabeth Peabody (1804–1894), had little knowledge of European theories or practices; their conviction that rigid discipline and rote learning were self-defeating arose largely from their own pedagogical experiences. Alcott, after a meager formal education and a brief career as a peddler, taught in several schools in New England and Pennsylvania before he opened the Temple School in Boston in 1834. Assisted by Miss Peabody, he emphasized moral education for young children through the conversational method; as members of Emerson's circle, they both endeavored to apply Transcendental insights to education. The publication of Miss Peabody's Record of a School and Alcott's Conversations with Children on the Gospels led to criticism of his discussions of religion and childbirth; attendance decreased, but the school survived until 1839, when a new controversy arose over Alcott's admission of a Negro girl. His later career was marked by one failure after another, his impracticality and idealism being overcome only by his daughter Louisa's success as an author. Miss Peabody meanwhile continued her educational activities, pioneering in the development of kindergartens in the United States.

Mr. Alcott re-commenced his school in Boston, after four years interval, September, 1834, at the Masonic Temple, No. 7. . . .

About twenty children came the first day. They were all under ten years of age, excepting two or three girls. I became his assistant, to teach Latin to such as might desire to learn.

Mr. Alcott sat behind his table, and the children were placed in chairs, in a large arc around him; the chairs so far apart, that they could not easily touch each other. He then asked each one separately, what idea she or he had of the object of coming to school?

SOURCE: [Elizabeth Peabody], Record of a School: Exemplifying the General Principles of Spiritual Culture (Boston: James Munroe and Co., 1835), pp. 1–3, 7–8, 14–15, 18–20.

To learn; was the first answer. To learn what? By pursuing this question, all the common exercises of school were brought up—successively—even philosophy. Still Mr. Alcott intimated that this was not all; and at last some one said "to behave well," and in pursuing this expression into its meanings, they at last decided that they came to learn to feel rightly, to think rightly, and to act rightly. A boy of seven years old suggested, and all agreed, that right actions were the most important of these three.

Simple as all this seems, it would hardly be believed what an evident exercise it was to these children, to be led of themselves to form and express these conceptions and few steps of reasoning. Every face was eager and interested. From right actions, the conversation naturally led into the means of bringing them out. And the necessity of feeling in earnest, of thinking clearly, and of school discipline, was talked over. School discipline was very carefully considered; Mr. Alcott's duty, and the children's individual duties, and the various means of producing attention, self-control, perseverance, faithfulness. Among these means, punishment was mentioned; and after a consideration of its nature and issues, they all very cheerfully agreed, that it was necessary, and that they preferred Mr. Alcott should punish them rather than leave them in their faults, and that it was his duty to do so. Various punishments were mentioned, and hurting the body was decided upon, as necessary and desirable in some instances. It was universally admitted that it was desirable whenever words were found insufficient to command the memory of conscience. After this conversation, which involved many anecdotes, many supposed cases, and many judgments, Mr. Alcott read from Krummacher's fables. . . . Nearly three hours passed away in this conversation and reading; and then they were asked, how long they had been sitting? None of them guessed more than an hour. . . . The whole effect of the day seemed to be a combination of quieting influences, with an awakening effect upon the heart and mind. . . .

It was soon found that Mr. Alcott, with all his mildness, was very strict. When sitting at their desks, at their writing, he would not allow the least inter-communication, and every whisper was taken notice of. When they sat in the semi-circle around him, they were not only requested to be silent, but to appear attentive to him; and any infringement of the spirit of this rule, would arrest his reading, and he would wait, however long it might be, until attention was restored. For some time the acquirement of this habit of stillness and attention was the most prominent subject, for it was found that many of the children had very little self-control, very weak attention, very self-indulgent habits. Some had no humility, and defended themselves in the wrong; a good deal of punishment was necessary, and some impressions upon the body (on the hand;) but still, in every individual instance, it was granted as necessary, not only by the whole school, but I believe, no bodily punishment was given without the assent of the individual himself; and they were never given in the room. In many of the punishments,—in the pauses of his reading, for instance, the innocent were obliged to suffer with the guilty. Mr. Alcott wished both parties to feel that this was the inevitable consequence of moral evil in this world; and that the good, in proportion to the depth of their principle, always feel it to be worth while to share the suffering, in order to bring the guilty to rectitude and moral sensibility.

On all these occasions, he conversed with them; and by a series of questions, led them to come to conclusions for themselves upon moral conduct in various particulars; teaching them how to examine themselves, and to discriminate their animal and spiritual natures, their outward and inward life; and also how the inward moulds the outward. . . . The youngest scholars were as much interested as the oldest, and although it was necessary to explain language to them rather more, it was found less necessary to reason on moral subjects. They did not so often inquire the history of an idea, or feeling; but they analysed the feelings which prompted action better. It was very striking to see how much nearer the kingdom of heaven were the little children, than were those who had begun to pride themselves on knowing something. We could not but often remark to each other, how unworthy the name of knowledge was that superficial acquirement, which has nothing to do with self-knowledge; and how much more susceptible to the impressions of genius, and how much more apprehensive of general truths were those, who had not been hackneyed by a false education. . . .

In teaching reading, . . . Mr. Alcott's method has . . . been much misunderstood; and because he thinks a child should never be hurried into or over the mechanical part of the process, many say and perhaps think, that he does not think it important for children to learn to read at all! It will probably, however, be difficult to find children, who know so well *how to use a book*, when they are eight years old, as those who have been taught on his method, which never allows a single step to be taken in any stage of the process, without a great deal of thinking on the part of the child. Perhaps a general adoption of Mr. Alcott's ideas on this subject, would lead to some check upon the habits of superficial reading, which do so much to counterbalance all the advantages arising from our profusion of books. . . .

. . . Mr. Alcott thinks that every book read, should be an event to a child; and all his plans of teaching keep steadily in mind the object of making books live, breathe, and speak; and he would consider the glib reading which we hear in most schools, as a preventive, rather than as an aid to his purposes. He has himself no doubt as to the ultimate result, not only upon the intellectual powers, but upon the very enunciation of the words; which cannot fail to borrow energy and life from the thoughts and feelings they awaken within the soul of the reader.

But the best reading which children can do for themselves, in the early stages of their education, cannot supersede the necessity of the teacher's reading a great deal to them; because it is desirable that they should early be put in possession of the thoughts of genius, and made to sympathise in the feelings inspired by their master works; as well as have their taste formed on the highest models. . . .

The first two months were given up almost entirely to this preliminary discipline. Two hours and a half every day were divided between the readings and conversations on conduct, and the comparative importance of things within and without. The government was decided and clear from the first; but was not hurried beyond the comprehension of the children; for Mr. Alcott is so thoroughly convinced that all effectual government must be self-government, that he much prefers that all the operations of school should obviously stand still, than they should go on *apparently*, while standing still or going back *really*, in any individual instance. If it should be objected to this principle, that the good are here made to wait upon the bad; it may be answered, that the good are learning the divinest part of human action, even the action of Christ, when they are taught to wait upon the bad for their improvement; and that there are seldom such actual discrepancies in children of but a few years difference of age, as that any harm can result to the best, from being brought to the contemplation of the worst; especially when the worst, as in every case in this school, express themselves sincerely desirous of becoming better; and not one is so bad as not to have been able to ask for punishment, at some gracious season.

One thing, however, should be remarked, as a caution to young teachers. It will be seen . . . that Mr. Alcott is very autocratic. But it must be remembered that this is dangerous ground for a young, or rather for an inexperienced teacher, to take. . . . Mr. Alcott has taught school for twelve years. During the first several years, he felt himself hardly any thing but a learner, on this sacred ground.—He did not, for many years, enforce authority in any instance, unless it was sanctioned by the unanimous voice of a school, sometimes of a school of an hundred pupils. So reverent was he of the voice of nature, that he chose to hear all its varying tones, before he ventured to feel that he sufficiently understood what he was dealing with, to raise his own voice above theirs, in confidence of harmonising them. That time of self-reliance, however, came at last; and he now is able to have faith in the moral response from the heart of the child, which he once only hoped for. This autocracy, therefore, is not derivative but original. It is drawn from experience and observation; and, I should add that it continually takes counsel from these, its sources. And is not this legitimate, in the moral sense of the word? Are not the laws of human nature sufficiently intelligible, to enable sensibility, and observation, and years of experience at last to construct a system, whose general principles need not to be reviewed, in every instance of application to every scholar? It is true that every scholar may afford new phenomena; and that the teacher who does not observe these as materials of thought, in private review of the principles on which he acts, thereby to enlarge them or rectify such small errors of application, as the wisest may fall into, omits the best means of perfecting himself and his art. Besides, a teacher never should forget that the mind he is directing, may be on a larger scale than his own; that its sensibilities may be deeper, tenderer, wider; that its imagination may be infinitely more rapid; that its intellectual power of proportioning and reasoning may be more powerful; and he should ever have the humility to feel himself at times in the place of the child, and the magnanimity to teach him how to defend himself against his own (i.e. the teacher's) influence. By such humility, he will also be in the best road towards that deeply felt self-reliance, which is founded on sober self-estimation, although entirely removed from vanity. . . .

22. A System of Republican Education
New York Workingmen's Party

WHEN the Workingmen's Party entered New York politics in 1829, one of its demands was the establishment of a system of "equal republican education," based largely upon proposals by Frances Wright and Robert Dale Owen in the Free Enquirer (Document 39). This demand represented the desire of the "mechanics and workingmen" to improve their status or that of their children, free public education being viewed as a means to guarantee social and political equality. The alleged infidelity of Owen and Wright, combined with attacks upon "state guardianship" for destroying the family, led to a schism within the Party early in 1830. The majority report of the subcommittee on education disavowed the proposal; the minority report, drafted by Paul Grout, a cabinetmaker and disciple of Owen and George Henry Evans (Document 13), was defeated narrowly in the Party's General Executive Committee. Even though the sentiments of the minority, stated below, were not adopted, they were influential in the movement to establish "common schools." The workingmen provided a stimulus to the educated and wealthy who saw education as a means of social control of the lower classes in a republic, rather than as a means to attain social equality.

. . . When your Committee propose a system of republican education for the people, . . . we propose that it should be the best. Not the most brilliant, not the most extravagantly expensive, not the most fashionable—but the best that the nation, in its wisdom, may be able to devise. We need not be told that it will be imperfect. Everything human is. But if it be only as scientific, as wise, and as judicious as modern experience can make it, it will regenerate America in one generation. It will make but one class out of the many that now envy and despise each other. It will make American citizens what they once declared themselves, "Free and Equal."
. . .

If State Schools are to be, as now in New England, common day-schools only, we do not perceive how either of these requisitions are to be fulfilled. In republican schools, there must be no tempta-

SOURCE: "Report of the Minority of the Sub-Committee on Education" [Workingmen's Party of New York], New York Sentinel and Working Man's Advocate, June 19, 1830, p. 4.

tion to aristocratical prejudices. The pupils must learn to consider themselves as fellow-citizens, as equals. Respect ought to be paid, and will always be paid to virtue, and to talent; but it ought not to be paid to riches, or withheld from poverty. Yet if the children from these State Schools are to go every evening, the one to his wealthy parents' soft carpeted drawing-room, and the other to his poor father's, or widowed mother's comfortless cabin, will they return next day as friends and equals? He knows little of human nature who thinks they will.

Again, if it is to be left to the parent's taste, and pecuniary means to clothe their children as they please and as they can, the one in braided broad-cloth and velvet cap, and the other in thread-bare homespun, will they meet as friends and equals? Will there be no envy on the one side, nor disdain on the other? And are envy and disdain proper and virtuous feelings in young Republicans? Yet if State Schools be day school only, how can there be uniformity of dress? Must not the poor widow dress her children as she can? . . .

For our own parts, we understand education to mean, every thing which influences directly or indirectly the child's character. To see his companions smoke segars is a part of his education; to hear oaths is a part of his education; to see and laugh at drunken men in the street is a part of his education; to witness vulgar merriment or coarse brawls is a part of his education. And if any one thinks that an education like this (which is daily obtained in the streets of our city) will be counteracted and neutralized by half a dozen hours of daily schooling, we are not of his opinion. . . .

But even if none of these reasons existed, how is the poor laborer or the poorer widow, to keep her children at a day school, until they have received an education equal to that of their richer neighbors? Can the laborer or the widow afford to support their children until they are twelve, fourteen, or sixteen years old, while they peruse the page of science, and obtain the acquirements and accomplishments which form the enlightened, well educated man? . . . If day schools alone are provided, therefore, would not those very children who most require instruction be virtually excluded?

Is not the development of social habits, of the dispositions, of the moral feelings, the most important of the teacher's duties? And what opportunity is there of fulfilling them, unless the pupils be at all times under his very eye and control? . . .

We conceive, then, that State Schools, to be republican, efficient and acceptable to all, must receive the children, not for six hours a day, but altogether; must feed them, clothe them, lodge them, must direct not their studies only, but their occupations and amusements; must care for them until their education is completed, and then only abandon them to the world, as useful, intelligent, virtuous citizens.

We do not consider this question regarding day schools and boarding schools as a non-essential matter that may be decided either way without ruin to the cause. We conceive that on its decision depends, in a manner, every thing. On its decision depends whether the system of education which the people call for, shall be a paltry palliative, or an efficient cure: whether aristocracy shall be perpetuated or destroyed; whether the poor man's child shall be educated or not; whether the next generation shall obtain their just rights or lose them. . . .

Your Committee propose therefore, a System of Public Education, which shall provide for all children, at all times, receiving them at the earliest age their parents choose to entrust them to the national care; feeding, clothing, and educating them to the age of maturity.

Your Committee propose that all children so adopted, should receive the same food; should be dressed in the same simple clothing; should experience the same kind treatment; should be taught (until their professional education commences) the same branches; in a word, that nothing savoring of inequality, nothing reminding them of the pride of riches, or the contempt of poverty, should be suffered to enter these republican safeguards of a young nation of equals. We propose that the destitute widow's child or the orphan boy should share the public care equally with the heir to a princely estate; so that all may become, not in word, but in deed and in feeling, free and equal.

Thus may the spirit of democracy, that spirit which Jefferson labored for half a century to plant in our republican soil, become universal among us; thus may luxury, may pride, may ignorance be banished from among us; and we may become what fellow citizens ought to be, a nation of brothers.

Your Committee propose that the food should be of the simplest kind, both for the sake of economy and temperance. A Spartan simplicity of regimen is becoming a republic, and is best suited to preserve the health and strength unimpared, even to old age. We suggest the propriety of excluding all distilled or fermented liquors of every description; perhaps, also, luxuries, such as tea and coffee, might be beneficially dispensed with. . . .

Thus might the pest of our land, intemperance, be destroyed—not discouraged, not lessened, not partially cured—but destroyed: this modern curse that degrades the human race below the beasts of the field; that offers her poison cup at every corner of our streets, and at every turn of our highways, that sacrifices her tens of thousands of victims yearly in these States, that loads our country with a tax more than sufficient to pay twice over for the virtuous training of all her children—might thus be deposed from the foul sway she exercises over freemen, too proud to yield to a foreign country, but not too proud to bow beneath the iron rod of a domestic curse. Is there any other method of tearing up this monstrous evil, the scandal of our republic, root and branch?

Your Committee propose that the dress should be a plain, convenient, economical uniform. The silliest of all vanities, (and one of the most expensive,) is the vanity of dress. Children trained to the age of twenty-one without being exposed to it, could not, in after life, be taught such folly. But, learnt as it now is, from the earliest infancy, do we find that the most faithful preaching checks or reforms it?

The food and clothing might be chiefly raised and manufactured by the pupils themselves, in the exercise of their several occupations. They would thus acquire a taste for articles produced in their own country, in preference to foreign superfluities. . . .

We propose that the teachers should be elected by the people. There is no office of trust in a republic, more honorable, or more important, nor any that more immediately influences its doctrines, than the office of a teacher. They ought to be chosen, and if we read the signs of the times right, they will be chosen with as much, nay with more care, than our representatives. The Office of General Superintendent of schools will be, in our opinion, an office at least as important as that of President. . . .

. . . every citizen ought to contribute his fair share towards the expenses of legislation; . . . [for] education is a most important branch of legislation; as much more important than the criminal law, as "prevention is better than cure." Would not even the rich old bachelor be individually benefitted (in the most selfish sense of the term) if, instead of having the rogue who broke into his counting-house shut up in the penitentiary, that rogue had been trained to be an honest man, and thus prevented from putting his fingers in the old man's coffers at all? And is it not as cheap, and much more rational and humane to pay for keeping men and women out of the penitentiary, than to pay for putting them in? . . .

Your Committee conceive, that Education is emphatically the business of the government. What is the first and chief end of Government, if not to produce peace and harmony among men? And what means are so effectual to produce peace and harmony, as an enlightened public education? . . .

We hold the opinion, therefore, that there is no call for the public money, more strictly, and immediately, and essentially for the public benefit, than in the case of public education. And we are further convinced, that there is no expenditure of the people's funds that would be more cheerfully sanctioned by them than this; provided they were satisfied with the system of education itself. . . .

In conclusion, your Committee would express their firm conviction, that in proportion as the Mechanics and Working Men of our City, of our State, and of our Republic generally, interest themselves in this subject, in proportion as they take a firm, decisive stand, and adopt enlarged and liberal views in regard to Public Education—in the same proportion will be the ultimate success of their cause.

23. The Great Equalizer
of the Conditions of Men
Horace Mann

MASSACHUSETTS, the first American colony to provide for education at public expense, lagged behind some of her neighbors in implementing this program in the early nineteenth century. Horace Mann (1796–1859), a lawyer and state legislator who had first associated himself with other reforms, took the lead in establishing a state board of education, resigning his seat in the state senate to accept the position of secretary of the board. For twelve years, from 1837 to 1849, Mann devoted all his energies to this task, collecting and disseminating information on the state of public education in Massachusetts, establishing institutes and normal schools to improve the education of teachers, and propagandizing the public on the necessity of improving public education in the state; his twelfth annual report is excerpted below. In 1849 Mann was elected to the seat in Congress formerly occupied by John Quincy Adams, and in 1852 was an unsuccessful Free Soil candidate for governor; he became president of Antioch College in Ohio the following year. His objective throughout his life was stated in an address to his students a few weeks before his death: "be ashamed to die until you have won some victory for humanity."

. . . Poverty is a public as well as a private evil. There is no physical law necessitating its existence. The earth contains abundant resources for ten times,—doubtless for twenty times,—its present inhabitants. Cold, hunger, and nakedness, are not, like death, an inevitable lot. . . . There is, indeed, no assignable limit to the capacities of the earth for producing whatever is necessary for the sustenance, comfort, and improvement of the race. Indigence, therefore, and the miseries and degradations incident to indigence, seem to be no part of the eternal ordinances of Heaven. . . .

According to the European theory, men are divided into classes, —some to toil and earn, others to seize and enjoy. According to the Massachusetts theory, all are to have an equal chance for earning,

SOURCE: *Twelfth Annual Report of the Board of Education, Together With the Twelfth Annual Report of the Secretary of the Board* (Boston: Dutton and Wentworth, 1849), pp. 54–60, 66–68, 74.

and equal security in the enjoyment of what they earn. The latter tends to equality of condition; the former to the grossest inequalities. Tried by any Christian standard of morals, or even by any of the better sort of heathen standards, can any one hesitate, for a moment, in declaring which of the two will produce the greater amount of human welfare; and which, therefore, is the more conformable to the Divine will? The European theory is blind to what constitutes the highest glory, as well as the highest duty, of a State. . . .

Our ambition, as a State, should trace itself to a different origin, and propose to itself a different object. . . . It should seek the solution of such problems as these: To what extent can competence displace pauperism? How nearly can we free ourselves from the low-minded and the vicious; not by their expatriation, but by their elevation? To what extent can the resources and powers of nature be converted into human welfare; the peaceful arts of life be advanced, and the vast treasures of human talent and genius be developed? How much of suffering, in all its forms, can be relieved; or, what is better than relief, how much can be prevented? Cannot the classes of crimes be lessened, and the number of criminals, in each class, be diminished? . . . When we have spread competence through all the abodes of poverty; when we have substituted knowledge for ignorance, in the minds of the whole people; when we have reformed the vicious and reclaimed the criminal; then may we invite all neighboring nations to behold the spectacle. . . . Until that day shall arrive, our duties will not be wholly fulfilled, and our ambition will have new honors to win.

But, is it not true, that Massachusetts, in some respects, instead of adhering more and more closely to her own theory, is becoming emulous of the baneful examples of Europe? The distance between the two extremes of society is lengthening, instead of being abridged. With every generation, fortunes increase, on the one hand, and some new privation is added to poverty, on the other. We are verging towards those extremes of opulence and of penury, each of which unhumanizes the human mind. A perpetual struggle for the bare necessaries of life, without the ability to obtain them, makes men wolfish. Avarice, on the other hand, sees, in all the victims of misery around it,—not objects for pity and succor,—but only crude materials to be worked up into more money. . . .

Now two or three things will doubtless be admitted to be true, beyond all controversy, in regard to Massachusetts. By its industrial condition, and its business operations, it is exposed, far beyond any other state in the Union, to the fatal extremes of overgrown wealth and desperate poverty. . . . If this be so, are we not in danger of naturalizing and domesticating among ourselves those hideous evils which are always engendered between Capital and Labor, when all the capital is in the hands of one class, and all the labor is thrown upon another?

Now, surely, nothing but Universal Education can counterwork this tendency to the domination of capital and the servility of labor. If one class possesses all the wealth and the education, while the residue of society is ignorant and poor, it matters not by what name the relation between them may be called; the latter, in fact and in truth, will be the servile dependants and subjects of the former. But if education be equally diffused, it will draw property after it, by the strongest of all attractions; for such a thing never did happen, and never can happen, as that an intelligent and practical body of men should be permanently poor. Property and labor, in different classes, are essentially antagonistic; but property and labor, in the same class, are essentially fraternal. The people of Massachusetts have, in some degree, appreciated the truth, that the unexampled prosperity of the State,—its comfort, its competence, its general intelligence and virtue,—is attributable to the education, more or less perfect, which all its people have received; but are they sensible of a fact equally important?—namely, that it is to this same education that two thirds of the people are indebted for not being, to-day, the vassals of as severe a tyranny, in the form of capital, as the lower classes of Europe are bound to in the form of brute force.

Education, then, beyond all other devices of human origin, is the great equalizer of the conditions of men—the balance-wheel of the social machinery. I do not here mean that it so elevates the moral nature as to make men disdain and abhor the oppression of their fellow-men. This idea pertains to another of its attributes. But I mean that it gives each man the independence and the means, by which he can resist the selfishness of other men. It does better than to disarm the poor of their hostility towards the rich; it prevents being poor. Agrarianism is the revenge of poverty against wealth. The wanton destruction of the property of others,—the burning of hay-ricks and corn-ricks, the demolition of machinery, because it supersedes hand-labor, the sprinkling of vitriol on rich dresses,—is only agrarianism run mad. Education prevents both the revenge and the madness. On the other hand, a fellow-feeling for one's class or caste is the common instinct of hearts not wholly sunk in selfish regards for person, or for family. The spread of education, by enlarging the cultivated class or caste, will open a wider area over which the social feelings will expand; and, if this education should be universal and complete, it would do more than all things else to obliterate factitious distinctions in society.

The main idea set forth in the creeds of some political reformers, or revolutionizers, is, that some people are poor *because* others are rich. This idea supposes a fixed amount of property in the community, which, by fraud or force, or arbitrary law, is unequally divided among men; and the problem presented for solution is, how to transfer a portion of this property from those who are supposed to have too much, to those who feel and know that they have too little. At this point, both their theory and their expectation of reform stop. But the beneficent power of education would not be exhausted, even though it should peaceably abolish all the miseries that spring from the coexistence, side by side, of enormous wealth and squalid want. It has a higher function. Beyond the power of diffusing old wealth, it has the prerogative of creating new. It is a thousand times more lucrative than fraud; and adds a thousand fold more to a nation's resources than the most successful conquests. Knaves and robbers can obtain only what was before possessed by others. But education creates or develops new treasures,—treasures not before possessed or dreamed of by any one. . . .

. . . The reason why the mechanical and useful arts,—those arts which have done so much to civilize mankind, and which have given comforts and luxuries to the common laborer of the present day, such as kings and queens could not command three centuries ago,—the reason why these arts made no progress; and, until recently, indeed, can hardly be said to have had any thing more than a beginning, is, that the labor of the world was performed by ignorant men. As soon as some degree of intelligence dawned upon the workman, then a corresponding degree of improvement in his work followed. At first, this intelligence was confined to a very small number, and, therefore, improvements were few, and they followed each other only after long intervals. They uniformly began in the nations, and among the classes, where there was most intelligence. . . . But, just in proportion as intelligence,—that is, education,—has quickened and stimulated a greater and a greater number of minds, just in the same proportion have inventions and discoveries increased in their wonderfulness, and in the rapidity of their succession. . . .

For the creation of wealth, then,—for the existence of a wealthy people and a wealthy nation—intelligence is the grand condition. The number of improvers will increase, as the intellectual constituency, if I may so call it, increases. In former times, and in most parts of the world even at the present day, not one man in a million has ever had such a development of mind, as made it possible for him to become a contributor to art or science. Let this development precede, and contributions, numberless, and of inestimable value, will be sure to follow. That Political Economy, therefore, which busies itself about capital and labor, supply and demand, interest and rents, favorable and unfavorable balances of trade; but leaves out of account the element of a wide-spread mental development, is nought but stupendous folly. The greatest of all the arts in political economy is, to change a consumer into a producer; and the next greatest is, to increase the producer's producing power;—an end to be directly attained, by increasing his intelligence. . . .

Now it is in these various ways that all the means of human subsistence, comfort, improvement,—or what, in one word, we call wealth,—are created;—additional wealth, new wealth,—not another man's earnings, not another nation's treasures or lands, tricked away by fraud, or wrested by force,—but substantially, and, for all practical purposes, knowledge-created, mind-created wealth. . . . To see a community acquiring and redoubling its wealth in this way; enriching itself without impoverishing others, without despoiling others, is it not a noble spectacle! And will not the community that gains its wealth in this way, ten times faster than any robber-nation ever did by plunder,—will not such a community be a model and a pattern for the nations; a type of excellence to be admired and followed by the world? Has Massachusetts no ambition to win the palm in so glorious a rivalry? . . .

24. The Advantages of a Liberal Education
Thaddeus Stevens

PUBLIC education, even where it was established, was often attacked for its cost and for its potential disruption of the social order. In 1834 the free school system of Philadelphia was extended throughout Pennsylvania; Thaddeus Stevens (1792–1868) was influential in the passage of this act and played a significant role the following year in defeating an attempt to repeal the system. Born in Vermont to a poor family, Stevens graduated from Dartmouth College and then moved to Pennsylvania, where he practiced law in Gettysburg, defending numerous fugitive slaves without fee while increasing his personal fortune through investments in ironworks. Elected to the Pennsylvania legislature as an Antimason, he served for eight years before retiring temporarily from politics. In addition to defending the "common" schools, Stevens urged appropriations for higher education: his 1838 speech quoted below gives his defense of a liberal arts education as a necessity for a democratic society. In 1848 he was elected to Congress as a Whig; within a few years he became a Republican and until his death was influential in the politics of the Civil War and Reconstruction. A humanitarian and a political fanatic, Stevens resists classification.

. . . I think it is generally admitted that within the last few years, Pennsylvania has acquired more honor by her legislation upon the subject of Education, than she had ever done before; and I cannot help believing, that those under whose auspices that legislation took place, will be gratefully remembered in after times. . . .

. . . But great and creditable as have hitherto been the efforts of Pennsylvania in the cause of Education, I trust she is not yet exhausted; but while she is only in the vigor of youth in her physical strength, she has not yet attained the maturity of manhood, much less the decrepitude of old age, in her mental energies. . . . The degree of civilization and intellectual cultivation of every nation on earth, may be ascertained, and accurately estimated, by

SOURCE: *Speech of Thaddeus Stevens, Esq. in Favor of the Bill to Establish a School of Arts in the City of Philadelphia, and to Endow the Colleges and Academies of Pennsylvania. Delivered in the House of Representatives at Harrisburg, March 10th, 1838* (Harrisburg: Theophilus Fenn, 1838), pp. 3–12.

the amount of encouragement which they give, not by individual contributions, for these only show private liberality, but by *permanent laws* to common schools and common education, and to the higher branches of knowledge. Nor does it seem possible to separate the higher from the lower branches of education, without injuring, if not paralizing the prosperity of both. They are as mutually dependant and necessary to each other's existence and prosperity, as are the ocean and the streams by which it is supplied. For while the ocean supplies the quickening principle of the springs, they in turn pour their united tribute to the common reservoir—thus mutually replenishing each other. So colleges, and academies, furnish and propagate the seeds of knowledge for common schools; and they transfer their most thrifty plants to these more carefully and more highly cultivated gardens of knowledge. I am aware that there are many honest, highly respectable, and somewhat intelligent gentlemen here, and elsewhere, who, while they fully appreciate, and frankly acknowledge the advantages of common schools, doubt or deny the utility of the higher branches of learning.

. . . I believe that a little careful and candid reflection, will convince gentlemen that in all their objections, they err. They object that colleges are schools for the rich, and not for the poor— that classical learning is useless in the common walks of life—that it is soon forgotten—that it tends to produce idleness by promoting pride and vanity. . . .

It may be true, that unendowed Colleges are accessible only to the rich; but that shows the necessity of endowing them, and thus opening their doors to the meritorious poor. Extend public aid to these institutions, and thus reduce the rate of tuition; in short, render learning cheap and honourable, and he who has genius, no matter how poor he may be, will find the means of improving it. It can hardly be seriously contended, that liberal education is useless to man in any condition of life. So long as the only object of our earthly existence is happiness, enlarged knowledge must be useful to every intellectual being, high or low, rich or poor—unless you consider happiness as consisting in the mere vulgar gratification of the animal appetites and passions. Then indeed that man, like the brute, is happiest who has the most flesh and blood, the strongest sinews, and the stoutest stomach. . . .

Never was there a grosser or more injurious error than to suppose that learning begets pride. Ignorance is the parent of pride and disgusting vanity; he only has censurable pride, who has too little knowledge to know that he is himself a fool. But he who has long and arduously labored up the hill of science, and then found himself but standing upon the threshhold of her temple—who, after a toilsome, and perhaps successful examination of the works of nature and of art, discovers that he has scarcely yet entered upon the confines of the inimitable works of an omniscient artist, will surely find nothing in his own weak, blind insignificance, to flatter pride or foster vanity. It is the illiterate, ignorant, senseless, witless coxcomb that struts and fumes, proud perhaps of his ignorance, himself, his baubles, and his folly.

. . . I trust I need add nothing more to show the advantages of a liberal education. I believe that the proposed permanent mode of providing for the higher institutions of learning, is more useful to the cause of science, and more economical to the State, than the present uncertain mode of appropriations by the legislature. . . .

It seems to me that true economy would be consulted by making appropriations small, but permanent. The present sum proposed is so small as almost to make a Pennsylvanian blush to find it opposed.—The thirty or forty thousand dollars, which is asked for all these institutions is a less sum than you appropriate annually to keep in repair a single section of your canals, to be disbursed and expended by a single agent. Though we have appropriated less in all, to Colleges and Acadamies, than single institutions of other States are worth, yet some of our institutions have received in money and lands, I believe 50, or $100,000; and being thus full of funds for a while, they flourished in luxury, if not in idleness, and neglected what was necessary for their future prosperity and preservation. But if the same amount had been sparingly, but permanently appropriated—combining the aid of Government with their own industry and economy, these institutions would have been perfectly prepared to meet the adversity of the times. They could have given a *certain living* to their Professors, and they could have been assured, that their situations were permanent. This would add much to the cause of science, and equally, I trust every gentleman here will think, to the glory of the State. These institutions being permanent and prosperous would reduce the price of education, and thus enable the aspiring sons of the poor man to become equally learned with the rich. Then should we no longer see the struggling genius, of the humble, obstructed, and as now, stopped midway in the paths of science; but we should see them reaching the farthest goal of their noblest ambition. Then, the Laurel wreath would no longer be the purchase of gold, but the reward of honest merit. Then the yeomanry of our country would shine forth in their grandeur, the proudest ornament of the nation. In these national workshops of science, the gem of the peasant would be polished, till it out-shone the jewel of the Prince.

I am aware that the too great increase of the number of Colleges is feared by some. I have no such apprehension. With a population increasing as fast as ours is—with a soil and a territory capable of supporting ten millions of inhabitants; with free schools to plant the seeds and the desire of knowledge in every mind; with discriminating parents to encourage and select those most anxious and best fitted for scientific acquirements, there is little danger that we shall have too many institutions for the education of our youth. . . .

. . . there is in this community too great and growing an inclination, to undervalue classical knowledge. If we foster this disposition, is there not danger that in some future revolution of the condition of the world, the light of science will be entirely extinguished? When the Barbarians made war, not only upon Rome but upon all learning, what, and who preserved the arts, and sciences, and knowledge of antiquity from utter oblivion? Not common schools, and gentlemen of common education, useful as they are. During the long and gloomy period of the dark ages, they were preserved and fostered, and finally restored by liberally educated priests, and learned monks; and if they did no other good, we owe the existence of science, as it now is, to them. This light of knowledge is so easily extinguished, and so hard and tedious to be re-kindled, that it ought to be as carefully guarded, night and day, as was ever the sacred fire by the vestal virgins.

But ought we not to look beyond the present moment, and inquire into the effect which the arts and sciences are to have upon the posthumous glory of our country? Nations, like individuals, sport but a brief scene upon this stage of action, and then pass away into the oblivion of their own ignorance, or into that immortality which their civilization and intellectual cultivation have provided for them. Little as we think of it now, such will, perhaps, at no distant day, be the fate of this nation. And who does not desire his country to live in the memory of posterity? Does any gentleman think that we shall not, like other nations, feel the frost of time and crumble to decay? . . .

. . . Viewing such ruin as the doomed fate of Nations, who does not desire to be able to look down this broad and desolating gulph of time, and amidst its destruction, behold his own country forever flourishing like the green and flowery oasis in the midst of a barren desert? Can any one be insensible to these motives? Is there a gentleman within these walls?—Is there a human being any where, whose tabernacle of clay is inhabited by a living soul, that does not anxiously desire to see the fair fame and noble deeds of his native land, instead of being blotted and blurred by Boetian ignorance, recorded in letters of living light, by the bright pen of the historic muse? . . .

How are we to secure for our country this great good—this meed of earthly immortality? Not by riches, which some gentlemen so highly value. . . . What was it that has given such fresh and durable renown to the comparatively circumscribed and barren territory of Athens, of Sparta, of all Greece? . . . Whatever may be said of her deeds of patriotic valor, her true and lasting glory will ever be found in her civil institutions—in the wisdom of her laws, her academic groves, the schools and porticos of her philosophers, the writings of her poets, and the forum of her orators. If we are not altogether insensible to such considerations, let us, in our humble way, do all in our power, not only to lay broad and deep the foundations, but to build the beautiful superstructure, and raise high the monuments of science. For, when everything else that belongs to this nation shall have yielded to the scythe of the destroyer, their smooth and polished surfaces alone shall withstand the rust, and bid defiance to the tooth of time. . . .

Will any gentleman urge, that any sum, much less this paltry trifle, is too much for such a high, and lofty, and glorious an object? . . . Let us go on to exercise the same liberality in this respect that has characterized Pennsylvania in every other, and we shall soon see these little fountains, scattered by our creative hands over this great state, sending forth perennially, forever, their sweet rivulets, till this whole Commonwealth shall become one mighty ocean of Pierean waters. Then will have arrived the true, genuine— the only real intellectual millennium. . . .

25. Negroes Everywhere Form a People Apart
Gustave de Beaumont

THE status of Negroes and Indians was noted by most nineteenth-century European visitors to the United States, although the former received most attention. The young French aristocrat Gustave de Beaumont, who in 1831 accompanied Alexis de Tocqueville on a tour of the country (Document 6), was especially concerned about this problem. While his compatriot was working on Democracy in America, a sympathetic but critical study of American society, Beaumont was writing a sentimental novel, Marie, depicting and analyzing the racial problems of the young Republic. He not only gathered data during his visit to the United States, but continued to acquire information on American racial attitudes after his return to France. The New York City race riot of 1834 provided grist for his mill and served as the basis of one of the most dramatic episodes of the novel: the hero, who has fallen in love with an American girl of mixed blood, is prevented by mob action from marrying her. The lovers flee to the frontier, but their expected happiness is frustrated by the death of Marie. In the novel Beaumont also castigated American Indian policy, having been particularly affected by the removal of the Five Civilized Tribes from their ancestral homeland.

FOREWORD

I owe the reader some explanation on the form and background of this book. . . .

During my stay in the United States, I observed a society which harmonizes and contrasts with ours; and it seemed to me that if I could manage to convey the impressions which I received in America, my narrative would not be entirely useless. It is these very real impressions which I have blended with an imagined story. . . .

There are two things principally to be observed among a people: its institutions and its customs.

SOURCE: Gustave de Beaumont, Marie, or Slavery in the United States, trans. Barbara Chapman (Stanford, Calif.: Stanford University Press, 1958), pp. 3–6, 123–125, 129–130, reprinted by permission of the publisher. Copyright 1958 by the Board of Trustees of the Leland Stanford University.

I shall remain silent on the first. At the very moment when my book will be published, another will appear which will shed the most brilliant illumination upon the democratic institutions of the United States. I refer to the work of M. Alexis de Tocqueville, entitled *Democracy in America*. . . .

It is, therefore, solely the customs of the United States which I propose to describe. Here again I must observe to the reader that he will not find in my work a complete picture of the customs of that country. . . . The truth is that a single idea dominates the work and forms the central point around which all the developments are arranged.

The reader is aware that there are still slaves in the United States; their number has grown to more than two million. Surely it is a strange fact that there is so much bondage amid so much liberty; but what is perhaps still more extraordinary is the violence of the prejudice which separates the race of slaves from that of the free men, that is, the Negroes from the whites. For the study of this prejudice, the society of the United States furnishes a double element which it would be hard to find elsewhere. Slavery reigns in the South of this country, while there are no longer slaves in the North. In the Southern states one sees the wounds inflicted by slavery in full force; and, in the North, the consequences of slavery after it has ceased to exist. Slave or free, the Negroes everywhere form a people apart from the whites. To give the reader an idea of the barrier placed between the two races, I believe I should cite an event which I myself witnessed.

The first time I attended a theater in the United States, I was surprised at the careful distinction made between the white spectators and an audience whose faces were black. In the first balcony were whites; in the second, mulattoes; in the third, Negroes. An American, beside whom I was sitting, informed me that the dignity of white blood demanded these classifications. However, my eyes being drawn to the balcony where sat the mulattoes, I perceived a young woman of dazzling beauty, whose complexion, of perfect whiteness, proclaimed the purest European blood. Entering into all the prejudices of my neighbor, I asked him how a woman of English origin could be so lacking in shame as to seat herself among the Africans.

"That woman," he replied, "is colored."

"What? Colored? She is whiter than a lily!"

"She is colored," he repeated coldly; "local tradition has established her ancestry, and everyone knows that she had a mulatto among her forebears."

He pronounced these words without further explanation, as one who states a fact which needs only be voiced to be understood.

At the same moment I made out in the balcony for whites a face which was very dark. I asked for an explanation of this new phenomenon; the American answered:

"The lady who has attracted your attention is white."

"What? White! She is the same color as the mulattoes."

"She is white," he replied; "local tradition affirms that the blood which flows in her veins is Spanish."

If this blighting viewpoint on the black race and on even those generations in which the color has disappeared gave birth only to a few frivolous distinctions, my study of it would present but a sightseer's interest, but this prejudice is of graver import. Each day it deepens the abyss which separates the two races and pursues them in every phase of social and political life; it governs the mutual relations of the whites and the colored men, corrupting the habits of the first, whom it accustoms to domination and tyranny, and ruling the fate of the Negroes, whom it dooms to the persecution of the whites; and it generates between them hatreds so violent, resentments so lasting, clashes so dangerous, that one may rightly say it will influence the whole future of American society.

It is this prejudice, born of both slavery and the slave race, which forms the principal subject of my book. I wished to show how great are the miseries of slavery, and how deeply it affects traditions, after it has legally ceased to exist. It is, above all, these secondary consequences of an evil whose first cause has disappeared which I have endeavored to develop. . . .

THE RIOT

. . . In New York, as in all North American cities, there are two distinct parties among the friends of the black race.

The first, judging slavery an evil for their country and perhaps also condemning it as contrary to the Christian religion, demand the emancipation of the black population, but, full of the prejudices of their race, do not consider freed Negroes to be the equals of the whites; they therefore wish to deport colored people as soon as they are liberated; and they hold them to a state of degradation and inferiority as long as they remain among the Americans. A large number of these friends of the Negroes are against slavery only because of national pride; it is distressing to them to be blamed for it by foreigners, and to hear it said that slavery is a relic of barbarism. Some attack the evil for the sole reason that they cannot bear to see it: these, while working for emancipation, accomplish little; they would destroy slavery without offering liberty. They are ridding themselves of an annoyance, an embarrassment, a wound to their vanity, but they are not healing the wounds of others; they have worked for themselves, not for the slaves. Freed from bondage, the latter are denied entrance into free society.

The other partisans of the Negroes are those who sincerely love them, as a Christian loves his brother men; who not only desire the abolition of slavery but also receive the freed men with open arms and treat them as equals.

These zealous friends of the black population are rare, but their ardor is indefatigable; for a long time it was fruitless, but some prejudices have vanished through their efforts, and white men have been known to marry women of color.

As long as philanthropy on behalf of the Negroes had resulted in nothing but useless declamation, the Americans tolerated it without difficulty; it mattered little to them that the equality of the Negroes should be proclaimed in theory, so long as in fact they remained inferior to the whites. But on the day when an American took a colored woman to wife, the attempt to mix the two races took on a practical character. It was an insult directed against the dignity of the whites; American pride was completely up in arms. This was the general state of mind in the city of New York at the time of my wedding with Marie.

On our way to the Catholic church, I noticed an unaccustomed restlessness in the city. It was not the regular activity of an industrial and commercial population: ill-dressed men of the working class roamed the streets at an hour when they were usually at work. They could be seen, scorning their habitual calm coolness, walking quickly, colliding with each other, accosting each other mysteriously, forming animated groups, and separating suddenly in contrary directions. . . .

Nelson asked a passerby the cause of the tumult. "Oh," said he, "the amalgamists are making the trouble; they want the Negroes to be the equals of the whites; so the whites are forced to revolt."

Another man, asked the same question, replied, "If the Negroes get killed, it's their own fault; how do the wretches dare to raise themselves to the rank of Americans?"

A third man gave a different answer: "They are going to tear down the blacks' houses and rid our city of their ugly faces! Though the whites are wrong to act like this, they acted wrongly in the first place: why did they give the Negroes their freedom?"

While we listened to these deplorable statements, a frightful spectacle struck our eyes.

. . . Several poor mulattoes happening to pass at that moment, we heard at once a thousand infuriated voices shouting: "Down with the Negroes! Kill them!" At the same instant, a hail of stones, flung by the crowd, fell upon the colored people; Americans armed with clubs flung themselves on the poor creatures and beat them pitilessly. Overwhelmed by this treatment, as cruel as it was unexpected, the mulattoes made no resistance, and seemed dazed at the sight of the angry crowd; their eyes, raised to Heaven, seemed to ask God whence came the wrath of a society whose laws they respected. . . .

Toward evening the rioting died down; the philanthropic society established in New York for the liberation of the Negroes published a declaration which attempted to calm the passions of the Americans against the colored people. It said, "We never conceived the insane project of mingling the two races; in this regard we could not fail to recognize the dignity of the whites; we respect the laws which uphold slavery in the Southern states."

Oh, shame! Who then are these free people, among whom one is not allowed to hate slavery? The Negroes in New York are not demanding liberty for themselves—they are all free; they appeal to the Americans to pity their brothers in slavery, and their prayers, and those of their friends, are crimes for which they must ask forgiveness! . . .

Everyone, after the event, condemned the rioters and their excesses. Most people, while deploring the wretchedness of the blacks, experienced a secret joy. However, I saw several good citizens, sincere friends to their country, who shed tears at the memory of that dreadful day; they saw, in that act of tyranny exercised by the majority on a weak minority, the most shameful abuse of strength, and they wondered if a people whose evil passions were stronger than the law could long remain free. . . .

26. Colonizing the Free People of Color
American Colonization Society

THOMAS JEFFERSON and others of his generation believed that slavery would eventually disappear in the United States, citing the 1808 Congressional ban on the importation of Negroes as a necessary first step. Therefore, during the first two or three decades of the nineteenth century few Americans were seriously concerned about slavery. One reason for the decline of abolitionist sentiment during this period was the increasing antipathy toward the free Negro. This attitude was most graphically illustrated by the organization in 1817 of the American Colonization Society, led by prominent slaveholders in the upper South who advocated resettlement of freedmen and emancipated slaves in Africa as the only solution to the race problem. While the colonizationists endeavored to encourage manumission, their activities were largely devoted to convincing free Negroes to migrate. In 1821 a colony was established in Liberia, about fourteen hundred Negroes being transported in the ensuing decade, but the cost of the enterprise soon proved prohibitive. Nevertheless, a small but devoted group of colonizationists continued up to the brink of the Civil War to maintain that this was the only rational solution. As indicated in the following selection, the Society had branches in the North as well as the South.

It is now only fourteen years since a small number of gentlemen met together, in the city of Washington, and formed themselves into a Society, under the denomination of "The American Society for colonizing in Africa the free people of color of these United States." . . .

The plan of colonizing the free people of color, in some place beyond the United States, was first conceived at the south. . . . The scheme, . . . was ever cherished, with interest, by the most eminent men of Virginia. Mr. Jefferson and Mr. Monroe expressed, in repeated terms, their warmest approbation of the plan, as the most desirable measure, which could be adopted for gradually drawing off this part of our population. . . .

SOURCE: *Report Made at an Adjourned Meeting of the Friends of the American Colonization Society, in Worcester County, Held in Worcester, Dec. 8, 1830, by a Committee Appointed for that Purpose, with the Proceedings of the Meeting, &c* (Worcester, Mass.: S. H. Colton and Co., 1831), pp. 3–7, 10–16.

The progress of the Society, after its organization, was in a short period, such as to excite the attention of the public, so far as to make its object and character a subject of inquiry. This scheme not only originated with the citizens of slave-holding States, but numbered, among its first projectors, those who were slave-holders themselves. It was therefore viewed with distrust and suspicion, by the opponents of slavery, at the North, and it was believed by many, to be but a wicked contrivance of slave-holders, themselves, to rivet the chains of slavery more firmly than ever. It was supposed . . . that, in their wish to remove the free people of color, they were simply actuated by a desire to remove the only example of liberty existing with this population, and thus obliterate, in the minds of their slaves, the last hope of freedom. In fine, the whole plan was denounced as a base conspiracy against the cause of emancipation. . . .

But the Society had hardly begun to recover from unfavorable impressions, thus entertained of it at the North, when it was destined to experience a more virulent and unexpected attack from the South. . . . some of its early friends in that region, fancying they saw in the scheme a disguised attack upon the rights of the slave-holding States, abandoned the Society, and turned their eloquence against it. In that quarter, it has, therefore, been denounced as an insidious attack on the domestic tranquillity of the South, and an unhallowed attempt of Northern abolitionists, to sow, in that region, "the seeds of anxiety, inquietude, and trouble." . . .

Although the Society suffered from the misrepresentations of its enemies, it still continued to add to the number of its friends, and to augment its resources. In the period of four or five years after its formation, the Society, by treaty and by purchase, procured a considerable extent of territory on the Western coast of Africa, to which, as expressive of its character, they gave the name of LIBERIA. . . .

. . . Here was the country, chosen to be the promised land of the free people of color of these United States. Here, the Society proposed to plant the Colony, which was to restore the broken hearted African to the land of his fathers,—heal his wounds, inflicted by a Christian and civilized world,—and, it was to be hoped, one day, redeem him from his present degraded and debased condition. . . .

It is impossible to trace the rapid rise and progress of this infant Colony, without once glancing at the past history of Africa, or indulging a single thought of her future destinies. . . . A portion of this ill-fated country was once the cradle of the arts and sciences: she could once boast of a Republic, famed for its wealth and its commerce, and the rival of Rome herself. But, long since, the sun of her glory and her greatness has gone down; and barbarity and ignorance established their dark and ruthless dominion. But the march of empire and of intellect, that has for ages been westward, may yet retrace its course. Through the humble agency of the American Colonization Society, the light of knowledge may be diffused over Africa, the chains of her bondage be broken, and her sons be regenerated. Her idolatry and superstition may yield to the pure and undefiled influence of our Holy Religion; her forests may be converted into fruitful fields, and the banks of her Senegal, her Gambia, and her Niger, may yet vie in splendor and in wealth with those of our beautiful Ohio, and majestic Mississippi. Events as great as these are within the compass of human possibilities, and cannot be contemplated without emotions of interest and admiration. The American continent now exhibits the proud spectacle, of twelve millions of free people, united into one great and enlightened Republic. Two hundred years ago, and who foresaw this great event? Fancy herself could not, in her boldest flights, have caught so bright a vision.

But the merits of the Society, and the utility of its plans, are not to be tested by the issue of distant, and perhaps, uncertain events. The advantages which the Society hold out, are immediate, certain, and permanent, in their character and operation.

The removal of those free blacks, which throng our cities and populous towns, to the coast of Africa, where they may find an asylum from their present degraded and debased condition, is, in itself, a scheme at once benevolent and patriotic.

. . . The existence of so large a number of free blacks, in the immediate neighborhood of their slaves, has always been a source of anxious solicitude and alarm in the slave-holding States. With us, they have always been a miserable and degraded race, and, as to all those lofty sensibilities, which give dignity and worth to human character, absolutely forsaken and forlorn. Although free, they are not permitted to enjoy the blessings of freedom. They are strangers and aliens in the land of their birth. . . . Protected indeed, they are, by the laws of the country, but excluded from any share in their administration, they feel none of those generous impulses, which prompt to virtue, or deter from vice. Without character, or any regular vocation, shunned, and even scorned, by the white man, they become reckless and abandoned. They furnish a large proportion of our malefactors. Indolent in their habits, vicious in their propensities, they become discontented with themselves, and excite discontent in others. . . .

To remove this class, therefore, beyond these unhappy influences, and embody them into one community, where distinctions of color will no longer exclude them from those endearing sympathies, which flow from social intercourse,—to place them, not only in a state of freedom, but in a condition of conscious independence, where industry and honesty shall carry with them the reward of influence and respect;—finally, to secure to them, not only the enjoyment, but the sole exercise, of political rights and privileges, is calculated, while it rids the country of a pest, to rescue this unfortunate race from their moral and intellectual debasement, and to inspire them with that hope, pride, and dignity, which freedom, connected with self-government, can alone excite.

But the Society, from its commencement, hoped to do something for the cause of emancipation. It holds out its benefits, therefore, to such, "as the humanity of individuals, and the laws of the different States might see fit to liberate from bondage." The existence of slavery in the United States has been, with every friend to his country, a constant theme of regret. The philanthropist and the friend of liberty deprecate it, as a stain upon the lofty character which a republic, like our own, ought to sustain. Our most distinguished statesmen acknowledge it to be a political evil, and a domestic scourge; a sort of morbid excrescence, destined to become more unsightly, and to grow more deformed with the growth of the country. . . . But, commensurate with the magnitude of the evil, has always been the difficulty of finding a remedy. To violate the rights and duties, which, under our constitution and laws, govern the relation between master and slave, cannot be justified upon any principle of justice, or precept of religion. The Society have, accordingly, at all times, unequivocally disclaimed any design of that character, and have always forborne to countenance any measure that would, in the least degree, impair the rights and obligations imposed by such a relation. To emancipate these unfortunate beings, and leave them to their fate, would be madness and folly.

To knock off their shackles, and turn them loose upon the community, would, not only be no kindness to them, but a palpable injustice to Society. . . .

The only remedy for the evil, has been applied by the Society. They have provided for the liberated slave, an asylum and a home. The friends of the Society expected that voluntary emancipation would follow in the train of colonization. It was believed that many masters would follow the natural dictates of justice and humanity, and manumit their slaves, when it could be done with safety to themselves, and without danger to the public. The anticipations of the Society have been more than realized. Many slaves have already been emancipated and transported to the colony. . . .

. . . Another important advantage, that was expected to result from the scheme of the Society, was, the aid which a civilized colony, established on the coast of Africa, would afford in the suppression of the Slave Trade. . . . The petty and deluded princes of Africa must be taught to feel the superiority, conferred by civilization and christianity, and deem it infamous to sell their brethren into bondage. . . . The continued example of a happy community, enjoying the peace and tranquillity, which civilization and christianity confers, must produce the desired effect; and the success of the Society's efforts in this part of its scheme, will yet be, it is believed, the brightest page of its history.

. . . We send back the natives to carry to their own countrymen, the liberty and religion taught them in the land of their captivity. Every individual emigrant becomes a missionary; and the whole community together constitute a fountain, from which streams of living waters will unceasingly flow. It promises to do more, in a few years, than has been accomplished by missionary labors for a century. . . .

Whether, therefore, we contemplate the magnificence of its plan, the beneficence of its design, or the unexampled success of its efforts, the Colonization Society must be, to every American citizen, an object of interest and admiration. . . .

The resources of the national Government alone are sufficient for the complete success and final accomplishment of so great an object; and the friends of the Society have always cherished a belief, that an enterprize, so intimately connected with the national welfare, would ultimately command the patronage and cordial support of our General Government. . . .

27. We Must and Shall Be Free
David Walker

MOST free Negroes rejected the appeal of the American Colonization Society, preferring to believe that their destiny was to be realized in the United States rather than Africa; in response, they created a movement of their own. At the beginning their most influential spokesman proved to be David Walker (1785–1830), a free Negro who had migrated from North Carolina to Boston, where he became an old-clothes dealer. He became an important figure in the Negro community, devoted to the abolition of slavery and the improvement of the status of his fellow freedmen. In 1829 he wrote and published his Appeal, a pamphlet that ran into three editions. A call to militant action by Negroes, North and South, it was quickly condemned by whites in all sections as an incendiary publication, and efforts were made to suppress its circulation. In 1830 Walker was found dead in front of his shop, presumably the victim of foul play. Yet the Appeal continued to be circulated, receiving much of the blame in the South for Nat Turner's insurrection in 1831; the pamphlet and the revolt led to a rigorous ban on discussions of slavery in the South after that date.

Having travelled over a considerable portion of these United States, and having, in the course of my travels, taken the most accurate observations of things as they exist—the result of my observations has warranted the full and unshaken conviction, that we, (coloured people of these United States,) are the most degraded, wretched, and abject set of beings that ever lived since the world began; and I pray God that none like us ever may live again until time shall be no more. . . .

. . . I am fully aware, in making this appeal to my much afflicted and suffering brethren, that I shall not only be assailed by those whose greatest earthly desires are, to keep us in abject ignorance and wretchedness, and who are of the firm conviction that

SOURCE: *Walker's Appeal, in Four Articles; Together with a Preamble, to the Coloured Citizens of the World, But in Particular, and Very Expressly, to Those of the United States of America; Written in Boston, State of Massachusetts, September 28, 1829*, 3rd ed., with additional notes, corrections, &c. (Boston: David Walker, 1830), pp. 3–5, 18–20, 70–80.

Heaven has designed us and our children to be slaves and *beasts of burden* to them and their children. . . . But I am persuaded, that many of my brethren, particularly those who are ignorantly in league with slave-holders or tyrants, . . . will rise up and call me cursed—Yea, the jealous ones among us will perhaps use more abject subtlety, by affirming that this work is not worth perusing, that we are well situated, and there is no use in trying to better our condition, for we cannot. I will ask one question here.—Can our condition be any worse?—Can it be more mean and abject? If there are any changes, will they not be for the better, though they may appear for the worst at first? Can they get us any lower? Where can they get us? They are afraid to treat us worse, for they know well, the day they do it they are gone. But against all accusations which may or can be preferred against me, I appeal to Heaven for my motive in writing—who knows that my object is, if possible, to awaken in the breasts of my afflicted, degraded and slumbering brethren, a spirit of inquiry and investigation respecting our miseries, and wretchedness in this *Republican Land of Liberty!* ! ! ! ! . . .

. . . Are we MEN! !—I ask you, O my brethren! are we MEN? Did our Creator make us to be slaves to dust and ashes like ourselves? Are they not dying worms as well as we? Have they not to make their appearance before the tribunal of Heaven, to answer for the deeds done in the body, as well as we? Have we any other Master but Jesus Christ alone? Is he not their Master as well as ours?—What right then, have we to obey and call any other Master, but Himself? How we could be so *submissive* to a gang of men, whom we cannot tell whether they are *as good as ourselves* or not, I never could conceive. . . .

The whites have always been an unjust, jealous, unmerciful, avaricious and blood-thirsty set of beings, always seeking after power and authority. . . . But some may ask, did not the blacks of Africa, and the mulattoes of Asia, go on in the same way as did the whites of Europe. I answer, no—they never were half so avaricious, deceitful and unmerciful as the whites, according to their knowledge.

. . . I therefore, in the name of fear of the Lord God of Heaven and of earth, divested of prejudice either on the side of my colour or that of the whites, advance my suspicion of them, whether they are *as good by nature* as we are or not. Their actions, since they were known as a people, have been the reverse, I do indeed suspect them, but this, as I before observed, is shut up with the Lord, we cannot exactly tell, it will be proved in succeeding generations.— The whites have had the essence of the gospel as it was preached by my master and his apostles—the Ethiopians have not. . . .

. . . They keep us miserable now, and call us their property, but some of them will have enough of us by and by—their stomachs shall run over with us; they want us for their slaves, and shall have us to their fill. . . . we can help ourselves; for, if we lay aside abject servility, and be determined to act like men, and not brutes—the murder[er]s among the whites would be afraid to show their cruel heads. But O, my God!—in sorrow I must say it, that my colour, all over the world, have a mean, servile spirit. They yield in a moment to the whites, let them be right or wrong—the reason they are able to keep their feet on our throats. Oh! my coloured brethren, all over the world, when shall we arise from this death-like apathy?—And be men! ! You will notice, if ever we become men, (I mean respectable men, such as other people are,) we must exert ourselves to the full. For remember, that it is the greatest desire and object of the greater part of the whites, to keep us ignorant, and make us work to support them and their families. —Here now, in the Southern and Western sections of this country, there are at least three coloured persons for one white, why is it, that those few weak, good-for-nothing whites, are able to keep so many able men, one of whom, can put to flight a dozen whites, in wretchedness and misery? It shows at once, what the blacks are, we are ignorant, abject, servile and mean—and the whites know it— they know that we are too servile to assert our rights as men—or they would not fool with us as they do. Would they fool with any other people as they do with us? No, they know too well, that they would get themselves ruined. Why do they not bring the inhabitants of Asia to be body servants to them? They know they would get their bodies rent and torn from head to foot. Why do they not get the Aborigines of this country to be slaves to them and their children, to work their farms and dig their mines? They know well that the Aborigines of this country, or (Indians) would tear them from the earth. The Indians would not rest day or night, they would be up all times of night, cutting their cruel throats. But my colour, (some, not all,) are willing to stand still and be murdered by the cruel whites. . . . Some of our brethren, . . . who seeking more after self aggrandisement, than the glory of God, and the welfare of their brethren, join with our oppressors. . . . They think, that they are doing great things, when they can get in company with the whites, to ridicule and make sport of those who are labouring for their good. Poor ignorant creatures, they do not know that the sole aim and object of the whites, are only to make fools and slaves of them, and put the whip to them, and make them work to support them and their families. . . . Will any of us leave our homes and go to Africa? I hope not. . . . Let no man of us budge one step, and let slave-holders come to beat us from our country. America is more our country, than it is the whites—we have enriched it with our *blood and tears*. The greatest riches in all America have arisen from our blood and tears:—and will they drive us from our property and homes, which we have earned with our *blood?* They must look sharp or this very thing will bring swift destruction upon them. The Americans have got so fat on our blood and groans, that they have almost forgotten the God of armies. But let them go on. . . .

. . . Americans! . . . you have and do continue to treat us more cruel than any heathen nation ever did a people it had subjected to the same condition that you have us. Now let us reason— I mean you of the United States, whom I believe God designs to save from destruction, if you will hear. For I declare to you, whether you believe it or not, that there are some on the continent of America, who will never be able to repent. God will surely destroy them, to show you his disapprobation of the murders they and you have inflicted on us. I say, let us reason; had you not better take our body, while you have it in your power, and while we are yet ignorant and wretched, not knowing but a little, give us education, and teach us the pure religion of our Lord and Master, which is calculated to make the lion lay down in peace with the lamb, and which millions of you have beaten us nearly to death for trying to obtain since we have been among you, and thus at once, gain our affection while we are ignorant? Remember Americans, that we must and shall be free and enlightened as you are, will you wait until we shall, under God, obtain our liberty by the crushing arm of power? Will it not be dreadful for you? I speak Americans for your good. We must and shall be free I say, in spite of you. You may do your best to keep us in wretchedness and misery, to enrich you and your children, but God will deliver us from under you. And wo, wo, will be to you if we have to obtain our freedom by fighting. Throw away your fears and prejudices then, and enlighten us and treat us like men, and we will like you more than we do now hate you, and tell us now no more about colonization, for America is as much our country, as it is yours.—Treat us like men, and there is no danger but we will all live in peace and happiness together. For we are not like you, hard hearted, unmerciful, and unforgiving. What a happy country this will be, if the whites will listen. What nation under heaven, will be able to do any thing with us, unless God gives us up into its hand? But Americans, I declare to you, while you keep us and our children in bondage, and treat us like brutes, to make us support you and your families, we cannot be your friends. And there is not a doubt in my mind, but that the whole of the past will be sunk into oblivion, and we yet, under God, will become a united and happy people. The whites may say it is impossible, but re-member that nothing is impossible with God.

The Americans may say or do as they please, but they have to raise us from the condition of brutes to that of respectable men, and to make a national acknowledgement to us for the wrongs they have inflicted on us. As unexpected, strange, and wild as these propositions may to some appear, it is no less a fact, that unless they are complied with, the Americans of the United States, though they may for a little while escape, God will yet weigh them in a balance, and if they are not superior to other men, as they have represented themselves to be, he will give them wretchedness to their very heart's content.

28. Immediate Emancipation
or Continued Slavery
William Jay

PROBABLY the most effective and widely circulated criticism of colonization as the solution to the Negro question was written by William Jay
(1789–1858), the son of John Jay, a prominent New York Federalist
and first Chief Justice of the United States. After graduating from Yale
and studying law, Jay served as a county judge for twenty-five years, but
spent most of his energies in reform activities, including the American
Bible Society and the peace and temperance movements. As a leader
of the New York City Anti-Slavery Society, he not only opposed
colonization but agitated for the abolition of the slave trade in the District of Columbia. Although agreeing with Garrison (Document 29)
on the necessity of immediate emancipation, he believed that this objective could be attained constitutionally through legislative action; in
contradiction to Garrison, Jay argued that the Constitution had not
legalized slavery in the United States.

If we have been successful in our endeavors to prove, that the
removal of slavery by colonization is both morally and physically
impossible, then it necessarily follows, that the slaves must be
emancipated here, or that slavery must be indefinitely continued.

Should the former alternative be adopted, the important question occurs: ought the emancipation to be *gradual* or *immediate?*

If this question is to be determined with reference to moral
obligation, it is certainly difficult for those who regard slavery as
sinful to justify its continuance even for a limited time. If, however, the question is to be decided on the ground of mere political
expediency, there are many and powerful objections to *gradual*
emancipation; and what may at first view appear paradoxical, the
strength of these objections is proportioned to the number of slaves
to be emancipated. . . .

. . . in those States, in which nearly all the laborers are slaves,
where every free black is regarded as a nuisance and an incendiary

SOURCE: William Jay, An Inquiry into the Character and Tendency of the American Colonization and American Anti-Slavery
Societies, 3rd edition (New York: Leavitt, Lord & Co., 1835),
pp. 192–198.

and where the planter would, on no consideration, permit him to labor in company with his slaves, much difficulty would necessarily attend a *gradual* relinquishment of slave labor. . . .

. . . The idea, that by gradual emancipation, the slaves will become fit for freedom, is visionary in the extreme. How is it possible that the liberation of a portion of the slaves, can qualify those who remain in chains, to become useful citizens? The house of bondage is not the school in which men are to be trained for liberty.

As then gradual emancipation, however desirable, if no other can be obtained, is so full of difficulty, and, in the opinion of slave holders, so *dangerous* that they have almost universally passed laws to prevent it, the only alternative is *immediate emancipation* or *continued slavery.* . . .

But we are met with the inquiry, how are the owners to be compensated for the loss of their property? This same objection was made to the suppression of the African slave trade. . . .

If a particular manufactory is found to be deleterious to the health of a city, it is not only the right, but the duty of the civil authority, to suppress it. If the national interests require an embargo, the measure is adopted, although it virtually wrests from the merchant his property, by depriving him of the use of his own ships. . . .

To contend that the slaves in the Southern States, ought not to be emancipated by law, except on the payment to their masters, of their market value, is to contend that slavery ought to be perpetual. Such a payment is MORALLY IMPOSSIBLE. By whom can it be made? The Federal Government have neither the will nor the constitutional power to make it. . . . To suppose that the free States, would be willing from motives of disinterested benevolence, to make a present to their neighbors of a THOUSAND MILLIONS OF DOLLARS is obviously absurd: nor is it less absurd to insist that this sum ought to be paid to the masters, by the Legislatures of the slave states; since the pockets of the masters, are the only sources whence those Legislatures could obtain the money. . . .

If the slaves are worth a thousand millions of dollars, it is evidence that their *labor* must be worth *much more*; because, to their price is to be added the cost of their maintenance, and the whole is to be reimbursed with profit out of their labor. Now Colonization, would utterly annihilate all this labor; it calls upon the South to surrender a commodity worth more than a thousand millions; and upon this surrender, which would convert the whole slave region into a wilderness, it rests all its hopes of the ultimate abolition of slavery! !

Emancipation on the contrary, instead of removing millions of laborers, would stimulate their industry, improve their morals, quicken their intelligence, and convert a dangerous, idle, and vicious population into wholesome citizens. Were all the slaves in South Carolina emancipated to-morrow, every branch of industry would derive new energy, and every species of property, an increased value from the additional security which such a measure would give to society. All dread of insurrection would vanish, and one half of the population, who are now regarded as implacable foes, would be converted into useful friends.

But it is objected, that the emancipated blacks will form a bad population. One would think, from this objection, that the slaves now form a *good* population, and that they are to be rendered ignorant and immoral by freedom. Unquestionably, the liberated slaves, like all other vicious and degraded people, will, while such, form a bad population; but if they are such while in bondage, and must ever remain such until liberated, then emancipation is the only process by which a bad, can be converted into a good population. As soon as they are free, they will be accessible to education and religious instruction, and all those various motives which operate as a wholesome restraint on the evil passions of our nature. It would be most unjust to estimate the future character of the emancipated slaves, supposing slavery to be immediately abolished, by the *present* character of the free negroes. These last, in the slave States, are a hated and persecuted race. They are *kept* not only in ignorance, but in idleness. The planters will not employ them, for fear they will contaminate the slaves; and the whole legislation of the Southern States, towards this people, is to degrade and brutify them. But these wicked efforts are the results of slavery, and would cease with it. Were slavery abolished, then it would be the obvious interest of the South to improve the black population, and the causes which necessarily render the free blacks vicious, would no longer operate. The same remark applies, although with less force, to the free blacks of the North. Colonization and slavery have both had their influence in keeping alive, and aggravating the prejudices against color, and these prejudices have led to that system of persecution and oppression to which the free blacks here are sub-jected. . . .

Abolitionists are constantly called on for a plan of emancipation. They have little encouragement to respond to the call. If they propose the simple plan of proclaiming by act of the State Legis-latures, the immediate and unqualified abolition of slavery, they are denounced as reckless incendiaries. If they intimate, that aboli-tion does not necessarily inhibit all compulsory labor, and point to the rural code of St. Domingo and the apprentice system of the West Indies, they are reproached with wishing to substitute one kind of slavery for another. But, in truth, they are under no obliga-tion of duty or policy to propose any specific plan. No Temperance Society has felt itself bound because it pronounced the traffic in ardent spirits to be sinful, to furnish venders with plans for employ-ing their capitals in other occupations.

The details of emancipation, and the various legal provisions proper to render it safe and convenient, are not prescribed by the great principles of justice and religion, but by considerations of local policy. It is not probable, that if all the Southern Legislatures were sincerely anxious to abolish slavery, any two of them would do it in precisely the same manner, and under the same regulations. We have seen one plan pursued in St. Domingo, another in Ber-muda and Antigua, a third in the other British West-Indies, and still different plans in South America.

Of all these plans, that adopted in Mexico, Bermuda and An-tigua, of immediate, total and unqualified emancipation, will, there is reason to believe, be found in all cases the most safe and expedient.

This plan removes from the slave all cause for discontent. He is free, and his own master, and he can ask for no more. Yet he is, in fact, for a time, absolutely dependent on his late owner. He can look to no other person for food to eat, clothes to put on, or house to shelter him. His first wish therefore is, to remain where he is, and he receives as a favor, permission to labor in the service of him whom the day before he regarded as his oppressor. But labor is no longer the badge of his servitude, and the consummation of his misery: it is the evidence of his liberty, for it is *voluntary*. For the first time in his life, he is a party to a contract. . . . Thus will the transition from slave to free labor be effected instantaneously, and with scarcely any perceptible interruption of the ordinary pursuits of life. In the course of time, the value of negro labor, like all other vendible commodities, will be regulated by the supply and demand: and justice be done both to the planter and his laborers. The very consciousness, moreover, that justice *is* done to both parties, will remove their mutual suspicions and animosities, and substitute in their place feelings of kindness and confidence. . . .

29. Moderation Is Deliberate Barbarity
William Lloyd Garrison

WILLIAM LLOYD GARRISON (1805–1879) was the most inflammatory of the white abolitionists and one of the few with a following among free Negroes. Educated largely in the print shop, he joined the moderate abolitionist Benjamin Lundy in 1829 as assistant editor of a Baltimore journal. His denunciation of the slave trade and his demand for immediate emancipation led to his imprisonment and his estrangement from Lundy. Two years later he moved to Boston where the Liberator, his mouthpiece for the next thirty-five years, was established, most of its subscribers being Negroes. Attempting moral suasion upon Northerners and Southerners alike, Garrison agitated the necessity of abolition with a vehemence and fervor that aroused a violent antipathy in both sections. The occasion for the following address was his impending visit to England in 1833 to gain the support of British abolitionists for the American movement; his reception abroad increased his prestige at home and contributed to the establishment of the American Anti-Slavery Society. Within a few years this organization split into Garrisonians and anti-Garrisonians, his intransigence and emphasis upon agitation rather than organization isolating him from many of his colleagues in the movement. Nevertheless, Garrison continued as an indomitable abolitionist until emancipation was achieved at the end of the Civil War.

BRETHREN AND FRIENDS:—

My pleasure, in meeting you on this occasion, would be perfect, were it not dashed with the knowledge that I am soon to be separated from you, in a distant country. Probably you are all aware that, in a few days, I propose to sail from New-York for England, on a high and important mission. . . .

But let not this be an occasion of sadness. I will make it rather an occasion of joy. . . . Do you not see the pitiless storm, which has so long been pouring its rage upon you, breaking away, and a bow of promise, as glorious as that which succeeded the ancient deluge, spanning the sky—a token that, to the end of time, the billows of prejudice and oppression shall no more cover the earth,

SOURCE: William Lloyd Garrison, *Address Delivered in Boston, New-York and Philadelphia, Before the Free People of Color, in April, 1833* (New-York: Printed for the Free People of Color, 1833), pp. 3–13, 15–16, 19–22.

to the destruction of your race; but seed-time and harvest shall never fail, and the laborer shall eat the fruit of his hands? Is not your cause ripening like the spring? . . .

Why should this not be an occasion of joy, instead of sorrow? Listen to those trumpet tones which come swelling on the winds of the Atlantic, and which shall bring an echo from every harp in heaven! If there is joy in that blissful abode over one sinner that repenteth, how mighty and thrilling must it be over a repentant nation! And Great Britain is that nation. Her people are humbling themselves before God, and before those whom they have so long held in bondage. Their voices are breaking, in peals of thunder, upon the ear of Parliament, demanding the immediate and utter overthrow of slavery in all the colonies; and in obedience to their will, the mandate is about being issued by Parliament, which shall sever at a blow the chains of eight hundred thousand slaves! . . .

Why should we not rejoice this evening, brethren? Find we nothing at home to raise our drooping spirits, to invigorate our hopes, and to engage our efforts? . . .

Look, in the first place, at the abolition standard—more gorgeous and spirit-stirring than the star-spangled banner—floating high in the air! . . . Around it, thousands are gathering with high and holy courage, to contend not with carnal but spiritual weapons against the powers of darkness. . . . They who are contending for the immediate abolition of slavery—the destruction of its ally, the American Colonization Society—and the bestowal of equal rights and privileges upon the whole colored population—well knew what would be the consequences of their advocacy to themselves. They knew that slander would blacken their characters with infamy—that their pleadings would be received with ridicule and reproach—that persecution would assail them on the right hand and on the left—that the dungeon would yawn for their bodies— that the dagger of the assassin would gleam behind them—that they would be branded as disturbers of the peace, as fanatics, madmen, and incendiaries—that the heel of friendship would be lifted against them, and love be turned into hatred, and confidence into suspicion, and respect into derision—that their worldly interests would be jeoparded, and the honor and emoluments of office be withheld from their enjoyment. Knowing all this, still they dared all things, in order to save their country, and abolish the bloody system of slavery. . . .

In the second place, we perceive for our encouragement, brethren, that the attention of the nation is now fixed upon the subject of slavery with an interest altogether unprecedented. . . . What has created the mighty discussion which has taken, or is taking place in almost every debating Society or Lyceum throughout the Union, and which cannot cease till the cause of it, SLAVERY, is overthrown? . . . May I not say that the Liberator has been a prominent medium through which this truth has obtained circulation? . . . Bitter enemies and luke-warm friends represent it as an incendiary publication. Well, I am willing to admit the propriety of the designation. It is, unquestionably, kindling a great fire; but it is the fire of sympathy and holy indignation, against the most atrocious system on earth, and will burn up nothing but the chaff. . . . Let those throw water upon it, who will—love to God and man shall feed it, and prevent its extinguishment.

But the Liberator is said to be destructive in its character and tendency. That charge, also, I admit is true. It is putting whole magazines of truth under the slave system, and I trust in God will blow it into countless fragments, so that not the remnant of a whip or chain can be found in all the south, and so that upon its ruins may be erected the beautiful temple of freedom. . . .

But the Liberator uses very hard language, and calls a great many bad names, and is very harsh and abusive. Precious cant, indeed! And what has been so efficacious as this hard language? Now, I am satisfied that its strength of denunciation bears no proportion to the enormous guilt of the slave system. The English language is lamentably weak and deficient, in regard to this matter. I wish its epithets were heavier—I wish it would not break so easily—I wish I could denounce slavery, and all its abettors, in terms equal to their infamy. . . .

How, then, ought I to feel, and speak, and write, in view of a system which is red with innocent blood, drawn from the bodies of millions of my countrymen by the scourge of brutal drivers;—which is full of all uncleanness and licentiousness; which destroys the "life of the soul;"—and which is too horrible for the mind to imagine, or the pen to declare? How ought I to feel and speak? As a man! as a patriot! as a philanthropist! as a christian! My soul should be, as it is, on fire. I should thunder—I should lighten. I should blow the trumpet of alarm, long and loud. I should use just such language as is most descriptive of the crime. I should imitate the example of Christ, who, when he had to do with people of like manners, called them sharply by their proper names—such as, an adulterous and perverse generation, a brood of vipers, hypocrites, children of the devil who could not escape the damnation of hell. Moderation, under such circumstances, is deliberate barbarity, both to the oppressor and the oppressed—calmness is marble indifference. . . .

But a graver charge is brought against me, brethren, and now I want your verdict. It is said that I am exciting your rage against the whites and filling your minds with revengeful feelings? Is this true? Have not all my addresses and appeals to you had a contrary effect upon your minds? Have they not been calculated to make you bear all your trials and difficulties in the spirit of christian resignation, and to induce you to return good for evil? Where is the calumniator who dares to affirm that you have been turbulent and quarrelsome since I began my labors in your behalf? Where is the man who is so ignorant as not to know or perceive that, as a people, you are constantly improving in knowledge and virtue? . . .

I will notice but one other charge which the enemies of our cause has brought against me. It is, that I am unduly exciting your hopes, and holding out to your view prospects of future happiness and respectability which can never be realized in this country. Pitiful complaint! Because I have planted a solitary rose, as it were, in the wilderness of suffering in which your race has so long wandered, to cheer your drooping hearts, I am sharply reproved for giving even this little token of good things to come—by those, too, who make loud professions of friendship for you, that is, if you will go to Liberia, but who are constantly strewing in your path briars and thorns, and digging pits into which you may stumble to rise no more. . . . Surely I may be pardoned, when so many are endeavoring to break down all your towering hopes and noble aspirations, if I urge you not to despair, for the day of redemption will assuredly come. . . .

It is proper, my dear friends, that you should understand the objects of my mission to England. . . . Although this is styled "the land of the free and the home of the brave,"—a land of pure democracy,—a christian land; and although the people thereof have met together in a national capacity, for the fifty-sixth time, solemnly to declare that all men are created free and equal—sternly to denounce tyranny, and, in imitation of their fathers, to pledge their lives, their fortunes, and their sacred honor, that they will perish sooner than submit to the yoke of bondage,—notwithstanding all this, there are MILLIONS OF SLAVES in the United States, and it is deemed a criminal act to plead for their deliverance. . . . For a short space, then, I propose to leave this free republican, christian country, and go to one in which there is a king and a proud nobility; but where my denunciations against the persecution and oppression of your color will be received, not as in this country with astonishment, and rage, and scorn, but with loud cheers—with thunders of applause! There, I cannot speak too plainly, nor betray too much zeal, nor be too uncompromising in my demands. . . .

. . . Although absent from you in body, I shall still be with you in spirit. I go away, not to escape from toil, but to labor more abundantly in your cause. If I may do something for your good at home, I hope to do more abroad. In the mean time, I beseech you fail not, on your part, to lead quiet and orderly lives. Let there be no ground whatever for the charge which is brought against you by your enemies, that you are turbulent and rude. Let all quarrelling, all dram-drinking, all profanity, all violence, all division be confined to the white people. Imitate them in nothing but what is clearly good, and carefully shun even the appearance of evil. Let them, if they will, follow the devices and perform the drudgery of the devil; but be ye perfect, even as your heavenly Father is perfect. Conquer their aversion by moral excellence; their proud spirit by love; their evil acts by acts of goodness; their animosity by forgiveness. Keep in your hearts the fear of God, and rejoice even in tribulation; for the promise is sure, that all things shall work together for good to those who love His name. . . .

30. The Case of Human Rights
Against Slavery
Theodore Dwight Weld

THE *most effective propagandist and lecturer for the American Anti-Slavery Society was Theodore D. Weld (1803–1895), a disciple of Charles Grandison Finney (Document 2). After being converted to a belief in immediate emancipation, he aided in establishing Lane Seminary in Cincinnati as a center for antislavery agitation, planning the famous Lane Debate of 1834. The condemnation of this action by the trustees led Weld and forty students to leave for newly established Oberlin College, a pioneer in both coeducation and Negro education. Weld then embarked upon a project to train "the Seventy," young and fervent propagandists for abolitionism who evangelized the Old Northwest. A few years later he married Angelina Grimké (see Document 17); by this time his voice was failing, so he deserted the lecture platform and with his wife and her sister began compiling data on slavery from newspapers and other sources. Slavery As It Is became the best selling tract of the American Anti-Slavery Society, consulted by critics of slavery from Charles Dickens to Harriet Beecher Stowe. Shortly after its publication Weld and his wife retired to private life, continuing their interest but curtailing their activities in behalf of the abolition movement.*

READER, you are empannelled as a juror to try a plain case and bring in an honest verdict. The question at issue is not one of law, but of fact—"What is the actual condition of the slaves in the United States?" A plainer case never went to a jury. Look at it. TWENTY-SEVEN HUNDRED THOUSAND PERSONS in this country, men, women, and children, are in SLAVERY. Is slavery, as a condition for human beings, good, bad, or indifferent? We submit the question without argument. You have common sense, and conscience, and a human heart;—pronounce upon it. You have a wife, or a husband, a child, a father, a mother, a brother or a sister—make the case your own, make it theirs, and bring in your verdict. The case of Human Rights against Slavery has been adjudicated in the court of conscience times innumerable. The same verdict has always been ren-

SOURCE: [Theodore Dwight Weld], *American Slavery As It Is: Testimony of a Thousand Witnesses* (New York: American Anti-Slavery Society, 1839), pp. 7–10.

dered—"Guilty;" the same sentence has always been pronounced, "Let it be accursed;" and human nature, with her million echoes, has rung it round the world in every language under heaven, "Let it be accursed. Let it be accursed." His heart is false to human nature, who will not say "Amen." . . . Whoever denies this, his lips libel his heart. Try him; clank the chains in his ears, and tell him they are for *him*; give him an hour to prepare his wife and children for a life of slavery; bid him make haste and get ready their necks for the yoke, and their wrists for the coffle chains, then look at his pale lips and trembling knees, and you have *nature's* testimony against slavery.

Two millions seven hundred thousand persons in these States are in this condition. They were made slaves and are held such by force, and by being put in fear, and this for no crime! Reader, what have you to say of such treatment? Is it right, just, benevolent? Suppose I should seize you, rob you of your liberty, drive you into the field, and make you work without pay as long as you live, would that be justice and kindness, or monstrous injustice and cruelty? Now, every body knows that the slaveholders do these things to the slaves every day, and yet it is stoutly affirmed that they treat them well and kindly, and that their tender regard for their slaves restrains the masters from inflicting cruelties upon them. We shall go into no metaphysics to show the absurdity of this pretence. The man who *robs* you every day, is, forsooth, quite too tender-hearted ever to cuff or kick you! True, he can snatch your money, but he does it gently lest he should hurt you. He can empty your pockets without qualms, but if your *stomach* is empty, it cuts him to the quick. He can make you work a life time without pay, but loves you too well to let you go hungry. He fleeces you of your *rights* with a relish, but is shocked if you work bareheaded in summer, or in winter without warm stockings. He can make you go without your *liberty*, but never without a shirt. He can crush, in you, all hope of bettering your condition, by vowing that you shall die his slave, but though he can coolly torture your feelings, he is too compassionate to lacerate your back—he can break your heart, but he is very tender of your skin. He can strip you of all protection and thus expose you to all outrages, but if you are exposed to the *weather*, half clad and half sheltered, how yearn his tender bowels! What! slaveholders talk of treating men well, and yet not only rob them of all they get, and as fast as they get it, but rob them of *them-*

selves, also; their very hands and feet, all their muscles, and limbs, and senses, their bodies and minds, their time and liberty and earnings, their free speech and rights of conscience, their right to acquire knowledge, and property, and reputation;—and yet they, who plunder them of all these, would fain make us believe that their soft hearts ooze out so lovingly toward their slaves that they always keep them well housed and well clad, never push them too hard in the field, never make their dear backs smart, nor let their dear stomachs get empty.

But there is no end to these absurdities. Are slaveholders dunces, or do they take all the rest of the world to be, that they think to bandage our eyes with such thin gauzes? Protesting their kind regard for those whom they hourly plunder of all they have and all they get! What! when they have seized their victims, and annihilated all their *rights*, still claim to be the special guardians of their *happiness!* Plunderers of their liberty, yet the careful suppliers of their wants? Robbers of their earnings, yet watchful sentinels round their interests, and kind providers for their comfort? Filching all their time, yet granting generous donations for rest and sleep? Stealing the use of their muscles, yet thoughtful of their ease? Putting them under *drivers*, yet careful that they are not hardpushed? Too humane forsooth to stint the stomachs of their slaves, yet force their *minds* to starve, and brandish over them pains and penalties, if they dare to reach forth for the smallest crumb of knowledge, even a letter of the alphabet!

It is no marvel that slaveholders are always talking of their *kind treatment* of their slaves. The only marvel is, that men of sense can be gulled by such professions. Despots always insist that they are merciful. . . . The guilty, according to their own showing, are always innocent, and cowards brave, and drunkards sober, and harlots chaste, and pickpockets honest to a fault. Every body understands this. When a man's tongue grows thick, and he begins to hiccough and walk cross-legged, we expect him, as a matter of course, to protest that he is not drunk; so when a man is always singing the praises of his own honesty, we instinctively watch his movements and look out for our pocketbooks. Whoever is simple enough to be hoaxed by such professions, should never be trusted in the streets without somebody to take care of him. . . .

As slaveholders and their apologists are volunteer witnesses in their own cause, and are flooding the world with testimony that

their slaves are kindly treated; . . . we propose—first, to disprove
their assertions by the testimony of a multitude of impartial witnesses, and then to put slaveholders themselves through a course of
cross-questioning which shall draw their condemnation out of their
own mouths. We will prove that the slaves in the United States are
treated with barbarous inhumanity; they are overworked, underfed,
wretchedly clad and lodged, and have insufficient sleep; that they
are often made to wear round their necks iron collars armed with
prongs, to drag heavy chains and weights at their feet while working in the field, and to wear yokes, and bells, and iron horns; that
they are often kept confined in the stocks day and night for weeks
together, made to wear gags in their mouths for hours or days, and
have some of their front teeth torn out or broken off, that they may
be easily detected when they run away; that they are frequently
flogged with terrible severity, have red pepper rubbed into their
lacerated flesh, and hot brine, spirits of turpentine, &c., poured over
the gashes to increase the torture; that they are often stripped
naked, their backs and limbs cut with knives, bruised and mangled
by scores and hundreds of blows with the paddle, and terribly torn
by the claws of cats, drawn over them by their tormentors; that
they are often hunted with blood hounds and shot down like
beasts, or torn in pieces by dogs; that they are often suspended by
the arms and whipped and beaten till they faint, and when revived
by restoratives, beaten again till they faint, and sometimes till they
die; that their ears are often cut off, their eyes knocked out, their
bones broken, their flesh branded with red hot irons; that they are
maimed, mutilated and burned to death over slow fires. All these
things, and more, and worse, we shall prove. . . . We shall show,
not merely that such deeds are committed, but that they are frequent; not done in corners, but before the sun; not in one of the
slave states, but in all of them; not perpetrated by brutal overseers
and drivers merely, but by magistrates, by legislators, by professors
of religion, by preachers of the gospel, by governors of states, by
"gentlemen of property and standing," and by delicate females
moving in the "highest circles of society." We know, full well, the
outcry that will be made by multitudes, at these declarations; the
multiform cavils, and flat denials, the charges of "exaggeration"
and "falsehood" so often bandied, the sneers of affected contempt
at the credulity that can believe such things, and the rage and
imprecations against those who give them currency. . . .

. . . All these pleas, and scores of others, are bruited in every corner of the free States; and who that hath eyes to see, has not sickened at the blindness that saw not, at the palsy of heart that felt not, or at the cowardice and sycophancy that dared not expose such shallow fallacies. We are not to be turned from our purpose by such vapid babblings. . . .

The foregoing declarations touching the inflictions upon slaves, are not hap-hazard assertions, nor the exaggerations of fiction conjured up to carry a point; nor are they the rhapsodies of enthusiasm, nor crude conclusions, jumped at by hasty and imperfect investigation, nor the aimless outpourings either of sympathy or poetry; but they are proclamations of deliberate, well-weighed convictions, produced by accumulations of proof, by affirmations and affidavits, by written testimonies and statements of a cloud of witnesses who speak what they know and testify what they have seen, and all these impregnably fortified by proofs innumerable, in the relation of the slaveholder to his slave, the nature of arbitrary power, and the nature and history of man.

31. Abolition Is a Necessary and Glorious Part of Democracy
William Leggett

MANY Americans, critical of slavery but unsympathetic with the tactics or the rhetoric of the abolitionists, gradually and often reluctantly joined their cause. One of the most significant of these was William Leggett (1801–1839), co-editor with William Cullen Bryant of the influential New York Evening Post. After a brief career in the Navy and an unsuccessful effort in editing a literary journal, he joined Bryant in converting the paper into a spokesman for radical Jacksonianism, opposing the conservatism of Tammany and its allies in the banking community. Their editorials, preaching the doctrines of free trade and anti-monopoly, encouraged left-wing Democrats and contributed to the Locofoco schism of 1835. Denounced in the Party press as an "agrarian" for his views on banking, Leggett was further ostracized for expressing sentiments favorable to the abolitionists; he then left the Post, now in financial difficulty because of his stand, to publish the Plaindealer. When some of his friends attempted to nominate him for Congress in 1838, Leggett eliminated himself from consideration by the letter quoted below; he later accepted appointment to a diplomatic post by President Van Buren, but died while preparing to leave. Selections from his editorials were collected and published by his friend and associate Theodore Sedgwick, Jr., after his death.

[New York Evening Post]
[August 8, 1835]
. . . While we believe most fully that the abolitionists are justly chargeable with fanaticism, we consider it worse than folly to misrepresent their character in other respects. They are not knaves nor fools, but men of wealth, education, respectability and intelligence, misguided on a single subject, but actuated by a sincere desire to promote the welfare of their kind. . . . Is it not apparent on the face of the matter, that invective, denunciations, burnings in effigy, mob violence, and the like proceedings, do not constitute the

SOURCE: A Collection of the Political Writings of William Leggett, selected and arranged, with a preface, by Theodore Sedgwick, Jr. (New York: Taylor & Dodd, 1840), vol. II, pp. 9–11, 53–55, 70–73, 329–330, 335–336.

proper mode of changing the opinions or conduct of such men? The true way is, either to point out their error by temperate arguments, or better still leave them to discover it themselves. The fire, unsupplied with fuel, soon flickers and goes out, which stirred and fed, will rise to a fearful conflagration, and destroy whatever falls within the reach of its fury. . . .

. . . it is the bounden duty of the Government to protect the abolitionists in their constitutional right of free discussion; and opposed, sincerely and zealously as we are, to their doctrines and practise, we should be still more opposed to any infringement of their political or civil rights. If the Government once begins to discriminate as to what is orthodox and what heterodox in opinion, what is safe and what is unsafe in its tendency, farewell, a long farewell to our freedom. . . .

[New York *Evening Post*]
[September 4, 1835]

. . . We do not approve of perseverance in sending pamphlets to the south on the subject of slavery in direct opposition to the unanimous sentiments of the slaveholders; but we do approve of the strenuous assertion of the right of free discussion, and moreover we admire the heroism which cannot be driven from its ground by the maniac and unsparing opposition which the abolitionists have encountered. . . .

We are not sure that the Harry Percys of the South, are not by their hot menaces and inconsiderate vaunts precipitating a discussion which must be entered into sooner or later, and may, perhaps, as well be undertaken at once. Be that as it may, their high and boastful language shall never deter this print from expressing its opinion that slavery is an opprobrium and a curse, a monstrous and crying evil, in whatever light it is viewed; and that we shall hail, as the second most auspicious day that ever smiled on our republic, that which shall break the fetters of the bondman, and give his enfranchised spirit leave to roam abroad on the illimitable plain of equal liberty.

We have no right to interfere legislatively with the subject of slavery in our sister states, and never have arrogated any. We have no moral right to stir the question in such a way as to endanger the lives of our fellow human beings, white or black, or expose the citizens of the north, attending to their occasions in the south, to the horrors of Lynch law. Nay, we repeat, what we have often asserted with as sincere earnestness as any loud-mouthed anti-abolitionist, that we deeply deplore all intemperate movements on this momentous subject, in view of the dreadful wrecks which the meeting tides of contrary fanaticism must spread around their borders. But while we truly entertain these sentiments, we know no reason that renders it incumbent on us to conceal how far our views are really opposed to slavery; and while we disclaim any constitutional right to legislate on the subject, we assert, without hesitation, that, if we possessed the right, we should not scruple to exercise it for the speedy and utter annihilation of servitude and chains. . . .

[New York *Evening Post*]
[September 19, 1835]
>   *From the Washington Globe, of yesterday.*

"The Evening Post has, on various occasions, shown a disposition to fly off from the democratic party, by running into extremes. . . . This Eutopian temper in the Post was perpetually running the Editor's head against a post—some established landmark set up by the experience and good sense of the people to designate the different interests among us and the principles by which they were to be protected. In its warfare upon the settled principles of Democracy, the Post has ever and anon found itself at loggerheads with the organs which have long been accustomed to reflect the public sentiment. . . . All this might possibly be set down to individual caprice—a sort of innocent ostentation, by way of displaying the independence of the editor. But he has at last (and we are glad of it) taken a stand which must forever separate him from the democratic party. His journal now openly and systematically encourages the Abolitionists. . . . The scheme of the Abolitionists involves the destruction of the Confederacy, and brings with it also, as a foretaste, the horrors of a servile and civil war. As this is the tendency of the Post's present course, it must be content, hereafter, to be numbered among those journals with which its extravagance has associated it. . . ."

We very much regret that the Globe has taken upon itself to denounce this journal, and to give all who believe in its infallibility to understand that they must hereafter consider and treat the Evening Post as belonging to the common herd of the enemies of the democracy. . . . But we by no means look upon it as the worst evil which could befall us, and while we remain true to the great interests of democratic freedom, we have little fear either that our own prosperity, or our just influence on public sentiment, will be materially diminished by the proscription or denunciation of a party journal which, in no quality that ought to distinguish the public press, rises much above the level of ordinary party papers, and which derives all its superiority from the mere accident of its semi-official character. . . .

[*Plaindealer*]
[July 29, 1837]
. . . If an extensive and well-arranged insurrection of the blacks should occur in any of the slave states, we should probably see the freemen of this quarter of the country rallying around that "glorious emblem" . . . and marching beneath its folds to take sides with the slaveholders, and reduce the poor negroes, struggling for liberty, to heavier bondage than they endured before. . . . We confess, with the keenest mortification and chagrin, that the banner of our country is the emblem, not of justice and freedom, but of oppression; that it is the symbol of a compact which recognizes, in palpable and outrageous contradiction of the great principle of liberty, the right of one man to hold another as property; and that we are liable at any moment to be required, under all our obligations of citizenship, to array ourselves beneath it, and wage a war, of extermination if necessary, against the slave, for no crime but asserting his right of equal humanity—the self-evident truth that all men are created equal, and have an unalienable right of life, liberty, and the pursuit of happiness. Would we comply with such a requisition? No! rather would we see our right arm lopped from our body, and the mutilated trunk itself gored with mortal wounds, than raise a finger in opposition to men struggling in the holy cause of freedom. The obligations of citizenship are strong, but those of justice, humanity and religion stronger. We earnestly trust that the great contest of opinion which is now going on in this country may terminate in the enfranchisement of the slaves, without recourse to the strife of blood; but should the oppressed bondmen, impatient of the tardy progress of truth urged only in discussion, attempt to burst their chains by a more violent and shorter process, they should never encounter our arm, nor hear our voice, in the ranks of

their opponents. We should stand a sad spectator of the conflict; and whatever commiseration we might feel for the discomfiture of the oppressors, we should pray that the battle might end in giving freedom to the oppressed.

[Letter]
[October 24, 1838]

. . . I am an abolitionist. I hate slavery in all its forms, degrees, and influences; and I deem myself bound by the highest moral and political obligations, not to let that sentiment of hate be dormant and smouldering in my own breast, but to give it free vent, and let it blaze forth that it may kindle equal ardour through the whole sphere of my influence. I would not have this fact disguised or mystified, for any office the people have it in their power to give.

. . . Abolition is, in my sense, a necessary and a glorious part of democracy; and I hold the right and the duty to discuss the subject of slavery, and to expose its hideous evils in all its bearings, moral, social, and political, as of infinitely higher moment than to carry fifty sub-treasury bills. That I should discharge this duty temperately, and should not let it come in collision with other duties; that I should not let hatred of slavery transcend the express obligations of the Constitution, or violate its clear spirit, I hope and trust you think sufficiently well of me to believe. But what I fear is, (not from you, however,) that some of my advocates and champions will seek to recommend me to popular support, by representing that I am not an abolitionist, which is false. All that I have written gives the lie to it. All I shall write will give the lie to it.

. . . To be an abolitionist, is to be an incendiary now, as three years ago, to be an anti-monopolist, was to be a leveller, and a Jack Cade. See what those three short years have done in effecting the anti-monopoly reform; and depend upon it, that the next three years—or, if not three, say three times three, if you please, will work a greater revolution on the slavery question. The stream of public opinion now sets against us; but it is about to turn, and the regurgitation will be tremendous. . . . I have written my name in ineffaceable letters on the abolition record; and whether the reward ultimately come in the shape of honours to the living man, or a tribute to the memory of a departed one, I would not forfeit my right to it. . . .

Excuse me for scribbling all this farrago to you; but I am really

anxious not to be placed before the public in a false and dis-
coloured light. I do not wish to cheat the people of their votes. I
would not get their support, any more than their money, under
false pretences. I am, what I am! and if that does not suit them, I
am content to stay at home, praying God in the meantime, to
mend their taste. . . .

32. Intemperance Is Worse
Than the Slave Trade
Heman Humphrey

THE early nineteenth-century temperance movement was largely fostered by the clergy, with New England taking the lead. At first, only the use of "ardent spirits" was denounced, wine and beer being recommended as substitutes, but by the 1820s total abstinence was being advocated by some. Heman Humphrey (1779–1861) was influential in this movement and typical of the early proponents of prohibition. A graduate of Yale who was ordained a Congregational minister in 1807, he joined the temperance crusade a few years later. In 1823 he became president of Amherst College, a position he held for twenty-two years; during his tenure more than half of the graduates entered the ministry. Humphrey not only exhorted his students, as in the following address, but organized an Antivenean Society at the College, whose members pledged to refrain from the use of alcohol, opium and tobacco; for fifteen years more than 80 per cent of his students subscribed to this pledge, most of whom continued the crusade for temperance in their professional and private lives.

The birth-day of our nation is the brightest era in the political history of the world; and may the fourth of July never dawn, without exciting in every American bosom the warmest gratitude to Heaven, for the blessings of civil and religious liberty. May the sun never shine between our ocean boundaries upon any other than a free, united and happy people. But the popular and stereotyped topics of the anniversary, I do not intend to introduce on the present occasion. . . .

The subject which I have chosen, though not invested with the rhetorical attributes of our revolutionary struggle, is nevertheless but too painfully appropriate. *Slavery* and not *Independence* will be my theme. Would that there was no such discord in the jubilant

SOURCE: Heman Humphrey, D. D., *Parallel Between Intemperance and the Slave Trade: An Address Delivered at Amherst College, July 4, 1828* (Amherst, Mass.: J. S. and C. Adams, 1828), pp. 3–6, 8, 12–18, 25–26, 28, 39–40.

sounds of the day we celebrate. But the mortifying truth is, and the world knows it, that after the lapse of nearly fifty years of undisputed political freedom, the blood-freezing clank of a cruel bondage is still heard amid our loudest rejoicings. You will naturally suppose I allude to that grievous anomaly in our free constitution, which darkens all the southern horizon; but I have a more brutifying and afflictive thraldom in view. . . .

Yes, there is a domestic tyrant now traversing the fairest districts of our country. . . . This man-devouring shape . . . is INTEMPERANCE. . . .

. . . I have long thought, that a great advantage might be gained, by comparing intemperance with some other terrible scourge of humanity, which has fallen under deep and universal reprobation. Such a scourge is the African Slave-trade; and the position which I mean to take is this, *that the prevalent use of ardent spirits in the United States, is a worse evil at this moment, than the slave-trade ever was, in the height of its horrible prosperity.* . . .

First; let us look at the *comparative aggregate of misery,* occasioned by the slave trade on one hand, and intemperate drinking on the other. . . .

Go then with me to that long abused continent, where the first act of this infernal tragedy is acted over every month, and you will gain some faint idea of the atrocities which it unfolds. In that thicket crouches a human tyger; and just beyond it, you hear the joyous voices of children at their sports. The next moment he springs upon his terrified prey, nor sister nor mother shall ever see them more. On the right hand, you hear the moans of the captive as he goes bleeding to his doom; and on the left, a peaceful village, all at once flashes horror upon the face of midnight; and as you approach the scene of conflagration you behold the sick, the aged and the infant, either writhing in the fire where they lay down, unconscious of danger, or if attempting to escape, you see them forced back into the flames, as not worth the trouble of driving to market. And then, O what shrieks from the bursting hearts of the more unhappy survivors! . . . How many would die if they could, before they have been an hour in the hands of those incarnate daemons, who are hurrying them away!

Shall I attempt to describe the horrors of the *middle passage*— the miseries which await these wretched beings in crossing the ocean? . . . see them literally packed alive by hundreds in a floating and pestilential dungeon—manacled to the very bone, under a treble-ironed hatchway—tormented with thirst and devoured by hunger—suffocated in their own breath—chained to corpses, and maddened by despair, to the rending of all their heartstrings. See mothers and young girls, and even little children, watching their opportunity to seek refuge in the caverns of the deep, from the power of their tormentors; and not to be diverted from their purpose, by the hanging and shooting of such as have failed in similar attempts. Behold the sick and the blind struggling amid the waves, into which avarice has cast them; and shrieking in the jaws of the shark, for the unpardonable crime of having sunk under their tortures, and lost their marketable value on the voyage. See them headed up in water casks and thrown into the sea, lest they should be found and liberated by the merciful cruiser. . . .

But while intemperance mixes ingredients equally bitter, if not similar, in the cup of trembling and woe which it fills up to the brim, . . . it fetters the immortal mind as well as the dying body. It not only blisters the skin, but scorches the vitals. While it scourges the flesh, it tortures the conscience. . . .

Who can enumerate the diseases which intemperance generates in the brain, liver, stomach, lungs, bones, muscles, nerves, fluids, and whatever else is susceptible of disease, or pain in the human system? How rudely does it shut up, one after another, all the doors of sensation, or in the caprice of its wrath throw them all wide open to every hateful intruder.

. . . mark that carbuncled, slavering, doubtful remnant of a man, retching and picking tansy, every morning before sunrise—loathing his breakfast—getting his ear bored to the door of a dram shop an hour after—disguised before ten—quarrelling by dinner time, and snoring drunk before supper. See him next morning at his retching and his tansy again; and as the day advances, becoming noisy, cross, driveling and intoxicated. Think of him thus dragging out months and years of torture, till the earth refuses any longer to bear such a wretch upon its surface, and then tell me, if any Barbadian slave was ever so miserable. . . .

Does your sickened and harrowed soul turn away with horror from such a scene? Go with me then to the alms house, and tell me whether you recognize that bloated figure, sitting all day and all night in his chair, because the dropsy will not suffer him to lie down, and thus lingering from week to week under the slow torments of strangulation. How piercing are his shrieks, as if he was actually drowning, from which, indeed, he can obtain a short reprieve only, by diverting from the seat of life the accumulating waters. He was once your neighbour, thrifty, reputable and happy —but he yielded to the blandishments of the great destroyer. He drank, first temperately, then freely, then to excess, and finally, to habitual inebriation. The consequences are before you. His daily and nightly sufferings no tongue can utter. His disease no skill can cure. The swelling flood in which he catches every precarious breath, no finite power can long assuage. The veriest wretch, chained and sweltering between decks in a Portuguese Guineaman, is not half so miserable. . . .

I might ask you in passing the Insane Hospital, just to look through the grated window, at the maniac in his straight-jacket— gnashing his teeth, cursing his keepers, withering your very soul by the flashes of his eye, disquieting the night with incoherent cries of distress, or more appalling fits of laughter. Here you would see what it is for the immortal mind to be laid in ruins, by the worse than volcanic belchings of the distillery; and what happens every day from these Tartarean eruptions. But I cannot detain you. . . .

. . . intemperance is beyond all comparison more destructive to the *souls* of men than the slave-trade. Diabolical as this traffic is, it does not deprive its victims of the means of grace, for they never enjoyed them. It seals not up the bible, nor blots out the sabbath, nor removes men from the "house of God and the gate of heaven." It hardens not their hearts. It sears not their consciences. They are not more likely to lose their souls in America, than they would have been in their native country. On the contrary, many are brought under the saving light of the gospel here, who, in all probability, would never have heard of a Saviour there. This I know, affords not the slightest apology for man-stealing; for we may never "do evil that good may come;" and even if we might, the saving of souls, is not among the motives, which have so long desolated the shores of Africa.

But how much more terrible are the effects of intemperate drinking, upon the character and destiny of men, born and educated in a christian land. If there is any evil which hardens the heart faster, or fills the mouth with "cursing and bitterness" sooner, or quickens hatred to God and man into a more rapid and frightful maturity, I know not what it is. . . .

. . . Our free institutions are more endangered by the love of ardent spirits, than they ever were by the slave-trade, or than they now are by the existing slavery of the south. . . .

. . . A sober people may possibly be enslaved; but an intemperate people cannot long remain free. They must have a master, to measure out their rations, and keep them in awe, at the point of the bayonet. And if the emblems of liberty are ever to be torn from our banner—if her statues are to be hurled from their pedestals—if the car of a despot is to be driven over our suppliant bodies, it will be by the aid of strong drink. For an army of sober men can never be raised to enslave their country. . . .

Finally; if intemperance is worse than the slave-trade, let every *christian*, every *patriot*, every *philanthropist*, gird himself up to the great work of reform, and never cease from it till it shall be accomplished. A fearful responsibility rests upon the men of this generation; especially upon the influential and the temperate—upon the guardians and teachers of youth in all our public and private seminaries; and above all, perhaps, upon the *young men* of our beloved country. Let this responsibility be deeply felt by my youthful audience. . . .

Wherever you go, in whatever profession or employment you may be called to serve God and your generation, let total abstinence be your own motto, . . .

Let this course be taken, by all the liberally educated youth of our country, and by all others of enlightened minds and benevolent hearts—let union and perseverance every where be the watchwords of the sober and the virtuous, and soon a drunkard will become as rare a monster, as he was in the days of our Pilgrim Fathers; and posterity will look back upon the present ravages and toleration of intemperance, with emotions of astonishment, grief and horror, similar to those which we now feel, in reading the most afflictive history of the Slave-trade.

33. Abstinence From the Use of Ardent Spirit
National Circular

THE temperance movement soon became a part of the "benevolent empire," headed for a time by the Tappan brothers of New York (see Document 4); the American Temperance Society, founded in Boston in 1826, became the national engine of reform. Like other units of the "empire," it was a militant organization enlisting clergy and laymen in a revivalistic and emotional appeal for total abstinence from spirituous liquors. The propaganda of this organization was funneled through periodicals, pamphlets and prize essay contests; as in the National Circular quoted below, emotion was combined with statistics to induce the moderate drinker and the apathetic non-drinker to sign a pledge and to organize or join a local temperance society. For a time the campaign was remarkably effective, five thousand societies with a million members being claimed by 1835, but within a few years the movement split on the issue of banning fermented as well as distilled liquors. Both the objectives and the tactics of the radicals were questioned, and the movement declined in the late 1830s.

NATIONAL CIRCULAR
ADDRESSED TO THE HEAD OF EACH FAMILY IN
THE UNITED STATES

RESPECTED FRIEND,

We are engaged in a great and good work; and, to accomplish it, we need your aid. It is the work of extending the principle of abstinence from the use of ardent spirit, as a drink, throughout our country, and throughout the world. By means of the press, and of living agents, a strong impression has already been made, and a great change effected with regard to this subject. More than a million of persons, in the United States, have ceased to use ardent spirit; more than a thousand distilleries have been stopped; more than three thousand merchants have ceased to traffic in the article, and more than three thousand drunkards ceased to use intoxicating drinks. More than ten thousand persons, as appears from numerous facts, have been saved from becoming drunkards, who, had it not

SOURCE: *National Circular, Addressed to the Head of Each Family in the United States* (Boston: Aaron Russell, n.d.), pp. 1–2, 5–9, 12.

been for the change of sentiment and practice in the community, had, before now, been involved in all the horrors of that loathsome and fatal vice. . . .

And what we ask of you, and of each member of your family, is that you will not only abstain from the use of ardent spirit, but, for the sake of doing good to others, unite with a temperance society; and for this purpose, that you will give your names, and the influence which is attached to them, to the pledge which is annexed to this paper. And we do this for the following reasons, viz.

1. Ardent spirit, as a drink, is not *needful*.

All the world lived without it, and all the business of the world was conducted without it, for more than five thousand years. It was not used, as a drink, in Great Britain, till within less than three hundred years; nor was it common in this country, till within less than one hundred years. . . .

2. It is not *useful*. The men that never use it suffer no evil for want of it. There is no natural appetite for it; but the appetite is created solely by the use of it. . . .

3. Alcohol, which forms the basis of ardent spirit, is a *poison*. When taken unmixed, in no very large quantity, it destroys life; and when taken even moderately, it induces disease, and forms an artificial, an unnatural, and a very dangerous appetite. This appetite, like the desire for sinning, in the man who sins, by gratification tends continually to increase; and requires continually increasing quantities to satisfy it. . . .

4. The use of ardent spirit impairs, and in many cases destroys reason. Of 781 maniacs in different insane hospitals, 392, according to the testimony of their own friends, were rendered maniacs by strong drink; and the physicians give it as their opinion, that this was also the case with many others.

. . . Nor is the effect in such cases confined to those who use it; it descends to their children and children's children; producing a predisposition to insanity and various diseases, which, if the cause is continued, will become hereditary, and be manifested in a diminution of size and stature; a decrease of bodily and mental strength and activity; a feebleness of vision and a trembling of limbs; an indecision and a fickleness of purpose; a general deterioration of character, and a premature old age; which will visit the iniquities of the fathers upon the children, from generation to generation. Nor does the effect stop here, but,

5. It weakens the power of motives to do right, and is thus shown decisively to be in its tendency *immoral*; and that no man, can consistently with his duty, either use it, or be accessory to the use of it by others.

. . . God, in his providence and his word, presents a great variety of motives to make men diligent; and motives in sufficient number and strength, in such a country as this, to secure the object; provided men do not use ardent spirit. But if they do, all these motives with thousands and thousands will utterly fail; and they will be idle; they will be paupers, and they will be vagabonds and nuisances after all. . . .

6. It strengthens the power of motives to do wrong. Temptation to crime, which men will withstand when they have not been drinking, will lead them when they have, in numerous cases, to go and commit it. Of thirty-nine prisoners in the jail of Litchfield county, Connecticut, thirty-five were intemperate men. In the jail at Ogdensburg, New York, seven eighths of the criminals were addicted to strong drink; of 647 in the state prison at Auburn, New York, 467 were intemperate; and 346 were under the influence of ardent spirit at the time the crimes, for which they were imprisoned, were committed; and of 120 in the state prison of Connecticut, more than ninety were of the same class. And a similar proportion may be found in other prisons. So obvious is it that it weakens the power of motives to do right, and strengthens the power of motives to do wrong. Of 690 children, imprisoned for crime, in the city of New York, more than 400 were from intemperate families. Suppose one family in ten were intemperate, more than four sevenths of the youthful criminals were from those one in ten, while not three sevenths were from all the other nine in ten, making the children of intemperate parents more than ten times as liable to crime, to the prison and to the gallows, as the children of temperate parents. . . . Not a year passes in which murders are not committed through the influence of ardent spirit. . . .

7. *It destroys the soul.* It makes sinners more sinful, and prevents them from experiencing God's illuminating and purifying power. It tends directly and strongly to make men feel, as Jesus Christ hates—rich spiritually, increased in goods, and in need of nothing; and for ever to prevent them from feeling as men must feel in order to be interested in the blessings of his salvation. The Holy Spirit will not visit, much less dwell with him who is under

the polluting, debasing effects of intoxicating drink. That state of mind and heart, which this occasions, is to Him a loathing, and an utter abomination. Not only does it darken the understanding, sear the conscience, pollute the affections, and debase all the powers of the soul; but it counteracts the merciful designs of Jehovah, and all that overflowing kindness of an infinitely compassionate Savior for its deliverance; binds the soul in hopeless bondage to its destroyers; . . . and drives the soul away in despair, weeping and wailing, to be punished with everlasting destruction from the presence of the Lord and the glory of his power.

And it is for these reasons that we most respectfully and most earnestly request, not only that you will abstain from it, but that you will also unite the influence of your example with that of others, to lead all to do the same. Should the use of ardent spirit be continued for thirty years to come, as it has been for thirty years past, it will cost the people of the United States more than $3,000,000,000, and it will bring down more than a million of people to the drunkard's grave. It will raise up more than a million more, and make them drunkards, to roll the burning curse on to the next generation, raising up other millions to roll it onward, and others still to roll it onward, blazing with a fire that no man can quench. . . .

And yet these evils, great as they are, rising up to heaven, and overwhelming, as if continued, they certainly will be, may, nevertheless, with perfect ease, all be done away. Let each individual cease to use intoxicating drinks, intemperance and all its abominations will vanish; and temperance, with all its blessings of body and soul, will universally prevail. And if only all sober persons will adopt and continue this course, drunkards, who will not reform, will all soon die; no new drunkards will be made, and the whole land will be free. Our 3,000,000 children may come forward into life, without the habit of using intoxicating liquors, without any appetite for it, or any expectation of benefit from the use of it. And such a generation they may be as this world never saw; to show, by their blessings, the glory of free institutions, and the brighter glories of the gospel of the Son of God, and to spread a light which shall cause ignorance and vice, desolation and wretchedness, over the whole earth, for ever to flee away. . . .

It is proposed, through the medium of state, county, town and district societies, and the efforts of friends of temperance, to put a copy of this, or a similar paper, into every family in the United States. In several states, the friends of temperance are now doing it; and with the most gratifying success. And could we exhibit to the world, the noble, the sublime spectacle, of thirteen millions of people rising in their strength, and voluntarily renouncing the tyranny of pernicious custom, and resolving henceforward not to be in bondage, even to themselves, but to be *doubly* free, we should be indeed the people which the Lord hath blessed. And it would do more than all which has ever yet been done, to render our free institutions *permanent*; and by the manifestation of their blessings, to spread their causes and their attendants, knowledge, virtue, and blessedness, throughout the world.

34. Early Impressions of Temperance
Juvenile Friends of Temperance

THE temperance movement endeavored to be both persuasive and educational. For this reason a special appeal was made to children, who were induced to sign the pledge and enlisted in juvenile societies, usually offshoots of the growing Sunday School movement. If this educational campaign were effective, it was believed, alcoholism and its attendant evils could be eliminated in the coming generation. Although "Cold Water Armies" of children, dressed in white and carrying banners, were to become a regular feature of temperance celebrations, the Temperance Jubilee described below was a more usual occurrence.

FOURTH SIMULTANEOUS ANNIVERSARY
By the Juvenile friends of Temperance, at the Odeon, on the afternoon of
February 28th.

At a meeting held in this city on the 15th of February, by delegates from the several temperance societies, it was voted, that, there be in addition to the adult evening celebration, a Juvenile meeting in the afternoon of the Simultaneous Temperance Jubilee. To carry the plan into full effect, the following application was made to the School Committee, and unanimously complied with:—

To . . . the gentlemen of the School Committee of the City of Boston.

At a meeting held in this city, . . . at which several Temperance Societies were represented, it was unanimously voted—

That a most respectful and earnest solicitation be presented to the Mayor and the gentlemen of the School Committee of the city, requesting that the several public schools in the city, with the exception of the Primary Schools, may be dismissed on the afternoon of the last Tuesday of the present month, (which is the day of the Simultaneous Temperance Meetings throughout the civilized world,) for the purpose of holding upon that afternoon, a Juvenile Temperance meeting at the Odeon.

SOURCE: William E. Channing, *An Address on Temperance* (Boston: Weeks, Jordan & Company, 1837), appendix, pp. 92–96.

Highly as we appreciate the intellectual and moral instruction, which the children of the city are receiving at its schools, we believe that they will not be less benefited by the early impressions in favor of Temperance, they may receive by appropriating one afternoon in the year to a subject, so promotive of the welfare of their whole lives. . . .

The Instructers in the public Schools, on being consulted, unanimously voted to attend at the Odeon with the pupils under their charge, which was done in a most orderly and proper manner. Places were assigned each school under the immediate charge of its Instructer. The girls occupied the lower floor, and the boys the upper boxes and galleries, and a more interesting exhibition has been seldom witnessed in this city. Delightful as it is at all times, to see the Odeon filled with human beings, congregated for some holy purpose, the present occasion was one of thrilling interest, and caused tears of joy to roll down the cheeks of the spectators; for instead of parents were to be seen the *children*. About twenty-five hundred children from our thirteen public schools, being the first and second classes, were present.

The Rev. Dr. PARKMAN commenced the exercises by Prayer. . . .

. . .

The children were then addressed on the subject of temperance, . . . after which the following Hymn was sung to the tune of Peterborough with fine effect:—

HYMN

" 'Tis but a drop," the father said,
   And gave it to his son;
But little did he think a work
   Of death was then begun.
The "drop" that lured him, when the babe
   Scarce lisped his father's name,
Planted a fatal appetite,
   Deep in his infant frame.

" 'Tis but a drop," the comrades cried,
   In truant schoolboy tone;
"It did not hurt us in our robes—
   It will not, now we're grown."
And so they drank the mixture up,
   That reeling, youthful band;
For each had learned to love the taste,
   From his own father's hand.

" 'Tis but a drop,—I need it now"—
  The staggering drunkard said;
"It was my food in infancy—
  My meat, and drink, and bread.
A drop—a drop—oh let me have,
  'Twill so refresh my soul!"
He took it—trembled—drank and died,
  Grasping the fatal bowl.

Each of the Instructers were presented with a volume of the very interesting and useful work, called the Temperance Documents of the American Temperance Society. . . . also a number of very appropriate kind of Temperance medals were placed at the disposal of each Instructer.

At 5 o'clock this great congregation of "little ones," retired in the same good order that they entered, having behaved throughout the services with much propriety, and reflecting honor on themselves as "Boston Boys and Girls," and great credit on their Instructers. . . .

35. All Men Are Created Temperate
Washington Temperance Society

THE early temperance movement implicitly believed that there was no hope for the confirmed drunkard; he was used only as a horrible example to persuade others to take the pledge. But in 1840 the crusade was reborn when six reformed drunkards organized the Washington Temperance Society in Baltimore. During the ensuing decade the Washingtonians established societies throughout the nation, reviving the dormant movement through dramatic testimony of personal degradation and subsequent regeneration. The pattern was the same that had been found successful in religious revivals: an appeal was made to intemperate drinkers and alcoholics, but their example and experience served to induce non-drinkers to take the pledge. The following address, written and delivered by Jesse W. Goodrich (1803–1857), is a less flamboyant example of the appeal of this group; a serious parody of the Declaration of Independence, it illustrates the use that was made of this document in the reform movements of the period.

When from the depths of human misery, it becomes possible for a portion of the infatuated victims of appetite to arise, and dissolve the vicious and habitual bonds which have connected them with *inebriety* and degradation, and to assume among the temperate and industrious of the community, the useful, respectable and appropriate stations, to which the laws of Nature, and of Nature's God entitle them, an anxious regard for the safety of their former companions; and the welfare of society requires, that they should declare the causes that impel them to such a *Reformation!*

We hold these truths to be self-evident; that all men are created *temperate*; that they are endowed by their Creator with certain natural and innocent desires; that among these are the appetite for COLD WATER and the pursuit of happiness! that to secure the gratification of these propensities fountains and streams are gushing and meandering from the hills and vales, benignly and abundantly abroad among men, deriving their just powers from their

SOURCE: *A Second Declaration of Independence: Or, The Manifesto of All the Washington Total Abstinence Societies of the United States of America* (Worcester, Mass.: Spooner and Howland, 1841), pp. 3–8.

beneficial adaptation to the natures of all the varieties of animal organization; that whenever any form of substituted artificial beverage becomes destructive of these natures, it is the right of the recipients to proscribe—to alter, or to abolish it and to return to the use of that crystal element, which alone of all that has come to us from Eden, still retains all its primitive purity and sweetness, demonstrating its benefits on such principles, and testing its powers in such quantities, and under such circumstances, as to them shall seem most likely to effect their safety and happiness.

Habit indeed will dictate, that indulgences long established cannot be forborne, or changed for slight and transient causes; and accordingly all experience hath shown, that "inebriates" are more disposed to suffer the evils of intoxicating drinks, while the temptations of intoxicating drinks are around them and sufferable, than to right themselves, by abandoning the *Dram Shops*, to which they are accustomed. But when a long train of abuses, and gradually excessive and habitual potations of these destructive stimulants, prompting invariably still greater and greater indulgences, evinces a tendency to reduce them under absolute despotism, despondency, and death, it is their right—it is their duty—and as they now by blessed experience know, it is their power, to throw off such habits, and to provide new guards for their future security in *total abstinence and pure water*. Such has been the cruel sufferance of these Inebriates; and such is now the necessity which constrains them to alter their former habits of using intoxicating drinks—to reform—and to refrain from the use of them all, henceforth and forever, *entirely*. The history of the *Reign of Alcohol* is a history of repeated injuries—brutalities—vices—diseases—and enormities, all having in direct object the absolute ruin, both temporal and eternal, of all his votaries! To prove this, let facts be submitted to a candid world. . . .

We, therefore, the Reformed Inebriates of the United States of America, for the celebration of the 4th of July, 1841, throughout the Union assembled, appealing to the Supreme Judge of the world for support in the maintenance of our pledges, do, in the name, and by the authority of all the *Washington Total Abstinence Societies* of these States, solemnly publish and declare, that the members of these blessed and blessing Washingtonian Fraternities, are, and of right ought to be, temperate, free and independent citizens; that they are absolved from all allegiance to the ALCO-

HOLIC CROWN, and that all social intercourse, or connection, or fellowship, between them and any and all of the numerous branches of the *Alcoholic Family*, is, and ought to be totally dissolved; and that as free, temperate, reformed, and independent citizens, they have full power to levy war against all the Alcoholic Legions—conclude peace when the same are vanquished and exterminated—contract alliances for the accomplishment of their objects—establish commerce in the deeds of benevolence and charity, and to do all other acts and things which reformed, temperate, free, and independent citizens may of right do.

And for the support of this Declaration, with a firm reliance on the protection of Divine Providence, we mutually pledge to each other our adhesion to PURE WATER, TOTAL ABSTINENCE, and the CAUSE OF HUMANITY.

36. The Temperance Revolution
Abraham Lincoln

LIKE abolitionism, temperance moved to the West, notorious for hard and heavy drinking. Abraham Lincoln (1809–1865) was atypical of frontier Illinois: a lifelong teetotaler who was neither particularly religious nor censorious of the foibles of his fellows. This characteristic, among others, led to his election as captain of a militia company in the Black Hawk War and to his subsequent election to the Illinois legislature, where he served from 1837–1841. Temporarily retiring from politics to marry and pursue his law practice, Lincoln accepted an invitation in 1842 to address the Springfield Washingtonian Temperance Society. Although the speech, revealing both his humor and his sympathy for the drunkard as an individual, met with a certain amount of disapprobation, he clearly demonstrated his understanding of the objectives of the movement. Yet his pragmatic humanitarianism fitted him more for politics, and he demonstrated little interest in reform movements as such for the remainder of his life.

Although the Temperance Cause has been in progress for nearly twenty years, it is apparent to all that it is just now being crowned with a degree of success, hitherto unparalleled. . . .

The warfare heretofore waged against the demon intemperance, has, somehow or other, been erroneous. Either the champions engaged, or the tactics they adopted, have not been the most proper. These champions, for the most part, have been preachers, lawyers and hired agents; between these and the mass of mankind, there is a want of *approachability*, if the term be admissible, partial at least, fatal to their success. They are supposed to have no sympathy of feeling or interest with those very persons whom it is their object to convince and persuade. . . .

But when one who has long been known as a victim of intemperance bursts the fetters that have bound him, and appears before his

SOURCE: "Address Before the Springfield Washingtonian Temperance Society, February 22, 1842," *Complete Works of Abraham Lincoln*, ed. John G. Nicolay and John Hay (New York: Francis D. Tandy Co., 1894), vol. I, pp. 193–198, 201–209. Reprinted from the *Sangamo Journal* (Springfield, Ill.), March 25, 1842.

neighbors "clothed and in his right mind," a redeemed specimen of long-lost humanity, and stands up with tears of joy trembling in his eyes, to tell of the miseries once endured, now to be endured no more forever, of his once naked and starving children, now clad and fed comfortably, of a wife, long weighed down with woe, weeping, and a broken heart, now restored to health, happiness and a renewed affection . . .; how simple his language; there is a logic and an eloquence in it that few with human feelings can resist. . . .

In my judgment it is to the battles of this new class of champions that our late success is greatly, perhaps chiefly, owing. But had the old-school champions themselves been of the most wise selecting? Was their system of tactics the most judicious? It seems to me it was not. Too much denunciation against dram-sellers and dram-drinkers was indulged in. This, I think, was both impolitic and unjust. It was impolitic, because it is not much in the nature of man to be driven to anything; still less to be driven about that which is exclusively his own business; and least of all, where such driving is to be submitted to at the expense of pecuniary interest, or burning appetite. When the dram-seller and drinker were incessantly told, not in the accents of entreaty and persuasion, diffidently addressed by erring man to an erring brother, but in the thundering tones of anathema and denunciation, . . . that they were the authors of all the vice and misery and crime in the land; that they were the manufacturers and material of all the thieves and robbers and murderers that infest the earth; that their houses were the work-shops of the devil, and that their persons should be shunned by all the good and virtuous, as moral pestilences,—I say, when they were told all this, and in this way, it is not wonderful they were slow, very slow, to acknowledge the truth of such denunciations, and to join the ranks of their denouncers, in a hue and cry against themselves. . . .

When the conduct of men is designed to be influenced, persuasion, kind, unassuming persuasion, should ever be adopted. . . .

On this point, the Washingtonians greatly excel the temperance advocates of former times. Those whom they desire to convince and persuade are their old friends and companions. They know they are not demons, nor even the worst of men; they know that generally they are kind, generous and charitable, even beyond the example of their more staid and sober neighbors. They are practical philanthropists; and they glow with a generous and brotherly zeal, that mere theorizers are incapable of feeling. Benevolence and charity possess their hearts entirely; and out of the abundance of their hearts their tongues give utterance, "Love through all their actions run, and all their words are mild:" in this spirit they speak and act, and in the same they are heard and regarded. And when such is the temper of the advocate, and such of the audience, no good cause can be unsuccessful. . . .

Another error, as it seems to me, into which the old reformers fell, was the position that all habitual drunkards were utterly incorrigible, and therefore, must be turned adrift, and damned without remedy, in order that the grace of temperance might abound, to the temperate then, and to all mankind some hundreds of years thereafter. There is in this something so repugnant to humanity, so uncharitable, so cold-blooded and feelingless, that it never did, nor never can enlist the enthusiasm of a popular cause. We could not love the man who taught it—we could not hear him with patience. The heart could not throw open its portals to it, the generous man could not adopt it, it could not mix with his blood. It looked so fiendishly selfish, so like throwing fathers and brothers overboard, to lighten the boat for our security—that the noble-minded shrank from the manifest meanness of the thing. And besides this, the benefits of a reformation to be effected by such a system, were too remote in point of time, to warmly engage many in its behalf. Few can be induced to labor exclusively for posterity; and none will do it enthusiastically. Posterity has done nothing for us; and theorize on it as we may, practically we shall do very little for it unless we are made to think, we are, at the same time, doing something for ourselves. . . .

By the Washingtonians this system of consigning the habitual drunkard to hopeless ruin is repudiated. They adopt a more enlarged philanthropy, they go for present as well as future good. They labor for all now living, as well as hereafter to live. They teach hope to all—despair to none. . . .

But if it be true, as I have insisted, that those who have suffered by intemperance personally, and have reformed, are the most powerful and efficient instruments to push the reformation to ultimate success, it does not follow that those who have not suffered have no part left them to perform. . . .

. . . For the man, suddenly or in any other way, to break off from the use of drams, who indulged in them for a long course of years, and until his appetite for them has grown ten or a hundred fold stronger and more craving than any natural appetite can be, requires a most powerful moral effort. In such an undertaking he needs every moral support and influence that can possibly be brought to his aid, and thrown around him. And not only so, but every moral prop should be taken from whatever argument might rise in his mind, to lure him to his backsliding. When he casts his eyes around him, he should be able to see all that he respects, all that he admires, all that he loves, kindly and anxiously pointing him onward, and none beckoning him back to his former miserable "wallowing in the mire."

But it is said by some, that men will think and act for themselves; that none will disuse spirits or anything else because his neighbors do; and that moral influence is not that powerful engine contended for. Let us examine this. Let me ask the man who could maintain this position most stiffly, what compensation he will accept to go to church some Sunday and sit during the sermon with his wife's bonnet upon his head? Not a trifle, I'll venture. And why not? There would be nothing irreligious in it, nothing immoral, nothing uncomfortable—then why not? Is it not because there would be something egregiously unfashionable in it? Then it is the influence of fashion; and what is the influence of fashion but the influence that other people's actions have on our own actions—the strong inclination each of us feels to do as we see all our neighbors do? . . . Let us make it as unfashionable to withhold our names from the temperance pledge, as for husbands to wear their wives' bonnets to church, and instances will be just as rare in the one case as the other.

. . . In my judgment such of us as have never fallen victims, have been spared more from the absence of appetite, than from any mental or moral superiority over those who have. Indeed, I believe, if we take habitual drunkards as a class, their heads and their hearts will bear an advantageous comparison with those of any other class. There seems ever to have been a proneness in the brilliant and warm-blooded to fall into this vice—the demon of intemperance ever seems to have delighted in sucking the blood of genius and generosity. . . .

Of our political revolution of '76 we are all justly proud. It has given us a degree of political freedom far exceeding that of any other nations of the earth. In it the world has found a solution of the long mooted problem, as to the capability of man to govern himself. In it was the germ which has vegetated, and still is to grow and expand into the universal liberty of mankind. . . .

Turn now to the temperance revolution. In it we shall find a stronger bondage broken, a viler slavery manumitted, a greater tyrant deposed—in it, more of want supplied, more disease healed, more sorrow assuaged. By it, no orphans starving, no widows weeping. By it, none wounded in feeling, none injured in interest; even the dram-maker and dram-seller will have glided into other occupations so gradually as never to have felt the change, and will stand ready to join all others in the universal song of gladness. And what a noble ally this, to the cause of political freedom, with such an aid, its march cannot fail to be on and on, till every son of earth shall drink in rich fruition the sorrow-quenching draughts of perfect liberty. Happy day, when all appetites controlled, all passions subdued, all matter subjugated, mind, all-conquering mind, shall live and move, the monarch of the world! . . .

And when the victory shall be complete—when there shall be neither a slave nor a drunkard on the earth—how proud the title of that *Land*, which may truly claim to be the birth-place and the cradle of both those revolutions that shall have ended in that victory. How nobly distinguished that people, who shall have planted, and nurtured to maturity, both the political and moral freedom of their species. . . .

37. The Supreme Virtue of a Life of Celibacy
The Shakers

ROOTED *in European pietism, religious communism first came to America in the eighteenth century, but sectarian immigrants continued to arrive until the eve of the Civil War to seek freedom to follow their own road to salvation. The Shakers, one of the earliest and most successful of these groups, originated in England; combining millennialism with a belief in sexual equality and the practice of celibacy, they sublimated violent physical manifestations of religious fervor into a ritualistic dance, from which the sect acquired its popular name. Led by Mother Ann Lee, who to her followers manifested the female principle in Christ, a small group of Shakers arrived in New York in 1774; in the ten years before her death, converts were won and communities established in New York and New England. As in other religious utopias, communism was adopted both through necessity and through the desire to emulate primitive Christianity. Leadership and discipline were supplied by elders and eldresses, one of whom was Frederick W. Evans, a brother of the agnostic labor editor George Henry Evans (Document 13); his conversion in 1830 demonstrates the attraction that the Shaker life had for many reformers and intellectuals of the period.*

Circumstances that need not be rehearsed, induced me to visit the Shaker Society at Watervliet, in the winter of 1842-3. Soon after my arrival, I was conducted to the Elder whose business it was to deal with inquirers. . . . I found him very intelligent, and soon made known to him my business, which was to learn something about the Shakers and their conditions of receiving members. . . . He propounded to me at considerable length their faith, "the daily cross" they were obliged to take up against the devil and the flesh, and the supreme virtue of a life of celibacy. . . . He then informed me of the conditions under which they received candidates: "All new comers have one week's trial, to see how they like; and after that, if they wish to continue they must take up the daily cross, and commence the work of regeneration and salvation, fol-

SOURCE: "Four Months Among the Shakers," in John Humphrey Noyes, *History of American Socialisms* (Philadelphia: J. B. Lippincott & Co., 1870), pp. 597–598, 600–604, 608.

lowing in the footsteps of Jesus Christ and Mother Ann." My first cross, he informed me, would be to confess all the wicked acts I had ever committed. . . . I agreed however before confession to make a week's trial of the place, and was accordingly invited to supper; after which I was shown to the sleeping room specially set apart for new members. I was not left here more than an hour when a small bell rang, and one of the brothers entered the room and invited me to go to the family meeting; where I saw for the first time their mode of worshiping God in the dance. I thought it was an exciting exercise, and I should have been more pleased if they had had instrumental, instead of vocal music. . . .

The hours of rising were five o'clock in the summer, and half-past five in the winter. The family all rose at the toll of the bell, and in less than ten minutes vacated the bed-rooms. The sisters then distributed themselves throughout the rooms, and made up all the beds, putting every thing in the most perfect order before breakfast. The brothers proceeded to their various employments, and made a commencement for the day. The cows were milked, and the horses were fed. At seven o'clock the bell rang for breakfast, but it was ten minutes after when we went to the tables. The brothers and sisters assembled each by themselves, in rooms appointed for the purpose; and at the sound of a small bell the doors of these rooms opened, and a procession of the family was formed in the hall, each individual being in his or her proper place, as they would be at table. The brothers came first, followed by the sisters, and the whole marched in solemn silence to the dining-room. The brothers and sisters took separate tables, on opposite sides of the room. All stood up until each one had arrived at his or her proper place, and then at a signal from the Elder at the head of the table, they all knelt down for about two minutes, and at another signal they all arose and commenced eating their breakfast. Each individual helped himself; which was easily done, as the tables were so arranged that between every four persons there was a supply of every article intended for the meal. At the conclusion they all arose and marched away from the tables in the same manner as they marched to them; and during the time of marching, eating, and remarching, not one word was spoken, but the most perfect silence was preserved.

After breakfast all proceeded immediately to their respective employments, and continued industriously occupied until ten min-

utes to twelve o'clock, when the bell announced dinner. Farmers
then left the field and mechanics their shops, all washed their
hands, and formed procession again, and marched to dinner in the
same way as to breakfast. Immediately after dinner they went to
work again, (having no hour for resting), and continued steady at
it until the bell announced supper. At supper the same routine was
gone through as at the other meals, and all except the farmers went
to work again. The farmers were supposed to be doing what were
called "chores," which appeared to mean any little odd jobs in and
about the stables and barns. At eight o'clock all work was ended for
the day, and the family went to what they called a "union meeting." This meeting generally continued one hour, and then, at
about nine o'clock, all retired to bed. . . .

I have thus given the routine for one day; and each week-day
throughout the year was the same. The only variation was in the
evening. Besides these union meetings, every alternate evening was
devoted to dancing. Sundays also had a routine of their own, which
I will not detail.

During the time I was with the Shakers, I never heard one of
them read the Bible or pray in public. Each one was permitted to
pray or let it alone as he pleased, and I believe there was very little
praying among them. Believing as they did that all "worldly
things" should be left in the "world" behind them, they did not
even read the ordinary literature of the day. Newspapers were only
for the use of the Elders and Deacons. The routine I have described was continually going on; and it was their boast that they
were then the same in their habits and manners as they were sixty
years before. The furniture of the dwellings was of the same old-
fashioned kind that the early Dutch settlers used; and every thing
about them and their dwellings, I was taught, was originally designed in heaven, and the designs transmitted to them by angels.
The plan of their buildings, the style of their furniture, the pattern
of their coats and pants, and the cut of their hair, is all regulated
according to communications received from heaven by Mother
Ann. I was gravely told by the first Elder, that the inhabitants of
the other world were Shakers, and that they lived in Community
the same as we did, but that they were more perfect.

At half-past seven P.M. on the dancing days, all the members
retired to their separate rooms, where they sat in solemn silence,
just gazing at the stove, until the silver tones of a small tea-bell

gave the signal for them to assemble in the large hall. Thither they proceeded in perfect order and solemn silence. Each had on thin dancing-shoes; and on entering the door of the hall they walked on tip-toe, and took up their positions as follows: the brothers formed a rank on the right, and the sisters on the left, facing each other, about five feet apart. After all were in their proper places the chief Elder stepped into the center of the space, and gave an exhortation for about five minutes, concluding with an invitation to them all to "go forth, old men, young men and maidens, and worship God with all their might in the dance." Accordingly they "went forth," the men stripping off their coats and remaining in their shirt-sleeves. First they formed a procession and marched around the room at double-quick time, while four brothers and four sisters stood in the center singing for them. After marching in this manner until they got a little warm, they commenced dancing, and continued it until they were all pretty well tired. During the dance the sisters kept on one side, and the brothers on the other, and not a word was spoken by any of them. After they appeared to have had enough of this exercise, the Elder gave the signal to stop, when immediately each one took his or her place in an oblong circle formed around the room, and all waited to see if any one had received a "gift," that is, an inspiration to do something odd. Then two of the sisters would commence whirling round like a top, with their eyes shut; and continued this motion for about fifteen minutes; when they suddenly stopped and resumed their places, as steady as if they had never stirred. During the "whirl" the members stood round like statues, looking on in solemn silence. . . .

The Elder would sometimes kindly invite me to his room and ask me what I thought of the meeting last night. . . . I could only reply that I was much astonished, and that these things were altogether new to me. He would then tell me that I would see greater things than these. But I replied that it required more faith to believe them than I possessed. Then he would exhort me to "labor for faith, and I would get it. He did not expect young believers to get faith all at once; although some got it faster than others." . . .

38. Bible Communism and Complex Marriage
John Humphrey Noyes

THE Oneida community was a home-grown American variety of religious communism; in many ways it was the most radical of the utopian societies and, next to Mormonism, the longest lived. John Humphrey Noyes (1811–1886), its founder, was a graduate of Dartmouth who decided to enter the ministry after hearing Charles G. Finney (Document 2). However, his adoption of perfectionism, the heretical belief that conversion brought a complete and final release from sin, prevented his ordination, so he organized an informal society in Putney, Vermont, based upon communism of property and "complex marriage." In 1848 he was arrested on a charge of adultery, forfeited his bail and migrated with his followers to Oneida, New York, where additional converts were made; Bible Communism, published in that year, was an exposition of his beliefs. At Oneida agriculture was combined with small industrial enterprises to produce a salable surplus, and the community flourished for more than thirty years. Noyes attributed success more to their religious views than to economic and social theories and practices, maintaining that Owen's and Fourier's secular communism (see Documents 1 and 41) had failed because of their inability to understand that socialism and perfectionism were inseparable. His experiment came to an end in 1880, after "complex marriage" was abandoned and the Oneida community was incorporated as a joint-stock company.

PROPOSITION 5.—In the Kingdom of Heaven, the institution of marriage, which assigns the exclusive possession of one woman to one man, does not exist. . . .

6.—In the Kingdom of Heaven the intimate union of life and interest, which in the world is limited to pairs, extends through the whole body of believers; i.e. complex marriage takes the place of simple. . . .

7.—The effects of the effusion of the Holy Spirit on the day of Pentecost, present a practical commentary on Christ's prayer for

SOURCE: "Leading Propositions of Bible Communism Slightly Condensed," in Noyes, History of American Socialisms, pp. 624–636.

the unity of believers. . . . "The multitude of them that believed were of one heart and of one soul; neither said any of them that aught of the things which he possessed was his own; but they had all things common." . . .

8.—Admitting that the Community principle of the day of Pentecost, in its actual operation at that time, extended only to material goods, yet we affirm that there is no intrinsic difference between property in persons and property in things; and that the same spirit which abolished exclusiveness in regard to money, would abolish, if circumstances allowed full scope to it, exclusiveness in regard to women and children. . . .

9.—The abolishment of appropriation is involved in the very nature of a true relation to Christ in the gospel. . . . Amativeness and acquisitiveness are only different channels of one stream. . . . the possessive feeling, whether amative or acquisitive, flows from the personal feeling, that is, it is a branch of egotism. Now egotism is abolished by the gospel relation to Christ. . . . From *I* comes *mine*, and from the I-spirit comes exclusive appropriation of money, women, etc. From *we* comes *ours*, and from the We-spirit comes universal community of interests.

10.—The abolishment of exclusiveness is involved in the love-relation required between all believers by the express injunction of Christ and the apostles, and by the whole tenor of the New Testament. "The new commandment is, that we love one another," and that, not by pairs, as in the world, but *en masse*. We are required to love one another fervently. The fashion of the world forbids a man and woman who are otherwise appropriated, to love one another fervently. But if they obey Christ they must do this. . . .

13.—. . . All experience testifies (the theory of the novels to the contrary notwithstanding), that sexual love is not naturally restricted to pairs. Second marriages are contrary to the one-love theory, and yet are often the happiest marriages. Men and women find universally (however the fact may be concealed), that their susceptibility to love is not burnt out by one honey-moon, or satisfied by one lover. On the contrary, the secret history of the human heart will bear out the assertion that it is capable of loving any number of times and any number of persons, and that the more it loves the more it can love. This is the law of nature, thrust out of sight and condemned by common consent, and yet secretly known to all.

14.—The law of marriage "worketh wrath." 1. It provokes to secret adultery, actual or of the heart. 2. It ties together unmatched natures. 3. It sunders matched natures. 4. It gives to sexual appetite only a scanty and monotonous allowance, and so produces the natural vices of poverty, contraction of taste and stinginess or jealousy. 5. It makes no provision for the sexual appetite at the very time when that appetite is the strongest. By the custom of the world, marriage, in the average of cases, takes place at about the age of twenty-four; whereas puberty commences at the age of fourteen. For ten years, therefore, and that in the very flush of life, the sexual appetite is starved. This law of society bears hardest on females, because they have less opportunity of choosing their time of marriage than men. This discrepancy between the marriage system and nature, is one of the principal sources of the peculiar diseases of women, of prostitution, masturbation, and licentiousness in general. . . .

17.—The restoration of true relations between the sexes is a matter second in importance only to the reconciliation of man to God. . . . The relation of male and female was the first social relation. . . . It is therefore the root of all other social relations. The derangement of this relation was the first result of the original breach with God. . . . Adam and Eve were, at the beginning, in open, fearless, spiritual fellowship, first with God, and secondly, with each other. Their transgression produced two corresponding alienations, viz., first an alienation from God, indicated by their fear of meeting him and their hiding themselves among the trees of the garden; and secondly, an alienation from each other, indicated by their shame at their nakedness and their hiding themselves from each other by clothing. These were the two great manifestations of original sin—the only manifestations presented to notice in the record of the apostacy. The first thing then to be done, in an attempt to redeem man and reorganize society, is to bring about reconciliation with God; and the second thing is to bring about a true union of the sexes. In other words, religion is the first subject of interest, and sexual morality the second, in the great enterprise of establishing the Kingdom of Heaven on earth. . . .

19.—From what precedes, it is evident that any attempt to

revolutionize sexual morality before settlement with God, is out of order. Holiness must go before free love. Bible Communists are not responsible for the proceedings of those who meddle with the sexual question, before they have laid the foundation of true faith and union with God.

20.—Dividing the sexual relation into two branches, the amative and propagative, the amative or love-relation is first in importance, as it is in the order of nature. God made woman because "he saw it was not good for man to be alone;" . . . i.e., for social, not primarily for propagative, purposes. . . . Amativeness was necessarily the first social affection developed in the garden of Eden. The second commandment of the eternal law of love, "Thou shalt love thy neighbor as thyself," had amativeness for its first channel; for Eve was at first Adam's only neighbor. Propagation and the affections connected with it, did not commence their operation during the period of innocence. After the fall God said to the woman, "I will greatly multiply thy sorrow and thy conception;" from which it is to be inferred that in the original state, conception would have been comparatively infrequent. . . .

22.—The propagative part of the sexual relation is in its nature the expensive department. 1. While amativeness keeps the capital stock of life circulating between two, propagation introduces a third partner. 2. The propagative act is a drain on the life of man, and when habitual, produces disease. 3. The infirmities and vital expenses of woman during the long period of pregnancy, waste her constitution. 4. The awful agonies of child-birth heavily tax the life of woman. 5. The cares of the nursing period bear heavily on woman. 6. The cares of both parents, through the period of the childhood of their offspring, are many and burdensome. 7. The labor of man is greatly increased by the necessity of providing for children. . . . the birth of children, viewed either as a vital or mechanical operation, is in its nature expensive; and the fact that multiplied conception was imposed as a curse, indicates that it was so regarded by the Creator. . . .

23.—The amative and propagative functions are distinct from each other, and may be separated practically. . . . if amativeness is, as we have seen, the first and noblest of the social affections, and if the propagative part of the sexual relation was originally secondary, and became paramount by the subversion of order in the fall, we are bound to raise the amative office of the sexual organs into a distinct and paramount function. . . .

25.—The foregoing principles concerning the sexual relation, open the way for Association. 1. They furnish motives. They apply to larger partnerships the same attractions that draw and bind together pairs in the worldly partnership of marriage. A Community home in which each is married to all, and where love is honored and cultivated, will be as much more attractive than an ordinary home, as the Community out-numbers a pair. 2. These principles remove the principal obstructions in the way of Association. . . . Amalgamation of interests, frequency of interview, and companionship in labor, inevitably give activity and intensity to the social attractions in which amativeness is the strongest element. The tendency to extra-matrimonial love will be proportioned to the condensation of interests produced by any given form of Association; that is, if the ordinary principles of exclusiveness are preserved, Association will be a worse school of temptation to unlawful love than the world is, in proportion to its social advantages. Love, in the exclusive form, has jealousy for its complement; and jealousy brings on strife and division. Association, therefore, if it retains one-love exclusiveness, contains the seeds of dissolution; and those seeds will be hastened to their harvest by the warmth of associate life. . . .

27.—In vital society labor will become attractive. Loving companionship in labor, and especially the mingling of the sexes, makes labor attractive. The present division of labor between the sexes separates them entirely. The woman keeps house, and man labors abroad. Instead of this, in vital society men and women will mingle in both of their peculiar departments of work. It will be economically as well as spiritually profitable, to marry them indoors and out, by day as well as by night. When the partition between the sexes is taken away, and man ceases to make woman a propagative drudge, when love takes the place of shame, and fashion follows nature in dress and business, men and women will be able to mingle in all their employments, as boys and girls mingle in their sports; and then labor will be attractive.

28.—We can now see our way to victory over death. Reconciliation with God opens the way for the reconciliation of the sexes. Reconciliation of the sexes emancipates woman, and opens the way for vital society. Vital society increases strength, diminishes work, and makes labor attractive, thus removing the antecedents of death. First we abolish sin; then shame; then the curse on woman of exhausting child-bearing; then the curse on man of exhausting labor; and so we arrive regularly at the tree of life. . . .

39. Human Liberty and Equality
Without Exceptions or Limitations
Frances Wright

Frances Wright (1795–1852), *a young Scotswoman with a private fortune, first visited the United States in 1818. Her uncritical enthusiasm on that occasion was modified when she returned in 1824, when she became particularly concerned about slavery and the condition of women. Inequality in a nation dedicated to liberty and equality, she concluded, was not only a paradox but a moral evil. Miss Wright's solution to the problem of slavery and racism was the establishment in 1825 of a model community at Nashoba in western Tennessee where former slaves could work with whites and acquire skills which would prepare them to live in freedom. She spent nearly half her fortune, but Nashoba was a disastrous failure: ill health forced her to leave for England, the managers she left in charge were inefficient, and rumors of miscegenation and "free love" in the colony deterred potential partners in the enterprise. The publication of her Explanatory Notes following her return to America only increased the opposition, so she colonized the few Negro residents of Nashoba in Haiti and embarked upon a career of writing and lecturing. Her attacks upon orthodox religion and education, as well as her brief association with the Workingmen's movement (Document 22), made her notorious to conservatives as the "Red Harlot of Infidelity."*

. . . The object of the founder was to attempt the practice of certain principles, which in theory had been frequently advocated. . . . All her observations tended to corroborate the opinion which her own feelings might possibly, in the first instance, have predisposed her to adopt—*that men are virtuous in proportion as they are happy, and happy in proportion as they are free.* . . .

But while human liberty has engaged the attention of the enlightened, and enlisted the feelings of the generous of all civil-

SOURCE: *Fanny Wright Unmasked by Her Own Pen: Explanatory Notes, Respecting the Nature and Objects of the Institution of Nashoba, and of the Principles Upon Which It Is Founded; Addressed to the Friends of Human Improvement, in All Countries and of All Nations* (New York: 1830), pp. 3–13.

ized nations, may we not inquire if this liberty has been rightly understood? . . . Liberty without equality, what is it but a chimera? and equality, what is it also but a chimera, unless it extend to all the enjoyments, exertions, and advantages, intellectual and physical, of which our nature is capable? . . .

Political liberty may be said to exist in the United States of America, and . . . *only there*. Moral liberty exists *no where*.

By political liberty we may understand the liberty of speech and of action without incurring the violence of authority or the penalties of law. By moral liberty may we not understand the *free exercise of the liberty of speech and of action*, without incurring the intolerance of popular prejudice and ignorant public opinion? . . . It is much to have *declared* men free and equal, but it shall be more when they are rendered so; when means shall be sought and found, and employed to develope all the intellectual and physical powers of all human beings, without regard to sex or condition, class, race, nation or color; and when men shall learn to view each other as members of one great family, with equal claims to enjoyment and equal capacities for labor and instruction, admitting always the sole differences arising out of the varieties exhibited in individual organization. . . .

Man has been adjudged a social animal. And so he truly is; equally, we might even hazard the assertion, *more capable of being moved to generous feeling and generous action, through his affections and his interests rightly understood*, than he is now moved to violence, rapine and fraud by hard necessity, and his interests falsely interpreted. Let us not libel human nature! It is what circumstance has made it. But, as profiting by experience, we shall change the education of youth, remould our institutions, correct our very ideas of true and false, of right and wrong, of vice and virtue, we may see human nature assume a new form and present an appearance rich in peace and enjoyment—yet more rich in future hope.

How great soever the differences stamped on each individual by original organization, it will readily be conceded, that by fostering the good, and repressing the evil tendencies, by developing every useful faculty and amiable feeling, and cultivating the peculiar talent or talents of every child, as discovered in the course of education, all human beings, (with the single and rare exceptions presented by the malconformation of the physical organs,) might be rendered useful and happy. . . .

The founder of Nashoba looks not for the conversion of the existing generation; she looks not even for its sympathy. All that she ventures to anticipate is, the cooperation of a certain number of individuals acknowledging the same views with herself. . . . From their union, their cooperation, their exertions, she ventures to expect a successful experiment in favor of human liberty and human happiness. . . .

This has been attempted at Nashoba. . . . the principles on which the institution is based are those of human liberty and equality without exceptions or limitations—*and its more especial object, the protection and regeneration of the race of color, universally oppressed and despised in a country self-denominated free.* This more immediate object was selected and specified by the founder, first, because her feelings had been peculiarly enlisted in behalf of the negro; and secondly, because the aristocracy of color is the peculiar vice of the country which she had chosen as the seat of her experiment. . . .

It is declared, in the deed of the founder, that no individual can be received as a member, but after a noviciate of six months, and then only by a *unanimous* vote of the resident proprietors. It is also provided that the admission of a husband shall not involve that of a wife, nor the admission of a wife that of a husband, nor the admission of either or both of the parents that of children *above the age of* fourteen. Each individual must pass through a separate trial, and be received or rejected on the strength of his or her merits or demerits. . . . The marriage law existing without the pale of the institution, is of no force within that pale. No woman can forfeit her individual rights or independent existence, and no man assert over her any rights or power whatsoever beyond what he may exercise over her free and voluntary affections. Nor, on the other hand, may any woman assert claims to the society or peculiar protection of any individual of the other sex, beyond what mutual inclination dictates and sanctions; while, to every individual member of either sex, is secured the protection and friendly aid of all.

The tyranny usurped by the matrimonial law, over the most sacred of the human affections, can perhaps only be equalled by that of the unjust public opinion, which so frequently stamps with infamy, or condemns to martyrdom, the best grounded, and most generous attachments which ever did honor to the human heart, simply because unlegalized by human ceremonies equally idle and offensive in the form and mischievous in their tendency. . . .

. . . how many of the moral evils, and numerous family of physical diseases, which now torture the human species, have their source in the false opinions and vicious institutions, which have perverted the best source of human happiness—the intercourse of the sexes, into the deepest source of human misery. Let us look into our streets, our hospitals, our asylums; let us look into the secret thought of the anxious parent, trembling for the minds and bodies of sons starting into life, or mourning over the dying health of daughters condemned to the unnatural repression of feelings and desires inherent to their very organization, and necessary alike to their moral and physical well being.

Or let us look to the victims—not of pleasure—not of love—nor yet of their own depravity, but of those ignorant laws, ignorant prejudices, and of that ignorant code of morals which condemn one portion of the female sex to vicious excess, another to as vicious restraint, and all to defenceless helplessness, and slavery; and generally the whole of the male sex to debasing licentiousness, if not to loathsome brutality. . . .

. . . Let us correct our views of right and wrong, correct our moral lessons, and so correct the practice of rising generations! Let us not teach that virtue consists in crucifying the affections and appetites, but in their judicious government! Let us not attach ideas of purity to monastic chastity, impossible to man or woman without consequences fraught with evil, nor ideas of vice to connections formed under the auspices of kind feeling! Let us inquire, not if a mother be a wife, or a father a husband, but if parents can supply, to the creatures they have brought into being, all things requisite to make existence a blessing. Let the force of public opinion be brought against the thoughtless ignorance or cruel selfishness which, either with or without the sanction of a legal or religious permit, so frequently multiplies offspring beyond the resources of the parents. Let us check the force of passions, as well as their precocity, not by the idle terror of imaginary crime in the desire itself, but by the just and benevolent apprehension of bringing into existence unhappy or imperfect beings! Let us teach the young mind to reason, and the young heart to feel; and, instead of shrouding our own bodies, wants, desires, senses, affections, and faculties in mystery, let us court inquiry, and show, that acquaintance with our own nature can alone guide us to judicious practice, *and that in the consequence of human actions exists the only true test of their virtue or their vice.* . . .

It is considered that the peculiar object of the founder, "The benefit of the negro race," may best be consulted by the admission and incorporation of suitable individuals of that, and of the mixed race, on the same principles of equality which guide the admission of all members; and farther, that such individuals may best be found among the *free citizens of color,* who form no inconsiderable, and frequently a very respectable body in the American population, more especially in that of the southern cities. . . .

It is not supposed that (with some rare exceptions) human beings raised under the benumbing influence of brutal slavery can be elevated to the level of a society based upon the principles of moral liberty and voluntary cooperation. The experiment, therefore, as respects *slave* population, it is intended to limit, at Nashoba, to the first purchase of the founder, excepting in cases where planters, becoming members, may wish to place their negroes under the protection of the institution. . . . the founder judged that she should best conciliate the laws of the southern states, and the popular feelings of the whole Union as well as the interests of the emancipated negro, by providing for the colonization of all the slaves emancipated by the society, in a free country, without the limits of the United States. Personal observation had taught her the danger of launching a freed slave into the midst of an inimical population. . . .

The strength of the prejudice of color, as existing in the U. States and in the European colonies, can in general be little conceived, and less understood in the old continent; yet, however whimsical it may there appear, is it, in fact, more ridiculous than the European prejudice of birth? The superior excellence which the one supposes in a peculiar descent, or merely in a peculiar name, the other imagines in a peculiar complexion or set of features; and perhaps it is only by considering man in many countries, and observing all his varying and contradictory prejudices, that we can discover the equal absurdity of all.

Those to whom the American institutions and American character are familiar, and who have considered the question of negro slavery in all its bearings, will probably be disposed to pronounce, with the writer of this address, that the emancipation of the colored population cannot be *progressive through the laws.* It must, and can only be *progressive through the feelings;* and, through that medium, be finally complete and entire, involving at once political equality and the amalgamation of the races. . . .

. . . The education of the race of color would doubtless make the amalgamation more rapid as well as more creditable; and so far from considering the physical amalgamation of the two colors, when accompanied by a moral approximation, as an evil, it must surely be viewed as a good equally desirable for both. In this belief, the more especial object of the founder of Nashoba is to raise the man of color to the level of the white. Where fitted by habits of industry and suitable dispositions to receive him as a brother and equal . . . ; to educate his children with white children, and thus approaching their minds, tastes and occupations, to leave the affections of future generations to the dictates of free choice. . . .

. . . It is conceived that, with some exceptions, the institution of Nashoba will be found most suited to young persons, of both sexes, of independent minds and liberal education. . . . All must bring hands as well as heads, and, above all, kind and willing *hearts,* ever disposed to make light of inconveniences, and to find the best enjoyment in promoting the happiness of others. Moreover, let none imagine that they can enter an institution based on the novel principle of cooperation, without experiencing inconveniences and difficulties both moral and physical. *They will experience many,* and nothing but a strong moral purpose—a real heart interest in the success of the undertaking, a deep conviction of the truth of the principles, which it aspires practically to illustrate, can strengthen them to weather such difficulties. Possessed of the moral requisites, they will succeed and ensure the success of the institution. . . .

40. A Natural Union Between Intellectual and Manual Labor
George Ripley and Ralph W. Emerson

BROOK FARM, the result of a Transcendentalist dream, was probably the most famous American utopian community. George Ripley (1802–1880), a Unitarian minister and member of Emerson's Transcendentalist Club, was the moving spirit, the community being established in the summer of 1841 on a farm nine miles from Boston. It was organized on a joint-stock basis, each shareholder having one vote, receiving one dollar per day for his labor, and being entitled to the tuition of one child in the community school. Publicized in the Dial and other periodicals, it became a mecca for the New England intelligentsia who enjoyed its atmosphere of informality and spontaneity; Emerson and Margaret Fuller were frequent visitors, although they were skeptical friends rather than members of the community, and Hawthorne remained critical after his brief experience (see Document 46). In 1844 Ripley was converted by Albert Brisbane to Fourierism (see Document 41) and induced the trustees to transform the community into a phalanx. A disastrous fire in 1846 doomed the experiment, and Brook Farm was sold at auction three years later; nevertheless, it remained a bright memory to most of those who had been associated with it.

Boston, November 9,
1840

My Dear Sir,—Our conversation in Concord was of such a general nature, that I do not feel as if you were in complete possession of the idea of the Association which I wish to see established. As we have now a prospect of carrying it into effect, at an early period, I wish to submit the plan more distinctly to your judgment, that you may decide whether it is one that can have the benefit of your aid and cooperation.

Our objects, as you know, are to insure a more natural union

SOURCE: Letter from Ripley to Emerson reprinted from O. B. Frothingham, George Ripley (Boston: Houghton Mifflin Company, 1882), pp. 307–312. Letter from Emerson to Ripley reprinted by permission of the publisher from The Letters of Ralph Waldo Emerson, ed. Ralph L. Rusk (New York: Columbia University Press, 1939), vol. II, pp. 368–371.

between intellectual and manual labor than now exists; to combine the thinker and the worker, as far as possible, in the same individual; to guarantee the highest mental freedom, by providing all with labor, adapted to their tastes and talents, and securing to them the fruits of their industry; to do away the necessity of menial services, by opening the benefits of education and the profits of labor to all; and thus to prepare a society of liberal, intelligent, and cultivated persons, whose relations with each other would permit a more simple and wholesome life, than can be led amidst the pressure of our competitive institutions.

To accomplish these objects, we propose to take a small tract of land, which, under skillful husbandry, uniting the garden and the farm, will be adequate to the subsistence of the families; and to connect with this a school or college, in which the most complete instruction shall be given, from the first rudiments to the highest culture. Our farm would be a place for improving the race of men that lived on it; thought would preside over the operations of labor, and labor would contribute to the expansion of thought; we should have industry without drudgery, and true equality without its vulgarity.

An offer has been made to us of a beautiful estate, on very reasonable terms, on the borders of Newton, West Roxbury, and Dedham. I am very familiar with the premises, having resided on them a part of last summer, and we might search the country in vain for anything more eligible. Our proposal now is for three or four families to take possession on the first of April next, to attend to the cultivation of the farm and the erection of buildings, to prepare for the coming of as many more in the autumn, and thus to commence the institution in the simplest manner, and with the smallest number, with which it can go into operation at all. It would thus be not less than two or three years, before we should be joined by all who mean to be with us; we should not fall to pieces by our own weight; we should grow up slowly and strong; and the attractiveness of our experiment would win to us all whose society we should want.

The step now to be taken at once is the procuring of funds for the necessary capital. According to the present modification of our plan, a much less sum will be required than that spoken of in our discussions at Concord. We thought then $50,000 would be needed; I find now, after a careful estimate, that $30,000 will purchase the estate and buildings for ten families, and give the required surplus for carrying on the operations for one year.

We propose to raise this sum by a subscription to a joint stock company, among the friends of the institution, the payment of a fixed interest being guaranteed to the subscribers, and the subscription itself secured by that real estate. No man then will be in danger of losing; he will receive as fair an interest as he would from any investment, while at the same time he is contributing towards an institution, in which while the true use of money is retained, its abuses are done away. The sum required cannot come from rich capitalists; their instinct would protest against such an application of their coins; it must be obtained from those who sympathize with our ideas, and who are willing to aid their realization with their money, if not by their personal cooperation. There are some of this description on whom I think we can rely; among ourselves we can produce perhaps $10,000; the remainder must be subscribed for by those who wish us well, whether they mean to unite with us or not.

I can imagine no plan which is suited to carry into effect so many divine ideas as this. If wisely executed, it will be a light over this country and this age. If not the sunrise, it will be the morning star. As a practical man, I see clearly that we must have some such arrangement, or all changes less radical will be nugatory. I believe in the divinity of labor; I wish to "harvest my flesh and blood from the land;" but to do this, I must either be insulated and work to disadvantage, or avail myself of the services of hirelings, who are not of my order, and whom I can scarce make friends; for I must have another to drive the plough, which I hold. I cannot empty a cask of lime upon my grass alone. I wish to see a society of educated friends, working, thinking, and living together, with no strife, except that of each to contribute the most to the benefit of all.

Personally, my tastes and habits would lead me in another direction. I have a passion for being independent of the world, and of every man in it. . . . But I feel bound to sacrifice this private feeling, in the hope of a great social good. I shall be anxious to hear from you. Your decision will do much towards settling the question with me, whether the time has come for the fulfillment of a high hope, or whether the work belongs to a future generation. All omens now are favorable; a singular union of diverse talents is ready for the enterprise; everything indicates that we ought to arise and build; and if we let slip this occasion, the unsleeping Nemesis will deprive us of the boon we seek. For myself, I am sure that I can never give so much thought to it again; my mind must act on other objects, and I shall acquiesce in the course of fate, with grief that so fair a light is put out. A small pittance of the wealth which has been thrown away on ignoble objects, during this wild contest for political supremacy, would lay the cornerstone of a house, which would ere long become the desire of nations.

. . . Pray write me with as much frankness as I have used towards you, and believe me ever your friend and faithful servant,

GEORGE RIPLEY

P.S. . . . I recollect you said that if you were sure of compeers of the right stamp you might embark yourself in the adventure: as to this, let me suggest the inquiry, whether our Association should not be composed of various classes of men? If we have friends whom we love and who love us, I think we should be content to join with others, with whom our personal sympathy is not strong, but whose general ideas coincide with ours, and whose gifts and abilities would make their services important. For instance, I should like to have a good washerwoman in my parish admitted into the plot. She is certainly not a Minerva or a Venus; but we might educate her two children to wisdom and varied accomplishments, who otherwise will be doomed to drudge through life. The same is true of some farmers and mechanics, whom we should like with us.

[December 15, 1840]

MY DEAR SIR,

It is quite time I made an answer to your proposition that I should join you in your new enterprise. The design appears to me so noble & humane, proceeding, as I plainly see, from a manly & expanding heart & mind that it makes me & all men its friends & debtors. It becomes a matter of conscience to entertain it friendly & to examine what it has for us.

I have decided not to join it & yet very slowly & I may almost say penitentially. . . .

The ground of my decision is almost purely personal to myself. I have some remains of skepticism in regard to the general practicability of the plan, but these have not much weighed with me. That which determines me is the conviction that the Community is not good for me. Whilst I see it may hold out many inducements for others it has little to offer me which with resolution I cannot procure for myself. . . .

The principal particulars in which I wish to mend my domestic life are in acquiring habits of regular manual labor, and in ameliorating or abolishing in my house the condition of hired menial service. I should like to come one step nearer to nature than this usage permits. But surely I need not sell my house & remove my family to Newton in order to make the experiment of labor & self help. I am already in the act of trying some domestic & social experiments which my present position favors. And I think that my present position has even greater advantages than yours would offer me for testing my improvements in those small private parties into which men are all set off already throughout the world. . . .

If the community is not good for me neither am I good for it. I do not look on myself as a valuable member to any community which is not either very large or very small & select. I fear that yours would not find me as profitable & pleasant an associate as I should wish to be and as so important a project seems imperatively to require in all its constituents. Moreover I am so ignorant & uncertain in my improvements that I would fain hide my attempts & failures in solitude where they shall perplex none or very few beside myself. The result of our secretest improvements will certainly have as much renown as shall be due to them. . . .

Whilst I refuse to be an active member of your company I must yet declare that of all the . . . philanthropic projects of which I have heard yours is the most pleasing to me and if it is prosecuted in the same spirit in which it is begun, I shall regard it with lively sympathy & with a sort of gratitude.

Yours affectionately
R W EMERSON

41. A Social System Perfectly Adapted to Human Nature

Albert Brisbane

THE theories of the French socialist Charles Fourier were brought to America by Albert Brisbane (1809–1890), who had known Fourier before his death in 1837. Brisbane first converted Horace Greeley, who published his articles in the New York Tribune, and then was instrumental in transforming Brook Farm into a Fourierist phalanx (see Document 40). His writings and Greeley's sponsorship led to the establishment of forty to fifty other phalanxes in ten states, most of them short lived; the most successful was the North American Phalanx in New Jersey, which operated for twelve years. Fourier's "scientific" scheme called for the reorganization of society into communal groups based upon a complicated division of labor; each phalanx was to be organized on the joint-stock principle, with wages credited for work done and profits divided annually. After leaving the Tribune, Brisbane edited the Phalanx and the Harbinger, the latter for several years the most important socialist journal in the United States.

We assert, and will prove, that LABOR, which is now MONOTONOUS, REPUGNANT and DEGRADING, can be ENNOBLED, ELEVATED and made HONORABLE;—or in other words, that INDUSTRY CAN BE RENDERED ATTRACTIVE!

Let this great and practical reform be once effected, and three-fourths of the evils, which oppress mankind, will be done away with as if by a magic influence.

What does man require to be happy? RICHES, and an ENNOBLING AND PLEASING ACTIVITY.

How is he to obtain riches, if Labor, which is the source of all WEALTH, be repugnant and degrading, and if its exercise has to be coerced by POVERTY AND WANT, OR BY THE FEAR OF THE WHIP? With the present miserable organization of Labor, it is useless to

SOURCE: Albert Brisbane, *Social Destiny of Man: or, Association and Reorganization of Industry* (Philadelphia: C. F. Stollmeyer, 1840), pp. vi–viii, 26, 29–30, 239, 241–243, 248–249, 252, 259–260.

think of general riches, that is, of an abundance for all: poverty will continue to be the lot of the great majority, so long as the present defective system of Industry is continued. . . .

ATTRACTIVE INDUSTRY is the first remedy to be applied to Social evils; it would replace the present poverty and anxiety by riches and contentment, and relieve the mass from those harrassing cares and physical wants, which deaden the intellect, and smother or.pervert all the higher sympathies and feelings.

It would open also a new and vast career to the genius and ambition of man, and employ usefully the passions, whose restless activity is now perverted in our societies, with their monotonous idleness, and their conflicts and discords.

We assert therefore, that the greatest and most important problem which can be proposed to Society, if Society be willing to occupy itself with any questions of a general nature, is a REORGANIZATION OF INDUSTRY, or a REFORM IN OUR WHOLE SYSTEM OF LABOR. It is here,—in the foundation of the Social edifice, that a reform should commence,—and not in the superstructure, in the administration, or the political power. . . .

Association is the most brilliant problem, which can occupy the mind of man. It is a means of uniting all individual forces and intelligences, now so miserably wasted and misapplied, and of directing them to great and important undertakings. Society, strong with the strength of all its members, its power not fretted away by the interminable conflicts of individuals, between whom no combination exists, could undertake, with intelligence and foresight, gigantic operations, which a Society like ours, circumscribed to the mere effort of individuals, cannot conceive, or which, if it does, it declares chimeras and illusions. . . .

Before entering into practical details upon the economies of Association, we have a favor to ask of our readers. We particularly request them not to confound the system of Association which we shall propose, with those monotonous and monastic trials which have been attempted or executed by Mr. Owen, the Rappites, Shakers, and others. Although well intended, the monotony, the absence of individual property (the greatest guarantee of individual liberty) which characterize them, have excited a distrust on the part of the public against Association. We wish particularly in the outset, to do away with any prejudices of the kind, which may exist against our plan in the mind of the reader.

Man is a being of a compound nature; to be happy, the field of intellectual and material enjoyment must be thrown open to him. The present social organization in which there is so much real and relative poverty, not only shuts out from the mass the world of intellectual enjoyment, but oppresses them with poverty and anxiety.

As attractive industry does not exist, as industry has not been ennobled, as but little encouragement and extension is given to the fine arts and the sciences, the rich themselves find few occupations which unite pleasure and health. Our defective Societies, with their monotony and staleness, circumscribe the individual, even in large cities, to a most narrow social circle, confine him to a single occupation without variety, and oppress in one way or other all classes, both rich and poor.

The systems of Association, which have been attempted, have merely aimed at a guarantee of physical sufficiency, with the aid of constraints and repulsive personal economies. Industry has remained repugnant and entirely devoid of emulation and charm. The intellectual world, the world of art and science, of poetry and imagination, have been neglected as incompatible with industry and the cares of life. The mind, with its higher aspirations and delights, has been sacrificed to procure the necessaries of life.

If we would organize an Association like these, we should wish as a consequence to sink or degrade mankind lower than they now are in our civilized Societies. So far from having this for our object, we wish to elevate them infinitely above their present condition in the most favored of countries. We wish to throw open to them the entire field of human activity, develop all their faculties and powers, guarantee to each member of the great human family equal social chances, which would result in the richest and most varied development of genius. Such a state would not produce a monotonous equality, but would call forth an infinite variety of tastes and capacities, adapted to all functions. Each individual would form a note in the great concert, and would perform his part in the mechanism of the whole. . . .

What is the DESTINY OF MAN? why was he placed upon the Earth? Was it to ravage and devastate its surface, to render it a scene of desolation and misery, to degrade his own nature and the creations around him?—or was it to cultivate and embellish it, to develop its varied resources and realize in his passional or social existence *those Laws of order and justice, which govern the Universe?* . . .

The ignorance of man of his Destiny, of the link which exists between him and his planet, is connected with the poverty and suffering, which have been his lot, and which characterize his social infancy. Men of science, occupied exclusively with the history of the past, and seeing the continuance for so many centuries of social misery, have considered it permanent, and supposed it to be the *unchangeable* destiny of the human race. They have sought for the cause of all this evil, and from superficial observation they have declared it to be in human nature—in the passions. . . . they declare that man was not made for happiness, that the evils he suffers are a consequence of his depraved nature, and that no higher Destiny is reserved for him than the present mingled disorder of moral and physical suffering. To conciliate this monstrous theory with the creation of the earth, and the existence of man upon it, they assert that it is a valley of tears, a place of probation, where he is placed to expiate by suffering the imperfection of his nature.— Life becomes a ceaseless combat, a mournful pilgrimage towards eternity.

This explication, so unsatisfactory and repugnant, is contradicted by every act of man, by every impulse of his soul. He seeks for happiness and enjoyment as a law of his nature, as a part of his destiny;—he seeks for riches and the goods of this earth, as a right. . . .

It is true, man is now a discordant note in the Universe, for while harmony is *its Law*, discord has marked *his Career*. But let us not suppose that the evil is in man individually, in his passions or nature; for they were created by the same Power whose wisdom regulates the most infinite, as well as the most minute harmonies. *The evil is in the collective action of the race*, in the false and heterogeneous social principles, which they have established. . . .

The passions of men are at present all more or less smothered, tantalized or misdirected; and it is for that reason that we find, not only so many criminals, but descending to a lower sphere of subversion, so many drunken, quarrelsome, scolding, petulent, backbiting creatures, whose unaccountable freaks can only be understood by those who possess a knowledge of the twofold mode of action of the passions. The discordant and perverted play of those springs of action is carried to a higher pitch in civilization than in the savage and barbarian societies, because its mechanism is more complicated, and because there is a broader development of the passions to be acted upon. But it is certain, that as great as is the discord and duplicity which reign in the present state of things, as great will be the harmony and unity in a social system perfectly adapted to human nature. . . .

The condemnation of human nature in order to exculpate society, has been a universal error of science. It is time it was rectified; man, the WORK of the Divinity, should become the standard whereby the social organization should be judged; he should not be sacrificed to, nor measured by the measure of our arbitrary societies, the work of accidental circumstances and human Legislation. . . .

It would seem . . . that thirty centuries of poverty and carnage, of political and administrative controversies, should have convinced men of the impotency of human legislation, and led them to set aside their prejudices for a time to seek for a remedy elsewhere than in party strife and legislative controversy. At any rate, as human legislation is all based on the theory of the depravity of human nature, its miserable practical results should have been alone sufficient to prove the falseness of this outrageous doctrine, insulting alike to the justice of the Divinity and to the dignity of man.

Either the passions *are bad*, or the social mechanism *is false*; for evil prevails, and to a melancholy extent. If the former be true, then there is no hope of a better state of things; for every means of repression and constraint that human ingenuity could invent, has been applied to regulate their action, but all in vain; they have remained unchanged, and in the eyes of the moralist, as perverse as ever. If, however, the latter be true—that is, if the social mechanism be false—then there is a chance of a better future; for our incoherent and absurd societies are changing more or less with every century. They are at the mercy of the whim of a tyrant, or of a revolution of the mass; they may therefore be reformed, or even done away with entirely. . . .

42. The Governments of This World Are Anti-Christ
William Lloyd Garrison

Although noted primarily as a radical abolitionist (Document 29), William Lloyd Garrison aspired to be a "universal reformer." Between 1837 and 1840 his commitment to equal rights for women in the abolition movement had estranged him from moderates, a tendency which was furthered by his denunciation of the corruption in both church and state which was responsible for their continued toleration of slavery. His adherence to the tenets of Noyes' perfectionism (Document 38) further estranged him from orthodox abolitionists. As a convinced pacifist and an advocate of "moral suasion," Garrison embraced non-resistance to government while burning copies of the Constitution as a "Covenant with Death and an agreement with Hell." Therefore, he continued to oppose political abolitionism and until the eve of the Civil War advocated dissolution of the Union as the solution to the slavery question.

. . . In entering upon our eighth volume, the abolition of slavery will still be the grand object of our labors, though, not, perhaps, so exclusively as heretofore. There are other topics which, in our opinion, are intimately connected with the great doctrine of inalienable human rights; and which, while they conflict with no religious sect, or political party, as such, are pregnant with momentous consequences to the freedom, equality, and happiness of mankind. These we shall discuss as time and opportunity may permit.

The motto upon our banner has been, from the commencement of our moral warfare, "OUR COUNTRY IS THE WORLD—OUR COUNTRYMEN ARE ALL MANKIND." We trust that it will be our only epitaph. Another motto we have chosen is, UNIVERSAL EMANCIPATION. Up to this time we have limited its application to those who are held in this country, by Southern taskmasters, as marketable commodities, goods and chattels, and implements of husbandry. Henceforth we shall use it in its widest latitude: the emancipation of our whole race from the

SOURCE: *The Liberator* (Boston), December 15, 1837.

dominion of man, from the thraldom of self, from the government of brute force, from the bondage of sin—and bringing them under the dominion of God, the control of an inward spirit, the government of the law of love, and into the obedience and liberty of Christ, who is "*the* same, yesterday, TO-DAY, and forever.". . .

Next to the overthrow of slavery, the cause of PEACE will command our attention. . . .

Now the doctrine we shall endeavor to inculcate is, that the kingdoms of this world are to become the kingdoms of our Lord and of his Christ; consequently, that they are all to be supplanted, whether they are called despotic, monarchical, or republican, and he only who is King of kings, and Lord of lords, is to rule in righteousness. The kingdom of God is to be established IN ALL THE EARTH, and it shall never be destroyed, but it shall "BREAK IN PIECES AND CONSUME ALL OTHERS:" its elements are righteousness and peace, and joy in the Holy Ghost: without are dogs, and sorcerers, and whoremongers, and murderers, and idolators, and whatsoever loveth and maketh a lie. . . .

As to the governments of this world, whatever their titles or forms, we shall endeavor to prove that, in their essential elements, and as at present administered, they are all Anti-Christ; that they can never, by human wisdom, be brought into conformity to the will of God; that they cannot be maintained except by naval and military power; that all their penal enactments, being a dead letter without an army to carry them into effect, are virtually written in human blood; and that the followers of Jesus should instinctively shun their stations of honor, power, and emolument—at the same time "submitting to every ordinance of man, for the Lord's sake," and offering no *physical* resistance to any of their mandates, however unjust or tyrannical. The language of Jesus is, "My kingdom is not of this world, else would my servants fight." . . .

Human governments are to be viewed as judicial punishments. If a people turn the grace of God into lasciviousness, or make their liberty an occasion for anarchy,—or if they refuse to belong to the "one fold and one Shepherd,"—they shall be scourged by governments of their own choosing, and burdened with taxation, and subjected to physical control, and torn by factions, and made to eat the fruits of their evil doings, until they are prepared to receive the liberty and the rest which remain on earth as well as in heaven, for

THE PEOPLE OF GOD. This is in strict accordance with the arrangement of Divine Providence.

So long as men condemn the perfect government of the Most High, and will not fill up the measure of Christ's sufferings in their own persons, just so long will they desire to usurp authority over each other—just so long will they pertinaciously cling to human governments, *fashioned in the likeness and administered in the spirit of their own disobedience.* Now, if the prayer of our Lord be not a mockery; if the Kingdom of God is to come universally, and his will to be done ON EARTH AS IT IS IN HEAVEN; and if, in that kingdom, no carnal weapon can be wielded, and swords are beaten into ploughshares, and spears into pruning-hooks, and there is none to molest or make afraid, and no statute-book but the Bible, and no judge but Christ; then why are not Christians obligated to come out NOW, and be separate from "the kingdoms of this world," which are all based upon THE PRINCIPLE OF VIOLENCE, and which require their officers and servants to govern and be governed by that principle? . . .

. . . We regret, indeed, that the principles of abolitionists seem to be quite unsettled upon a question of such vast importance, and so vitally connected with the bloodless overthrow of slavery. It is time for all our friends to know where they stand. If those whose yokes they are endeavoring to break by the fire and hammer of God's word, would not, in their opinion, be justified in appealing to physical force, how can they justify others of a different complexion in doing the same thing? And if they conscientiously believe that the slaves would be guiltless in shedding the blood of their merciless oppressors, let them say so unequivocally—for there is no neutral ground in this matter, and the time is near when they will be compelled to take sides. . . .

43. The Mass of Men
Serve the State as Machines
Henry D. Thoreau

THE Mexican War was fervently opposed by New England intellectuals, but only Henry David Thoreau (1817–1862) both preached and practiced resistance to the government, accepting imprisonment for non-payment of taxes. An associate of Emerson in the Transcendental Club, he was more of an individualist than his mentor. In 1845 he retired from the world and lived for two years at Walden Pond, proving to himself and hopefully to others that man could live independent of human society. Thoreau was not an abolitionist and had little use for reformers, but he regarded John Brown as a true man of principle. In 1859 he wrote A Plea for Captain John Brown, an apparent refutation of his earlier argument in favor of non-violent civil disobedience; yet to Thoreau there was no contradiction between adherence to the higher law and a belief in the majority of one. His essay on Civil Disobedience was delivered as a lecture at the Concord Lyceum in 1847 and first published by Elizabeth Peabody two years later under the title of "Resistance to Civil Government"; it was not reprinted until after his death.

I heartily accept the motto,—"That government is best which governs least"; and I should like to see it acted up to more rapidly and systematically. Carried out, it finally amounts to this, which also I believe,—"That government is best which governs not at all"; and when men are prepared for it, that will be the kind of government which they will have. Government is at best but an expedient; but most governments are usually, and all governments are sometimes, inexpedient. . . .

After all, the practical reason why, when the power is once in the hands of the people, a majority are permitted, and for a long period continue, to rule is not because they are most likely to be in the right, nor because this seems fairest to the minority, but because they are physically the strongest. But a government in which the majority rule in all cases cannot be based on justice, even as far as

SOURCE: "Resistance to Civil Government; a Lecture delivered in 1847 by H. D. Thoreau, Esq.," *Aesthetic Papers*, ed. Elizabeth P. Peabody (New York: G. P. Putnam, 1849), pp. 189–192, 195–200, 203, 208, 211.

men understand it. Can there not be a government in which majorities do not virtually decide right and wrong, but conscience?—in which majorities decide only those questions to which the rule of expediency is applicable? Must the citizen ever for a moment, or in the least degree, resign his conscience to the legislator? Why has every man a conscience, then? I think that we should be men first, and subjects afterward. It is not desirable to cultivate a respect for the law, so much as for the right. The only obligation which I have a right to assume is to do at any time what I think right. . . . Law never made men a whit more just; and, by means of their respect for it, even the well-disposed are daily made the agents of injustice. A common and natural result of an undue respect for law is, that you may see a file of soldiers, colonel, captain, corporal, privates, powder-monkeys, and all, marching in admirable order over hill and dale to the wars, against their wills, ay, against their common sense and consciences, which makes it very steep marching indeed, and produces a palpitation of the heart. They have no doubt that it is a damnable business in which they are concerned; they are all peaceably inclined. Now, what are they? Men at all? or small movable forts and magazines, at the service of some unscrupulous man in power? . . .

The mass of men serve the state thus, not as men mainly, but as machines, with their bodies. . . . In most cases there is no free exercise whatever of the judgment or of the moral sense; but they put themselves on a level with wood and earth and stones; and wooden men can perhaps be manufactured that will serve the purpose as well. . . . Yet such as these even are commonly esteemed good citizens. Others—as most legislators, politicians, lawyers, ministers, and office-holders—serve the state chiefly with their heads; and, as they rarely make any moral distinctions, they are as likely to serve the Devil, without *intending* it, as God. A very few, as heroes, patriots, martyrs, reformers in the great sense, and *men*, serve the state with their consciences also, and so necessarily resist it for the most part; and they are commonly treated as enemies by it. A wise man will only be useful as a man, and will not submit to be "clay," and "stop a hole to keep the wind away," but leave that office to his dust at least. . . .

. . . O for a man who is a *man*, and, as my neighbor says, has a bone in his back which you cannot pass your hand through! Our statistics are at fault: the population has been returned too large.

How many men are there to a square thousand miles in this country? Hardly one. Does not America offer any inducement for men to settle here? The American has dwindled into an Odd Fellow,— one who may be known by the development of his organ of gregariousness, and a manifest lack of intellect and cheerful self-reliance; whose first and chief concern, on coming into the world, is to see that the Alms-houses are in good repair; and, before yet he has lawfully donned the virile garb, to collect a fund for the support of the widows and orphans that may be; who, in short, ventures to live only by the aid of the Mutual Insurance company, which has promised to bury him decently.

. . . The soldier is applauded who refuses to serve in an unjust war by those who do not refuse to sustain the unjust government which makes the war; is applauded by those whose own act and authority he disregards and sets at naught. . . . Thus, under the name of Order and Civil Government, we are all made at last to pay homage to and support our own meanness. After the first blush of sin comes its indifference; and from immoral it becomes, as it were, unmoral, and not quite unnecessary to that life which we have made. . . .

Unjust laws exist: shall we be content to obey them, or shall we endeavor to amend them, and obey them until we have succeeded, or shall we transgress them at once? Men generally, under such a government as this, think that they ought to wait until they have persuaded the majority to alter them. They think that, if they should resist, the remedy would be worse than the evil. But it is the fault of the government itself that the remedy *is* worse than the evil. *It* makes it worse. Why is it not more apt to anticipate and provide for reform? Why does it not cherish its wise minority? Why does it cry and resist before it is hurt? Why does it not encourage its citizens to be on the alert to point out its faults, and *do* better than it would have them? Why does it always crucify Christ, and excommunicate Copernicus and Luther, and pronounce Washington and Franklin rebels? . . .

If the injustice is part of the necessary friction of the machine of government, let it go, let it go: perchance it will wear smooth,— certainly the machine will wear out. If the injustice has a spring, or a pulley, or a rope, or a crank, exclusively for itself, then perhaps you may consider whether the remedy will not be worse than the evil; but if it is of such a nature that it requires you to be the agent of injustice to another, then, I say, break the law. Let your life be a counter friction to stop the machine. What I have to do is to see, at any rate, that I do not lend myself to the wrong which I condemn.

As for adopting the ways which the state has provided for remedying the evil, I know not of such ways. They take too much time, and a man's life will be gone. I have other affairs to attend to. I came into this world, not chiefly to make this a good place to live in, but to live in it, be it good or bad. A man has not everything to do, but something; and because he cannot do *everything*, it is not necessary that he should do *something* wrong. . . .

I meet this American government, or its representative, the state government, directly, and face to face, once a year—no more—in the person of its tax-gatherer; this is the only mode in which a man situated as I am necessarily meets it; and it then says distinctly, Recognize me; and the simplest, the most effectual, and, in the present posture of affairs, the indispensablest mode of treating with it on this head, of expressing your little satisfaction with and love for it, is to deny it then. . . . I know this well, that if one thousand, if one hundred, if ten men whom I could name,—if ten *honest* men only,—ay, if *one* HONEST man, in this State of Massachusetts, *ceasing to hold slaves*, were actually to withdraw from this copartnership, and be locked up in the county jail therefor, it would be the abolition of slavery in America. For it matters not how small the beginning may seem to be: what is once well done is done forever. But we love better to talk about it: that we say is our mission. Reform keeps many scores of newspapers in its service, but not one man. . . .

Under a government which imprisons any unjustly, the true place for a just man is also a prison. The proper place to-day, the only place which Massachusetts has provided for her free and less desponding spirit, is in her prisons, to be put out and locked out of the State by her own act, as they have already put themselves out by their principles. It is there that the fugitive slave, and the Mexican prisoner on parole, and the Indian come to plead the wrongs of his race should find them; on that separate, but more free and honorable ground, where the State places those who are not *with* her, but *against* her,—the only house in a slave State in which a free man can abide with honor. . . . A minority is powerless while it conforms to the majority; it is not even a minority then; but it is irresistible when it clogs by its whole weight. If the alternative is to keep all just men in prison, or give up war and slavery, the State will not hesitate which to choose. If a thousand men were not to pay their tax-bills this year, that would not be a violent and bloody measure, as it would be to pay them, and enable the State to commit violence and shed innocent blood. This is, in fact, the definition of a peaceable revolution, if any such is possible. . . . But even suppose blood should flow. Is there not a sort of blood shed when the conscience is wounded? Through this wound a man's real manhood and immortality flow out, and he bleeds to an everlasting death. I see this blood flowing now. . . .

I have paid no poll-tax for six years. I was put into a jail once on this account, for one night; and, as I stood considering the walls of solid stone, two or three feet thick, the door of wood and iron, a foot thick, and the iron grating which strained the light, I could not help being struck with the foolishness of that institution which treated me as if I were mere flesh and blood and bones, to be locked up. I wondered that it should have concluded at length that this was the best use it could put me to, and had never thought to avail itself of my services in some way. I saw that, if there was a wall of stone between me and my townsmen, there was a still more difficult one to climb or break through before they could get to be as free as I was. . . . As they could not reach me, they had resolved to punish my body; just as boys, if they cannot come at some person against whom they have a spite, will abuse his dog. I saw that the State was half-witted, that it was timid as a lone woman with her silver spoons, and that it did not know its friends from its foes, and I lost all my remaining respect for it, and pitied it.

Thus the State never intentionally confronts a man's sense, intellectual or moral, but only his body, his senses. It is not armed with superior wit or honesty, but with superior physical strength. I was not born to be forced. I will breathe after my own fashion. Let us see who is the strongest. . . .

However, the government does not concern me much, and I shall bestow the fewest possible thoughts on it. It is not many moments that I live under a government, even in this world. If a man is thought-free, fancy-free, imagination-free, that which *is not* never for a long time appearing *to be* to him, unwise rulers or reformers cannot fatally interrupt him. . . .

The authority of government, even such as I am willing to submit to,—for I will cheerfully obey those who know and can do better than I, and in many things even those who neither know nor can do so well,—is still an impure one: to be strictly just, it must have the sanction and consent of the governed. It can have no pure right over my person and property but what I concede to it. . . . There will never be a really free and enlightened State until the State comes to recognize the individual as a higher and independent power, from which all its own power and authority are derived, and treats him accordingly. I please myself with imagining a State at last which can afford to be just to all men, and to treat the individual with respect as a neighbor; which even would not think it inconsistent with its own repose if a few were to live aloof from it, not meddling with it, nor embraced by it, who fulfilled all the duties of neighbors and fellow-men. A State which bore this kind of fruit, and suffered it to drop off as fast as it ripened, would prepare the way for a still more perfect and glorious State, which also I have imagined, but not yet anywhere seen.

44. Dethrone the Sanguinary Monster, War
Elihu Burritt

THE peace movement in the United States developed after the War of
1812, but made little headway for a time because the possibility of war
seemed remote to a generation which was mainly concerned with settling
a continent. In 1828 William Ladd founded the American Peace Society, which was devoted to furthering international arbitration and the
eventual abolition of war. Although the society split on the issue of non-
resistance, Garrison arguing against the validity of defensive as well as
offensive wars, it was able to form a united front against the Mexican
War. The most influential leader of the movement in the 1840s and
1850s was Elihu Burritt (1810–1879), the "learned blacksmith," who
had taught himself nearly fifty languages. After lecturing on the Lyceum
circuit, he supported the abolition of slavery but devoted most of his
energies to the problem of international peace. Burritt organized several
peace congresses in Europe between 1848 and 1852, though his efforts
were frustrated by the Crimean War and the imminence of civil war in
the United States. The following article was first published in England in
1847.

BRETHREN,—The London *Times* recent stated that nine-tenths
of the revenue of the British Government came, directly or indirectly, from the labouring classes of the kingdom. If this be
true with regard to our brethren in Great Britain, it is equally true
with regard to the labouring classes of every country in Christendom; it is true in the United States, France, Germany, and in all
the Continental nations. Let us pin that fact upon the wall over
against our work-benches and mantel-pieces; for it is a fact that has
something to do with every meal of our food and every hour of our
labour. We working men of Christendom supply our respective
governments with nine-tenths of their revenues. Remember that.
Then nine-tenths of all the national debts of Christendom are our

SOURCE: A Working Man of America [Elihu Burritt], "A Way-
Word to the Working Men of Christendom," *The Herald of
Peace; A Monthly Journal, Published Under the Auspices of the
Peace Society* (London: Office of the Peace Society, May 1,
1857), vol. III, New Series, 1856–1857, no. LXXXIII, pp. 202–
203.

own debts, and we must pay them to the utmost farthing. . . . What is our share of these national debts? Why, their sum total, at the lowest calculation, cannot be less than £1500,000,000 or 7500,-000,000 dollars! And all for wars, every farthing of it. There is not a government in Christendom that can show a single school-house, a mile of railway or canal, against this tremendous expenditure. Well, nine-tenths of this vast sum the working classes owe; as much as if every man of us had given his note of hand for his share of it. . . . And this for war, brethren, for the glorious wars of the past! This is our debt; remember that. Shall we ever work it off? shall we ever pay it? That is a question our governments care but little about. They know that the working classes "are good" for the amount, or at least good for the interest of it. We may send the principle down from generation to generation of our posterity, to be a great mill-stone about the neck of industry; but we cannot get rid of the *interest* in that way. That we must pay, not at the end of the year, as in other cases of debt, but at the purchase of every article of food and clothing, and even at every glance at heaven's gratuitous sky through our windows. . . . Let us see how much we must pay every year on this old score of bloodshed. The interest of the working man's share of the war-debt of Christendom, at 5 per cent., is £67,500,000, or about 337,000,000 dollars. This is the sum they have had to pay annually ever since the sun went down upon the carnage of Waterloo. Since that day of blood they have paid in interest on the war-debts which it left upon their industry more than £2,000,000,000, or 10,000,000,000 dollars. During the next thirty years, fellow working men of Christendom, we shall have to pay £2,000,000,000 more in *interest* on this debt of ours. . . . Now, think of that to-day, to-morrow, next week, and all the weeks of the year. All you men in the fields, in the factories, in the forests, mines, and mountains, and you who do business in the great deep, think of that sober fact. Think what one million is, when cut up into days' wages; then what TWO THOUSAND MILLIONS sterling must be, for the working men of Europe alone to pay during the next thirty years! How many days' work, at three shillings a-day, must be given to sweep off this interest score?

Surely this tremendous burden must be all that the system of war can have saddled upon the labouring classes of Christendom? No; far from it. . . . We have been weighing the burden of wars past; let us now weigh, in the same scale, the burden of wars prospective. For, ever since the great slaughter-day of Waterloo, wars prospective have been reddening the horizon of the future, with their bloody omens, in the eyes of our respective governments; wars to be prepared for and paid for in time of peace. Well, nine-tenths of this preparing and paying, of course, have devolved upon the labouring classes again, and make up the other burden saddled upon their necks. Let us see if it be an ounce lighter than the first.

At the lowest calculation admissible, the governments of Christendom, including that of the United States, have expended £150,-000,000 a-year in mere preparations for war, since 1815. Nine-tenths of this sum amount to £135,000,000. This is the working men's part of the annual "preparations," which, being multiplied by 32, the number of years since the peace in 1815, gives us the snug little sum of £4,320,000,000, or about 21,500,000,000 dollars, which we labouring men of Christendom have paid out of our earnings merely for preparing for future wars during the last thirty-two years! Why, this burden is heavier than the other! . . . But stop! we have not put the whole of it into the scale yet. There are at least 2,500,000 able-bodied men in the standing armies of Christendom—all able-bodied men these, according to the surgeon's certificate, which is never asked when men are merely wanted to mow, plough, and sow, and make stone wall, or for any vulgar utilitarian purpose. Every common soldier is taken from the labouring class, we may be sure of that. . . . Now, instead of being drilled into mere machines for murder, suppose these 2,500,000 able-bodied men had been employed in some productive labour, even at the low rate of one shilling a-day per head. Allowing 300 working-days to the year, then they would have earned £37,-500,000 yearly; which, multiplied by 32, gives us £1,200,000,000 as the dead loss in labour to the labouring classes of Christendom, by the withdrawal, from their productive ranks, of two millions and a half of hardy, healthy men, in the bloom of life since 1815! . . .

Fellow working men of Christendom, are not these things so? If they be, has not war been a ruinous game to us, either in its prosecution or preparation? Without estimating the loss of life which we have suffered, what an amount of hard-earned money have we thrown into the bottomless gulf of war? . . . Working men of Europe! working men of America! shall the sword devour us and our substance for ever? . . . Shall we go on in this way, from year to year, to take the bread from our children and throw it to the dogs of war?

Working men of the United States! voters of a young republic! what example will you set at the polls to the hard-working myriads of your brethren in the Old World who lack your right of suffrage to dethrone the sanguinary monster, War! Shall your great officers of the nation "be peace, and your exactors, righteousness?" or shall "garments rolled in blood," and fiendish feats of human butchery, qualify your candidate for the highest honour within a nation's gift?

Working men of Great Britain! "shall the sword devour for ever?" Shall its suicidal edge fall daily and for ever upon the sinews of your industry? . . . What say you to the war-ridden millions of Christendom, whose substance is plucked from the very thorn of their poverty to batten this great red dragon of sin? Is your voice still for war? or will you subscribe with them to a covenant of everlasting peace?

Working men of France, brethren of the Continent! shall the sword devour for ever? What one good thing have you ever gained by its murderous edge? Of what avail is it to you to keep it sharpened in time of peace, at such a tremendous cost?

Working men of Christendom! let us put away from us the worship of this pagan Mars. Let us offer the beast no more oblations of our blood and treasure; and then an abundance of peace shall be within our borders.

III

Criticisms of the
Reform Impulse

45. We Are Overrun With Quackery
Orestes A. Brownson

REFORMERS and their movements were attacked with vehemence in the press, in the pulpit and in the Halls of Congress. Yet most of these criticisms are not helpful in understanding or analyzing the impact or success of the reform movement. More significant are the criticisms of those who had been involved with reform, but had come to reject either the assumptions or the aims of the movement. Orestes Brownson (see Document 15), after an early career supporting a variety of radical causes, became increasingly skeptical after 1840 of social reform and democracy; like Edmund Burke, he was hostile to any movement or program which rejected the past. His address at Wesleyan University, delivered two months before he announced his conversion to Catholicism, a development which shocked his former liberal associates, is essentially a diatribe against the entire concept of social reform.

. . . The cry for social reform rings upon our ears from every quarter, and whole armies of real or pretended reformers swarm over the land. They meet us in highways and byways; they come into our houses, into our sleeping chambers, and our kneading troughs. There is no escaping them, and they give us no rest by day or by night. . . .

. . . The age in which we live is the age of quackery. We are overrun with quackery, with quackery of every description. I refer not merely to quack medicines, which, though bad enough in all conscience, are by no means the worst or most deleterious species of quackery with which we are infested. We have quack economics, quack politics, quack law, quack learning, and quack divinity; quackery everywhere, and sometimes one, in a fit of despair or spleen, fancies nowhere anything but quackery. All are bringing forward every species of nostrums, for every real or imaginary disease, and no one brings forward any nostrum, likely to effect even an imaginary cure. I propose, therefore, to bestow the remainder of

SOURCE: O. A. Brownson, *Social Reform: An Address Before the Society of the Mystical Seven in the Wesleyan University, Middletown, Conn. August 7, 1844* (Boston: Waite, Peirce & Company, 1844), pp. 4, 10, 13, 18–20, 22–25, 27–31, 33, 39–40.

my remarks, my attention on several species of the *genus* QUACK REFORMERS. . . .

. . . the effort *to cut loose from the past,* and to create an entirely new social and industrial order . . . is the species of quackery practised by our professed social reformers, of which there are several varieties. . . .

. . . these systems of reform disown the past, condemn what has been, and propose the creation of an entirely new social order. In this fact alone we may read their common condemnation. It is to no man's credit that he disowns what has gone before him. There may be, and there probably is, a period in the lives of most of us, when we feel ourselves restrained, "cabined, cribbed, confined," by the existing order, galled in the most sensitive parts of our being by the old institutions which have come down to us, and the reason of which in our ignorance and inexperience we see not. We feel that we are wronged; we are outraged; we rise up in our own majesty, and utter one long, loud, indignant protest against all that is and has been. . . .

But what is this past which we in our folly condemn? It is that which has made us what we are. It is our mother. And shall we turn round and curse it? Alas! he is a bad son who curses his own mother, and no good can come of him. I distrust that man's virtue who sees nothing in the past to love and reverence, whose heart is not moved as he contemplates the old, that over which the tide of ages, especially the tide of human affection, has flowed. . . .

There is no greater defect in our own age than its want of reverence. Its grand characteristic is the absence of a deep reverential spirit. Especially is this true of our own country. With us all is new. Our institutions are of yesterday, and the work of our own hands. There is nothing we venerate. We have nothing amongst us that we hold sacred and venerable. We lose respect one for another. We acknowledge nothing above us. Reverence to superiors is regarded as meanness, as a vice. *Superiors,* did I say? I forget myself; we acknowledge no superiors. Is not this the land of equality? Are we not all equals? Is not one man as good as another? Who are you, that you put on airs, as my superior? Know I am your equal, I am as good as you. So far do we carry our notions of equality, that youth forgets, nay, disdains, to uncover itself in the presence of age, and our children hold it to be gross tyranny that they should respect their parents. . . .

. . . We must seek in the institutions of the past, our point of support. Our reformers forget that man cannot lift himself. Give me, said Archimedes, a stand-point outside the world, and I will raise it. Your fulcrum must rest on another body than the one you propose to raise. This is as true in morals as in mechanics. Man never suffices for himself. . . . What he calls his act is the resultant of two factors, himself and that which is not himself, and can never surpass the combined powers of the factors themselves. Hence, whenever you wish to elevate man from what he is, to give to his action a higher worth, a truer excellence, you must bring to his aid, into conjunction with his activity, a higher object. . . .

It is the neglect of this great and essential truth that causes the failure of so many brilliant schemes of reform. The new must always have its support in the old, and grow out of it, and be merely its fulfilment, or it will fail. . . .

. . . No man, in politics, in society, in morals, in religion, will ever succeed in any attempt at reform who does not pursue the same method. Our Socialists, then, are suicidal in attempting to cut themselves loose from the past, and to create a new order. They are attempting to make brick without straw; throwing away their materials, and attempting to create,—forgetful that to create without materials, to create out of nothing, is the prerogative of God alone.

. . . [Another] species of quack reformers I mention are the NO GOVERNMENT MEN, or those who would reform all abuses by getting rid of civil government. . . . They find evil in the world, co-existing with government, and because government has not suppressed it, they sagely infer that government has caused it; and, therefore, the way to root out the evil is to get rid of the government. . . .

. . . Liberty, rightly understood, is the true end of man. All the institutions of society, all the dispensations of Providence, have for their mission the freedom of man, to make him free indeed: free through the Son of God, and able to look into the perfect law of liberty. But there can be no liberty without order. Order is not the end, but the means. Where there is not the most perfect order, where each is not in his place, there is no free movement; there is confusion, a clashing and crossing of interests, and the rubbing of one against another, the thwarting of one by another. And order can be maintained only by means of government which reduces all to their places, each to his proper sphere, and maintains him in it. Order is essential to liberty; but order is impossible without government; therefore, government is essential to liberty. I do not demand government to suppress or restrain liberty, but to maintain it.

The necessity of government is to be found in the fact that men are naturally unequal. The great talk we hear about men being born equal is all moonshine. There is no natural equality. Men are born unequal, with unequal powers of body, mind, and heart. Some are by nature strong, others weak; some cunning, others simple. And depraved as human nature is since the Fall, governed as men are by lust, avarice, covetousness, pride, ambition, the strong will oppress the weak, and the cunning overreach the simple; wrongs and outrages will prevail, and man be both the plague and the victim of man. Disorder, confusion, all manner of injustice will obtain. What need we? Government, government which shall step in as a beneficent Providence, protect the weak and simple, befriend the friendless, help the helpless, and reduce the stubborn and disobedient to submission, and compel each to respect the equality of all before the Law. . . .

We misinterpret liberty. The great mass understand by liberty the right of each man to an equal share in the government; that is, the right of each man to govern—which is tantamount to the right of each man *not* to be governed; that is, again, the right of each man to do as he pleases; which is not liberty but license. But so long as men retain their present evil and corrupt passions, there can be no liberty where all are as free to do wrong as right. Restraint is necessary. Liberty is freedom to do whatever is lawful; all beyond is not freedom but license, and is to be compressed, not indulged; and, when not otherwise, to be compressed by the sword of the magistrate.

I cannot, then, agree with those who think to reform society by removing the restraints imposed by government. Man needs to be governed, for without government he will either outrage his brother or be outraged by him. Left to his natural liberty, that is, to his natural *might*, he is inadequate to the protection of his own rights and interests. These loose notions of government, which are rife in the land, are fraught with danger. The first lesson we should be taught is to obey, reverence for authority, obedience to law. . . . The world has not been governed enough. Wrongs and outrages have always obtained and still obtain; the strong even yet oppress the weak, the cunning circumvent the simple, and we need more and stronger government to prevent it. It is madness to war upon government. . . .

. . . the . . . last species of quacks I shall notice, are those who propose to reform the world by getting rid of RELIGION. . . . Almost every young enthusiast, who steps forth to attempt the realization of a higher good for his country or his race, fancies he must begin by denouncing the Church and making war upon the clergy, sometimes in the name of infidelity, avowedly, sometimes under cover of reviving what he is pleased to call "primitive Christianity," "Christianity in its purity"; which is rarely any thing more than infidelity baptized with the Christian name, at best Christianity divested of its supernatural character, deprived of its life and power, and reduced to a mere speculative philosophy and a barren system of ethics.

I look upon this as the most dangerous species of quack reformers it is possible to imagine. For what, after all, is the real cause of the evils I began by pointing out? . . . The real cause must be sought in the fact that Mammon, the representative of wealth, in our modern society, reigns without a rival. As our society now is we have no antagonist power to wealth. It is in the want of this power, a power that can, not only compete with wealth, but subordinate it, that originates the terrible evils to which I began by drawing your attention. . . .

. . . Mammon has taken possession of our hearts, and instituted his worship almost universally. There is, therefore, no check on his rule. The government cannot check the power of wealth, because it becomes its factor, and must do its bidding. The rich themselves cannot because they are the power itself. The poor cannot, because they are dependent on the rich for employment, and, therefore, for the means of subsistence. The Church cannot do it, for it has no hold on the conscience, no authority in the living faith of the age. Where then is your power to control wealth, and to make it subservient to the well-being of society! . . .

We must bring back the faith which exclaims, blessed are the poor, and blessed are the poor in spirit, for theirs is the kingdom of heaven; we must restore the blessed ages of Faith, when men lived for eternity, not for time; when poverty was deemed honorable;

when kings and princes, and nobles, joyed to lay aside their earthly dignity, and wealth, and become humble followers of him, who though rich, for our sakes became poor. . . .

When we have recalled this faith, when we have made poverty once more honorable, and made it believed that voluntary poverty is even meritorious, and that the rich are no otherwise to be respected in their riches than as they obtain them honestly, and devote them to the service of God in the service of man, we shall begin to remedy the terrible evils which now obtain, but not till then. Till then, . . . all your patent nostrums, will prove ineffectual, and only serve to extend the ravages of the disease that is preying upon our vitals. . . .

46. Godlike Benevolence Debased into All-Devouring Egotism
Nathaniel Hawthorne

ANOTHER criticism of reform arose from a concern with the individual and his values, subordinated to the movement and its aims. Emerson (see Documents 3 and 40) used this argument as a justification for his reluctance to become involved in reform, yet he supported many objectives of the movement and accepted the perfectionist assumptions about human nature adopted by most reformers. Nathaniel Hawthorne (1804–1864), a onetime associate of the Transcendentalists and a member of the Brook Farm community during its first summer, questioned reform on different grounds: its failure to acknowledge the sense of sin as a basic ingredient of human nature. Ten years after his summer at Brook Farm, he used this experience as a vehicle to demonstrate the flaws in the genus reformer. Despite Hawthorne's protestations, his heroine Zenobia, "the high-spirited Woman, bruising herself against the narrow limitations of her sex," is obviously modeled in part upon Margaret Fuller. Hollingsworth, the narrow-minded and fanatical "philanthropist" who is morally responsible for her suicide, is an essentially unrealistic figure, but is at the same time a composite portrait of the characteristics which Hawthorne, the neo-Puritan, found most reprehensible. It was the incongruity between the philanthropist and philanthropy, between the humanitarian and humanity, that he wished to emphasize in this work.

. . . We had left the rusty iron frame-work of society behind us; we had broken through many hindrances that are powerful enough to keep most people on the weary tread-mill of the established system, even while they feel its irksomeness almost as intolerable as we did. We had stept down from the pulpit; we had flung aside the pen; we had shut up the ledger; we had thrown off that sweet, bewitching, enervating indolence, which is better, after all, than most of the enjoyments within mortal grasp. It was our purpose . . . to give up whatever we had heretofore attained, for the sake of showing mankind the example of a life governed by other than

SOURCE: Nathaniel Hawthorne, *The Blithedale Romance* (Boston: Ticknor, Reed & Fields, 1852), chapters III, IX, XV, XXVIII, abridged.

the false and cruel principles on which human society has all along been based.

And, first of all, we had divorced ourselves from pride, and were striving to supply its place with familiar love. We meant to lessen the laboring man's great burthen of toil, by performing our due share of it at the cost of our own thews and sinews. We sought our profit by mutual aid, instead of wresting it by the strong hand from an enemy, or filching it craftily from those less shrewd than ourselves . . . or winning it by selfish competition with a neighbor. . . . And, as the basis of our institution, we purposed to offer up the earnest toil of our bodies, as a prayer no less than an effort for the advancement of our race.

. . . I rejoice that I could once think better of the world's improvability than it deserved. It is a mistake into which men seldom fall twice in a lifetime; or, if so, the rarer and higher is the nature that can thus magnanimously persist in error. . . .

. . . I loved Hollingsworth. . . . But it impressed me, more and more, that there was a stern and dreadful peculiarity in this man, such as could not prove otherwise than pernicious to the happiness of those who should be drawn into too intimate a connection with him. He was not altogether human. There was something else in Hollingsworth besides flesh and blood, and sympathies and affections, and celestial spirit.

This is always true of those men who have surrendered themselves to an overruling purpose. It does not so much impel them from without, nor even operate as a motive power within, but grows incorporate with all that they think and feel, and finally converts them into little else save that one principle. When such begins to be the predicament, it is not cowardice, but wisdom, to avoid these victims. They have no heart, no sympathy, no reason, no conscience. They will keep no friend, unless he make himself the mirror of their purpose; they will smite and slay you, and trample your dead corpse under foot, all the more readily, if you take the first step with them, and cannot take the second, and the third, and every other step of their terribly straight path. They have an idol, to which they consecrate themselves high-priest, and deem it holy work to offer sacrifices of whatever is most precious; and never once seem to suspect—so cunning has the devil been with them—that this false deity, in whose iron features, immitigable to all the rest of mankind, they see only benignity and love, is but a spectrum of the very priest himself, projected upon the surrounding darkness. And the higher and purer the original object, and the more unselfishly it may have been taken up, the slighter is the probability that they can be led to recognize the process by which godlike benevolence has been debased into all-devouring egotism.

. . . in solitude I often shuddered at my friend. In my recollection of his dark and impressive countenance, the features grew more sternly prominent than the reality, duskier in their depth and shadow, and more lurid in their light; the frown, that had merely flitted across his brow, seemed to have contorted it with an adamantine wrinkle. On meeting him again, I was often filled with remorse, when his deep eyes beamed kindly upon me, as with the glow of a household fire that was burning in a cave. "He is a man, after all," thought I; "his Maker's own truest image, a philanthropic man!—not that steel engine of the devil's contrivance, a philanthropist!" But in my wood-walks, and in my silent chamber, the dark face frowned at me again. . . .

Thus the summer was passing away;—a summer of toil, of interest, of something that was not pleasure, but which went deep into my heart, and there became a rich experience. I found myself looking forward to years, if not to a lifetime, to be spent on the same system. The Community were now beginning to form their permanent plans. . . . Altogether, by projecting our minds outward, we had imparted a show of novelty to existence, and contemplated it as hopefully as if the soil beneath our feet had not been fathom-deep with the dust of deluded generations, on every one of which, as on ourselves, the world had imposed itself as a hitherto unwedded bride.

Hollingsworth and myself had often discussed these prospects. It was easy to perceive, however, that he spoke with little or no fervor, but either as questioning the fulfilment of our anticipations, or, at any rate, with a quiet consciousness that it was no personal concern of his. . . . while he and I were repairing an old stone fence, I amused myself with sallying forward into the future time. . . .

[Hollingsworth responded:] ". . . Your fantastic anticipations make me discern all the more forcibly what a wretched, unsubstantial scheme is this, on which we have wasted a precious summer of our lives. Do you seriously imagine that any such realities as you, and many others here, have dreamed of, will ever be brought to pass?

"Certainly, I do," said I. "Of course, when the reality comes, it will wear the every-day, commonplace, dusty, and rather homely garb, that reality always does put on. . . ."

"You only half believe what you say," rejoined Holingsworth; "and as for me, I neither have faith in your dream, nor would care the value of this pebble for its realization, were that possible. And what more do you want of it? It has given you a theme for poetry. Let that content you. But now I ask you to be, at last, a man of sobriety and earnestness, and aid me in an enterprise which is worth all our strength, and the strength of a thousand mightier than we."

There can be no need of giving in detail the conversation that ensued. It is enough to say that Hollingsworth once more brought forward his rigid and unconquerable idea; a scheme for the reformation of the wicked by methods moral, intellectual and industrial, by the sympathy of pure, humble, and yet exalted minds, and by opening to his pupils the possibility of a worthier life than that which had become their fate. It appeared . . . that Hollingsworth held it at his choice . . . to obtain possession of the very ground on which we had planted our Community. . . . It was just the foundation that he desired. . . .

"And have you no regrets," I inquired, "in overthrowing this fair system of our new life, which has been planned so deeply, and is now beginning to flourish so hopefully around us? How beautiful it is, and, so far as we can yet see, how practicable! The ages have waited for us, and here we are, the very first that have essayed to carry on our mortal existence in love and mutual help! Hollingsworth, I would be loth to take the ruin of this enterprise upon my conscience."

"Then let it rest wholly upon mine!" he answered, knitting his black brows. "I see through the system. It is full of defects,—irremediable and damning ones!—from first to last, there is nothing else! I grasp it in my hand, and find no substance whatever. There is not human nature in it."

"Why are you so secret in your operations?" I asked. "God forbid that I should accuse you of intentional wrong; but the besetting sin of a philanthropist, it appears to me, is apt to be a moral obliquity. His sense of honor ceases to be the sense of other honorable men. At some point in his course—I know not exactly when or where—he is tempted to palter with the right, and can scarcely forbear persuading himself that the importance of his public ends renders it allowable to throw aside his private conscience. O, my dear friend, beware this error!". . .

"I will not argue the point," said he. "What I desire to know of you is,—and you can tell me in one word,—whether I am to look for your cooperation in this great scheme of good? Take it up with me! Be my brother in it! It offers you (what you have told me, over and over again, that you most need) a purpose in life, worthy of the extremest self-devotion,—worthy of martyrdom, should God so order it! . . . Strike hands with me, and from this moment you shall never again feel the languor and vague wretchedness of an indolent or half-occupied man. . . . We shall have done our best for this miserable world; and happiness (which never comes but incidentally) will come to us unawares."

. . . I saw in his scheme of philanthropy nothing but what was odious. A loathsomeness that was to be forever in my daily work! A great, black ugliness of sin, which he proposed to collect out of a thousand human hearts, and that we should spend our lives in an experiment of transmuting it into virtue! . . .

"In Heaven's name, Hollingsworth," cried I, getting angry, and glad to be angry, because so only was it possible to oppose his tremendous concentrativeness and indomitable will, "cannot you conceive that a man may wish well to the world, and struggle for its good, on some other plan than precisely that which you have laid down? And will you cast off a friend for no unworthiness, but merely because he stands upon his right as an individual being, and looks at matters through his own optics, instead of yours?"

"Be with me," said Hollingsworth, "or be against me! There is no third choice for you."

"Take this, then, as my decision," I answered. "I doubt the wisdom of your scheme. Furthermore, I greatly fear that the methods by which you allow yourself to pursue it are such as cannot stand the scrutiny of an unbiassed conscience."

"And you will not join me?"

"No!"

I never said the word . . . that cost me a thousandth part so hard an effort as did that one syllable. . . .

. . . The moral which presents itself to my reflections, as drawn from Hollingsworth's character and errors, is simply this,—that, admitting what is called philanthropy, when adopted as a profession, to be often useful by its energetic impulse to society at large, it is perilous to the individual whose ruling passion, in one exclusive channel, it thus becomes. It ruins, or is fearfully apt to ruin, the heart, the rich juices of which God never meant should be pressed violently out, and distilled into alcoholic liquor, by an unnatural process, but should render life sweet, bland, and gently beneficent, and insensibly influence other hearts and other lives to the same blessed end. I see in Hollingsworth an exemplification of the most awful truth in Bunyan's book of such;—from the very gate of heaven there is a by-way to the pit! . . .

The Reform Impulse, 1825–1850

Printed by offset lithography by Halliday Lithograph Corporation on 55# Warren's University Text. This acid-free paper, noted for its longevity, has been watermarked with the University of South Carolina Press colophon. Binding by Halliday Lithograph Corporation in Scott Graphics' Corinthian Kivar 9.